CITY OF BLACK GOLD

CITY
OF
BLACK
GOLD

Oil, Ethnicity, and the Making
of Modern Kirkuk

ARBELLA BET-SHLIMON

STANFORD UNIVERSITY PRESS
Stanford, California

STANFORD UNIVERSITY PRESS

Stanford, California

© 2019 by the Board of Trustees of the Leland Stanford Junior University.
All rights reserved.

This book has been partially underwritten by the Stanford Authors Fund. We are grateful to the Fund for its support of scholarship by first-time authors. For more information, please see www.sup.org/authorsfund

Printed in the United States of America on acid-free, archival-quality paper

Library of Congress Cataloging-in-Publication Data

Names: Bet-Shlimon, Arbella, author.

Title: City of black gold : oil, ethnicity, and the making of modern Kirkuk / Arbella Bet-Shlimon.

Description: Stanford, California : Stanford University Press, 2019. | Includes bibliographical references and index.

Identifiers: LCCN 2018043067 (print) | LCCN 2018045044 (ebook) | ISBN 9781503608122 (cloth :alk. paper) | ISBN 9781503609136 (pbk. :alk. paper) | ISBN 9781503609143 (ebook)

Subjects: LCSH: Ethnicity—Political aspects—Iraq—Karkuk—History—20th century. | Karkuk (Iraq)—Ethnic relations—Political aspects—History—20th century. | Petroleum industry and trade—Iraq—Karkuk—History—20th century. | Ethnic conflict—Iraq-Karkuk—History—20th century. | Karkuk (Iraq)—Politics and government—20th century.

Classification: LCC DS79.9.K37 (ebook) | LCC DS79.9.K37 B48 2019 (print) | DDC 956.7/4—dc23

LC record available at https://lccn.loc.gov/2018043067

Cover designer: Angela Moody

Cover photo: Kirkuk, a street scene in the older town, 1932. Library of Congress.

Typeset by Kevin Barrett Kane in 10/14 Minion

CONTENTS

ACKNOWLEDGMENTS

This book was made possible, first and foremost, by people from Kirkuk: those with roots there and those who spent many years of their lives there. They generously invited me into their living rooms, responded to my emails and text messages, answered obvious and obscure questions alike, acted as impromptu translators in multilingual conversations, and helped me keep going by conveying their enthusiasm for this project. My mother and her family, especially my maternal grandmother, were my earliest inspirations as I began to explore the history of their hometown. I am indebted to Kamal Muzhir Ahmad, Fadhil al-Azzawi, the late Daniel Benjamin, Ferida Danyal, Nineb Lamassu, Kamal Majid, Edward Odisho, Banu Saatçi, Suphi Saatçi, Adnan Samarrai, Nineb Shamoun, Karzan Sherabayani, George Yacu, and a number of others who would prefer to remain anonymous or whose names I cannot recall. These linguists, historians, writers, scholars, scientists, homemakers, and oil workers offer many differing perspectives on Kirkuk's history and identity, all of which I have learned from. But ultimately the views I express in this book are mine alone.

I am grateful to Kate Wahl and the team at Stanford University Press for turning this project into the volume you are currently reading. Kate's editorial observations and suggestions have made it a better work of scholarship and a more readable book. Stephanie Adams, Rob Ehle, Anne Fuzellier, Leah Pennywark, and many others behind the scenes at the press have helped bring this book to fruition. I thank Angela Moody for the cover design and John Culp for making the maps.

The late Roger Owen guided this project for several years in its earliest stages at Harvard University. I thank him for nurturing all my best ideas, quietly insisting that I pursue certain leads, and reading so many drafts promptly. Nelida Fuccaro's advice also shaped this book when I began to research it while I was affiliated with the University of London. I benefited immensely from her detailed feedback. Alison Frank Johnson's incisive perspectives on my work made me look at it in new ways, bringing me to a better sense of the relationship between identity formation and oil. At Harvard and in London I also received advice and key opportunities from Vivian Bickford-Smith, Ben Fortna, Bill Granara, and Mary D. Lewis.

At the University of Washington I have found an inspirational intellectual home that I am glad to be a part of. I extend my gratitude to all the UW staff, faculty, graduate students, and undergraduate students who have shown me kindness, offered suggestions, and done favors for me over the last five years. I thank especially the most recent chairs of the Department of History, Lynn Thomas and Anand Yang, for their unflagging support. The Department of History's current and former administrative staff did essential logistical work in support of this project; in particular, I thank Josh Apfel, Jessica Claycomb, Wanjiku Gitahi, Brendon Lee, Star Murray, and Jeri Park. My colleagues Purnima Dhavan and Joel Walker have provided frequent advice and reassurance. Michael Degerald provided thorough feedback on short notice on a chapter draft. I also received feedback on chapter drafts, writing accountability checks, and other beneficial efforts on my behalf from Samad Alavi, Danny Bessner, Jordanna Bailkin, Elena Campbell, Vanessa Freije, Liora Halperin, Selim Kuru, James Lin, Matthew Mosca, Devin Naar, Margaret O'Mara, Arzoo Osanloo, Cabeiri Robinson, and Michael Sims. I thank all my past and present students at UW, Harvard University, and Tufts University who offered endless observations and questions on the histories of Iraq, the Persian Gulf, and Middle Eastern urbanism. Their energetic engagement has helped me hone many of my ideas.

The research that went into this book was funded by Harvard University, the University of London's Institute of Historical Research, the Academic Research Institute in Iraq, the UW Royalty Research Fund, and the UW Department of History's Hanauer and Keller funds. The process of researching this book started in Cambridge, Massachusetts, and took me to Ankara, Arbil, Athens, College Park, Coventry, Exeter, Istanbul, London, Oxford, Palo Alto, and Washington, DC. I am indebted to the efforts of library and archive staff in all these places. For their extensive, personalized assistance, I especially thank Mary St. Germain of the UW Libraries; Michael Hopper of Widener Library's Middle Eastern Division, Harvard University; the staff of the National Archives of the United States at College Park; Debbie Usher of the Middle East Centre Archive, St. Antony's College, Oxford; Joanne Berman and Peter Housego of the BP Archive at the University of Warwick, Coventry; the staff of the Arab World Documentation Unit at the University of Exeter; and Giota Pavlidou of the Constantinos A. Doxiadis Archives in Athens.

Over the course of this project, I have relied on the wisdom of many people on several continents. I deeply appreciate the extensive comments provided by Toby Jones and an anonymous reviewer for Stanford University Press on the full manuscript. My colleagues Reem Alissa, Farah Al-Nakib, Orit Bashkin, Güldem Büyüksaraç, Mona Damluji, Bridget Guarasci, Dina Khoury, Sreemati Mitter, Suneela Mubayi, Zainab Saleh, and Bob Vitalis have provided key insights time and time again. I thank Hashem Ahmadzadeh, Khaled Al-Masri, Wisam Alshaibi, Idan Barir, Lee F. Dinsmore, Toby Dodge, Nadia Hamdan Gattan, Joost Hiltermann, Clive Holes, Kamil Mahdi, Kanan Makiya, Maysoon Pachachi, Sarah Panizzo, John Sheffield, the late Peter Sluglett, Gareth Stansfield, Lefteris Theodosis, Charles Tripp, and Sami Zubaida for taking the time to meet or correspond with me at length and answer many of my questions. I thank Ziad Abu-Rish, Kevin Jones, Augustus Richard Norton, and Nova Robinson for inviting me to their universities to speak about this project. My year spent in London would have been much poorer without the intellectual curiosity and warm hospitality of Ulla Kjellstrand. Sargon Donabed and Shamiran Mako have opened their home to me repeatedly and talked me through many half-formed ideas. Alda Benjamen, herself both a historian and a Kirkuk native, has been a consistent source of insights, assistance, and encouragement.

I reserve my last and most profound thanks for those closest to me. My aunts, uncles, and cousins are a constant reminder of why the history of this region matters. I wish that my maternal grandmother, Seranoush Elias, and my maternal aunt, Marlyne Soro, both of whom spent much of their lives in Kirkuk, had lived to see this book published. Kyle Haddad-Fonda has shared this project with me, from conception to completion, for more than a decade. He was this book's first and last editor. More important, he has been my pillar of moral support through the writing process, even when we were living thousands of miles apart. I am grateful to my brilliant and funny brother, Sargon Bet-Shlimon, for setting an ethical example through his care for patients and, in lighter moments, providing much-needed breaks from academic life. Finally, I thank my parents, George Bet-Shlimon and Dolphine Oda. When they traveled across continents and oceans to make new lives in North America, I do not think they anticipated that their American-born eldest child would, upon reaching adulthood, promptly start traveling back to their countries of origin to understand where they came from. All the same, they have sustained me and facilitated my work on this project in every way possible. This book is for them and for the people of Kirkuk.

NOTE ON LANGUAGES AND TRANSLITERATION

Writing about a place as multilingual as Kirkuk presents unique linguistic challenges. In this book I have broadly adhered to the standards of *The International Journal of Middle East Studies* (IJMES). I have used the IJMES transliteration guide for the transliteration of words and names from Arabic and Kurdish that do not have common English spellings. Words in modern Turkish, which uses the Latin alphabet, have been rendered as is; Ottoman names have been rendered in their modern Turkish forms. If a name has a common alternative form, I have included it in parentheses after its first mention.

I have made exceptions to IJMES rules for some Kirkuki names that are of multilingual or linguistically ambiguous origin. For instance, Naftchizada, the name of a prominent Kirkuki Turkmen family, combines an Arabic word with Turkish and Persian suffixes. To transliterate it as though it were a fully Arabic (Naftjizada) or fully Turkish (Neftçizade) name would be problematic. Therefore in these instances I have rendered the names as closely as possible to IJMES standards while maintaining readability and faithfulness to the names' polyglot origins. In addition, I have followed individuals' preferences, where known, for the spelling of their own names in English, including whether or not they capitalize the Arabic definite article al-.

In accordance with prevailing practice in the English-language historical literature on Iraq and for the sake of simplicity, I have consistently used the Arabic names of Iraqi places as a basis for transliteration in instances where the names do not have a single dominant English form. For instance, the name of the city of Arbil is rendered as such, rather than as Erbil, an equally common English spelling that more closely approximates the city's name in Kurdish and Turkish.

The common English spelling of Kirkuk, which I have used here, is an early-twentieth-century Anglicization of its name in Turkish, Kerkük. In Arabic and Aramaic it is Karkuk, a transliteration that virtually never appears in English. In Kurdish it is Kerkûk. The title of the city's municipal newspaper, which is simply the city's name, reflects some of the specific nuances of transliteration that arise in a project like this one. When the paper was established in 1926, it was a trilingual Turkish-Kurdish-Arabic publication whose title (in Arabic script) was spelled in a manner consistent with Turkish and Arabic; it can therefore be Latinized as *Kerkük* or *Karkuk* and was probably pronounced both ways. Later in the twentieth century, the same newspaper was published solely in Arabic, so the single transliteration *Karkuk* makes the most sense if one is following IJMES standards. Throughout this book, such terms may appear with multiple possible transliterations separated by a slash, or one transliteration may appear in lieu of another if it makes more sense for that particular document.

The quotations included in this book come from sources in several different languages. Some were originally in English, which I quote verbatim. Some sources were originally in a language other than English but were translated into English by someone other than me, such as translated Iraqi press excerpts included in British archival files, which I also quote verbatim. Other archival materials and sources were originally in Arabic, French, or Turkish, which I have translated into English myself. In general, it is clear from a combination of context and the citation whether a quotation of a particular text is translated from a language other than English and whether, if translated, the translation is my own or someone else's. Where this is ambiguous, I have clarified it in an endnote.

PREFACE

Kirkuk is a city in crisis. It is ethnically segregated and politically stagnant. Mutual mistrust between its communities runs deep. For decades its residents have had to contend with a constant war of words over the city's status, punctuated by episodic violence. Under the Baʿth government of Saddam Hussein, Kirkuk was a key target of the campaign of ethnic cleansing that ravaged northern Iraq (Figure 1). After a U.S.-led military operation overthrew the Iraqi Baʿth regime in 2003, the disputes over Kirkuk's future stymied attempts to construct a democratic legal and political system for the entire country. Iraqi lawmakers and foreign policymakers have spent the years since attempting to address the urgent need to resolve rival claims to control Kirkuk—and, by extension, rival claims to the city's identity.

The first such effort to settle lingering conflicts over Kirkuk was written into Iraq's provisional legal document, the 2004 Transitional Administrative Law. Article 58 of that document detailed a process by which authorities would mitigate and remedy Baʿth atrocities in Iraq's disputed territories, of which Kirkuk is by far the most prominent. First, the Iraqi government would conduct a full census for the first time since 1957. Then, officials would begin resettling and compensating Kirkuki residents who had been displaced. Most important, Article 58 affirmed that those affected could "determine their own national identity and racial (*'irqi*) affiliation without coercion or pressure."[1] After that process was complete, the article declared, Kirkukis would vote on their desired political status. When the formal Constitution of Iraq was ratified by a national vote a year later, its Article 140 reiterated this plan and called for "a referendum in Kirkuk and the other disputed territories to determine the will of their citizens"; the referendum was to be held no later than 31 December 2007.[2]

More than a decade later, the process of resolving the disputes over Kirkuk has not begun in any meaningful way. There has been no census. The exact parameters of the promised referendum—what, exactly, are the options for Kirkuk's

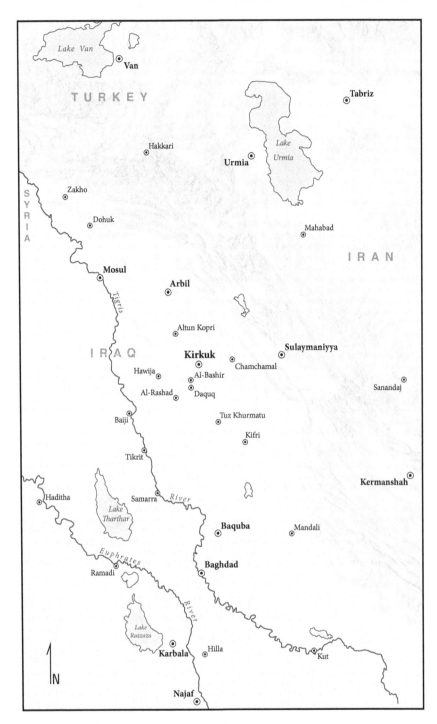

FIGURE 1. Kirkuk and its surrounding region.

political status?—were never defined. Because the constitution failed to account for what would happen if the official deadline was not met, 31 December 2007 came and went without consequence.

Meanwhile, the uncertainty over Kirkuk's future was holding back Iraq's national politics. The country's provincial elections, scheduled for 2008, were delayed until 2009 because the Iraqi parliament could not pass an election law that included Kirkuk in a way that met the differing demands of Kurdish, Turkmen, and Arab lawmakers.[3] In the end, the Kirkuk province sat out the 2009 provincial elections altogether. With tensions still high, it did so again in 2013.

Throughout these years Iraq's national security forces repeatedly faced off with Kurdish troops, known as *pêşmerge*, in tense standoffs on the outskirts of the city. In 2014, amid a power vacuum created by the Islamic State's takeover of nearby Mosul, *pêşmerge* seized Kirkuk and all but officially declared it to be part of Kurdistan. In 2017 the Iraqi army seized the city back.

Amid all this conflict it has been easy for most Iraqis, as well as international diplomats, mediators, and journalists, to accept that Kirkuk is Iraq's Sarajevo or Nicosia—a tinderbox of ethnic tensions. The assumption of ethnic conflict as an inevitable characteristic of a place, however, should not foreclose further questions about where that state of contestation came from. Identifying a conflict's origins—and the origins of its disputants' claims—can also reveal its limits.

According to the most common perspectives on Kirkuk, its three major ethnic groups are Kurds, Arabs, and Turkmens, each of which has a competing claim to own the city. Kurds, hoping to attach Kirkuk to the autonomous Kurdistan region in Iraq's northeast, refer to the city as the "Kurdish Jerusalem" and the "heart of Kurdistan."[4] On the other side of the dispute, Turkmens, Arabs, and members of the city's smaller minorities dread the prospect of being integrated into Kurdistan and would rather remain aligned with Baghdad.

Accordingly, when elections are held in Kirkuk, pundits assume that members of each ethnic group have voted for their corresponding ethnic parties: Kurds for the Patriotic Union of Kurdistan (PUK) or the Kurdistan Democratic Party (KDP), Turkmens for the Iraqi Turkmen Front (ITF), and Arabs for parties that present themselves as nonethnic. These assumptions are so widely accepted that political scientists have asserted that the results of national parliamentary elections in Kirkuk can be used as a "rough and ready census" that can "reveal Kirkuk's ethnic makeup for the first time" since the last full Iraqi census in 1957.[5]

The politics of ethnicity are so thoroughly embedded in Kirkuk's every-day functioning that security forces use ethnic labels as a form of shorthand when apprehending suspects. In a 2007 documentary about Kirkuk by the Kirkuki Kurdish filmmaker and actor Karzan Sherabayani, the viewer witnesses the gruesome aftermath of an October 2005 car bomb attack on the Kirkuk police force that killed two officers and wounded two others. Nearby, three handcuffed, blindfolded men are dragged into the back of a flatbed truck by Arabic-speaking soldiers of the Iraqi army. Each of the men has a large placard hanging around his neck bearing handwritten information—in English—for several categories: name, age, location, and ethnicity. According to the placards, all the men are Arabs. Blindfolded and uncertain of their fate, they weep in despair and protest, in Arabic, that they are innocent.[6] What does the ethnic categorization of a terrorism suspect reveal about the likelihood of his guilt? It is not entirely clear, but the very act of this public labeling betrays the extent to which positions in Kirkuk's conflict are presumed by all involved to rely on an individual's ethnicity.

Scholars who have focused on Kirkuk since 2003 have mainly studied the city from the perspective of conflict resolution and have operated almost exclusively within an ethnopolitical paradigm.[7] Political scientists and journalists writing about Kirkuk have typically held that the crisis is best understood as a clash of three main narratives, each primarily associated with an ethnic self-identity. The Kurdish narrative asserts that Kirkuk is rightfully a part of Kurdistan, and its proponents often try to make the case that the city has always been Kurdish. The Turkmen narrative holds that Kirkuk is a historically Turkmen city that has undergone demographic changes but has retained its Turkmen character. The Arab narrative does not try to claim that Kirkuk has ever been an Arab-majority city but instead insists that the city is a multiethnic "Iraqi" city first and foremost and hence that it must retain its pluralistic identity.[8]

Why do these groups fight over Kirkuk? Most commentators, whether implic-itly or explicitly, offer a simple answer: oil. After all, the city rests atop a supergiant oil field. For much of the twentieth century, before the development of larger fields in southern Iraq, Kirkuk was the heart of the country's oil industry. Kirkuk's oil fueled its growth. It also made both the city and its hinterland a strategically crucial region for Baghdad, which went to great lengths—sometimes quietly, sometimes brutally—to integrate the largely non-Arab area into mostly Arab Iraq. One would be hard-pressed to find a discussion of Kirkuk's political crisis since 2003 that does not contain the modifier "oil-rich" to describe the city.

Yet the idea of oil as a cause of Kirkuk's ethnic conflict is seldom explored in any great detail. What does it mean, specifically, for a dispute to be about oil?

It is not only "about oil" in the simplistic sense that Kirkukis have no stakes in other forms of control and legitimacy. Indeed, claims to Kirkuk's history and culture are a powerful factor in the dispute over its status even in parts of Iraq far from the city itself. For example, in 2011, while driving through a rural part of Arbil Governorate about 130 kilometers north of Kirkuk, I saw the words "Kirkuk is the heart of Kurdistan" spray-painted in Arabic and Kurdish on a cliff near a Kurdistan Regional Government (KRG) military checkpoint. And when the Kurdish nationalist leader Jalal Talabani invoked the idea that Kirkuk is the "Kurdish Jerusalem" in 2011 during his term as Iraq's president, many residents of Baghdad were so deeply affronted by this notion that they took to the streets in protest.[9]

The city of Kirkuk is also an omnipresent theme in Iraqi Turkmen discourses, both popular and literary. Turkmen writers, representing a much smaller group than the Kurds, have referred to Kirkuk as the "ancestral capital" of their people.[10] A viewer of the Turkish-language Iraqi satellite television channel Türkmeneli TV will notice that it features bilingual Arabic and Turkish advertisements for businesses that are almost exclusively located in Kirkuk, an indication that the city is the dominant social and economic center of the Iraqi Turkmen community.

To someone familiar with the ethnic and sectarian violence of Iraq's recent history, all these contemporary problems may seem obvious and expected. But the assumptions about Kirkuk's ethnic politics just outlined, while not always inaccurate, are ahistorical and thus superficial. Emotive comparisons to Jerusalem and the disturbing sight of suspected criminals burdened with ethnicity-identifying placards would have been baffling to a Kirkuki observer around the turn of the twentieth century. At that time, Kirkuk was a site of relative stability in northern Mesopotamia, a key stop on travel routes between Baghdad and Syria's major cities, and the location of an Ottoman garrison.

In a memoir of a visit to Kirkuk in 1909, a British military officer named E. B. Soane celebrated the presence of a diverse array of people—"Jew, Arab, Syrian, Armenian, Chaldean, Turk, Turkoman, and Kurd"—in the city. He described Kirkuk's urban public spaces as "indifferently" multilingual and asserted that this state of affairs afforded the city "considerable freedom from fanaticism."[11] Similarly, in a 2001 interview, the late Kirkuki poet Sargon Boulus recalled that the city in his youth had been a "crucible" of parlances whose multilingualism nurtured his development as a writer.[12] It is clear that communal social-linguistic identities—what scholars today usually call ethnicities—have long existed in Kirkuk. They were not, however, constant in definition, nor were they sites of political mobilization or the cleavage lines in a territorial status dispute until relatively recently.

How, then, did ethnic identities in Kirkuk develop into the institutionalized Kurdish-Arab-Turkmen schema with which Iraqis are so familiar today? How did these ethnicities become politically salient?

And what role did oil really play in that process? In his documentary, Karzan Sherabayani, like many Kirkukis, condemns Kirkuk's oil for the trouble it has brought to the city. He calls oil a "black curse," tacitly referring to a common nickname for Kirkuk in its native languages, City of Black Gold. "In a way, I wish we never had it," he says to the camera. "The only thing this brought to us is disaster." Yet the film also makes clear that oil is inextricably bound up in the city's identity. In another scene the manager of a fueling station gives his friend free gasoline ahead of a long line of cars waiting to purchase it. With a laugh, he explains, "In Europe, people give flowers to their friends as gifts. Here, we give petrol." Oil is central to Kirkukis' popular imagination and everyday interactions, including their interactions with ethnicity. This phenomenon is what this book aims to understand.

CITY OF BLACK GOLD

INTRODUCTION

IN KIRKUK THE PAST IS SO DEEPLY CONTESTED that the archival paper trail has repeatedly been burned. A longtime employee of Kirkuk's municipality once recalled that, immediately before the 2003 coalition invasion, she received an order from Saddam Hussein's government in Baghdad to purge records pertaining to ethnic cleansing. She remembered watching most of the documents go up in flames in a vast, daylong bonfire outside the municipality office.[1] The records that remain are scattered and fragmented. A petroleum geologist now living in Arbil told me that he personally salvaged (or, depending on one's perspective, looted) some old Iraq Petroleum Company geological files from the headquarters of Iraq's North Oil Company in Kirkuk during a period of lawlessness after the city's fall in 2003. When I appeared startled, he pulled out the dusty folders and piled them in front of me to prove his story. In another conversation a friend of mine recalled having witnessed Kurdish forces, the *pêşmerge*, taking over government offices and destroying records when they briefly occupied the city in 1991. A well-placed scholar commented to me during my research that there has been an effort in Iraq to buy and sell "historical documents" about Kirkuk as a result of the widespread obsession with the topic, given that rival versions of Kirkuk's history now form the basis for political claims. The authenticity of the documents being traded is doubtful, and they are being purchased by people who are not interested in making them available to external researchers.

History is, of course, in the memories of people as much as it is on paper. But many Kirkukis hesitate to give interviews to researchers, because they understand that speaking freely about politically sensitive issues could have consequences. And potential visitors who are not Iraqi citizens face visa limitations. A Turkish citizen of Kirkuki origin told me that she and her parents slipped into Kirkuk to visit relatives in 2012 by entering the autonomous Kurdistan Regional Government (KRG) area, which, unlike Iraq, permits visa-free entry to many passport holders, and then hiring two cars. One car transported their bags, and the other took them, luggage-free, through the military checkpoints on the highway to Kirkuk, where they pretended they were residents of the city returning home after a brief trip. Because the political situation in northern Iraq deteriorated in the following years, they did not return to Kirkuk. Even in the safety of diaspora, Kirkukis often do not want to talk in detail about past experiences. They are especially reluctant to relive memories of the troubling years of intercommunal violence after 1958 and the highly repressive era of Ba'th Party rule that began in 1968. Kirkuk may be a city where ideas about history inform every facet of civic identity, but it is also a place where many prefer not to delve too deeply into the traumas of the past.

When it is so hard to tell stories of the past and to stake historical claims, it may be no surprise that histories become disputed. In this book I reconstruct the political, social, and economic history, as well as the collective memories, of Kirkuk in order to question the assumptions behind present-day social and political practices. Since 2003, differing notions of Kirkuk's history, its inherent "ethnic character," and its rightful ownership have combined with sustained low-level violence to create profound tensions between Kirkuki communities. These tensions have raised the stakes of a crisis already exacerbated by a sclerotic process of political reconciliation.

Kirkuk is not unique in this respect. A historian's view of the politicization of identities in Kirkuk contributes to a fuller understanding of how local politics can become organized around ethnicized claims to a polyglot, culturally syncretic city. Kirkuk also illustrates that examining industrialization is not solely the domain of economic history and that understanding ethnicity is not just a concern of political and intellectual history. In urban history, economic, societal, and intellectual trends are tightly bound together. In twentieth-century Kirkuk, oil, urbanization, and colonialism guided the processes of nation building and collective identity formation, and the city that these forces built gave rise to fragmented, contentious local politics.

ETHNIC GROUPS, OR HOW ETHNICITY HAPPENS

Here, I use the English word *ethnic* to mean "ethnolinguistic."[2] This word has been widely used in its current sense only since the mid-twentieth century.[3] In Kirkuk, as in the rest of Iraq and many other parts of the Middle East, a person's or a community's primary language is the foremost constitutive element of their ethnicity. "Ethnicity" is an English-language concept that Kirkukis today use synonymously with many terms for collective identity in their local languages, including *qawm* (nation), *qawmiyya* (nationality), and *ʿirq* (race) in Arabic, *netewe* (nation) in Kurdish, and *millet* (nation or sect) and *etnik grup* (ethnic group) in Turkish. In general, Kirkukis who self-identify as members of a particular ethnicity speak the language associated with that group at home and among others of that group, or they were born into a family that does so. Thus, in certain social contexts, Kurds speak Sorani Kurdish. Similarly, Turkmens speak a distinct Turkish dialect, which they often refer to as Turkmani in the vernacular. Arabs speak Iraqi Arabic, and Chaldo-Assyrians speak vernacular Neo-Aramaic.

Of course, many particularities of lineage, custom, and political affiliation render the meaning of such terms as *Kurdish, Turkmen,* or *Arab* more complex than a linguistic signifier, both to those who identify with those labels and to those who apply them to others. Also, regardless of one's "ethnic" or "national" language, multilingualism is nearly universal in Kirkuk. A Kirkuki of any background who writes a letter to a Baghdad-based newspaper, for example, will do so in Arabic; an elderly Kirkuki who grew up in an era when primary education was mainly taught in Turkish might speak that language freely with Turkmani-speaking friends regardless of her own descent.

It is also inevitably the case that, as a result of multilingualism, intermarriage, and the many ways that one can self-identify, more than a few Kirkukis consider themselves members of more than one ethnic group or do not primarily identify with their ethnolinguistic heritage. Yet ethnicity, when it is politicized, is not just a matter of self-fashioning; it also affects how an individual is perceived by others. Any Kirkukis with a Kurdish parent could have been subjected to deportation during the "Arabization" ethnic-cleansing campaign by the Baʿthist government, which may have perceived them as "Kurdish" regardless of how they thought of themselves.

As a result, it is important to treat ethnicities as dynamic processes, or things that happen, rather than as static phenomena.[4] At times, they can even happen suddenly, turning a particular momentary altercation into an ethnic conflict.[5]

Some analysts of Kirkuk's ethnic politics in the present day have been careful to note that Kirkuki ethnicities and the rivalries between groups that result from them are not ancient and unchanging. They do so in deference to a social science literature that decades ago recognized that identities are subjectively constructed.[6] Still, there is currently too little discussion of how ethnicity, rather than a rigid set of categories, might be a way that Kirkukis articulate their political interests, a process of ethnicity that has become more prevalent over time. In popular forums such as the news media, writers often wrongly state or imply that the conflict over Kirkuk's status has been ongoing between three unitary ethnic groups for at least as long as the Iraqi state has existed, or even for thousands of years.[7] In reality, ethnic conflict in Kirkuk is a relatively new political practice.

OIL AS A SOCIAL, POLITICAL, AND CULTURAL FORCE

It is also time to rethink the role of oil in disputed oil-producing territories. The centrality of oil in Kirkukis' lives arose from the immense influence of the British-led Iraq Petroleum Company and (after 1972) its nationalized successor, the North Oil Company, in the city. Oil workers and their families made up nearly half the population of urban Kirkuk by the late 1940s. The company therefore dominated Kirkuk's labor affairs, drove its urban development, and wielded enormous leverage in its local politics. The city's urban fabric changed rapidly over the course of the twentieth century as a result of oil-fueled growth, intensifying communal segregation. Kirkukis came into contact with petroleum all the time, even in the most literal sense: major thoroughfares were paved with locally derived asphalt, and dirt roads were sprayed with viscous bitumen to maintain their solidity after rainfall. The experience of being a Kirkuki was, and is, suffused with oil. These kinds of cultural, material, and political-economic dynamics can never be fully separated from economically and strategically motivated claims to wealth-generating, resource-bearing areas. It is possible, even inevitable, for disputes over oil-rich regions to be competitions for a coveted commodity, a political domain, and a cultural imaginary simultaneously.

The prevailing discussion of the politics of oil in the Middle East, both historically and in the present, often fails to account for oil's social and cultural life. Instead, it usually functions within a false dichotomy that views actions such as staking a claim to Kirkuk as being either "about the oil" or motivated by something more "authentic." According to this framework, those who claim Kirkuk are either cynically aiming to gain access to its oil or are emotively connected to the city as part of their identity. In the first case, writers characterize the politics in question as avaricious and immoral and therefore illegitimate; in the second, they are pure and genuine and hence legitimate.[8]

This dichotomy is profoundly misleading. It oversimplifies the role of oil in the places where it is produced by presuming that it is either greedily desired as a source of wealth or totally immaterial. Instead, oil should be conceived of as an "oil complex"—not simply as a revenue-generating product but as a composite of institutions and as a means of political, social, and economic activity from which many different kinds of community, conflict, and culture can emerge.[9] Like many resources that require extraction, oil is linked to industries, technology, colonialism, urbanization, and pricing systems based on often-illusory perceptions of supply and demand. In Kirkuk oil was the central mediating factor that transformed how other forces throughout the twentieth century—urban growth, British influence, and consolidation of Iraqi state power—affected the city.

In other words, Kirkuk's dispute is certainly about the oil. But that does not mean that politicized ethnicity is a flimsy pretense masking a fundamentally mercenary conflict. Rather, it means that oil has shaped the self-identity of Kirkukis and their political practices by dominating their city's economy, running through their mundane interactions, and altering the physical geographies that they inhabit and traverse.

THE MAKING OF A DISPUTED CITY

Group identities in Kirkuk were more fluid when the Iraqi state was formed in the early 1920s. Local politics did not align clearly with ethnicities or other kinds of self-identities; instead, politics were largely subsumed under relations between more powerful external entities. The political interests of the people of Kirkuk were primarily determined by their ties to one or more of three patrons: the British administrators of Mandate Iraq, the fledgling Iraqi central government, or Turkey. Before Kirkuk's formal incorporation into Iraq, Kirkukis chose sides in an international status dispute over northern Mesopotamia based on which entity best served their interests—or, as was often the case, positioned themselves against a side based on its perceived hostility to their concerns.

These preexisting political dynamics began to shift with Kirkuk's integration into Baghdad's domain in 1926 and with the establishment of the Iraq Petroleum Company headquarters just northwest of urban Kirkuk after the company struck oil at Baba Gurgur in 1927. The Iraqi central government made efforts to promote Arab influence in the mostly non-Arab city, a process that exacerbated fault lines between emergent ethnic communities. At the same time, the city's population and its urban fabric grew rapidly. The oil industry, which provided the livelihood of a substantial percentage of Kirkuk's population, became the focus of labor organization led by the Iraqi Communist Party. The British government had retained a significant degree of informal imperial influence in Iraq. Consequently, the Iraqi government, the British government, and the oil company attempted to counter Communist influence through urban development schemes, including the construction of housing.

The combination of urban expansion and the growth of discursive activities, such as writing and printing, produced a distinct Kirkuki civic identity and an accompanying arena of local politics in which Kirkukis were deeply invested. In this environment Kirkukis became both ethnicized people and "people of oil," the two subjectivities inextricably linked. After the Iraqi revolution in 1958 and the resulting radical instability in Kirkuk's urban politics, a cycle of intercommunal violence began along increasingly apparent ethnic lines. The escalation of conflict between Baghdad and the Kurdish movement for control of Kirkuk and its hinterland after 1958 fueled these tensions further.

It was at this point that, for the first time in Iraq's modern history, Kirkuk *itself* became a battleground rather than an incidental part of a disputed surrounding region. Both internal communities and external forces fought over Kirkuk's status and rightful identity. The city became contested in its own right and remained that way for decades as the Ba'th regime brutally institutionalized ethnic groups through party expansion, ethnicity-based surveillance, and outright ethnic cleansing of non-Arabs. Baghdad also consolidated its power in Kirkuk through the nationalization of the oil industry in 1972, quickly subsuming the North Oil Company and its urban spaces under the Ba'th Party's strict loyalty-based control. The split of the Kurdish nationalist movement into distinct party factions also introduced a new layer of political contention. By the time of the 2003 coalition invasion, Kirkuk was already a divided, traumatized city.

OIL CITIES, PROVINCIAL HISTORY, AND CIVIC IDENTITIES

Kirkuk is an oil city, and this fact is salient to an understanding of its social relations and urban and provincial politics. The concept of the oil city contains two separate but equally important features: the role of industry, specifically oil production, as a sociopolitical agent, and the urban arena as an analytical scope.[10] Older histories of oil industries in the Middle East were prone to being descriptive and typically disregarded the experiences of local employees and communities in the places where firms operated.[11] Lately, a number of more rigorous academic works on the Middle East, Europe, and Latin America have examined oil industries as a way of combining analytical approaches to social, cultural, political, and environmental history in a specific place and time.[12] Similarly, traditional studies of urbanism in the oil-producing countries of the Persian Gulf region tended to overlook these cities' characteristics in the pre-oil era and did little more than document their development under the assumption that modernization is a steady, linear process advancing logically from the accrual of oil revenues.[13] Since the early 2000s, several studies have moved past these limitations, including Farah Al-Nakib's history of the erosion of social ties through oil urbanization in Kuwait City, Nelida Fuccaro's history of Manama before and after the discovery of oil, and Mandana Limbert's ethnography of the transformation of conceptions of time and memory in an Omani town.[14]

My work contributes to these efforts to understand the claiming, extraction, refinement, and export of oil as a crucial aspect of local, urban social and political processes. Furthermore, oil is not a predictable agent. It does not always lead to prosperity and modernity in the capitalist sense. Even when it does, it does so unevenly, and the development of an oil industry certainly does not benefit all the local inhabitants it affects. This is particularly true of Kirkuk, which is unusual among Middle Eastern cities that house oil company headquarters and operations. Kirkuk had a long history of expansion, bureaucratization as part of Ottoman governmental centralization, and the growth of a local political apparatus before the discovery in 1927 that it was resting atop an oil field capable of large-scale commercial production.[15] Kirkuk was not a planned "company town" in the same way that, for instance, Dhahran was in Saudi Arabia. Its physical and human geographies were not built from the ground up on the basis of a foreign company's inclinations, but evolved out of decades of interaction between local, external, and imperial forces. In this book I therefore extensively analyze Kirkuk's local politics, arrays of self-identity, and relationships with external politics in the decades before the Iraq Petroleum Company's presence. I then consider the ways that the oil industry *interacted* with this dynamic local domain, contributing to both its growth and its consolidation. Oil did not create Kirkuk, but oil was a key aspect of its reorientation toward Baghdad as a political center of gravity and of the reorganization and disaggregation of its ethnic communities.

Focusing on a place like Kirkuk also recenters national history—in this case, the history of the modern state of Iraq—in order to understand national integration and colonialism from a provincial perspective. National histories of lesser-studied countries tend to actually be about their capitals. Whether "Iraq" denotes the modern state or the historical region, histories of the area are usually written from the perspective of Baghdad. More research has been done on provincial Iraq in the Ottoman era than in the twentieth century, most likely because the relevant Ottoman archival sources on such places as Mosul and Basra are relatively easy to access in Istanbul.[16] There are also several histories of the Kurds that primarily discuss the areas where most of them reside in northeastern Iraq, though these tend to focus on the Kurdish nationalist movement rather than on other political elements of provincial-center relations.[17] The divide between the metropolis and provincial cities is particularly visible in studies of Iraqi urbanism; these works are forming a growing and increasingly sophisticated literature, but they focus almost exclusively on Baghdad.[18]

The prioritizing of territorial nationalisms, in Prasenjit Duara's words, currently leaves other "spatial formation[s] buried under the national space" in many regions of the world.[19] Duara published his first book on rural North China in 1988; the following year, Peter Sahlins published his landmark study of the Pyrenees borderland between France and Spain.[20] The historiographies of most major countries and regions have long since adopted this approach of decentering and recentering historical scopes. Yet it remains uncommon in the histories of smaller, formerly colonized countries such as Iraq. It is critical to closely examine provincial areas, like Kirkuk and its hinterland, in colonized countries to achieve a fuller understanding of how colonialism and decolonization work outside the halls of the central government. In Kirkuk the Iraq Petroleum Company was initially a node for British interests and private international interests, and the interaction of those forces had a profound local impact. Later, as a nationalized, decolonized operation, the oil company became one of the institutions through which the Ba'th government expanded its influence into the city.

Provincial areas also provide a window into the process of state building from the perspective of an area where such efforts were particularly troubled and proved to be divisive, not unifying, to the local population. Scholars specializing in Iraqi studies have created a robust literature in recent years on the subjects of Iraqi identity formation and nation building.[21] These scholars offer nuanced analyses of identities in a variety of Iraqi discourses, whether collective or factional, simple or "hybrid," or unifying or divisive. A common finding of this scholarship has been that one of the most potent identity-based divergences in Iraqi politics for most of the twentieth century was that between pan-Arabists and Iraqi-territorial nationalists. Another is that divisions fell along ideological, class, and rural-urban lines more often than along sectarian ones.

Altogether, scholars writing on the topic of Iraqi identity have thus far usually focused on conceptualizing identities that are coterminous, whether harmoniously or contentiously, with the boundaries of the nation-state. Although they do look at identity-based fault lines and "othering" within Iraqi society,[22] they tend to conclude that even these divided and divisive group identities formed a cohesive, yet complex, Iraqi whole in some form—that is, they were "fragments imagining the nation."[23] As a result of their focus on the formation of a communal Iraqi identity, these scholars often rely on Benedict Anderson's concept of the imagined community as a point of reference, whether for agreement or departure.[24] In their analyses they carefully avoid oversimplifying Iraqi group identities in the past and present, but they also tend to imply or state outright, with evident regret, that Iraq's legacy of pluralistic discourse in an earlier era contrasts with the present-day reality of pervasive sectarianism brought about by the Saddam Hussein era and the Iraq War.[25] Sectarianism, in this view, is especially apparent in the political rivalry between Arab members of Islamic confessional sects: Sunni Arabs and Shi'i Arabs. The Kurds, regardless of religion or sect, are often considered an analogous third group.[26]

My examination of the politics of identity in Kirkuk, while taking into account previous analyses of Iraqi identity formation, departs from this literature in two ways. First, I examine the coalescence of *ethnicized* politics in an unusually multilingual area. The political practice of ethnicity can be nationalistic, but that is not necessarily the case—and it is a phenomenon distinct from confessional sectarianism. (There are Sunni and Shi'i confessional communities in Kirkuk that cut across ethnic groups, but this divide had remarkably little political salience there until recently.) Second, I look at centralizing, integrative trends emanating from Baghdad at a distance. I view them as an external force in Kirkuk that did not have unifying effects and was more divisive than it was hybridizing.

Group identities in Kirkuk are unique among those in Iraq's major urban areas because the popularly perceived distinctions between communities fall along the lines of ethnolinguistic position. No other large urban area in Iraq is as thoroughly multilingual without a predominant majority group as Kirkuk, and few other major cities in the Middle East are as linguistically pluralistic. The average Kirkuki is accustomed to a polyglot environment in which public signs, for example, are routinely rendered in at least four languages (Figure 2). This diversity does not naturally imply, however, that Kirkuk was always a "city of ethnic harmony," an idea that suggests the existence of a shared, convivial sense of being Kirkuki that is "hyphenated" with ethnic identities.[27] Although many Kirkukis today sincerely profess hybrid identities, ethnic groupings in Kirkuk were simply not politically salient enough in the early twentieth century for hybridity to make sense. This circumstance was a result of the fluidity and the relative irrelevance of ethnicity, combined with universal multilingualism.

Throughout the period I am examining, there was never a strong unifying *national* identity in Kirkuk, whether Iraqi, Kurdistani, or otherwise. This is even true of the local notables who aligned themselves with Baghdad early in the process of Kirkuk's integration into the Iraqi state; they did not do so out of an articulated affinity with Baghdad. Instead, Kirkukis were largely "nationally indifferent."[28] In Kirkuk, as in other culturally and socially heterogeneous places, popular nationalism was not necessarily a natural outcome of the post–World War I era of newly created Middle Eastern nation-states. The extension of state influence and accompanying local bureaucratization can, and often does, precede the penetration of any kind of popular identification with the nation-state into peripheral areas. The two processes—state making and nation building—are distinct.[29]

British attempts to govern Kirkuk in the eras of military and Mandate rule relied on rigid and inaccurate assumptions about the area's "racial" composition (in their words at the time) and the distinct political interests of each "race," dividing its population into Kurds, Turkmens, Arabs, and Christians for this purpose. The eventual coalescence of these groups was, in part, the result of a symbiotic relationship between the practices of British and Baghdad authorities on the one

FIGURE 2. A sign in Arabic, Kurdish, Turkish, and English at Kirkuk University. Photo by Rawyar Ehsan. © Google.

hand and the practices of local notables on the other as the separate communities became invested in a growing domain of urban politics. With the advent of the oil industry, a reoriented Kirkuki civic identity emerged that was bound to oil, development, and Western-influenced notions of modernity, but this too became a basis for competition rather than purely being a source of conviviality. These kinds of intercommunal divisions are produced in the interplay between local dynamics and external forces that exert their influence in the local arena.[30]

My goal in this book is not to find a sort of compromise between the idea of ethnicity as a primordial trait and the idea of ethnicity as a fictive construction, but rather to locate and analyze the origins, components, and mechanisms of ethnicized politics. Phenomena such as ethnicity do not spring up out of an objective truth about a person's life, such as the language that a person speaks, and then become spontaneously politicized. Industry, work, space, and everyday practice also play a role in shaping them.

SOURCES AND TERMINOLOGY

This book is the first sustained history of Kirkuk in the era of the modern Iraqi state based on extensive, multisited primary-source research. The existing scholarship on Kirkuk's history in English consists mainly of small sections of projects that have a larger scope. Most notably, Hanna Batatu, in his definitive political and social history of Iraq, wrote an unparalleled account of the July 1959 massacre in Kirkuk using municipal police records that he was able to access in 1964.[31] In addition, there is a substantial literature on Kirkuk's history in Arabic, Turkish, and Kurdish written by both professional and amateur scholars who are often themselves from Kirkuk or nearby areas. Some of these works have been translated or adapted into English; occasionally, the author has written primarily in English. The consistent pattern in these works is that they are almost always written from either a Turkmen or a Kurdish ethnopolitical viewpoint and aim to make a case for what the authors perceive to be the city's inherent ethnic character. Therefore, even though they may muster thought-provoking material from a variety of sources, they are selective and sometimes misleading in their reading of that historical evidence rather than comprehensive and critical.[32]

Kurdish historians such as Kamal Muzhir Ahmad tend to rely to a great extent on Western, particularly British, sources and on published sources in Arabic and Kurdish. By contrast, Turkmen scholars writing about Kirkuk, such as Ata Terzibaşı, often compile information from more obscure primary sources, such as local newspapers in Turkish, or from their own ethnographic fieldwork.[33] These writings by Turkmens therefore constitute useful examples of what might generally be termed works of memory; they comprehensively document various aspects of the experience of the Turkmen community and are therefore of interest to historians regardless of the limitations and biases inherent in their approach.

One prominent example of scholarship on Kirkuk that is mostly by Middle Eastern scholars and transcends these limitations to some extent is a volume of conference proceedings featuring papers delivered at an Arabic-language conference about Kirkuk held in London in 2001. These essays feature explorations of some fascinating primary sources and are slightly subtler in their use of ethnopolitical frameworks. Nevertheless, despite the deliberate selection of the English title *Kirkuk, the City of Ethnic Harmony* (which loosely translates the original Arabic phrase *al-qawmiyyat al-muta'akhiyya*, or "fraternal nationalities"), exclusionary ethnicized lenses still predominate. Most of the authors explicitly identify themselves in the volume as either Kurdish or Turkmen, and the papers correspondingly tend to emphasize either Kurdish or Turkmen aspects of Kirkuk's history.[34]

The litterateurs of the Kirkuk Group (Jama'at Karkuk), a collective of novelists, poets, and scholars, have also produced compelling works of memory about Kirkuk. Two members of this group, Fadhil al-Azzawi and the late Anwar Al-Ghassani, have written essays about Kirkuk's literary scene and local politics in the early revolutionary era.

The late poet Sargon Boulus, another member of the collective, also publicly discussed his life in the city, including in an extensive autobiographical interview published in 2001.[35] As previously mentioned, Boulus recalled with regard to his youth in mid-twentieth-century Kirkuk that when he and his friends spoke with one another, deriving expressions from all of the city's languages as they bantered, what happened was "really a kind of poetic chemistry . . . if we consider these vocabularies as metals that theurgists put in that crucible where they fuse and become something else." It was in this environment, Boulus said, that they became litterateurs, devoted to the many possibilities of language.[36]

Some of these authors have written about Kirkuk in their literary works. The most notable example is al-Azzawi's novel *Akhir al-Mala'ika* (The Last of the Angels), which, though fictional with satirical and fantastical elements, creates a detailed portrait of the city from the late 1950s to the mid-1960s, complete with lovingly meticulous descriptions of its neighborhoods.[37]

My findings are based on research in a variety of types of sources in many different locations. I worked at several archives in the United Kingdom, including the National Archives and the BP Archive, as well as the National Archives of the United States, the Constantinos A. Doxiadis Archives in Athens, and the Iraqi Ba'th Party records at the National Defense University and the Hoover Institution. I also gathered published primary sources in Arabic, English, and Turkish, including works of memory, magazines, and newspapers, from libraries in the United States, the United Kingdom, and Turkey. I filled in critical details with personal correspondence and interviews, including those conducted on trips to Arbil in 2011 and Istanbul in 2014. (The ethical dilemmas raised by some of these sources, particularly the Ba'th Party records located in the United States, are discussed in the Note on Sources and Archives at the end of this book.) I also use secondary sources in Arabic and English, along with a handful in Turkish and French. In addition to written sources, the many maps and photographs found in these archives and publications have proven to be vital in portions of my analysis. Figures on Kirkuk found in the Iraqi censuses of 1947 and 1957 form the basis of my examination of urban demographic change.

I did not ultimately do any research in Kirkuk for this project. My conversations with friends and interlocutors who have lived there or conducted research on Iraq, as described previously, indicate that many municipal, oil company, and provincial records were destroyed or went missing during the Ba'th era and the looting that followed the fall of the city to coalition-affiliated Kurdish pêşmerge forces in 2003.[38] Other records are available on the black market or, as I found, in the possession of private individuals. Some Ba'th Party documents from Kirkuk are evidently in the custody of the KRG's ruling parties, the Kurdistan Democratic Party (KDP) and the Patriotic Union of Kurdistan (PUK), and are not widely publicly available.[39] To my knowledge, the only historian of any nationality who has cited archival materials accessed *in* Kirkuk in a published work in any language is, as previously mentioned, the late Hanna Batatu, who did so more than half a century ago.

Future researchers of Kirkuk's history would do well to seek out materials relevant to Kirkuk in the Iraq National Library and Archive in Baghdad, a city where I have not yet attempted to conduct research (in large part because I carry only a U.S. passport). This vital institution's holdings were badly damaged in the looting in the aftermath of Baghdad's capture by American-led forces in 2003. It has rebuilt since then, despite its reduced collection, and is open to researchers.[40] There must also be some essential Iraq Petroleum Company papers from Kirkuk archived in the Iraqi Ministry of Oil, which is also in Baghdad. Finally, it appears that there is crucial information in Turkish- and Kurdish-language memoirs and other published works of memory that have had limited distribution and are presently obscure to most scholars, both foreign and local.[41]

Because of the scope of this project, the challenges of doing research in multiple countries, and my own linguistic limitations, I have included relatively few Turkish-language sources and no Kurdish-language sources to supplement the English- and Arabic-language sources I have used. This book is not, of course, the final word on Kirkuk's twentieth-century history. There is also much more to learn about Kirkuk's history in the Ottoman era, before the establishment of the Iraqi state. I look forward to seeing scholars eventually tap into the kinds of materials I was unable to access. Doing so will require extensive multilingual skills and unfettered use of libraries and archives in Iraq. Ideally, historians native to Kirkuk will be in a position to do this research themselves. Those scholars will advance our understanding of modern Kirkuk beyond the analysis that I have presented here.

The problems with accessing any remaining archival sources in Kirkuk itself and of collecting oral histories there, approaches that are virtually impossible for outside researchers in the current political environment and risky even for the city's inhabitants, are unlikely to be resolved soon. Even among Kirkukis in the diaspora, ethnicized mutual mistrust runs so deep that interviews and other forms of person-to-person research can be difficult to conduct. My own positionality therefore merits explanation, as it has certainly played a role in shaping the archive of data I have created. I was born in the United States to Assyrian parents from Syria and Iraq; my mother was born in Kirkuk. Both of my grandfathers, like so many Assyrians in the twentieth century, worked at one point for the Iraq Petroleum Company. As someone with personal ties to Kirkuk who is associated with an ethnic minority outside the usual tripartite schema, I have been welcomed and enthusiastically assisted by a diverse group of Kirkukis, though not always without suspicion of my motives. In a typical encounter, one Kirkuki Turkmen asked me bluntly on my first visit to talk to him, "What is your agenda?" He warmed to me quickly when I explained that I was not making an ethnic-nationalist case for Kirkuk's ownership but rather was interested in oil and colonialism as forces that had shaped ethnicity and conflict. It is possible that he, and my Chaldo-Assyrian and Arab interlocutors, would not have been as forthcoming with assistance if I had a Kurdish name; similarly, some of my Kurdish contacts might have hesitated if I had a name that suggested I was Turkmen or Arab. At the same time, Kirkukis and other Iraqis I spoke to were aware that I was an American and therefore perceived me, with my non-native spoken Arabic, as somewhat foreign. This meant that they often assumed I knew little about Iraq or Kirkuk and tended to reiterate the basic elements of their respective nationalist (or "city of ethnic harmony") cases for Kirkuk until I surprised them with more detailed questions. The answers I received to those questions were sometimes warm, generous, and thorough. Sometimes they were puzzled and brief.

The terminology of ethnicity I use in this work requires its own explanatory note. It is particularly difficult to use ethnic descriptors with fixed definitions in a work that proceeds from the premise that identity, ethnicity, and ethnic differentiation are politicized processes and practices, not innate features of Kirkuki society. It is also worth questioning why a scholar would assign ethnic labels to groups of people when certain individuals commonly considered to be associated with those groups may prefer to profess another identity first and foremost or may have other equally relevant subject positions. Indeed, as discussed earlier, Kirkukis are routinely multilingual, and the language in use in any given situation varies depending on a large number of factors. For instance, it is noteworthy that, in Kurdish filmmaker Karzan Sherabayani's 2007 documentary of Kirkuk, self-identified Turkmens tend to speak to him in Arabic. Arabic is the most widespread common language in Iraq and is the language in which the vast majority of Iraqis (outside the KRG region) are educated. Turkmens' use of Arabic while talking to a Kurdish Kirkuki who is filming them for a Kurdish-nationalist documentary therefore suggests a conscious underscoring of their opposition to Kurdish control. Moreover, further complicating the picture of ethnolinguistic identity, intermarriage between ethnolinguistic communities in Kirkuk certainly exists, though its prevalence has never been measured.

In response to these kinds of dilemmas, some historians have chosen to avoid the idea of ethnicity or the use of the word *ethnic* altogether when writing about multilingual, multicultural regions, regarding it as a problematic concept that they would rather disrupt than reify.[42] In the case of Kirkuk, however, Kirkukis themselves use such a concept—including use of the English word *ethnic* and neologisms adapted from it—and there is no question that "ethnicity," in this sense, is central to the city's political, social, and physical fabric. Therefore I have had to find a way to talk about it.

The self-identity of any given individual in Kirkuk who warrants a mention in archival sources is typically unknown. It is impossible to know for certain whether, for instance, a particular British intelligence report describing an urban notable as a "Turk," "Turkmen," "Kurd," or "Arab" is doing so based on that individual's professed ethnicity or on the basis of European racial theories that considered someone of a particular "stock" to belong to that group regardless of other factors such as language, sociality, and class. The line between "Turks" and "Turkmens" is also indistinct. Early- to mid-twentieth-century sources often use these terms interchangeably, depending on whether or not the author regarded Turkish-speaking Iraqis, with their regional culture and dialect, as distinct from Turkish-speaking Anatolians. I have therefore been careful to differentiate between individuals' and groups' primary language, their most likely ethnic self-identity, and the way that others perceive their ethnicities. I also convey a sense of the frequent slipping in historical sources between terms that translate literally as "nationality" or "race."

I use adjectives such as "Turkish-speaking" and "Kurdish-speaking" and the corresponding nouns ("Turkish speaker," "Kurdish speaker") when the primary language is all that is known about an individual's or group's differentiation from others and when their ethnic self-identity, if they indeed have a distinct one, is not clear from the context. At the same time, when quoting or paraphrasing a source that uses a particular ethnoracial terminology, I follow its usage. If I know or am reasonably certain that a person or group would call themselves Kurdish, Turkmen, or Arab—or if they would be perceived that way because of certain markers of subjectivity such as geography and clothing, as in the case of the violence of July 1959—I use those ethnic terms.[43] Readers will notice that the straightforward use of the nouns *Kurd*, *Turkmen*, and *Arab*, along with their corresponding adjectival forms to describe people and groups, will become more frequent in chronologically later sections. This is one of many indications of the solidification of ethnic categories in Kirkuk over time.

The term *Chaldo-Assyrian* also merits a separate explanation.[44] The term *Christian*, though obviously not a linguistic designation, is often used as a quasi-ethnic descriptor for Christians from Iraq in general and from Kirkuk in particular. However, Iraqis who profess belief in Christianity, practice Christianity, or come from a family of Christians may belong to one of several linguistic-cultural spheres. The largest ethnic group in Iraq whose members are overwhelmingly Christian consists of those who speak Neo-Aramaic or, if they have personally assimilated into another language group, whose recent ancestors spoke Neo-Aramaic. Members of this Iraqi Christian group, who retain a linguistic heritage that long predates the advent of Islam and of the Arabic, Kurdish, and Turkish languages in Iraq, tend to call themselves Chaldeans if they belong to the Chaldean Catholic Church and Assyrians if they belong to the Assyrian Church of the East.[45] The combination of these names results in the collective term *Chaldo-Assyrian*.

Yet, in a Kirkuki context, this collective term can be misleading. Most Christians native to Kirkuk in the immediate post–World War I era were members of the Chaldean Catholic Church and spoke Turkish as their first language. Some sources even go so far as to describe them simultaneously as Chaldeans and as ethnic Turkmens. Chaldeans who lived in Kirkuk's citadel were known in Turkmani as *qalagawuru*, or "nonbelievers of the citadel" (a colloquially accepted term with derogatory origins). Neo-Aramaic-speaking people in Kirkuk who identified as Assyrian were, after World War I, most often refugees from other areas or their descendants. This difference was frequently significant because self-identified Assyrians were, rightly or not, perceived as outsiders in Kirkuk. The consequences of this tension could prove to be disastrous. Self-identified Assyrians also tended to have closer connections, for better or for worse, to the British presence in Iraq before 1958—whether the Royal Air Force, Mandate authorities, or the Iraq Petroleum Company. I have therefore used the separate terms *Chaldean* and *Assyrian* when the distinction between these communities is salient and the collective term *Chaldo-Assyrian* when it is not.

These subjective decisions that I have made with regard to terminology may be objectionable to some readers. More broadly, some may find it concerning that situating the origins of ethnicity in recent history calls into question the notion that any single linguistic-cultural community is unitary or stable. This, in turn, undermines the idea that any group possesses a hereditary right to a particular territory. In a region that has seen forced assimilation and ethnic cleansing, this kind of academic pursuit, undertaken by an American scholar living comfortably far away from the territory in question, might come across as reckless. From this perspective, asserting that terms such as *Kurdish, Turkmen, Arab, Chaldean*, and *Assyrian* have recent, contingent meanings could bolster the identity denialism of genocidaires. I hope readers of all backgrounds will recognize that I am not trying to suggest that ethnicity is not "real" or has no history—social constructs are, after all, very real and do not emerge out of vacuums. Rather, my goal is to reimagine the history of a city whose recent memory has been swallowed whole by the presumption of ethnopolitical conflict. If a historian, following the lead of Kirkukis like Sargon Boulus, instead begins with the premise that a multilingual city is a "crucible" of its citizens, how can she explain the volatile interaction and mutual separation of some of its elements? This is the question I seek to answer.

1 THE FORGING OF IRAQ

KIRKUK'S INTEGRATION INTO modern Iraq began in the final stages of the British Mesopotamian campaign of World War I in 1918. Troops under British command occupied the city and its hinterland, and Kirkuk remained under British military administration until 1921. To understand Kirkuk's political, social, and economic trajectory over the next several decades, it is necessary to address two main questions about this three-year period. First, in what political, social, and economic context were British authorities operating? Second, how did those authorities attempt, and fail, to integrate Kirkuk into the process of contriving the modern Iraqi state? Unlike some of the oil "company towns" of the Gulf, Kirkuk was already a sizable town with a preexisting history as a site of commerce and of Ottoman influence. The British government, which was aware that the Kirkuk area was rich with oil and had commercial potential, aimed to control it as part of a modern colony in the Iraqi region as they fought the Ottoman Empire in World War I.

Influential Kirkukis, typically family patriarchs and tribal leaders, built and maintained links with British authorities soon after troops under British command first occupied Kirkuk. British officials used these relationships to solidify their control over the area. Meanwhile, Kirkuki tribal leaders were able to more deeply entrench their power in local politics than had been the case under Ottoman rule. This approach to colonial governance created relationships of patronage that were useful to the British but also had serious shortcomings. In 1921, despite the ongoing ambiguity of Kirkuk's status in relation to Iraq, British officials unsuccessfully tried to incorporate prominent Kirkuki locals into a procedure to unanimously confirm the Iraqi monarch. The failures of early British administration stemmed from a lack of understanding of the interdependence of urban and rural Kirkuk, Kirkuk's distinctness from nearby Kurdish-majority areas, and the fluid nature of Kirkuk's group identities.

KIRKUK BEFORE THE LATE OTTOMAN ERA

The Kirkuk area is among the oldest continuously inhabited areas in the world, showing evidence of human settlement dating back more than three millennia. Kirkuk is located on the Khasa River, a tributary of the Tigris, in the northeastern part of the Tigris-Euphrates river system; traditionally known as Mesopotamia, this region is located between Anatolia, Persia, and the Levant. The city is just under 100 kilometers west of the Zagros mountain range. Scholars generally believe that the modern city is located on the site of the ancient city of Arrapha. The site of the ancient city of Nuzi, which was excavated by a team of Western archaeologists during the British Mandate era, is several kilometers away.

Kirkuk's oldest feature is a citadel built on the east bank of the Khasa River. Archaeological evidence indicates that the citadel, which remains in the center of the modern city, was probably constructed sometime in the middle of the third millennium BCE. As late as the Islamic era, writings by geographers indicated that the settlement that is now Kirkuk consisted solely of the citadel. Because of the frequent attacks that were the inevitable consequence of its frontier location, the town did not expand significantly beyond the fortified hill and onto both sides of the Khasa River until the seventeenth century.[1]

In its earliest era of settlement, the area including Arrapha and Nuzi was inhabited by two groups, the Akkadians and the Hurrians, both of whom controlled it at various times.[2] Over many centuries numerous other polities conquered and controlled the town that eventually became Kirkuk. It was an especially significant town in the Neo-Assyrian Empire. When it was part of the Sasanian Empire, its Syriac name was Karkha d-Beth Slokh, a likely source for the modern name; the town was noteworthy for being a place where Christianity, particularly the Church of the East, flourished.[3] In the seventh century the Kirkuk area and its surrounding regions came under the control of the Islamic caliphate along with most of the rest of the Sasanian domains. The Abbasid caliph al-Mansur founded Baghdad, which is located on the Tigris River about 240 kilometers south of Kirkuk, as the capital of the caliphate in the eighth century. Throughout the many conquests in the centuries that followed, the political status of the Kirkuk area typically corresponded to Baghdad's. The modern name of Kirkuk first appears in a fifteenth-century source.[4]

For reasons related to the twentieth- and twenty-first-century dispute over Kirkuk's status, the subject of when each of its major ethnic groups first appeared in the town is highly contentious. For instance, some scholars posit that the Turkmens of Kirkuk are descended from Turkic troops of the early Islamic era or from Turkic immigrants who arrived during the period of Seljuq rule beginning in the eleventh century, whereas others suggest that their antecedents did not arrive in Kirkuk until the sixteenth or even the eighteenth century.[5] Significantly, Kurdish nationalists have used the late-arrival theories to attempt to discredit the Turkmens' presence in Kirkuk, as will be discussed later. In addition, still other scholars have proposed a variety of highly inventive claims about the origins of Kirkuki ethnicities, especially among the Kurds and the Assyrians, that assert impossibly that they, as continuous and distinct groups, have been present in Kirkuk for many millennia.[6] That said, it is certainly the case that speakers of predecessor languages to modern Neo-Aramaic and Kurdish have been living in the region of Kirkuk since antiquity. Arabic-speaking people first came to Kirkuk during the Islamic conquest of Iraq in the seventh century.

Although some scholars have made thoroughgoing attempts to trace and summarize what is known about the origins of Kirkuk's modern ethnic groups through available sources and have weighed the plausibility of different claims,[7] I contend that this practice anachronistically implies that present-day ethnicities are a reflection of group identities that existed in Kirkuk many centuries ago. At worst, it perpetuates the idea that a particular ethnic community can claim a more legitimate presence in Kirkuk on the basis of perceived longevity, which in turn entails chauvinistic assumptions about the racial purity of each modern group. It should go without saying that, although many, perhaps even most, Kirkukis are partially descended from people who lived in the city or its surrounding region in antiquity, there is no telling what languages any given Kirkuki's ancestors spoke in this polyglot region or what communal identifying terms they would have used to describe themselves. Digging into ancient and medieval history for more information on the origins of modern Kirkukis also ignores the fact that enormous immigration into the city took place in the twentieth century, swelling the numbers of almost every linguistic community with colinguists from other regions. Finally, the process of tracing communities' origins in Kirkuk by working backward from today's prevalent ethnic groups erases the experiences of Kirkukis from groups that are no longer present in the city—most notably the Jewish community, virtually all of whom departed for Israel under duress in the mid-twentieth century—and disregards bases of community outside an ethnic paradigm, such as confessional identity, that were probably much more salient at different points in history.[8]

In all, though the details of Kirkuk's political history throughout its first two or three millennia remain hazy, the fact that the town has perpetually been located on frontiers between peoples suggests that a close analysis of this history, if possible, would reveal many heretofore untold episodes of contestation whose human costs could have been much greater than those of the violence driven by ethnic conflict in the city in the twentieth and twenty-first centuries. Furthermore, the linguistic and religious composition of Kirkuk's population has changed dramatically in the past several centuries. These changes have taken place not only because of shifts in Kirkuk's political status but also because of multilingualism and fluctuations in dominant languages and identities over a long period of time.

PATRONAGE AND THE PERILS OF THE
FRONTIER IN LATE OTTOMAN KIRKUK

Kirkuk became part of the Ottoman Empire in the sixteenth century, when Ottoman troops gradually conquered the region that is now the modern state of Iraq. Istanbul changed the administrative boundaries around Kirkuk frequently during this time, but it was generally part of an administrative unit called Şehrizor. In 1879 Şehrizor became part of the new *vilayet*, or province, of Mosul.[9] The three *vilayet*s of Mosul, Baghdad, and Basra would eventually correspond, for the most part, to the borders of the modern state of Iraq.

In the late Ottoman era Kirkuk was a point of intersection for Ottoman, Persian, and independent Kurdish tribal interests and influences. For centuries Şehrizor was a site of frequent fighting between Ottoman and Persian forces because of its proximity to Iran. Along with Sulaymaniyya (Silêmanî) to its east, the Şehrizor division was predominantly populated by Kurdish-speaking tribes. In general, Ottoman policy in Iraq relied on a system of the patronage of local notables, or prominent people with independent local influence, to maintain control and to collect taxes.[10] Consequently, beginning early in the era of Ottoman control of Iraq, authorities in Istanbul appointed Kurdish families to govern Şehrizor and Sulaymaniyya through semi-autonomous, hereditary tribal principalities.[11] Although their intention was, in part, to use these links to keep Şehrizor secure from Persian invasions, the Kurds remained largely independent from Istanbul's influence and sometimes made alliances with Persian leaders.[12] Persian forces entered Şehrizor frequently, and the town of Kirkuk even briefly surrendered to the Persians on a few occasions.[13] The fact that Kurdish tribal leaders in the area had a long history of openly allying themselves with both the Ottomans and the Persians, frequently switching sides, and of aligning with different sides within the same family is especially significant to an understanding of twentieth-century politics in Kirkuk.[14] The town of Kirkuk itself, unlike its hinterland, was predominantly Turkish speaking and was, as a result, "conspicuous as a nursery of the official class" of Turkish-speaking elites, according to British military officer and historian Stephen Longrigg.[15] Longrigg served as one of the first British military officials in charge of Kirkuk beginning in 1918.

Ottoman policy in Kirkuk under Sultan Abdülhamid II (1876–1909) was preoccupied with the fact that the town and its surrounding region were part of more than one linguistic and political frontier; the basic task of maintaining security there was a priority for Istanbul. In this time period the first frontier was between the Ottomans and Kurdish tribes. Early in the nineteenth century, Istanbul began an active campaign to bring the Kurdish tribes in Ottoman domains under their control, mainly by repressing and sidelining the leaders of the semi-autonomous principalities.[16] During the era of the Tanzimat reforms, which began in 1839, the extension of central government influence to frontier regions became an integral aspect of Ottoman policy. In eastern Anatolia, for example, the Ottoman government created a Kurdish cavalry force for social and political purposes in addition to its strategic functions as a way of integrating those provinces into the nation-state.[17] As for Kirkuk, its tribal hinterland and neighboring regions, including the town of Sulaymaniyya just under 100 kilometers to its east, came to be prominent sites of tribal Kurdish resistance to Istanbul's interference.

Kirkuk's second frontier was the violently disputed one between the Ottomans and the Persians. These two frontiers were inextricably linked in Ottoman policy, as the extension of central government control to Kurdish areas was associated with efforts to define and harden the ambiguous and fluid borderlands between Ottoman-controlled and Persian-controlled areas that had begun with the drawing of an Ottoman-Persian boundary in the mid- to late nineteenth century.[18] As a result of the fluctuating relationships between locally influential Kurdish tribes, Ottoman authorities, and the Persians, Şehrizor and Sulaymaniyya were the most unstable areas in the Iraqi region. This problem was exacerbated by the decline of central government influence caused by the Russo-Turkish War of 1877–1878, a blow to their leverage from which Ottoman authorities did not fully recover.[19]

In addition, the Ottomans' suppression of the secular and hereditary leaders of the former Kurdish semi-autonomous principalities created a power vacuum that various tribal chiefs in the Mosul *vilayet* exploited for their own gain. The Kurdish Hamawand tribe, which controlled areas between Kirkuk and Sulaymaniyya, became especially infamous for habitually undertaking raids. The void in secular leadership also allowed the rise in power of Kurdish shaykhly families. Of these, the Talabani sayyids of the Qadiriyya, a Sufi order, were especially important in the Kirkuk area. The Talabanis wielded influence over other Kurdish tribes around Kirkuk and owned a large amount of land. Indeed, one of the most famous Kirkukis of the time period was Shaykh Rida (Riza) Talabani (d. 1910), a popular poet originally from a village on the outskirts of Kirkuk who eventually settled in Baghdad and wrote poems in several languages, including Kurdish.[20] The Talabanis' Qadiri rivals, the Barzinji family, dominated Sulaymaniyya in a similar way. The fierce antagonism between these families further destabilized the region between Kirkuk and Sulaymaniyya and persisted after the fall of the Ottoman Empire.[21]

In 1879 the newly created Mosul *vilayet* had its seat in predominantly Turkish-speaking Kirkuk, but the governor was transferred to the mainly Arabic-speaking city of Mosul in 1883. In the years that followed, the troubled Mosul governorship saw a succession of inadequate officeholders as Istanbul repeatedly dismissed governors and appointed new ones. In addition to failing to prevent the continuous tribal unrest around Kirkuk and Sulaymaniyya, these governors were often accused of crimes, such as exploiting the tax collection system.[22] Around 1900 the central government sent a committee and subsequently an investigative commission to the Mosul *vilayet* to try to address these issues. Their findings confirmed the existence of official corruption and various types of tribal disturbances, but Istanbul failed to intervene effectively to solve these problems.[23] The violent resistance of Kurdish tribes therefore worsened.

The Hamawand tribe escalated its raids, at times disrupting or completely stopping trade and transportation between Kirkuk, Sulaymaniyya, and Baghdad.[24] In 1909 Sulaymaniyya's foremost Kurdish leader, Shaykh Sa'id Barzinji, who had married into the Hamawand tribe (thereby gaining further influence) and encouraged their uprising, was killed in a riot in Mosul that may have been instigated by Ottoman authorities. This event only further provoked the Hamawands, whose insurrection was still ongoing as of the beginning of World War I in 1914.[25] At that point, Kirkuk's administrative subdivision still extended to the Ottoman-Persian border. Persian currency, which remained in use in Sulaymaniyya, appears to have circulated in Kirkuk as well.[26] A Persian consul and an Ottoman garrison were also stationed in Kirkuk, indicating that the town continued to be an important site both politically and strategically on the Ottoman-Persian frontier.[27]

Ottoman-Kurdish and Ottoman-Persian interactions in and around Kirkuk in the twilight of the Ottoman Empire therefore established two consequential political precedents that continued to play a role in Kirkuk's politics in the era of British military control after World War I, at which point the Persians ceased to be an important political factor in the area. First, Kurdish tribes in the Kirkuk area desired a return to the relative autonomy to which they were accustomed and, as a result, they continued their revolt against centralized rule. Second, Ottoman authorities attempted to maintain their authority, collect taxes, and thwart external influence in the Kirkuk area through a system of patronage of local notables. Despite its overall ineffectiveness for Istanbul's purposes,[28] this was an idea that the British would soon adopt and modify according to their own interests and their own ideas of the political model that best suited the people of Kirkuk and its surrounding regions.

KIRKUK CIRCA 1918: URBAN FABRIC AND RURAL HINTERLAND, COMMERCE, AND GROUP IDENTITIES

Significant portions of what we currently know about Kirkuk's circumstances around the time of the British occupation come from Western accounts. Beginning in the late eighteenth century, European explorers traveling through the Ottoman and Persian domains sometimes stopped in Kirkuk, as did a few Christian missionaries.[29] Western travel in the Middle East became much more common in the mid-nineteenth to the early twentieth century for a variety of reasons, usually based on either religious or strategic interests. For many provincial parts of the region these explorers' travel memoirs, their shortcomings and inaccuracies notwithstanding, are among the few extant records from the late Ottoman era to contain fine-grained details about local societies and economies; they are therefore essential to understanding the contexts in which post–World War I authorities would operate.[30]

Most of the explorers who wrote about Kirkuk were British. Many of them, especially those who were military officers, would eventually play a role in the

Anglo-Iraqi administration after World War I. For example, before his political career and stint in the War Office, Sir Mark Sykes wrote an account of stopping in Kirkuk during a trip through the Ottoman domains in 1903.[31] E. B. Soane, who would later serve in the postwar military administration of Iraq, published a description of Kirkuk based on his travels in the Iraqi region in 1909 dressed as a Persian; he evocatively titled his memoir *To Mesopotamia and Kurdistan in Disguise*.[32] Gertrude Bell, later the Oriental secretary in Mandate Iraq, traveled to Kirkuk in 1911 with the aid of an existing War Office map of the region that was, she complained, "very imperfect."[33] Several British travelers presented their findings on the geography of Mesopotamia and Kurdistan to the Royal Geographical Society in the late nineteenth and early twentieth centuries; at least one military officer, F. R. Maunsell, explored the Kirkuk area and other nearby regions specifically for information on oil resources.[34]

Although referring to these British travelers as spies may be an overstatement, their travel was often officially sanctioned, and the British military used the information they gathered for various strategic and practical purposes.[35] In the case of the evidence of the presence of oil, these details even played a role in British maneuverings to maintain control of certain parts of the Mosul *vilayet* region, including Kirkuk, beginning with the Sykes-Picot Agreement of 1916.

Late-nineteenth-century and early-twentieth-century European accounts describe Kirkuk primarily as a market center for goods from the surrounding region and also sometimes mention that it housed an Ottoman army division. Most descriptions of Kirkuk, in keeping with European Orientalist ways of writing about the Near East, make special note of its reputed biblical connections. Locals described a tomb in the citadel as that of the prophet Daniel, and the natural gas fires burning outside the city correspondingly represented the "fiery furnace" of Shadrach, Meshach, and Abednego. Estimates of Kirkuk's population varied widely. A British military handbook from the World War I era states that the Kirkuk area had been "devastated by plague" about a century earlier.[36] The consensus indicates that Kirkuk had about 25,000 inhabitants in 1918; furthermore, it had "doubled in size" since 1890.[37] The town was connected by main roads to Baghdad in the south, Mosul (via Arbil) in the northwest, and Sulaymaniyya in the east, but was only indirectly connected to other major urban areas. The military estimated that, traveling by foot or by animal, as caravans at the time would have done, the distance between Baghdad and Kirkuk on the roads then in use was 187.5 miles.[38] Kirkuk's growth may have been related in part to an increase in trade activity; starting in the second half of the nineteenth

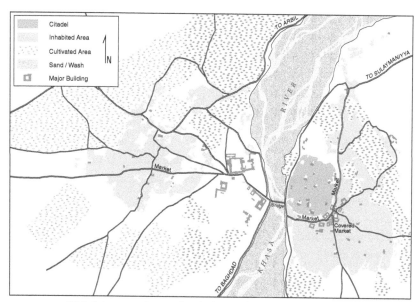

FIGURE 3. Kirkuk in 1919. Source: "Kirkuk City," 1919, National Archives of the United Kingdom, Records of the War Office, WO 302/553.

century, trade caravans going to Baghdad via Aleppo and Damascus began to travel much more frequently on a northern route through Mosul, which would have also taken them through Kirkuk, for reasons of safety.[39] One British report suggested that Kirkuk's trade networks, like those in other parts of Iraq, extended as far as Britain and India.[40]

By 1919 Kirkuk's urban fabric had grown not only around the citadel but also to the west side of the Khasa River, where the military barracks and government offices were located (Figure 3). A narrow stone bridge beginning at the southwestern edge of the citadel, known as Taş Köprü ("stone bridge" in Turkish), connected the two halves of the town. Extensive areas on the outskirts of the town's inhabited areas and even between its neighborhoods were cultivated. In March 1911 Gertrude Bell described the residential dwellings on the western side of Kirkuk as "houses set in gardens."[41] Similarly, in 1910 Captain Bertram Dickson described Kirkuk as "a veritable oasis in the desert, with palm-trees and fruit-gardens."[42] In addition to its urban cultivation, Kirkuk's rural surroundings contained fertile ground for agriculture, producing large quantities of wheat for export and various other grains, vegetables, and cotton for local use. In the town Christians produced well-known liquors for export that were taxed by Ottoman authorities.[43]

The town, which was still limited in size, was defined by the citadel at its core. An early French traveler who visited Kirkuk in 1735 described the town as split into two distinct sections: the citadel, which was relatively sparsely populated, and the plains surrounding the citadel, where commerce took place.[44] In another description of Kirkuk two centuries later, the British engineer A. M. Hamilton demonstrated his careful eye for man-made structures.

> It is an ancient place. Successive cities, built one upon the other, have raised a mound which stands well above the surrounding plain. . . . Only the main residential quarter is today contained within the wall built upon the mound, for the straggling bazaar has long ago overflowed on to the flat land by the river where it is at times threatened by widespread floods. In spite of the bombardment of flood-waters, the bridge, of a series of short-span masonry arches, is one of the few built during the Turkish régime that still stands.[45]

On a Friday during her 1911 visit, Gertrude Bell took a photograph from Taş Köprü while facing the citadel (Figure 4). This image offers a rare glimpse of the Ottoman-era town from the ground, including several pedestrians and beggars. Bell, who had worked as an archaeologist, found Kirkuk's scope for archaeological study fascinating, but she was repulsed by the lack of hygiene in the confined spaces of the oldest part of the town: "Kerkuk is perhaps the dirtiest town I have ever seen. An open drain, smelly and disgusting, runs down the middle of each narrow street and the exiguous space on either side of it on which you walk is filthy beyond words."[46] Bell's contempt for urban Kirkuk would later be echoed in official British reports from the town during the period of military rule.

Among Kirkuk's more prominent buildings were numerous mosques on both sides of the Khasa, some dating as far back as the early Islamic era and others relatively newly established and bearing the names of prominent locals.[47] Kirkuk was also home to many *takiyya*s, or Sufi establishments. Some of these were established in the nineteenth century as the influence of the Qadiriyya order over the area grew; the Talabani sayyids had built a large *takiyya* on the northeastern outskirts of Kirkuk in the 1840s.[48] There were several houses of worship for the Christian and Jewish communities as well. A French Catholic mission had recently built a cathedral for Kirkuk's Chaldean Catholics.[49]

Along with some other areas in the Mosul *vilayet*, Kirkuk's hinterland was also the site of a minor oil enterprise that had existed for as long as the area had been inhabited. Petroleum, where it seeped out of the ground of its own accord, sometimes with the added assistance of digging or boring, was collected in tins

FIGURE 4. Gertrude Bell's photograph of the Kirkuk citadel taken from the stone bridge across the Khasa River, 31 March 1911. Reproduced with permission from the Gertrude Bell Photographic Archive, Newcastle University, United Kingdom.

and transported by donkey or camel for sale.[50] People in the Ottoman domains, like their antecedents, used petroleum and associated substances such as bitumen for a variety of everyday and commercial functions, including fueling lamps and waterproofing rafts. After the opening of the Suez Canal in 1869, oil was also used to power steamboats on the Tigris River, run by both British and Ottoman companies, which greatly increased the Iraqi region's international trade.[51] The Ottoman government also used Kirkuk's oil for military purposes and had considered it a significant resource for centuries. Reflecting this fact, the central government had issued a decree in 1639 formally granting the rights to the Kirkuk division's oil-bearing areas to the Naftchizadas, an elite Turkish-speaking family.[52] The Naftchizadas claimed that they had been selling oil for generations before the Ottoman conquest of Iraq, a fact suggested by their name; *naftchi*, combining an Arabic word with a Turkish suffix, means "oilman." As will be discussed in a later chapter, the Naftchizadas continued to claim the rights to these lands in the twentieth century.

Travelers' accounts verify the claim that Kirkuk was predominantly Turkish speaking. Soane humorously described Kirkuk as being famous for "Turkomans, fruit, and crude oil, all of which abound."[53] It should be noted, however, that in this era the communal self-identity of those who spoke Turkish in Kirkuk was ambiguous. British accounts use the terms *Turk* and *Turkmen* (the latter in a variety of archaic spellings) interchangeably to refer to Kirkuk's Turkish-speaking community. Moreover, according to C. J. Edmonds, Kirkuk's "leading aristocratic families" considered themselves "Turks" even if they were believed to be of Kurdish origin.[54] Even the phrase "Turkish speaking" is not entirely accurate as a coherent description of a community. Kirkuk's Chaldeans also typically spoke Turkish as their first language but, being Christians who still retained some use of Neo-Aramaic and liturgical Syriac among themselves, they sometimes identified themselves as part of the community of Christians who spoke Neo-Aramaic as a vernacular.[55]

As the title of Soane's memoir implies, these foreign writers typically characterized Kirkuk as part of a region they called Kurdistan, describing the town's Turkish-speaking majority as a point of contrast with its surroundings. The name Kurdistan, meaning "land of the Kurds," has been used since at least the Seljuq period to describe the parts of Anatolia, Mesopotamia, and Persia that are majority Kurdish.[56] The borders of Kurdistan have not been strictly defined in any era and remain contentious. British portrayals of Kirkuk in the early twentieth century generally placed the town on the southern frontier of Kurdistan; by this definition, Kurdistan's center was in the Hakkari region of southeastern Anatolia.[57] Accordingly, Longrigg called Kirkuk one of the "main entrepôts for Kurdistan."[58]

There is little evidence that this description of Kirkuk's location reflected the regional self-identity of people in the town. Rather, it mainly indicated the British tendency to define regions first and foremost based on the linguistic and sectarian makeup of the majority of their rural tribes. Indeed, writers such as Edmonds sometimes also included the majority-Arabic-speaking city of Mosul in their definition of Kurdistan because of the Kurdish tribes in its hinterland.[59] Kirkuk's hinterland was not exclusively Kurdish; there were also Arab tribes in the area and polyglot villages that were not affiliated with tribes. Altogether, Kirkuk and its hinterland probably had a Kurdish-speaking plurality but no linguistic majority.[60] There were also Kurdish-speaking inhabitants of urban Kirkuk, some of whom were even trained as Ottoman officials and would therefore have also been fluent Turkish speakers.[61] Despite Edmonds's observation that such elites tended to think of themselves as Turks or Turkmens, it is impossible to know for certain whether or not their political status typically affected these individuals' communal self-identity.

Kirkuk's urban notables came from all of these groupings and could derive their authority from their political, economic, or religious standing, or some combination thereof. The most influential families in urban Kirkuk—that is,

the families to whom Ottoman authorities usually turned to appoint local officials—were primarily speakers of Turkish regardless of their descent. As a result
of the strong native presence of Turkic culture, Kirkuk had a solid foundation
for political connections to Istanbul. Edmonds described the town as a "centre
of Ottoman influence" within the mainly Kurdish *vilayet* of Mosul.[62] Members of
the Naftchizada family were among the most powerful Turkish-speaking elites.
Two other Turkish-speaking Kirkuki aristocratic families whose patriarchs were
politically prominent were the Ya'qubizadas and the Kırdars. Around the turn
of the twentieth century, a member of the Kırdar family, Mehmet Ali Kırdar,
served as the mayor of the town in addition to representing Kirkuk in the Ottoman parliament's Chamber of Deputies.[63]

Sufi religious leaders, who were typically members of the Kurdish Talabani
and Barzinji families, were also influential in urban Kirkuk. In addition, Chaldean Christian and Jewish traders and landowners sometimes held positions in
the provincial government.[64] In rural areas tribes other than the Talabani and
the Hamawand whose leaders were noteworthy included the Dawudi, the Jaf,
and the 'Ubayd; contemporary British sources and later Iraqi ones characterize
the 'Ubayd as an Arab tribe and all the others as Kurdish, though these catego-
rizations may not have been as relevant or simple to the tribesmen themselves.[65]
All these notables would continue to play important roles in the governance of
Kirkuk after the British invasion, though many would find themselves at odds
with British authorities at various times.

An important and subtle element of Kirkuk's social and economic life that is
captured in these early accounts is that the mainly Turkish-speaking town was
closely bound to a principally tribal and mostly Kurdish and Arab hinterland.
Travelers and officials would talk about both entities together as "Kirkuk" and then
emphasize the most obvious differences between the urban and rural areas, which
bore little resemblance to one another structurally or culturally, in the same breath.
As Sarah Shields argues, this was a common pattern throughout the Ottoman domains, where cities and their hinterlands became increasingly interdependent over
the course of the nineteenth century both politically and economically.[66] Shields
observes that hinterlands often adjoined markets on the edges of the urban fabric
where products from rural areas were sold, creating economic continuity between
rural and urban areas, and this observation accurately applies to Kirkuk.[67] The
town's main centers of commerce were along the edges of the citadel, which was
historically the center of its population, and roads from Arbil and Sulaymaniyya
led directly into markets on both sides of the Khasa River (see Figure 3).[68]

These realities run counter to simplistic notions of a division between urban and rural Kirkuk that are sometimes encountered in travelers' writings. For instance, Soane made a point of contrasting the town's "excellent state of affairs" with a dangerously unstable hinterland that began "only a mile or two outside the town."[69] Although tribal violence was a problem in late Ottoman Kirkuk by all accounts, these circumstances did not mean that urban and rural Kirkukis were unitary and separate groups. Rather, there were close links among them, including familial bonds. For instance, Ahmad-i Khanaqa, the leading Sufi sayyid in urban Kirkuk, was a member of the Barzinji family, which was based in the countryside of the Sulaymaniyya area. Sayyid Ahmad was particularly influential among rural Kurdish cultivators in Kirkuk.[70] Another prominent religious figure in urban Kirkuk and a member of the rival Talabani family, Habib, was the brother of Shaykh Hamid Talabani, who was one of the most powerful rural tribal chiefs in the Kirkuk area and controlled some productive oil wells in Gil, southeast of Kirkuk.[71]

At the same time, Kirkuk and its hinterland were not as strongly influenced by the politics of nearby urban areas. In his study of urban notables, Albert Hourani advances the argument that the city of Mosul functioned like a small "city-state" in the late Ottoman era, failing to exert political pull over much of the countryside in the *vilayet* of which it was the seat. This contention is confirmed by the fact that urban Mosul's reorientation toward the Arabic-speaking world during the late Ottoman era—reflected in its flourishing Arabic-language culture—seems to have had little effect in Kirkuk.[72] Instead, the town of Kirkuk circa 1918 could be described as having its own uniquely heterogeneous hinterland distinct from those of other towns and cities. The politics of urban and rural Kirkuk at this time are best understood as developing in connection with one another.

Starting in 1918, the British military administration did not adequately take into account the links between urban and rural Kirkuk and the fluidity of ethnolinguistic indicators among Kirkuk's population. British accounts, which initially focused on Turks (or Turkmens) and Kurds as the most distinct groups, would eventually construe Kirkuk's smaller communities of Arabs, "Christians," and sometimes "Jews" as analogous categories. Previous depictions of the town's many group identities thus coalesced into a perception that Kirkuk had four, or perhaps five, discrete communities in total.[73] Nuances in self-identity notwithstanding, this rudimentary anthropological sketch of Kirkuk, and of the Mosul *vilayet* in general, would persist after World War I and would inform British policy throughout both military and Mandate rule. By classifying Kirkukis in this manner, British authorities were following the lead of the late Ottoman nation-building project of the past few decades through which contentious ethnic and sectarian political identities emerged in many regions of the empire, from southern Anatolia to Lebanon.[74] What extant accounts of the late nineteenth and early twentieth centuries in Kirkuk convey upon a close reading, however, is that ethnicity was not yet a political or social practice there. Rather, self-identities and political subjectivities were determined by a complex and shifting combination of language, religion, class, and perceived lineage.

EXPLORING AND CONTROLLING KIRKUK'S OIL
IN THE EARLY TWENTIETH CENTURY

British travelers to Kirkuk in the late nineteenth and early twentieth centuries sometimes exhibited an interest in its oil. In the second half of the twentieth century, the "hydrocarbon era" of personal automobile usage, ubiquitous petrochemical products, and commercial air travel would make oil a crucial global resource. Although oil had not yet attained this level of importance in the nineteenth century, this resource was already essential to the expansion of steam-powered seafaring. The use of petroleum expanded commercial enterprise by enabling longer-distance trade by sea; as previously mentioned, steamboats became a factor in Middle Eastern trade after the opening of the Suez Canal. Even more important, it became a major resource for naval operations, as oil-powered fleets were widespread by the time World War I began. The United States dominated world oil production in this era, and the perceived necessity of reducing their dependence on the Americans and controlling oil resources on their own spurred British prospecting in other parts of the world.[75] Most notably, a British businessman, William Knox D'Arcy, obtained a concession from the shah of Iran for oil exploration at the turn of the century.

Upon the discovery of oil in the southwestern part of Iran, D'Arcy formed the Anglo-Persian Oil Company (APOC) in 1909. The British government purchased a majority of shares in the company and signed a contract to supply the Royal Navy with fuel just before the outbreak of war in 1914.[76] D'Arcy's British contemporaries included the aforementioned military officer F. R. Maunsell, who gathered information on oil in the Iraqi region in the late nineteenth century. In an 1897 paper titled "The Mesopotamian Petroleum Field," Maunsell detailed the composition and commercial potential of a "petroleum-bearing belt" in the Mosul *vilayet*; he specifically mentioned "petroleum springs" near the town of Kirkuk that were especially "extensive." Maunsell concluded that the Ottoman

Empire's political instability at the time could facilitate British obtainment of concessions "to develop some of these remarkable mineral riches."[77] By 1919 official information about potentially valuable oil drilling sites was considerably more extensive and included a thorough assessment of "oil in the Kirkuk anticline" among other areas.[78]

As a result of Maunsell's expedition and others by European explorers, the oil wealth of the Mosul *vilayet* became well known to Germany and France as well as to Great Britain. Istanbul was also aware of the Europeans' growing interest in Middle Eastern petroleum and thus started the process of creating a commercial oil industry with the involvement of the great powers. In 1888 Sultan Abdülhamid II took control of the known oil-bearing areas of the Mosul and Baghdad *vilayet*s through the Civil List, the first step in preparation for making concessions. He then commissioned Calouste Gulbenkian, an Armenian businessman from Istanbul, to undertake an expedition to Mesopotamia to assess its prospects for oil production.[79] Many European companies attempted and failed to secure oil concessions in Mesopotamia before World War I. The Turkish Petroleum Company (TPC) was eventually formed under Gulbenkian's tutelage in 1912. Various oil firms wrangled over shares in the TPC, and in 1914 the APOC prevailed: the British company would hold a 50% interest, with the other shares held by Deutsche Bank, Shell, and Gulbenkian himself.[80] The outbreak of war in 1914 put an immediate hold on the TPC's concession.

Just over a year later, Sir Mark Sykes, then an adviser to the War Office, and the French diplomat François Georges-Picot began secret negotiations to partition Ottoman territory into zones of direct control and "influence" for Britain and France. Although these talks took place while the Mesopotamian campaign was still in its early stages, Sykes and Picot undertook them in anticipation of a full victory over Germany and the Ottoman Empire. Their agreement, signed in 1916, placed the city of Mosul in the French zone of influence and the Kirkuk area in the British zone of influence (Figure 5).[81] In Sykes's own words, he wished to "draw a line from the 'e' in Acre to the last 'k' in Kirkuk," south of which the British would have their domain.[82] Many scholars inaccurately imply that the Sykes-Picot Agreement put the entire Mosul *vilayet* in the French zone, therefore giving the French future control over all the region's oil, and that the French subsequently relinquished Mosul to the British zone of influence in return for a share of its oil revenues.[83] The problem with this prevalent imprecision is that it suggests that the British were not interested in controlling oil resources in the Middle East in the early twentieth century, whereas the French were.

FIGURE 5. Map of the Sykes-Picot Agreement, 1916.

In fact, Picot did not specifically pursue including the Kirkuk area in the French zone of influence during the negotiations despite French awareness of its oil deposits.[84] Sykes, unlike Picot, had a clearly established opinion both of the importance of incorporating Kirkuk into the British zone of influence and of the significance of controlling Middle Eastern petroleum resources. Although he did not specify that he intended to include Kirkuk for its oil,[85] he emphasized in a secret memorandum dated soon after the signing of the Sykes-Picot Agreement that a "vast pocket of oil, the future propellant of the Navy," was at stake in Mesopotamia if the Germans ended up controlling it at the end of the war.[86] The Sykes-Picot Agreement ceded the city of Mosul and its surrounding area to the French because the War Office was willing, at the time, to create a strategic French wedge between their zone and Anatolia. Therefore they drew the partitioning line in the Mosul *vilayet* at the Lesser Zab River.[87] Sykes had ensured, in accordance with the wishes of the War Office, that the city of Kirkuk and its known oil-rich surrounding area were in the British zone of influence.[88]

However, once British troops occupied the Mosul *vilayet* in full in 1918, including the city of Mosul, the British government aimed to control the Iraqi region in its entirety. At the San Remo Conference in the spring of 1920, which formally established the British Mandate of Mesopotamia, the British recognized that the French had an interest in Iraqi oil revenues. They therefore agreed to give 25% of TPC shares to French business in return for French recognition of British control over the whole Mosul *vilayet*; the newly formed Compagnie Française des Pétroles would eventually take over these allotted French shares. The French interest in the Mosul *vilayet*'s oil was of secondary importance to their diplomats and was always purely commercial in nature. The British, on the other hand, demonstrated an early strategic interest in gaining control over Kirkuk. The San Remo agreement also stipulated that France would receive 25% of Iraq's oil revenue should the oil industry instead end up being run by the Iraqi state, but Foreign Secretary Lord Curzon in London and British officials in Iraq maneuvered to ensure that the TPC would, in fact, be the entity that would develop Iraq's oil privately.[89]

EARLY BRITISH MILITARY POLICY IN KIRKUK: TRIBAL PATRONAGE AND URBAN AND RURAL AFFAIRS

In their campaign against Ottoman troops during World War I, British-led troops occupied Baghdad in March 1917. By late 1917 they controlled the Iraqi region up to Khanaqin, a town close to the Persian border roughly halfway between Baghdad and Kirkuk, and began to establish contacts with influential Kurdish tribes soon thereafter. The British subsequently took control of Kirkuk in May 1918 but were forced to withdraw because of logistical difficulties. They continued to control territory up to the town of Tuz Khurmatu, about 55 miles to Kirkuk's southeast. They then reentered Kirkuk in late October. On 29 October 1918, officer C. C. Garbett wrote about the moment when British troops had entered the town a couple of days earlier.

> The town was completely quiet. There were very few people about, but in the bazaar the food shops were open. Capt. Longrigg had already interviewed the notables and made arrangements for the policing of the town. There was no plunder and none of the tendency to disorder which attended the occupation of Baghdad.[90]

British officials soon realized that the town's population had declined by nearly half, from about 25,000 to 14,000, during the Mesopotamian campaign. Many of those who had left Kirkuk had fled to refuge in British-controlled areas to the south. The town's Christian community in particular had "all hurried to Baghdad," according to officer Humphrey Bowman. Other Kirkukis had died of starvation. Early reports indicated that about one-seventh of the city's houses were in disrepair and that starvation remained widespread, both in Kirkuk and in surrounding regions. Agriculture and commerce were at a standstill. For months the inhabitants of Kirkuk had relied on inadequate supplies of imported wheat from the city of Arbil and the Lesser Zab River region to the north.[91]

Amid this dire situation British officers urgently set out to import more grain from Arbil. As Kirkuk's population slowly returned, they also supplied the town doctor and opened an orphanage. The abiding British colonial concern with hygiene led to the establishment of a sanitation system and to the registration and quarantining of prostitutes and the evacuation of some of them to Baghdad.[92] Kirkuk's limited printing activities also quickly restarted under British supervision. Beginning in December 1918, a local printing press that had produced Kirkuk's first newspaper under the Ottomans began publishing a daily newspaper in Turkish, *Necme* (Star). By the end of 1919, the newspaper printed three times a week and had a circulation of 300–400, mostly among local officials.[93]

Another urgent task was to analyze and document prevailing local systems of landownership and revenue collection and to solidify the general organization of authority within the Kirkuk division. As documented in his "Land Revenue Note on Kirkuk," C. C. Garbett found that the Ottomans had left an array of different local administrative systems in the area. The towns of Kirkuk and Altun Kopri had mayors, councils, and courts. The smaller settlements were typically villages and consisted almost entirely of *miri*, or state lands. Most tenants had obtained "prescriptive rights" to their land resembling individual ownership, usually because one family would cultivate a plot for generations.[94] These village heads were sometimes tribal chiefs, whereas in other cases they were "overlords" overseeing loosely defined collectives of area farmers. Despite the formalization of Kurdish tribal authority for much of the Ottoman era, some villages in Kirkuk's hinterland were not affiliated with tribes at this time.[95] These villages were under the independent control of peasants or large landowners who had interacted directly with Ottoman governors.[96]

As Garbett noted, trained civil servants known as *memurs* had coordinated the collection of taxes in the Kirkuk area under the late Ottoman system. Reports dating from some months before the second occupation of Kirkuk in October 1918 suggest that the British had initially planned to continue a *memur*-led system of administration there. For example, British officials in Baghdad had established separate Turkish-language classes specifically for Kirkuki refugees at a school for the training of *memurs*.[97] However, this plan soon evolved into a policy to replace all existing administrative systems in predominantly Kurdish rural areas of Iraq, including Kirkuk's hinterland, with a single, simplified system based on tribal units. The British political officer in Kirkuk, E. W. C. Noel, articulated this change in course in a directive to assistant officers in the region dated two weeks after the occupation of Kirkuk.

> It is our policy to foster the tribal system of government and with that object every effort should be made to strengthen the authority and develop the initiative of the recognised tribal chiefs. . . . It is essential that the executive staff of our administration should be Kurds, that no ex-Turkish officials should be employed in connection with Kurdish tribal areas, and that our proclamations, notices, etc. should be printed in Kurdi and not in Turkish or Arabic. [Assistant Political Officers] should obtain the services of relatives or members of the families of the big Shaikhs in their districts as their assistants in revenue and other work.

Noel explained that the ultimate goal of this policy would be to form a "Kurdish confederation" under the aegis of Britain. He also outlined a plan for paying tribal leaders for these services.[98]

Noel was an unusually strong proponent of creating an independent Kurdish state.[99] Nevertheless, other officials accepted the general principle of actively cultivating the loyalty of Kurdish tribes and vesting authority in tribal leaders to maintain British control. The concept of elevating familial structures would also become prevalent in British neocolonial policies outside Iraq, including in the Mandate administration of Palestine.[100] This idea was popular among British officials for several reasons. A primary reason was the notion that an administrative system that relied on tribal authorities was inherently better suited to the primitive nature of the rural people of the region than something that replicated the Tanzimat-era Ottoman administrative system. For instance, in his land revenue report, Garbett described the tribal unit as a "simple form of responsible community" and a system of government based on tribes as a "form of constitution in which the general desire for self-expression and for freedom can find fulfilment."[101] Many of the British officials who served in Iraq throughout the military and Mandate administrations had previously worked in colonial India, where they had operated according to a similar conception of rural tribesmen. They transplanted certain forms of governance they had developed there to Iraq with no regard for differences in local conditions, considering rural people in both regions to have been untouched by modernity and therefore essentially similar.[102] For example, the idea of paying tribal leaders was probably informed by the British precedent of indirect rule through tribal subsidization in India and other colonies.[103]

There was also an important short-term strategic reason for promulgating a unitary policy that privileged tribal shaykhs in all northern rural areas. Namely, as long as the British hold over the former *vilayet* of Mosul was tenuous, it was crucial to maintain the favor of individuals who held influence over the frontier—and in Kirkuk these figures were unusually amenable to anti-British ideas. This was particularly true once British control over the region came to be actively challenged by the nascent Republic of Turkey through the National Pact of January 1920, which claimed the former Mosul *vilayet*, among other areas, as Turkish territory.[104] As part of their campaign to challenge British authority in the region, Turkey fomented Kurdish unrest on the Turkish-Iraqi frontier north of Kirkuk by distributing anti-British propaganda in the former Mosul *vilayet*.[105] Turkish propaganda was especially effective among Kirkuki tribal leaders who had come to distrust the British after their initial withdrawal from Kirkuk in the spring of 1918.[106] Therefore British officials had to actively counter this influence, even though Kirkuk was relatively distant from the unstable edges of the frontier.

Nevertheless, the British tribal policy initially backfired in Kirkuk during the short-lived attempt at indirect rule in Kurdistan through collaboration with Shaykh Mahmud Barzinji, the son of the aforementioned late Shaykh Sa'id Barzinji. Shaykh Mahmud had inherited his father's immense influence in Sulaymaniyya as well as his active opposition to Ottoman authorities. The shaykh offered his assistance to British troops as they approached full control of the Mosul *vilayet* in 1918.[107] Less than a week after the capture of Kirkuk, the civil commissioner in Baghdad, Arnold Wilson, authorized Noel to appoint Shaykh Mahmud as the representative of British authorities in Sulaymaniyya.[108] Soon thereafter, in December 1918, Wilson informally granted Shaykh Mahmud authority over the region between the Greater Zab and Diyala Rivers, which included Kirkuk.[109] In a January 1919 report Wilson reported to the India Office in London that, though the system of maintaining security and collecting revenues was proceeding smoothly overall, notables in Kirkuk were alarmed by the strengthening British relationship with Shaykh Mahmud and the possibility that he could become the governor of an independent Kurdistan that included Kirkuk.

> All parts of the Kirkuk area make emphatic protest against the possibility of Shaikh Mahmud Qaradaghli [sic] of Sulaimaniyah being appointed Wali of Kurdistan. It is felt that the path of progress lies in the direction of Baghdad and not in that of Sulaimaniyah. Moreover there is no trace of Kurdish national feeling in Kirkuk. British control and protection is strongly desired as well as the absence of any administrative frontier between the Kurd and the Arab.[110]

This passage demonstrates that the notables of Kirkuk exhibited two tendencies from the beginning of the British occupation: a strong aversion to Sulaymaniyya-based Kurdish politics despite Sulaymaniyya's geographic proximity to Kirkuk compared to other major urban areas, and a desire for external patronage. Kirkukis' opposition to unification with Sulaymaniyya stemmed at least in part from the preexisting rivalry between the Barzinjis and the Talabanis; for instance, another January 1919 report communicated that the lands of the Jabbari tribe, whose ruling family were Barzinjis, were being removed from the administration of the Kirkuk district and attached to the Sulaymaniyya district.[111]

In March 1919 British officials, who were facing the obvious fact that Shaykh Mahmud was profoundly unpopular in Kirkuk, formally established a new district encompassing Kirkuk and neighboring Kifri outside the shaykh's purview.[112] Internal opposition to Shaykh Mahmud's consolidation of power had also developed among British officers. Aware of his decline in standing with British authorities, Shaykh Mahmud forcibly seized Sulaymaniyya and proclaimed himself the ruler of Kurdistan in May 1919. After initially suffering a disastrous defeat at the hands of Shaykh Mahmud's troops just outside Sulaymaniyya, British troops converged at Kirkuk and Khanaqin to advance on the town again. Of the many Kurdish tribes in the Kirkuk division, only one section of one tribe sided with Shaykh Mahmud; the Talabani family even offered their services to the British. British troops retook Sulaymaniyya in June 1919, badly wounding Shaykh Mahmud in the process. The region between the Greater Zab and Diyala Rivers therefore once more came fully under the civil commissioner's direct control. Shaykh Mahmud was treated and eventually allowed to return to Sulaymaniyya, where he continued to wield influence.[113]

Kirkuk's response to Shaykh Mahmud's first rebellion is an illustrative example of its often uneasy relationship with its neighboring areas. Scholars who have written about Kurdish-majority areas in the period of British administration have often framed their analyses in terms of Kurdish ethnic politics, thereby indiscriminately treating Kirkuk, a diverse area with no linguistic majority, as unified with Kurdistan. This approach overlooks the often contentious ways in which Kirkuk interacted with these districts.[114]

Although the British alliance with Shaykh Mahmud and the experiment of an independent Kurdish-led region did not last, the broader concept of privileging tribal ties and organizing politics along familial lines continued to dominate British administration of the Mosul *vilayet* and led to the development of a political system based on networks of patronage. British alliances with and sponsorships of Kurdish tribes often arose from improvised solutions to immediate problems relating to security, often turning to officials' experiences in colonial India for ideas. An important example of one such solution was the creation of a police force of *sowars*, or armed men who maintain control over roads and answer directly to their respective tribal leaders; *sowar* is an Indian term that was used to refer to similar forces under the British Raj. Garbett's earlier note that Longrigg had already "interviewed the notables and made arrangements for the policing of the town" in October 1918 implies that British forces relied on Kirkuk notables' prevailing links to maintain stability in the area from the very moment of occupation. Officers then proceeded to recruit and pay several *sowars* from each of nine major tribes or tribally based groups in the Kirkuk area.[115] Tribal notables from Kirkuk who had established relationships with British authorities through the *sowar* system would eventually be more likely to support Anglo-Iraqi interests in the dispute between Turkey and Iraq over the Mosul *vilayet* region.

The practice of empowering tribes and tribal leaders in a variety of ways prevailed despite internal acknowledgments of the shortcomings of the approach. One early report from Kirkuk exhibited a slight concern that the policy ignored the desires of nontribal rural villages and did not account for the fact that tribal leaders tended to treat cultivators, in particular, poorly.[116] The foremost British critic of the focus on tribes, E. B. Soane, asserted, based on his experiences in Sulaymaniyya, that the policy invested undue influence in "petty village headmen" in places that had long since "detribalised."[117] Even Noel recognized from the beginning that putting power in the hands of tribal leaders meant bolstering a system that would not function well for cultivators, but he dismissed this potential problem as a concern of overly indulgent Westerners that was irrelevant to the Kurdish tribes of Kirkuk and other areas.

> In this feudal system which we are striving to preserve, there must necessarily be a good deal that is repugnant to our western ideals of democracy and justice,

and there is a natural temptation to intervene on behalf of the peasant tribesman vis a vis his feudal chief and landlord; but this temptation must be resisted.[118]

In addition to the chaotic collapse of Shaykh Mahmud's scheme and the continued mistreatment of those of a lower social status, another consequence of the tribal focus was a lack of a coherent policy in urban Kirkuk because of its lower priority with regard to British interests. Structurally, the town's urban political and security status quo appears not to have changed significantly under British military rule from the circumstances that prevailed in the late Ottoman era. For instance, in contrast to the *sowar* system, British authorities reconstituted Kirkuk's urban police force with many of the "old Kirkuk police," even though they had "an unsavoury reputation."[119] In urban Kirkuk, as in rural areas, British authorities concentrated primarily on building relationships with existing notables; most often, these were the patriarchs of major families, merchants with local prominence, or religious leaders. However, they combined this approach with an unusual level of scorn for residents of the town. In the most common British official view of Iraq, which stemmed from discourses that were common in Britain, there was an urban-rural divide wherein the people of the countryside were "noble" and "natural" and the people of the cities and towns were "degenerate" and tainted by modernity. Of course, given the rapid rate of rural-to-urban migration that began in the late nineteenth century (in Kirkuk as well as in Baghdad and other urban areas), any kind of rigid distinction between the two made little sense.[120]

British anti-urbanism further combined with standard paternalistic notions of the time regarding Islam's unsuitability for modern progress and capitalist work standards. For instance, Longrigg remarked in November 1918 that Kirkuk's applicants for municipal employment and local religious leaders alike were averse to "hustle and efficiency" and found the idea of committed work "dreadful," though he was more forgiving of "the Jew, Christian, and pushful Muslim merchant." He also described the town's religious leaders as "extraordinarily mercenary."[121] Later, using similar language, an annual administration report on Kirkuk in 1919 dismissed the opposition of the urban population to British administration as part of their inherent tendency to be hostile to "an efficient Occidental Christian power."[122] In his minutes of a 1920 meeting of the Kirkuk divisional council, which consisted mostly of urban notables, Longrigg characterized the body as incoherent and impotent, concluding, "It explicitly asks, and patently requires, to be lead [*sic*]."[123] The relentless contempt for urban Kirkukis evident in British authorities' correspondence constituted a political failure that undoubtedly contributed to their inability to control the outcome of the Faysal referendum of 1921 in Kirkuk.

The British tendency to inflexibly separate urban and rural politics also be-
lied the close relationship between the city of Kirkuk and its hinterland and the
fact that the political concerns of the Kirkuk area were most clearly definable
if viewed as distinct from those of other areas. The effects of the Iraqi revolt of
1920 in Kirkuk illustrate these dynamics. Populations all over the Iraqi region,
especially tribes in the mid-Euphrates area, began to express grievances with
British authorities in the spring of 1920. Armed insurgents rose up against the
military administration beginning in June of that year for a number of different reasons stemming from widespread opposition to direct British rule of the
emerging state of Iraq. Because of Kurdish discontent with the lack of resolution of the question of Kurdish independence, the revolt spread to the Arbil
and Mosul divisions north of Kirkuk, where some Kurdish tribal leaders briefly
overpowered British officials.[124] Kirkuk itself, however, was "phenomenally quiet"
as agitation began in the spring, according to Longrigg.[125] By the summer of
1920, when neighboring Arbil was in disarray, Kirkuk was also experiencing the
effects of "a wave of political restlessness emanating from Baghdad." However,
Longrigg was most concerned about the "increased liveliness in political talk,"
which British officials attempted to curb by halting their payments to a particularly vocal Kirkuki religious leader. Specifically, Kirkuk's political discourse
had a common theme "throughout the townships and the Kurdish tribes" alike:
"dread of an Arab government."[126] The apparent unity of Kirkuki townspeople
and tribespeople in opinion on this issue contradicts the argument made by Sir
Aylmer Haldane, the general officer commanding Mesopotamia at the time, that
the 1920 insurrection was primarily the work of a restless and troublemaking
Iraqi urban elite.[127] An opposition to Arab-led, Baghdad-based Anglo-Iraqi rule
that cut across community and urban-rural divides had therefore emerged in
Kirkuk by 1920, becoming prominent at the very moment that British officials
were trying to forge the new state of Iraq under an Arab monarch.

THE FAYSAL REFERENDUM AND THE LIMITS
OF COLONIAL CONTRIVANCE

One of the most significant milestones during the transition to civilian rule
in Iraq was the Cairo Conference. In March 1921 the secretary of state for the
colonies, Winston Churchill, convened a conference in Cairo to discuss, among
other topics, British policy in Mandate Iraq and in Kurdistan. Sir Percy Cox,
who had arrived in Iraq in the fall of 1920 with the new civilian title of high
commissioner, led the Anglo-Iraqi delegation. The conference participants de-

termined that the Hashemite prince Amir Faysal, a son of Sharif Hussein of
Mecca and a leading figure of the World War I Arab Revolt, would be made
king of Iraq. High Commissioner Percy Cox made sure to extract an agreement from Faysal, before his accession, that he would allow British officials
"free rein" in the administration of predominantly Kurdish districts in the former Mosul *vilayet*.[128] Cox's insistence indicated the ongoing ambiguity of the
region's status. In addition to Turkish claims to the Mosul *vilayet* lands threatening security on the frontier, British authorities had not yet determined what
form Kurdish independence would take, or whether it would be fostered at all.
They were especially uncertain with regard to whether the Kirkuk area, with its
distinctive diversity and contentious relations with nearby Kurdish-majority
districts, should be included in an independent Kurdish entity.

Like many meetings, reports, and memoranda before it, the Cairo Conference
ultimately left the issues of Kirkuk's status and Kurdish independence unresolved.
At the conference Churchill and the delegation from Iraq broadly agreed that
the predominantly Kurdish areas of the Mosul *vilayet* should be administered
separately from the rest of Iraq in order to create a so-called buffer north of
Iraq proper, a variation on a theme first imagined by the War Office in the era
of the Sykes-Picot negotiations. Furthermore, the 1920 Treaty of Sèvres, though
negotiated and signed with an Ottoman government on its last legs, had put
into writing the stipulation that an independent Kurdistan would be created.
Despite this apparent (if limited) consensus, the Cairo Conference did not settle
the confusion surrounding the question of Kurdistan. A few months later, Cox
and Churchill would exchange correspondence in which they disagreed as to
whether or not the "balance of opinion" at the conference had been in favor of
creating an independent Kurdish state or integrating the Kurdish districts into
Iraq. Churchill also could not recall afterward whether Cox had intended to
include Kirkuk in the Kurdish region or in Iraq proper and suggested, barring
the objection of local opinion, that a case could be made for the former, as the
"buffer state" he envisioned would be broadly composed of "non-Arab elements"
rather than simply of Kurdish tribes.[129] Cox countered that Kirkuk would not "be
content to lapse into insignificance" among "mainly Kurdish units."[130]

The procedure by which Faysal would accede to the throne was not established at the conference because Cox felt that, because of the Kurdistan stipulation in the Treaty of Sèvres, it was first necessary to formulate an election law
that would account for the special status of the mainly non-Arab northern districts that Britain was then administering as part of Iraq.[131] It was not until after

returning to Baghdad that Cox came under pressure from Churchill to establish Faysal as king as soon as possible. Churchill, who was himself under pressure in London to prove that Iraq was on its way to independence and that the expensive task of maintaining troops there could soon come to an end, insisted that Faysal's coronation was a more pressing matter than resolving the ambiguities of Kirkuk and the Kurdish-majority districts.[132] Heeding the demands of the "vernacular papers" in Iraq, the high commissioner's office devised a plan for what they referred to as a "referendum" to legitimize Faysal's accession.[133]

Scholars have often stated or implied that the Faysal referendum, in which nearly every division overwhelmingly confirmed the amir, was plainly rigged, therefore only mentioning the event in passing in analyses of early British civilian administration. However, the referendum was a fallible process that failed dramatically in Kirkuk despite its successful implementation elsewhere. Characterizing it as fraudulent therefore obscures the nature of the procedure and overlooks the agency of those who participated in it. Although the referendum had the predetermined and explicitly stated goal of obtaining Iraqi approval of Faysal, it consisted of a series of negotiations carried out by lower-level officers throughout provincial Iraq with local notables about a variety of issues concerning their relations with Baghdad. For instance, in Mosul the divisional adviser reported success in getting Yazidi and Kurdish figures to sign, indicating their approval of Faysal, when they were allowed to add clauses related to minority rights.[134] In Arbil, Divisional Adviser Wallace Lyon recalled the negotiations as a "very long, hot and tiring day" during which he had to convince the area's reluctant tribal and urban notables that there was no need for opposing candidates. Lyon, like many other lower-level officials, had a poor understanding of the reasoning behind Iraq policies formulated in Baghdad and London and was not even aware of why his superiors had selected Faysal to be king.[135]

These local officials had to rely on their ties to certain powerful individuals to ensure a favorable result for the chosen monarch. To sway Kirkuk toward approval of Faysal, British officials decided to invest their efforts in the Kirkuki Turkmen notable and former Ottoman official 'Izzat Pasha Karkukli, whom they had appointed minister of education the previous fall.[136] The placement of 'Izzat Pasha in the Ministry of Education was meant solely to keep him in the patronage of the British and had nothing to do with his suitability for the position, as officials privately acknowledged. Gertrude Bell, the Oriental secretary, sent her father an indelicate limerick written by an unnamed person in the high commissioner's office in reference to 'Izzat Pasha's lack of fluency in formal Arabic.

There was an old man of Kirkuk,

Who knew nought of the pen and the book,

And was not good at speech,

So they set him to teach

All the ignorant boys in the suq.[137]

Perhaps unsurprisingly, by the fall of 1921 'Izzat Pasha had been transferred to the post of minister of public works.[138] While in Baghdad, 'Izzat Pasha became friends with Bell, who was aware that Kirkuk would be a particularly difficult district to control in the upcoming referendum. At a dinner party held in Faysal's honor in July 1921, 'Izzat Pasha sat next to Bell and, during the course of conversation, asked her why the British had chosen Faysal to be Iraq's king. Bell responded, "It's because he is the best Arab of his day. Is that enough?" According to Bell's account, 'Izzat Pasha responded, "Yes, that's enough." The following morning, he had "a long private conversation" with Faysal. Bell wrote in a letter to her father, "Faisal thinks he has got him. If he has, he has got Kirkuk."[139]

Meanwhile, events in Kirkuk suggested that the idea of being ruled by an Arab government continued to be as deeply unpopular as it had been during the agitation spurred by the 1920 revolt. Turkey, for its part, had actively been circulating propaganda throughout the former Mosul *vilayet* asserting that their military position on the Mosul frontier was particularly strong and emphasizing the Turkish role as protectors of the caliphate.[140] The town of Kirkuk had already emerged as a center of operation for those who favored the Mosul *vilayet* region's inclusion in Turkey. Colonial Office officials feared that such propaganda would further sway the Turkmen population of Kirkuk against inclusion in Iraq.[141]

In July 1921 the administrative adviser in Kirkuk circulated the district's official referendum protocol. This document made the British government's desires known, asked those opposed to Faysal to "reconsider their position," and excluded the possibility of Turkish rule. In response, anti-Faysal proclamations were posted in the town.[142] Sayyid Ahmad-i Khanaqa, the prominent Kirkuki religious figure, used his public addresses to denounce the Arab-ruled government.[143] Shortly before the referendum was to take place, a meeting at the home of another local religious leader concluded that a fatwa should be issued branding Faysal a "Yazidi"—essentially, an apostate—and that if he were chosen, "they would demand union with Kurdistan." The next day, a notice in Turkish was posted in Kirkuk's central market castigating Faysal for destroying the Islamic Ottoman government as part of the Arab Revolt. It concluded, "The

Arabs have always disliked the Turks," and, invoking the language used in pro-
Turkish propaganda, called for inclusion in the caliphate.[144]

The Colonial Office had hoped to get "the barest majority" in support of
Faysal in Kirkuk.[145] Ultimately, the tide of opinion went completely against him.
Out of just over 2,800 people approached for polling in the district, only 64 voted
in favor of Faysal's accession.[146] Although no account of the exact proceedings of
the referendum in Kirkuk is extant, British official C. J. Edmonds later wrote that
Turkmens there typically expressed support for the selection of a Turkish ruler
and that Kurds indicated that they favored some form of Kurdish administration.
However, the Kurds of Kirkuk remained hostile to Sulaymaniyya, especially to
Shaykh Mahmud's continued influence, and therefore did not favor unification
with other parts of Kurdistan.[147]

The precise role that 'Izzat Pasha played in the referendum in Kirkuk is also
unknown, but what is clear is that Kirkukis resented his interference. After the
referendum another notice appeared in Kirkuk's central market mocking 'Izzat
Pasha for his inability to manipulate the results—"because," it said, "our people
here are too good to give away to the words of such a man."[148] In the end, 96%
of respondents in the Faysal referendum throughout Iraq heeded the British
demand to vote in favor of his accession, and the dissenting 4% were almost
entirely from Kirkuk. "I hold the Kirkuklis to be asses," a disappointed Bell wrote
to her father in August 1921.[149]

The events of 1921 therefore demonstrated the limits of Britain's neocolonial
enterprise in Iraq. The success of the Mandate relied on divisional-level officials
and their close relationships with local patrons, especially urban notables and
tribal leaders; this tactic, carried over from military administration, failed to
effect Britain's desired outcome in Kirkuk. The Faysal referendum also marked
the beginning of a trend in Kirkuk of activity against centralized, external government. Despite being little more than a historical footnote in most works on
Iraq, the referendum is frequently mentioned as an important event in writings
about Kirkuk's history by Iraqi Turkmens. Today, these authors characterize
their antecedents' rejection of Faysal as a bold, dangerous move that incurred
the wrath of British authorities and brought about violence against their community, beginning with the massacre of 1924. The perception that British authorities targeted Turkmens because of their rejection of Faysal may also have
been prevalent among Kirkukis at the time.[150]

In general, Kirkuk's position in relation to the nascent Arab-led Anglo-Iraqi
government is best understood in terms of Kirkukis' attitudes toward power

centered in Baghdad—a fact that is also true of the Kurdish-majority districts. The district of Sulaymaniyya, which retained a separatist viewpoint, had refused to participate in the referendum altogether. The notables of the district of Arbil, despite the anti-British unrest that had taken place there the previous year, were forthright about their desire for British protection and therefore did not harbor the same level of hostility to Faysal as the notables of Kirkuk and Sulaymaniyya did. Indeed, their relations with Kirkuk were not friendly, making them equally unlikely at this stage to favor Kurdish unification.[151] Altogether, even though the discourses surrounding the Faysal referendum occasionally took on an ethnicized cast, identity-based communal divisions were less salient than pro- and anti-centralization forces in the earliest phase of Iraqi state making.

In a final act of defiance, Kirkuk and Sulaymaniyya did not send delegations to Faysal's coronation ceremony. Moreover, Kirkuki officials did not fly the Iraqi flag in the district until 1924.[152] Recognizing the fraught nature of Baghdad's relationship with Kirkuk, a few months after Faysal's accession Bell wrote, "It's best to have the Kirkuk situation undefined."[153]

CONCLUSION

By the fall of 1921, Kirkuk was a de facto part of the British Iraq Mandate, but neither Kirkukis nor British officials were certain where it belonged, administratively, politically, or otherwise. The single most consistent feature of politics in Kirkuk at the beginning of the Mandate was an opposition to the government in Baghdad, whether headed by the British or by King Faysal and Arab civil servants. This tendency was more present, albeit in different forms, in both the town of Kirkuk and its hinterland, reflecting the extent to which urban and rural interests and affairs were intertwined. The question of Kirkuk's status would persist as long as Turkey and British Iraq were actively wrangling over the status of the Mosul *vilayet* and as long as the remote possibility of the creation of an autonomous Kurdish region existed. But once the Kingdom of Iraq was formally established in 1921, an inexorable process of integration with the predominantly Arab state was already under way. Kirkuk's potential as an oil-bearing area enhanced the importance, as far as the British and Iraqi governments were concerned, of integrating the Mosul *vilayet* region into Iraq.

Kirkuki opponents of centralization competed with patronage networks fostered by British authorities, continuing a pattern of contentious local autonomy and reliance on external sponsors that had been present in the area since the Ottoman period. Kirkuk's political discourse in the early 1920s, though distinct from that of other areas, also showed signs of being swayed by external influences, especially Turkish and Kurdish nationalism. Linguistic-communal positions played a role in these political stances, especially with regard to the fact that Kirkukis, who were mostly non-Arab, straightforwardly denounced Arab rule in their rhetoric. However, these identities were not clear-cut categories but rather dynamic arrays of language, lineage, religion, and class. The debate surrounding the Mosul *vilayet*'s status in the 1920s would contribute to the consolidation of ethnicity as a political practice.

2 THE BRITISH MANDATE

FROM FAYSAL'S CORONATION UNTIL 1932, British officials administered Iraq under the League of Nations mandate system, a twentieth-century update of traditional colonial structures that relied on cultivating native authorities (such as the Hashemite monarchy) with the built-in expectation of eventual independence. One of the primary defining features of politics in Kirkuk during this neocolonial period was the constantly shifting nature of relationships between Kirkukis and Anglo-Iraqi authorities who responded to or were based in Baghdad. As British officials in Iraq transitioned to the mandate system, they sought to cut costs by devolving a certain amount of power to some notables and employing local forces for security while nevertheless maintaining effective control—a system they also used in other colonial and neocolonial territories, most notably India.

Individual Kirkukis' loyalties to the Anglo-Iraqi government had implications for Kirkuk's local politics amid a dispute between Iraq and Turkey over the former Mosul *vilayet*, a conflict that destabilized the region until 1926. These loyalties—pro-centralization or anti-centralization—were prone to change with differing political circumstances, particularly after the resolution of the "Mosul question" solidified Kirkuk's status as part of the new Iraqi state. British and other Western officials expected Kirkuki political loyalties to align predictably with factors such as ethnolinguistic identity. Kirkukis did not hold the same set of assumptions.

At crucial moments in Kirkuk's history, however, insipient group identities interacted suddenly with patronage politics in a manner that created tensions and violence between social communities. These intercommunal conflicts were only a marginal feature in Kirkuk's politics during the Mandate era, but they illustrate how local politics were inextricably linked with state making and other national and international dynamics, evolving along with their fluctuations. They also evince some of the roots of ethnicized conflict in Kirkuk, a phenomenon that was produced partly in local interactions with the state and with neocolonial authorities. By the end of the Mandate in 1932, these interactions revealed a number of fault lines between gradually coalescing ethnic communities.

VIOLENCE, INSTABILITY, AND KIRKUKIS' RELATIONS WITH ANGLO-IRAQI AUTHORITIES

At the beginning of British Mandate administration of Iraq, the former Mosul *vilayet* remained under Anglo-Iraqi governance. The contentiousness of British control of the region brought about a combination of destabilizing circumstances that engendered anxiety in Kirkuk and exposed the structures of patronage that the post-Ottoman reorientation of authority had created. The Turkish Republic continued to claim the entire Mosul *vilayet* region as part of its territory, exacerbating tensions by amassing troops on its frontier. In an attempt to weaken British control over the former Mosul *vilayet*, Turkey also dispatched agents to the region, including one who arrived in Rawanduz in March 1922 and described himself as the *kaymakam* (provincial governor) of the district. Turkish agents fomented unrest by promising Kurdish tribesmen the backing of Turkish forces if they resisted British control.[1] Furthermore, Kurdish tribesmen periodically rose up against British authorities and their patrons independently of Turkish influence because of ongoing widespread hostility to centralized authority.[2] Therefore, even though the new state of Iraq was formally in the process of transitioning to a civilian Mandate administration with an Arab monarch, the northern third of the state—if, in fact, it could be called part of Iraq—remained a site of active military operations after 1921. These realities aggravated the existing uncertainty of the Kirkuk area's relationship with British and Iraqi authorities.

British methods of controlling the former Mosul *vilayet* became progressively more violent in 1922, when a system of air control, led by the Royal Air Force (RAF), was established throughout Iraq. After much internal debate the British government adopted a policy of policing unstable areas in Iraq through aerial bombings, which were used as a way to reduce the expenses associated with maintaining a large ground force. Controlling Iraq without occupying it in the traditional sense also suited the structure of the Mandate system, whereby

British officials administered the country in collaboration with a less powerful but more visible Arab government.[3] Moreover, as Priya Satia argues, contemporary British notions of "Arabia," a broadly defined cultural category, undergirded the use of brutally repressive tactics in Iraq by regarding them as especially effective in relation to the local population's "Oriental" mentality.[4] Urban Kirkuk did not directly experience the effects of the region's mostly rural rebellions or British military operations to counter them, but its proximity to the violence—especially through its direct links with Sulaymaniyya, which remained outside centralized control—created an omnipresent unease in the town, according to the detailed contemporary accounts of C. J. Edmonds.

These British operations were psychologically devastating to rural communities. Edmonds wrote approvingly of this aspect of air control, while downplaying the overall damage it caused, in his description of a bombing campaign in late 1922 in the restive northeastern division of Marga, an area near the Persian frontier.

> The new incendiary bombs having arrived—seven Ninaks flew up from Baghdad and attacked Marga; all machines from here cooperated with ordinary bombs. Four large fires were observed in the morning but evidently did not spread far since they were out by the afternoon; mud houses are very unpromising material. . . . If the actual damage inflicted was not great the moral effect was, and for several weeks on end the Bristols and the Snipes were out every day on operations which were progressively extended from Marga.[5]

Similarly, at an early point in the debate over air control, a 1920 memorandum considering its use in predominantly Kurdish areas acknowledged that it was "a harsh and brutal instrument of force" and concluded that, before targeting humans, it would best be initially used against targets such as livestock, crops, and property "which the tribal mind might consider valuable."[6] British officials considered the tactic of inspiring fear in local populations useful to their mission, but they also saw it as a hallmark of the "humaneness" of an air control policy that would ostensibly lead to less loss of life than its alternatives. Needless to say, those who subscribed to this notion ignored the ruinous effects on villagers of the loss of their homes and resources as well as the inevitability of human casualties when explosive and incendiary bombs were dropped on populated areas.[7]

In the former Mosul *vilayet* the worst of this violence took place in areas north and east of the Kirkuk division, particularly around Sulaymaniyya. In comparison, Kirkuk and its rural hinterland were relatively peaceful. In the 1920 memorandum

British officials specifically ruled out the use of aerial bombings in the town of Kirkuk itself unless extreme circumstances were to arise, and British records of Kurdish unrest in the 1920s do not specifically indicate that tribes in rural Kirkuk joined in these revolts against central authority.[8] However, because of its relative proximity to Sulaymaniyya, Kirkuk usually served as the base where British-led troops would converge to carry out military operations in that division.[9] At one point in early 1923, Shaykh Mahmud, based in Sulaymaniyya as usual, even positioned his forces in such a way as to directly threaten Kirkuk.[10] A regiment of Indian Sikh troops under British command also continued to be stationed in the town. These troops were accompanied by a regiment of the Iraq Levies, a force made up predominantly of Assyrian refugees from southeastern Anatolia; the British found them especially useful as a replacement for their own ground forces because of their military background, their ready loyalty to British patronage, and the reduced expense of employing them in lieu of British or Indian troops. The Iraq Levies eventually replaced Indian troops in Kirkuk entirely in 1923.[11] Therefore continued military presence and persistent violence ensured that Kirkukis were well aware of the volatility of their surrounding region while simultaneously at a distance from the most brutal aspects of the unrest.

As mentioned, the instability of the Mosul *vilayet* region created a tense atmosphere among Kirkuki townspeople in the early years of the Mandate. This mood became especially pronounced after the multilateral Lausanne Conference was convened in November 1922. The Lausanne Conference, the last peace conference of World War I, mainly aimed to forge a definitive peace with Kemalist Turkey. The British were determined to maintain the Iraqi status quo, whereas the Kemalists rejected the terms of the Treaty of Sèvres and proceeded to formally assert what they perceived as their rightful sovereignty over the entirety of the former Mosul *vilayet*. The disagreement between Britain and Turkey made Kirkukis anxious about what would happen next. Edmonds wrote in January 1923 that people all over the Kirkuk division were preoccupied with the proceedings and that "even the most unsophisticated tribesmen constantly ask after the progress of the European conference." Rumors regarding the movement of Turkish troops were "rife." In one particularly frightening incident the same month, Turkey amassed an unusually large number of troops in an area near Zakho, a town in the extreme northwest of the Mosul *vilayet* region's frontier. In Edmonds's telling, Kirkuk's atmosphere reached "fever heat," and local authorities collaborating with the British were "pallid with terror." A British-led redistribution of the Indian troops stationed in Kirkuk in response to these actions led to widespread fear of renewed warfare.[12]

In the midst of this fraught situation, British officials in Iraq returned to the issue of incorporating the predominantly non-Arab governorates of the former Mosul *vilayet* into the election law, a problem that had preoccupied them in the months leading up to King Faysal's coronation. In the fall of 1922, Kirkuk, despite its uneasy relations with Baghdad, was obliged to undergo electoral registration along with every other Iraqi division except Sulaymaniyya. Kurdish tribesmen met the electoral registration process with considerable suspicion of British designs for areas that were predominantly Kurdish.[13] British officers stationed in Kirkuk and in other non-Arab areas were subsequently required to negotiate with influential local figures to secure their participation in the elections. In Kirkuk local notables initially demanded that the dispute with Turkey over the Mosul *vilayet* region be resolved as a condition of their participation in the elections, which was clearly not possible if the elections were going to be held in a timely manner. Adding to the difficulty of this process was the fact that civil servants of the Iraqi central government in Baghdad continuously roused the ire of the mayor of Kirkuk, 'Abd al-Majid Ya'qubizada, and the *mutasarrif* of the Kirkuk governorate, Fattah Pasha, by attempting to play a role in matters of local administration. Edmonds wrote in June 1923 that the election negotiations had been "neutralized by the grievances of the municipality which feels that it is being subjected to much arbitrary and illegal interference from Baghdad." In one provocative instance, a nepotistic central government minister in Baghdad dismissed and replaced a local appointee. Soon afterward, however, both sides reached an acceptable compromise: Kirkuk would participate in the elections on the condition that appointed positions in the district would be filled by local figures and that Turkish would remain the district's official language. The high commissioner officially recognized these rights in July 1923.[14]

The conclusion of the Lausanne Conference that same month failed to resolve the destabilizing dispute over the Mosul *vilayet* region, ensuring that complex pro-centralization and anti-centralization dynamics stemming from a vexed relationship with Baghdad would continue to dominate Kirkuk's politics for the foreseeable future. Instead, by agreement between the British and Turkish delegations, the Treaty of Lausanne stipulated that a year's worth of Anglo-Turkish talks would take place and that if they did not settle the dispute, the matter would be referred to the League of Nations for arbitration. In the meantime, the military status quo on the frontier, including British control over the former *vilayet*, would be maintained. The treaty was therefore a victory for the British, because they could make their case for retaining the region as part of

Iraq from the position of ongoing administration of the area, not to mention from a position of strength within the League of Nations.[15] British and Iraqi authorities also managed to partly calm Kurdish tribal unrest by reoccupying Sulaymaniyya with a combination of Iraqi army and Iraq Levy forces in July 1924, forcing Shaykh Mahmud to flee.[16]

Notably, the unrest stemming from the Mosul *vilayet* region's volatility and the uncertainty surrounding Kirkuk's status exposed the main factors that influenced the loyalties of its inhabitants, namely, the existence of client-patron relationships between British authorities and some Kirkuki notables and the competing perception among other notables that the British and Iraqi governments were opposed to their interests. For instance, British officials' eventual success in getting Kirkuk to participate in the elections was in large part due to a good personal relationship between the deputy administrative inspector A. F. Miller, who spoke fluent Turkish, and 'Abd al-Majid Ya'qubizada, the town mayor.[17] The Ya'qubizada family was a prominent urban Kirkuki family who were thought to be of Kurdish descent but who nevertheless self-identified as Turkish-speaking elites.[18] Although 'Abd al-Majid cultivated close links with British authorities, his younger brother, Mustafa, was one of many people from Kirkuk's prominent families who formed clandestine groups that opposed Anglo-Iraqi administration. These groups formed amid the questions about the Mosul *vilayet* region's political future that the Lausanne Conference raised. British authorities termed these groups "pro-Turkish committees."[19]

One of the most influential personalities to be involved with anti-Anglo-Iraqi activities was the leading local religious figure of the Naqshbandi Sufi order, Sayyid Ahmad-i Khanaqa. A Kurd both in terms of descent and self-identification, Sayyid Ahmad was a relative of the Barzinji family of Sulaymaniyya, which held particularly robust authority among fellow Kirkuki Kurds.[20] British authorities and their local patrons therefore quickly moved to expel him from Kirkuk. In early February 1923 Edmonds and Fattah Pasha arranged a meeting with Sayyid Ahmad to inform him of their suspicions about his clandestine activity, which he denied. He was then arrested, transported to a plane waiting for him at the city's airfield, and deported. Several other people fled Kirkuk in alarm at this apparent crackdown on activities in opposition to Anglo-Iraqi authority. One of these was the patriarch of the Naftchizada family of Turkmen notables, Nazim Beg, a former Ottoman official whom Edmonds called "the leading citizen of Kirkuk." Nazim Beg left Kirkuk for Turkey, where he would continue to be based for years to come.[21]

British sources from the Mandate era tend to assume that because Kirkuk was majority Turkmen, or at least majority Turkish speaking, it was more prone to being a center of purportedly "pro-Turkish" activity. However, although some Turkish-speaking elites, such as Nazim Beg, might have had a close relationship with the nascent republic of Turkey, these activities were not an indication of loyalty to Turkey as a country so much as they were part of the general trend in Kirkuk against being subjected to the whims of a distant administration. As Edmonds noted in a 1923 letter to the British adviser of the Iraqi Ministry of the Interior, the Mosul *vilayet*'s municipalities were accustomed to being "almost entirely independent and left entirely to run their own show" and resented the fact that, following the formation of the Iraqi central government, they were "never free from Baghdad dictation."[22] Furthermore, a closer examination of the details of local politics indicates that the affiliations of Kirkuk's notables depended more reliably on their patronage networks than on any source of communal identity; even brothers from the same prominent family, the Ya'qubizadas, were working toward different goals with regard to Iraqi centralization. Similarly, Nazim Beg Naftchizada's uncle, Salih Beg Naftchizada, who represented Kirkuk in the central government's Constituent Assembly after the elections were carried out, reportedly opposed Nazim Beg's defection to Turkey. A report in the Baghdad-based newspaper *al-Istiqlal* in 1925 went so far as to claim that Salih Beg was "bitterly angered" by his nephew's "lack of faith to his country."[23] Altogether, the era of the Mosul dispute would prove to be the apex of the politics of patronage in Kirkuk in the modern Iraqi state. It was the period in which, more than at any other time in the twentieth century, personal relationships and direct client links—or a disadvantageous lack thereof—between notables and more powerful external forces played a role in determining popular opinion.

SUDDEN SECTARIANISM: THE ASSYRIAN LEVIES MASSACRE

The explosive capacity of the friction between Kirkukis and centralized Anglo-Iraqi authority manifested in a violent series of events in May 1924. The incident that sparked these events, a massacre of townspeople by Assyrians in the Iraq Levies, receives very little treatment in the writings of the officials involved, evidently because it was a tremendous embarrassment to the British establishment in Iraq. C. J. Edmonds and R. S. Stafford, another British official, downplayed the significance of the massacre in their memoirs by simply saying that the Levies "ran amok" after a disagreement in Kirkuk's central market on 4 May 1924. Historians who have described the event, though usually only mentioning it in passing, have repeated this formulation with remarkable regularity.[24] Yet the prominent role that these events continue to play in the collective memory of Kirkukis in the present day, especially in Turkmen histories, demands a detailed analysis.

Accounts of the incident written by Turkmens consistently characterize it as a massacre (*katliam*) orchestrated by the British, who, in their view, were specifically targeting the Turkmen community of Kirkuk in retaliation for their rejection of King Faysal's leadership in the 1921 referendum on the monarchy. Turkmen authors refer to the killings of 4 May as the "Levy Massacre" or something similar.[25] In fact, Güldem Büyüksaraç has found that Iraqi Turkmens now living in Turkey often remember the massacre erroneously as the "Armenian Massacre," reflecting the extent to which its association with Assyrians has been supplanted by an emphasis on its perceived British—and Christian—backing.[26] Although the idea that these killings were a British act of revenge is highly dubious, the fact that it has passed into memory that way merits examination. Furthermore, the events of 5 May—the intercommunal conflict that ensued after the initial attack by the Levies—demonstrate the potential of the relationship between authorities, their patrons, and their local opponents to become intertwined with popular group identities. In this particular moment the groups that emerged revolved around Muslim and Christian confessional background, reflecting a type of social categorization that had become salient in areas outside Kirkuk during the late Ottoman era.

The Iraq Levies were local forces under British command who were key to Britain's neocolonial enterprise in Iraq. Many sources use the alternative name Assyrian Levies to refer specifically to the detachments of these forces that were made up entirely of Assyrian refugees. Assyrians made up the majority of the Iraq Levies by 1924 and constituted all of the infantry in urban Kirkuk. There was also a cavalry unit of the Iraq Levies in Kirkuk made up of Kurds, but the British typically employed the Assyrians exclusively in operations against Kurdish unrest in rural areas. The Assyrian refugees among the Levies had fled from the genocidal operations in Anatolia during World War I that claimed hundreds of thousands of Assyrian and Armenian lives, often in shockingly brutal ways. Although these operations were designed and ordered by Ottoman authorities, they were typically carried out by local Kurds, and Assyrian refugees associated the Mosul region's Kurds with their colinguists to the north.[27] As agents of British authority, as Christians, and as frequent partners in the quelling of uprisings, the Assyrian Levies were particularly closely associated with centralized

Anglo-Iraqi authority in the view of local populations throughout the former *vilayet*. Therefore, animosity between Assyrians and the rest of the population of the region was intense on both sides. These tensions nearly came to a head after a 1923 incident in Mosul in which two Assyrian children were killed; much to the Assyrian Levies' dismay, nobody was held responsible.[28] On the other side, Kurds in rural areas were angered by the fact that the Levies' operations in their villages often failed to distinguish between rebels and civilians.[29]

The details of the events of 4 May 1924 can be approximated on the basis of records of British officers' and some Kirkukis' testimonies as part of the later inquiry into the massacre.[30] That day, of the Assyrian Levies stationed in Kirkuk, two companies were in Chamchamal, a Kurdish village east of Kirkuk along the road to Sulaymaniyya, and two other companies were still in the town and under orders to march to Chamchamal by 5 May.[31] Various accounts agree that on the morning of 4 May, an argument broke out between some of the Assyrian Levies remaining in urban Kirkuk and a Muslim shopkeeper in Kirkuk's central market, which flanked the southern and eastern sides of the citadel on the eastern half of the town.[32] The argument, which apparently began over the price of a purchase of sugar, subsequently became charged with hostile language against the feuding parties' religions. Some British sources even suggest that it was significant that 4 May was the day before the beginning of 'Id al-Fitr, the religious holiday at the end of the Islamic month of Ramadan, and that the shopkeepers were consequently nearing the end of a "trying fast."[33]

Although religious animosity appears to have been one underlying factor of the confrontation, the 4 May events must also be understood in the context of Kirkuki discontent with Anglo-Iraqi administration and the violent operations that the Levies carried out on its behalf in the Mosul *vilayet* region. For instance, Lieutenant P. Paulet King, who was in charge of the Levies in Kirkuk, recalled that in addition to making derogatory comments about their Christianity, the shopkeepers had allegedly taunted the Assyrians "with their probable failure in assumed future operations against Shaikh Mahmud."[34] This reference indicates that the shopkeepers were aware that the Levies were in the process of gradually leaving the town and marching toward Sulaymaniyya, which, as mentioned before, they would eventually take part in reoccupying in July 1924. The Kirkukis in the market therefore correctly deduced that the Levies' movements indicated impending central government action against Shaykh Mahmud's rebellion. According to one report, rumors of the reoccupation of Sulaymaniyya had recently been the subject of a great deal of discussion among people in Kirkuk's traditional social centers, further supporting this interpretation of the comment.[35] The fact that Kirkuki notables and tribes tended to be hostile to Shaykh Mahmud at this time suggests that the shopkeepers' derision in this instance did not stem from support for Mahmud but from resentment of the Levies and the British-dominated authority they represented.

What occurred next is disputed. One British witness, referred to in his testimony as Officer Burgess, attested that the Assyrian Levies, who were not armed at the time, had then beaten some of the shopkeepers in the market. On the other hand, Lieutenant Paulet King stated that the shopkeepers had attacked the Levies, striking two on the head and one on the hand. Regardless of who began the physical altercation, Kirkuk police, led by Officer Burgess, arrested the three shopkeepers involved.[36] Paulet King thereafter ordered the two Levy companies to assemble. Using an Assyrian officer as an interpreter, he ordered that they were not to reenter the market or to cross the nearby stone bridge spanning the Khasa; this seems to have been an attempt to prevent them from returning to their barracks, which were on the western side of the town directly across the river from the citadel. He then sent a picket of Levies to enforce the ban on crossing the bridge and dismissed the remaining soldiers.[37] As they were proceeding away from the parade ground where they had gathered, some of the Levies stormed into a nearby coffee shop, destroying furniture and beating the customers. One British officer reported seeing two people with bloodied faces thrown from the shop.[38] The extant testimonies do not suggest any reason for this action and imply that it was random. Afterward, defying Paulet King's orders, the Levies began to force their way across the bridge to the west side of the town, fighting the picket of soldiers stationed on the bridge. In the midst of the melee the Kirkuk police fired rifle shots from their station near the west side of the bridge, striking and killing an Assyrian Levy sergeant.[39] Although these were probably not the first shots fired that day, they appear to have been the first to result in a death.[40] After the police opened fire and news of the sergeant's death spread among the crowd, the Levies rushed across the bridge to their barracks, where they gathered their arms. They then returned to the center of town and began to shoot indiscriminately at Kirkuki townspeople. A British officer testified that, while near the coffee shop on the east side of the river that had been the site of the earlier altercation, he saw one of the Levies pursue and shoot a "poorly dressed" civilian at point-blank range after the man had dropped to his knees and held up his hands.[41]

A well-known Chaldean merchant and landowner named Toma Hindi, whose large and prominent house was in the southwestern part of the citadel and thus within firing range of the bridge and west riverbank, testified:

> I was in my house on the morning of the 4th May when I heard some firing and almost immediately afterwards someone shouted in Turkish to be let in the front door. In spite of my objection a number of Assyrian soldiers succeeded in forcing an entrance. They went straight to the roof (about a dozen) where they were joined by others. . . . Two of the soldiers who came in the door seized me. . . . [An Assyrian] Officer gave some orders in his own tongue to the two men which was apparently to the effect that they were to leave me alone. . . . Firing had been going on from the roof of the house from the moment when the first soldiery reached it and continued for about 10 minutes after the Officer had reached the roof.[42]

It is noteworthy that Toma Hindi, although a Christian like the Levies, underscored in his brief testimony the differences between himself, a native Kirkuki Chaldean,[43] and the Assyrians, an external force. This emphasis is especially clear with regard to the language barrier between them. Despite the fact that he was presumably a descendant of Aramaic speakers, as were the Assyrians, Toma Hindi was most likely a Turkish speaker first and foremost, like the majority of Kirkuk's notables and Chaldean inhabitants of the citadel. This fact is indicated by the Levies' use of Turkish when trying to enter his house and by Toma Hindi's reference to the Levies' use of their "own tongue" as though it was not a language he knew. Among themselves the Assyrian soldiers would presumably have been speaking their vernacular dialect of Neo-Aramaic.

As it happened, the Levies had taken up positions on more than one strategically important rooftop other than that of Toma Hindi's house and were firing at civilians from several directions. A Kirkuki police inspector testified that he had seen gunfire from the roof of the school on the west riverbank and from the "Bridge head" in addition to the shots coming from the citadel and that the Kirkuk police were returning fire from the roof of their station on the west riverbank.[44] According to a British captain with the Levies, a police sniper fired numerous shots that hit the east riverbank and also fired in the direction of women relatives of the Levies in the area of the barracks.[45]

The violence of 4 May therefore took place entirely in the town's historical, political, social, and commercial core, centering on the bridge across the Khasa River (Figure 6). The significance of this location is reflected in the fact that, although the area in which the firing took place was relatively small, the shooting victims originated from fifteen different neighborhoods or quarters of Kirkuk.[46] Furthermore, in another attack on an emblematic, traditional node of social and economic interaction, some of the Assyrian Levies set fire to the market where their initial fight with Kirkuki townspeople had occurred. The Kirkukis in the

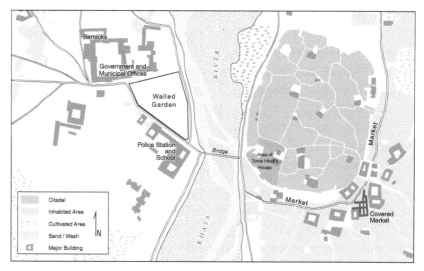

FIGURE 6. The traditional core of central Kirkuk illustrating where the events of 4 May 1924 took place.

vicinity of the market who later testified about this occurrence claimed that the Levies had created the large fire with the assistance of fuel and pumps. These Kirkukis consistently described the Levies as "Tiaris," or people from the Tiyari region of southeastern Anatolia, differentiating them from local Christians and emphasizing their status as unwelcome outsiders.[47]

By the end of 4 May, at least thirty-six and up to fifty Kirkukis had been killed in the chaos, and dozens more had been wounded.[48] Some Turkmen authors have claimed that the number of people killed was far higher.[49] Two witnesses, including the British civil surgeon in Kirkuk, F. M. Halley, testified that three of the dead were local police officers.[50] Sixteen or so of the casualties were women, at least four of whom died; Halley reported that whereas most of the victims suffered or died from rifle wounds, one of the women killed had been stabbed in the face.[51] Halley also testified that six Assyrian Levies died, presumably including the sergeant who was the first person to be shot, and that one member of the Kurdish Iraq Levy cavalry unit—which did not side with the Assyrian infantry—was killed.[52] On the afternoon of 4 May, British and Levy officers managed to bring the Assyrian soldiers under control and march them back to their barracks across the dry riverbed while the Kirkuk police continued to fire in their direction.[53] British authorities also flew in Sikh troops from Baghdad as reinforcements.[54] That evening the officers marched all of the Assyrian Levies and their families out of Kirkuk.[55] The next day the British high commissioner in Baghdad, Sir Henry Dobbs, issued a proclamation for distribution in Kirkuk reassuring the townspeople that the Assyrian Levies had been sent "to a place distant from Kirkuk" and promising an inquiry into the events.[56]

The testimonies collected as part of the subsequent inquiry, which provide most of the available details about these events as given here, concern only the massacre of 4 May. The events of 5 May, though less thoroughly chronicled, are equally significant to a fuller understanding of Kirkuk's local political and social circumstances in the early Mandate era because they constitute an evolution of the chaos into a clear pattern of intercommunal violence. One reason for this development may have been an impression on the part of Kirkuki townspeople, apparently fueled by rumors, that local Christians had sided with the Assyrian Levies in the various altercations of 4 May. For instance, two Kirkukis who later testified about the arson attack on the market claimed that they had seen some local Christians accompanying the "Tiaris" and providing the fuel.[57] In any case, by the morning of 5 May, some members of Kirkuk's Muslim population had turned against the local, and predominantly Chaldean, Christian community and begun to attack them and to loot their homes and businesses. Special Service Officer H. A. Anson summarized the incidents in a report to Baghdad, exhibiting a characteristic British scorn for Kirkuk's urban classes that appears to have been stronger than any sense of disquiet he might have felt about the killings of civilians.

> During the course of the day some 8 or 9 Christians were murdered and any Moslem so disposed applied himself vigorously to the task of getting something for nothing. A more revolting spectacle could not have been afforded than the streets of Kirkuk on that day. Every scoundrel in the town procured for himself some article of value from the houses and shops broken into. Singer Sewing machines were to be seen being carried away on donkeys by troopers from the Iraq levies, effendis staggering under bundles of clothing, scum from the bazaar decked out in silks and satins, and street urchins haggling over bales of cloth. . . . Many of the Iraq Levies were openly in partnership with townsmen, the former doing the looting while the latter removed the booty to their houses.[58]

The looting and violence of 5 May targeted people and businesses that were "Christian" in a broad sense, including the Kirkuk office of the U.S.-based Singer Manufacturing Company, which sold sewing machines. These actions signified a momentary shift to a politics of identity. In the view of some of Kirkuk's Muslim population, being Christian comprised an association with the Assyrian Levies and consequently with Anglo-Iraqi authority.

The concept of a split between Muslims and Christians, in which the Christians were popularly and violently construed as threatening outsiders, had a precedent in the late Ottoman era, especially among Kurds and Armenians in eastern Anatolia, which culminated in the genocide of World War I.[59] Even though the Muslim-Christian divide had not previously taken hold in Kirkuk to a significant degree, recent memories of trauma provided fertile ground for an instance of, to follow Max Bergholz's formulation, "sudden" sectarianism.[60] In this moment, patronage politics was temporarily subordinate, as indicated by the Kurdish Iraq Levy troopers' participation in the anti-Christian looting despite being under British command. The status of intercommunal relations in Kirkuk on 5 May 1924 therefore demonstrated the possibility that tensions between a provincial area and Iraqi centralized authority could interact with and exacerbate previously latent tensions between divided communities on a local level.

The spasm of violence in Kirkuk came to an end after 5 May. However, unrest spread as far as Sulaymaniyya, where Shaykh Mahmud declared a "jihad" against the British and the Assyrians. In accordance with the ongoing policy of using air control to weaken local morale and to bolster British influence, the RAF bombed Sulaymaniyya in response.[61] Lower-level agitation against local Chaldo-Assyrian Christians also continued. In cooperation with British authorities, 'Abd al-Majid Ya'qubizada, by then the governor of the Kirkuk district, had three people arrested on 10 May for "making inflammatory remarks" against Christians.[62] The animosity between Kirkukis and the Iraqi public on the one hand and the Assyrian Levies and Anglo-Iraqi administration on the other was further intensified when the official inquiry into the events of 4 May did not lead to a conclusive conviction of any of the individual Assyrian Levies involved. The court of inquiry was able, on the basis of the detailed witness accounts, to cite several officers by name, whom it recommended should be put on trial for murder and who were subsequently arrested.[63] However, the court that tried them, though determining that they had fired at civilians and sentencing most of them to life in prison as a result, did not pursue the death sentence because "it could not be proved that they had actually killed any" particular person.[64]

This confusing close to the affair led to a widespread perception among Iraqis that British authorities were intentionally harboring the guilty Levies,[65] a conjecture that is plausible but cannot be confirmed. Extant documents demonstrate that officials in London, at least, expressed interest in punishing both the Levies involved and their British officers.[66] There is also no evidence in archival sources to support the common Iraqi Turkmen contention that British

authorities intentionally unleashed the Assyrian Levies on the Turkmen community of Kirkuk as an act of revenge for their rejection of King Faysal. On the
contrary, frustrated British officials fancifully speculated in the first few days
after 4 May that the Levies' initial acts might have taken place as a result of
some sort of interference by Shaykh Mahmud.[67] In addition, although most of
the 4 May victims were indeed likely to have been Turkish-speaking Kirkukis,
this fact reflects the town's demographic composition at the time rather than an
organized campaign against a single ethnic group.

Nevertheless, the events of 4 and 5 May 1924 revealed the potential for tensions and violent actions among Kirkuk's communities that would persistently
be linked with the British presence in Iraq and with relations between Kirkuk
and Baghdad for years to come. For instance, the anger at Assyrians and at
the British that the massacre of 4 May provoked among Muslim inhabitants of
Kirkuk was so strong that when the Iraqi army massacred scores of unarmed
Assyrian civilians in the village of Simele, near the northern city of Dohuk, in
1933, Kirkukis recalled the incidents of 1924 and reacted with "excitement."[68]
The relationship between Iraqi Christians, especially Chaldo-Assyrians, and
British neocolonial authority would also continue to develop and to engender
a specific intercommunal fault line in urban Kirkuk. This relationship became
especially significant after the British-led Iraq Petroleum Company was established in Kirkuk and during the company's subsequent growth and period of
influence in the municipality.

RESOLVING THE MOSUL QUESTION: KIRKUK'S "RACES"
AND THE ENTRENCHMENT OF OIL INTERESTS

It was in this tense atmosphere that Anglo-Iraqi and Turkish delegations met in
Istanbul in May and June of 1924 to settle what had come to be known as the
Mosul question. The Turkish public had been galvanized by the dispute over
the former Mosul *vilayet*, and public opinion of the British as expressed in local newspapers was highly unflattering. François Georgeon observes that during the 1920s, the Turkish satirical press—a good indicator of Turkish popular
opinion because of its popularity, even though Kemalists had mostly appropri-
ated it—was particularly active in the media campaign against the British. One
paper, *Karagöz*, portrayed Britain as an absurd character inseparably attached
to an oil drum, representing the region's reputed oil wealth, and controlling
the strings of League of Nations figures and King Faysal, who were depicted as
puppets. This charge was meant to question the legitimacy of the Iraqi claim to

the former Mosul *vilayet*, suggesting that it was driven by British interests and was based entirely on a Western desire to control oil resources.[69] Kirkuk, which had long been one of the most famous oil-bearing sites in the Mosul region, was therefore a subtext to one of the most sensitive aspects of the dispute.

Indeed, the Constantinople Conference revolved primarily around conceptions of legitimacy. It became an opportunity for the figure at the head of each party—Fethi Bey, president of Turkey's Grand National Assembly, on the Turkish side and Sir Percy Cox on the Anglo-Iraqi side—to express his delegation's perception of the nature of the dispute (and how to settle it) and to articulate his side's concept of what constituted rightful claims to the region. The arguments that Fethi and Cox presented relied in large part on the idea of race and assumed that the legitimacy of a claim to the region rested on which "race" had demographic primacy in it. The conference's discourse therefore delimited ethnolinguistic categories that were actually ambiguous. The elevation of the concept of race also contradicted Cox's own previous position, based on the observations of officers on the ground in the Mosul *vilayet* region, that the lines between Kurds, Turkmens, and Arabs were, in his words, "very blurred" and that political allegiances were not easily predictable on the basis of such identities.[70]

Both Fethi and Cox also used the idea of race to tout their fairness and inclusiveness while simultaneously lambasting the other side for supposedly lacking this principle. For instance, Fethi challenged the British government's preoccupation with the settlement of Assyrian refugees; he asserted that the Assyrians were a "tiny" minority and that, in light of that fact, the British were obliged to pay more attention to those who constituted the large majority of the population of Mosul, or "the Turks and the Kurds." Fethi then mentioned the fact that the Assyrians were Christians. He provocatively assured Cox that he understood the British government's inclination to support the Assyrians, especially as a result of this religious affinity, but that the Turkish delegation recognized the same rights for all, regardless of "race" and religion, and that the Assyrians would, "on Turkish territory," enjoy the rights they had had for centuries. Cox, who was conscious of the fact that he was at the conference to represent an ostensibly sovereign Iraq rather than Britain, sidestepped the issue of religion and turned the racial argument against Fethi. In a later meeting he asserted that Fethi was trying to co-opt the Kurds so as to make Kurds and Turks seem racially indistinguishable and therefore give the impression that the Turks had a large majority in the Mosul *vilayet* region.[71] In the end, the talks made no progress, but the ideas and terminology used by the Turkish and

Anglo-Iraqi delegations, which prioritized the perceived interests of "racial" groups as coherent entities, built the scaffolding for the ensuing League of Nations arbitration of the dispute.

During the course of this arbitration, the idea of race evolved into a form of strict categorization and determinism. For instance, in support of the Anglo-Iraqi position on the issue, the Foreign Office submitted a memorandum to the League of Nations in August 1924 laying out the case for attaching the Mosul *vilayet* region to Iraq through four categories of argument: "Racial," "Political," "Economic," and "Geographical and Strategic." The political category was actually an analysis of the alleged political interests of the different "races." In addition, when describing these groups, British officials for the first time began to put the colloquially used adjective *Turks* in quotation marks when describing Turkish-speaking inhabitants of the region and emphasized that these "Turks" were racially distinct from those of "Osmanli" descent, because they were, in fact, "Turkomans." The British government clearly intended for this conception of racially based politics to diminish as much as possible the number of people in the Mosul *vilayet* region who could be considered likely to be loyal to Turkey.[72]

Ironically, this approach undercut their argument in the case of Kirkuk, as illustrated by a later British memorandum to the League of Nations on the Mosul question. In that document British officials underscored the fact that, upon their initial occupation of the Mosul *vilayet*, they had issued proclamations in Arabic in most areas but that their proclamations in Kirkuk had been in Turkish. More critically, while trying to argue that the people of the region had demonstrated loyalty to the new Iraqi state, the memorandum had to concede the fact that Kirkuk had rejected King Faysal in the 1921 referendum.[73] The fact that inhabitants of the Mosul *vilayet* region, especially in Kirkuk, had often shown a tendency to oppose any kind of centralized authority required British arguments in the Mosul dispute to rely on a simplistic idea of racial preferences rather than accounting for demonstrated loyalties.

The League of Nations solution to the dispute was to send a multilateral commission to the former Mosul *vilayet*. In accordance with the idea of the "self-determination of peoples," which was especially prevalent in the discourse of international institutions at the time and had been most famously articulated by American president Woodrow Wilson, the Mosul Commission aimed to discern whether the people of the region wanted to be part of Turkey or part of Iraq.[74] The three primary commissioners were Colonel Albert Paulis, a Belgian military officer who had served in the Congo Free State; Einar af Wirsén, a Swedish diplomat; and Count Paul Teleki, a former prime minister of Hungary. The Commission was accompanied by secretaries, British and Turkish representatives, and designated "experts" on Iraq and Turkey. C. J. Edmonds, whose papers provide some of the most detailed information on the Commission's activities, served as a British liaison. Nazim Beg Naftchizada, who, as previously mentioned, had fled to Turkey in 1923, served as the Turkish delegation's "expert" on Kirkuk. The Commission carefully considered economic, geographic, racial, strategic, and historical arguments, drew up elaborate maps, and conducted many interviews with notables to ask them if they were "for Iraq" or "for the Turk."

The Mosul Commission arrived in Baghdad in mid-January 1925 for just over two months of work. After proceeding to Mosul, they decided that it would be best to split up and evaluate smaller regions separately. They determined that Colonel Paulis would take on the Kirkuk area, accompanied by one Iraqi and one Turkish expert along with C. J. Edmonds. Kirkuk had already been the scene of overt "pro-Turkish" activity in January, when a brother of Nazim Beg Naftchizada had spread rumors that the *vilayet* had already been granted to Turkey and that Nazim Beg would be its *mutasarrif*. Soon afterward, meetings of the clandestine committees opposed to Anglo-Iraqi rule began to plan street demonstrations for when the Commission came to Kirkuk. In one of these meetings, a suggestion was made that demonstrators should carry Turkish flags dipped in sheep's blood to represent the blood of the citizens of Kirkuk who had died at the hands of the Assyrian Levies the previous May. British authorities had started the process of recompensing townspeople for their damaged property as a result of those events. But contrary to disposing the claimants to a positive opinion of British administration, they tended to assume British generosity in this regard was a result of the presence of the Commission. The Kirkuk *mutasarrif*, 'Abd al-Majid Ya'qubizada, ordered the arrest of several people associated with anti-British and anti-Iraq activities in order to restore "calm" to the city before Paulis's arrival.[75] Paulis expressed support for these repressive measures, noting in a letter to Edmonds that the quelling of street demonstrations allowed him to assess people's opinions in what he viewed as an authentic fashion.[76]

Throughout the many interviews he conducted in rural villages and urban Kirkuk, Paulis continued to harbor a colonialist, racist mind-set, overtly drawing on his experiences as part of Belgium's brutal regime over the Congolese. He repeatedly indicated in staggeringly blunt language that he did not take Kirkukis' opinions seriously. At one point during the process, he remarked in exasperation, "A child is not asked whether it would like to go to school . . . it is just sent."[77] The answers that his interviewees gave to what the commissioners called the "secret question"—Iraq or Turkey?—were not easily predictable and were therefore, in his view, arbitrary. In his diary about his activities with the Commission, Paulis noted that 'Izzat Pasha, who had previously enjoyed a close relationship with the British and had even tried to promote support for Faysal in Kirkuk in 1921, now supported unification with Turkey. On the other hand, the *mutasarrif* of the province and the mayor of Kirkuk both supported continued unification with Iraq, citing the region's closer economic ties with Baghdad. Nazim Beg Naftchizada, Paulis wrote, had supported Anglo-Iraqi administration before his defection to Turkey.[78] In his own diary entry of 21 February 1925, C. J. Edmonds wrote that the tribal parts of Kirkuk that were under the influence of the Talabanis had expressed support for Iraq and that the Kirkuk area was evenly divided so far.[79] Opinions in Kirkuk were not even consistent within families; for instance, the Ya'qubizada brothers continued to be divided. One British official later dryly suggested that at least one member of this family had to keep "a foot in the Turkish camp" as part of "the family Insurance Policy."[80] Despite having many reasons not to, Paulis stubbornly continued to conceive the dispute through a racial paradigm, suggesting at one stage that perhaps the Commission should recommend granting the predominantly Arab areas of the former Mosul *vilayet* to Iraq while attaching predominantly Turkmen and Kurdish areas to Turkey.[81]

The Commission's persistent attempts to understand public opinion in terms of race are remarkable in light of their own conclusion in their final report to the League of Nations that throughout the Mosul *vilayet* region, multilingualism and intermarriage rendered impossible such a simplified approach. In this report the Commission presented a "racial" analysis of the Kirkuk *liwa'* that divided its population into "Kurds," "Turks," "Arabs," and "Christians," notably excluding any people who fell outside their definitions of those categories, including the Jewish community, from serious consideration. They reported that while virtually all Christians favored inclusion in Iraq and a majority of Turks favored inclusion in Turkey, the opinions of Arabs and Kurds were divided. The Commission did recognize that patronage played a role in the opinions of certain respondents. For instance, they noted that the Kurdish tribal leaders of Kirkuk who favored inclusion in Iraq were often those who were being paid to police the roads in the Kirkuk area under the *sowar* system. However, they termed this factor "opportunism," thereby implying that any expression of loyalty that was not based on race was somehow not legitimate.[82]

In light of the ambiguities of local opinion, the Mosul Commission's conclusions ended up hinging to a great degree on their opinion of the Mosul *vilayet* region's economic needs. Because the region's economy was mainly based on agriculture and trade, the question the Commission considered was whether its inhabitants mainly conducted trade with Turkish cities or with Baghdad. In particular, the ongoing construction of a railway from Baghdad to Mosul played a pivotal role in Colonel Paulis's reasoning with regard to Kirkuk's economy. The railway was a British-led project dating back to the early occupation of Iraq. Its extension into the north was ahead of schedule, most likely for the very purpose of impressing the Commission about the importance of the region's trade and communications with Baghdad. In Paulis's view the railway was a crucial component of the Mosul *vilayet* region's future trade prospects. He was so thoroughly fascinated with the railway that once it became a dominant factor in his thinking, he even imprudently told people he was interviewing in Kirkuk that he already thought the Mosul *vilayet* region should be attached to Iraq. The railway had nearly reached Kirkuk at that point and would, he surmised, transform the town's commerce, allowing Kirkuk's farmers and merchants to take greater advantage of the Baghdad market by exporting their goods more efficiently.[83]

As the Commission noted in its report, though, most of Kirkuk's trade already took place with Baghdad rather than with any cities to the north. This was partly a matter of the inexpensiveness of exports using river rafts on the Tigris, which ran south, but it was also a result of postwar circumstances. Tensions on the Mosul *vilayet* frontier made it difficult or impossible for anyone in the region to take advantage of markets in Anatolia.[84] It does not appear that merchants in Kirkuk or the Mosul *vilayet* region in general shared Paulis's unbridled enthusiasm for the project, because the impact the railway would have on the prices of goods, for example, was uncertain.[85] Such was Paulis's eagerness that when one openly pro-Turkish Kirkuki notable voiced his disapproval of the railway project, Paulis "put him down as a rogue and a fool."[86] Although the Mosul Commission professed to gauge popular opinion, its conclusions ultimately rested on a deterministic set of assumptions about the region's nature and needs.

Another factor in the Mosul Commission's final decision was the region's potential for large-scale oil production and the implications of this possibility with regard to the Iraqi government's ongoing negotiations with the Turkish Petroleum Company (TPC). The TPC's proposed activities and the legal framework under which they would take place were of particular significance to Kirkuk, which would naturally be one of the early sites of exploration. Although the

Commission did not express an official opinion on the concession negotiations between the TPC and the Iraqi government, two of the commissioners, Paulis and Teleki, made it clear to Sir Henry Dobbs in separate private conversations that their decision would be affected by whether or not Iraq granted the TPC a concession to explore for oil in the Mosul *vilayet* region. The role of oil in the Commission's thinking is not readily obvious because the diplomatic correspondence and memoranda surrounding the Mosul question, including the Mosul Commission's report, only seldom mention the region's oil wealth.[87]

As far as native inhabitants and lower-level British officials operating on the ground were concerned, oil was not a major consideration in the Mosul *vilayet* region at this stage because their immediate concerns were with local commerce. The existing oil industry in villages near Kirkuk, in which output was measured in tins rather than barrels and transported by donkey rather than pipeline, was a minor component of the region's economy as a whole. Maintaining control over the former Mosul *vilayet*'s oil was important from the perspective of London, as previously discussed, but higher-level British officials recoiled at the fact that the legitimacy of their claim to the *vilayet* was questioned in the press as a result of their perceived greed.[88] These officials therefore took pains to distance themselves from the oil issue during the Mosul dispute. Their hesitant attitude was an early sign of what would prove to be a symbiotic but often uncomfortable relationship between the British government and the Iraqi oil industry. Nevertheless, there is little doubt that the strategic importance of controlling oil-bearing areas in the Middle East was one of the most important underlying factors in the British endeavor to ensure that the former Mosul *vilayet* became part of the state of Iraq.[89]

Furthermore, strategic and commercial considerations were intertwined, as demonstrated in the British government's determination to ensure that the TPC's rights to a concession from the prewar era would be honored. Negotiations between the TPC and the Iraqi government for a concession began once the state had been established in 1921 and therefore took place under the shadow of the Mosul question; the possibility, however remote, that the Mosul *vilayet* region might yet end up under the control of the Turkish government remained. All parties involved also wanted to establish a concession before an Iraqi parliament was formed, as the involvement of a legislative body would complicate the process. Despite the air of urgency surrounding the negotiations, talks were drawn out until 1925 because of several points of contention between the Iraqi government and the Western oil companies, especially the commitment the Iraqis had obtained at the San Remo Conference to a 20% ownership share in the

TPC.[90] The talks were therefore approaching their conclusion when the Mosul Commission began its work.

During the Commission's time in Iraq, both Paulis and Teleki, on different occasions, indicated to Dobbs that they thought the Iraqi government should grant the TPC concession. Baghdad's signature on the contract would bind the company to Iraq, thereby all but guaranteeing that Paulis and Teleki were prepared to make a decision in favor of Iraq's claim to Mosul.[91] Dobbs, of course, agreed; in his view, a signed Iraqi oil convention would secure greater international support for Iraq's position in the Mosul dispute as a result of American and French firms' shares in the TPC.[92] Soon afterward the TPC declined to allow the Iraqi government its previously promised 20% share in the company, and the Iraqi negotiators acquiesced before a more favorable compromise could be reached. The TPC concession was signed on 14 March 1925, several days before the work of the Mosul Commission came to an end. Digging began near Kirkuk soon afterward.[93]

The Commission left Iraq in March 1925 and issued its final report on the dispute that August, recommending that the former Mosul *vilayet* be awarded, with certain conditions, to British Iraq. The British government briefly feared that Turkey would attempt to challenge this decision by force, and some months of diplomatic tension ensued. Eventually, the Foreign Office was able to elicit Turkish cooperation in the settlement by promising that the Iraqi government would pay the Turkish government 10% of their royalties received from oil production for twenty-five years. This stipulation was written into the Anglo-Iraqi-Turkish Treaty of 1926 that settled the Mosul question.[94]

For Kirkuk the legacy of the dispute over the region was twofold. First, the process by which the dispute was resolved solidly established the limited paradigm, still prevalent today, in which members of Kirkuk's population are considered to fall into one of four separate categories—Kurdish, Turkmen, Arab, or Christian—each of which is each thought to have distinct political interests. To be clear, that paradigm did *not* immediately take hold as the underlying framework and set of practices shaping Kirkuk's politics. Although racial, ethnic, and sectarian divisions in many parts of the world can often be traced to a colonial encounter, it is usually *not* the case that colonialists directly create identity-based disputes among the colonized. The fact that this paradigm was initially mostly irrelevant in Kirkuk makes its durability over time all the more remarkable.

Second, the way that the TPC and British authorities forced the Iraqi government's hand in negotiations was a harbinger of the future political roles that the oil company, British diplomats, and Iraqi oil workers would play in Kirkuk. The coercion inherent in the TPC concession created a precedent whereby the oil company, in close collaboration with British governmental authorities, wielded political influence in service of its commercial interests and often at the Iraqis' expense. The company would continue to act according to this pattern once it became an important political and economic force in Kirkuk.

SHIFTING LOYALTIES AND EMERGING FAULT LINES AT THE END OF THE MANDATE

While the integration of Kirkuk and the rest of the Mosul *vilayet* region into Baghdad's domain had been an ongoing process since the creation of the monarchy in 1921, the political developments that took place after the settlement of the Mosul question underscored the fact that this was the overarching goal of Anglo-Iraqi policy in predominantly non-Arab areas. As the Baghdad-based Iraqi government progressively became more involved in affairs at the provincial and municipal levels in Kirkuk, changes in patronage led to shifting loyalties among its communities. The fact that the Iraqi government was Arab-led strengthened the linguistic-communal dimension of these affiliations and antagonisms in a way that did not occur when Kirkukis who supported the Baghdad-based government were more heavily reliant on the patronage of the British, a wholly external and (at least ostensibly) temporary power. In addition, the gradual hardening of defined ethnic and ethnoreligious categories in Kirkuk, which had begun during the Mosul dispute partly as a result of the impression among various officials that each group had particular concerns and loyalties, had the effect of generating more interests that were specific to self-identified communities. Efforts to bring the British Mandate to an end and pursue Iraq's admittance to the League of Nations, which began as early as 1927, compounded the effects of these trends by creating an atmosphere of instability.

Turkish-speaking elites were one of the groups that came to have a more coherent set of political views. This may have been in part because in the Mandate era self-identified Turkish speakers or Turkmens constituted a majority of Kirkuk's provincial officials appointed by Baghdad; thus, once the Republic of Turkey lost most of its influence in Kirkuk and its surrounding region, these elites would have found centralized authority to be the next logical patron. This shift is exemplified by Mustafa Ya'qubizada, who had previously engaged in clandestine anti-centralization activity and, unlike his brother, supported the Turkish claim in the Mosul dispute. Mustafa was acting in full support of the Iraqi government by 1931, even distributing pro-government propaganda to tribal chiefs in

Kirkuk.[95] The nature of loyalty to centralized authority was also gradually changing as British officials withdrew from direct control of Iraqi institutions. In the
process of fostering support for Baghdad's Arab-led government, Mustafa would
continue to criticize the perceived nefariousness of British authorities, much as
he had done when he was agitating against Baghdad. For instance, one British
intelligence report alleged that Mustafa was trying to discredit the newly formed
opposition Ikha' Party by spreading rumors that it was an element promoted by
the British to destabilize the Iraqi government.[96]

Because Turkmen figures such as the Ya'qubizadas had typically been influential notables and administrators under the Ottomans, their dominance in the
early Kirkuki government was not unexpected. Nonetheless, the comparative
lack of Kurdish representation in a *liwa'* that had a Kurdish plurality caused
consternation among Kirkuki Kurds and some concern among British officials.[97]
The impending end of Mandate administration also caused considerable unease
among Iraq's Kurds. By 1929 the British government had definitively indicated
that it would support Iraq's admission to the League of Nations on the condition that Britain would retain a strong position of informal influence in the
country. To this end, British officials negotiated a new treaty with the Iraqi
government, ratified in 1930, which rendered Iraq officially independent of
British control while maintaining the presence of British military personnel and
advisers.[98] The Kurds feared that inattention to their interests, especially their
concern with the continuous Arabization of local governments and schools
in predominantly Kurdish areas, would be a permanent policy under a fully
sovereign Arab government.[99] For its part, the Iraqi government denied that
this was the case while simultaneously resisting Kurdish efforts to ensure that
the majority of appointees to local government posts in predominantly Kurdish
*liwa'*s would be Kurds.[100]

After British authorities applied pressure on the Iraqi government to solve the
problem, the Iraqi parliament passed the Language Law of 1931, which ensured
that the official language of administration, courts, and schools in Kurdish-
dominated parts of these governorates would be Kurdish.[101] Many Kurds were
dissatisfied with this compromise, which only ensured that local officials would
know the Kurdish language, an unexceptional requirement in a multilingual
region.[102] The Language Law was particularly controversial in Kirkuk, where
multilingualism was so prevalent that knowledge of languages did not necessarily correspond to communal identities in a predictable way. Indeed, of the 232
officials in the Kirkuk governorate in 1931, only 42 were self-identified Kurds.

About 40 to 50 of the non-Kurds did not know Kurdish and would therefore have to be replaced; none of the officials in the latter category, however, were self-identified Turkmens. Virtually all the self-identified Turkmen officials had enough knowledge of Kurdish to satisfy the legal requirement.[103] Therefore even the implementation of the Language Law would do little to rectify the problem, from the Kurdish viewpoint, of Kurdish underrepresentation in local government. Moreover, the law had no effect on the continued entrenchment of the power of Turkmen elites in Kirkuk. These circumstances would engender tensions between Kirkuk's Kurdish and Turkmen communities.

The lack of Kurdish representation among officials implied that the steady Arabization of primary and secondary education in Kirkuk and throughout predominantly non-Arab areas of Iraq in general, which began in earnest toward the end of the Mandate, would continue unabated. Amir Hassanpour has argued that Mandate- and monarchy-era educational policies in Iraq endangered Kurdish language usage and may have even hindered Kurdish students' ability to obtain a postsecondary education.[104] It was also especially important for self-identified Kurds in rural areas to have some recourse to influence in the local government because of Iraq's Mandate-era political and economic system in which landowning elites who were in the service of the central government wielded considerable autonomous power over taxation.[105] The latter problem is illustrated in a forceful petition that the chiefs of the Dawudi tribe, who lived in an area south of urban Kirkuk, submitted to the League of Nations when the League was considering the question of Iraq's membership and its subsequent independence. The Dawudi chiefs complained that they were "subject to a pitiless and ruthless treatment" by Arab and Turkmen officials of the Kirkuk governorate, who treated them as "aliens" and imposed exorbitant taxes. They also explicitly demanded inclusion in a Kurdish state.[106]

It is therefore clear that even though Kurdish grievance was less "pronounced" among Kirkuk's thoroughly multilingual population compared to other largely Kurdish areas, it was nonetheless present, according to one official.[107] Kurds throughout the region sent numerous petitions to the Iraqi prime minister and to the League of Nations advocating the creation of an independent Kurdish province or state. The Dawudi petition was the only major petition to originate in Kirkuk, although various Kirkuki Kurds put their names to other petitions.[108] Furthermore, British intelligence reports from Kirkuk indicated that some Kurdish tribes were sympathetic to Shaykh Mahmud, to whom most of the Kurds of Kirkuk had previously been hostile.[109]

That said, despite these signs of consolidation of ethnolinguistic groups' political positions, complexities resulting from the influence of powerful forces external to Kirkuk continued to abound. The Talabani notables, for example, continued to exhibit loyalty to centralized authority amid a Kurdish revolt in 1931 and were rewarded with a gift of arms from Kirkuk's *mutasarrif* as a result.[110] On the other hand, anti-centralization sentiment continued to manifest itself to the extent that some Kirkuki Turkmens, including members of the Naftchizada family, were inclined to sympathize with those who advocated the creation of an independent Kurdish region or state.[111] One British intelligence report from 1929 went so far as to allege that the long-influential Turkmen notable 'Izzat Pasha was cooperating with local Kurdish tribal leaders to spread propaganda in support of Shaykh Mahmud as a step toward the reinstatement of Turkish rule.[112] Some aspects of this claim are undoubtedly exaggerated, but an underlying assumption of common political interests between some Turkmens and Kurds is apparent.

As Arab-led Iraq approached independence, a combination of increased centralization and language-based policies that failed to effectively expand Kurdish representation in local government strengthened the divide between Arabs and Kurds in Kirkuk. With so many Turkmen civil servants now unequivocally answering to the Baghdad government, these policies also led to the emergence of a distinct fault line between Turkmens and Kurds. Nevertheless, Kirkukis' political interests were still not necessarily tied to their communal identities in such a way as to pit linguistic communities against each other inexorably. The examples given here demonstrate that as of the end of British Mandate rule of Iraq in 1932, Kirkuk's communities continued to often share political concerns and did not, at this time, develop specific goals that were antithetical to one another.

CONCLUSION

The era of the British Mandate in Kirkuk was a period during which both relations with authorities and the nature of external influence evolved and changed. By the end of the Mandate, British governmental interests, which were also bound up in private commercial interests, had diverged from those of the Iraqi central government, such that those in the patronage of the Iraqi central government often remained opposed to the British government. Negotiations between Anglo-Iraqi authorities and the Republic of Turkey over the status of the Mosul *vilayet* region emphasized "racial" elements that were imagined by Western arbitrators to be mostly immutable, but the affiliations of the people of Kirkuk over the course of the British Mandate can best be understood in terms of their relations with external patrons whose positions of influence were themselves in a state of flux. Previously obscure fault lines were occasionally revealed in this process, as in the intercommunal violence of May 1924. Another shift took place when the elites of the Turkmen community, many of whom had previously opposed Anglo-Iraqi administration, became the bedrock of establishment power in Kirkuk once its surrounding region was definitively integrated into Iraq. However, by the time Iraq was admitted to the League of Nations in 1932, Kirkuk's communities were not on a clear path toward ethnic antagonism as a political practice. The complex interplay between group identities and local, provincial, and national politics would continue to develop as the growth of Kirkuk's oil industry beginning in the 1930s created new local political dynamics and accelerated the city's integration into Baghdad's domain.

3 OIL AND URBAN GROWTH

THE DISCOVERY OF OIL on a commercial scale near Kirkuk in 1927 transformed the city's geography, economy, and social life. Once the British Mandate
ended in 1932, the industry developed in the context of semi-official British
imperial influence in Iraq under the terms of the Anglo-Iraqi Treaty of 1930.
The presence of the oil company in Kirkuk shaped local politics and would
eventually have profound implications for urban development. In particular,
the presence of a large number of foreign, especially British, workers and executives in an isolated, luxurious company camp created social tensions. This dis-
regard for local concerns, combined with the employment of much of Kirkuk's
population in a physically dangerous heavy industry monopolized by a single
foreign company, helped lead to the emergence of popular opposition in the
form of organized labor.

Meanwhile, Kirkuk's demographics changed dramatically as the city's population multiplied in the post-Mandate era. The oil company was attractive to
laborers and former cultivators from rural areas who were seeking a way to make
a living amid an exploitative agricultural system and economic depression. In
Kirkuk's hinterland these rural poor who became urban migrants were disproportionately Kurdish. Kirkuk's deepening relationship with Baghdad intensified
the steady crystallization of Kirkuki Kurdish, Turkmen, and Arab communal
groupings in local politics as the numbers of these communities, especially the
Kurdish community, grew. But up to the 1940s ethnicity had not yet become
a primary method of political mobilization. As of 1946 the single, most visible

popular political movement in Kirkuk was the diverse, nonsectarian Iraqi Communist Party, whose appeal in Kirkuk was a direct result of the presence of the oil industry. The Communists orchestrated a strike within the Iraq Petroleum Company (IPC) that year, and it would have repercussions for years to come.

THE STORIES, TOLD AND UNTOLD, OF WELL NO. 1

In his 1959 history of British Petroleum,[1] Henry Longhurst refers to 14 October 1927 as Iraq's "Day of Destiny." Longhurst offers a gripping account of the first gusher at Baba Gurgur, just northwest of urban Kirkuk, marking the discovery of its supergiant oil field. Of the moment at which the American and Iraqi drilling crew working for the Turkish Petroleum Company (TPC) struck oil during a midnight shift very early on 15 October, Longhurst writes:

> At the psychological moment, unaware of what was going on 1500 feet below, the driller decided to pull out the bit. . . . He had raised the tools to within 20 feet of the derrick floor when a piercing hiss drowned the noise of the engine. Gas and oil, released from the tremendous pressure in the limestone, were rushing up the hole. . . . A fountain of oil gushed up through the floor and high over the top of the derrick into the darkness. It was heard rather than seen, for nobody dared light a lamp.[2]

According to a retrospective in an Arabic-language magazine, rumors then spread among the local population that the explosion was a sign of God's anger at them for straying from the rightful path.[3] For the next nine days the oil surged out of the ground at an extraordinary rate, estimated to be 95,000 barrels per day. The accompanying clouds of gas created the frightening possibility of a conflagration in villages near Baba Gurgur and even in Kirkuk itself. If the oil had flowed into the Tigris, it would have caused an environmental catastrophe far beyond Kirkuk. A team of workers, including reinforcements rapidly brought in from elsewhere in Iraq, did not manage to bring the gusher under control until 23 October.[4] In his account Longhurst quotes a TPC official discussing the danger of this task, extolling the valor and perseverance of the workers.

> With gas masks on, and oil dripping from their hats, the drillers worked feverishly in the cellar. . . . All day long men were collapsing and being hauled up unconscious to be revived outside in the comparatively fresh air. Some of the men were gassed two or three times a day, and yet staggered back to their jobs. It was inspiring to watch them, and the courage they displayed.[5]

What Longhurst fails to mention in his triumphant telling of the story is that not all the people who were overcome by the gas ultimately recovered to come back to work. Two American workers suffocated despite the best efforts of three Iraqis to rescue them. All three of these Iraqi workers died as well.[6]

In *Cities of Salt*, the acclaimed novel about Arab oil workers and foreign executives modeled after similar events in Dhahran, Saudi Arabia, Abdelrahman Munif poignantly describes the accidental death of an oil worker who was assigned to a dangerous job and the anguish that this incident caused his friends and co-workers, who already resented their expatriate employers.[7] This fictional episode is a rare example of an account of the hazards of large-scale oil extraction in the modern Middle Eastern petroleum industry from the (in this case, imagined) perspective of native workers. Munif's novel, which highlights the fear, confusion, and outrage of the local population toward the people and apparatuses of the nascent oil industry, stands in stark contrast to the exultant tone of British and other Western accounts of Middle Eastern oil production.

The Western versions of the story focus on the economic prosperity that oil had the potential to bring about, stressing the idea that oil companies pulled backward areas into modernity. For instance, a BBC broadcast covering the opening of Kirkuk's pipeline to the Mediterranean Sea in 1935 stated that the oil industry brought "one of the outstanding achievements of modern engineering skill" to "a remote and sterile corner of Iraq."[8] Longhurst typifies British writers of his era who mention reactions from members of the local population only inasmuch as they reflect these themes. He quotes one Iraqi as having said that the discovery of oil at Kirkuk made his compatriots "happy and grateful, knowing how it would open up a new way of life for our people."[9] During the course of my own conversations with Iraqi former employees of the oil company, one former staff member mentioned that he occasionally joins an annual meeting at BP's global headquarters in St. James's Square, London, that takes place every October to celebrate Well No. 1.[10] The more tumultuous, even painful, versions of the story that are likely to have been written or told by the local population in or soon after 1927 remain obscure.

The gulf between the Western perception of Kirkuk's oil and the difficulties faced by local oil workers is representative of the broader divide between Kirkukis and expatriates that constituted the greatest local political problem of the first few decades of the Iraqi oil industry.

DIVERGENCES BETWEEN THE OIL INDUSTRY AND KIRKUK

The discovery of a large amount of oil in Kirkuk necessitated the immediate settlement of a number of outstanding problems within the TPC to enable the progress of large-scale petroleum extraction, production, and export. In July 1928, several months after the strike at Baba Gurgur, the TPC's constituent companies and Calouste Gulbenkian finally signed an agreement that established the percentage of shares held by each entity. The D'Arcy Exploration Company (in which the Anglo-Persian Oil Company [APOC] held controlling shares), the Compagnie Française des Pétroles, Royal Dutch Shell, and a newly formed American consortium called the Near East Development Corporation each held 23.75% of the company's shares, and Gulbenkian negotiated a 5% cut for his role in structuring the company.[11] British shareholders, including the British government, held shares in the APOC and in Royal Dutch Shell; the British government therefore had a direct and significant interest in the TPC as well. The TPC was incorporated in the United Kingdom and had an office in London in addition to its headquarters in Iraq.[12] Consequently, although the company was formally a private entity that, in the end, was predominantly owned by non-British shareholders, the TPC's close relationship with the British government meant that the company pursued both corporate and British imperial interests.

In its early years the TPC's problems included disputes over its claim to exploitation rights in Iraq's oil-bearing areas.[13] The 1925 concession granted the TPC the "exclusive right," contingent on certain conditions, to "explore, prospect, drill for, extract and render suitable for trade petroleum, naphtha, natural gases, ozokerite, and the right to carry away and sell the same and the derivatives thereof" in the concession area.[14] The TPC's concession, signed in Baghdad, had no legitimacy in the view of the Naftchizada family of Kirkuk. The Naftchizadas had been exploiting the Kirkuk region's oil for centuries and had held formal rights to oil seepages in the Kirkuk area by Istanbul's decree since the seventeenth century. Even though these rights were superseded by the TPC's concession in the eyes of the Iraqi government after 1925, the Naftchizadas were still extracting and selling Kirkuk's petroleum exclusively when the TPC began prospecting for oil in the same area.[15]

Around the time that the TPC began exploring, the Iraqi government began to challenge the Naftchizadas' rights to oil-bearing lands. In March 1926 a land registry official acting on behalf of the Kirkuk *liwa'* took legal action against a member of the Naftchizada family and fourteen of his associates for "usurping" a particular naphtha mine, demanding that they surrender it to the provincial government.[16] Another controversy arose over the TPC's well digging at Baba Gurgur. In July 1927, a few months before the first oil gusher, the TPC's general manager in Iraq wrote a letter to Salih Beg Naftchizada to assure him that the company's work would "not in the least interfere" with his family's wells, because the wells the company created were "some thousands of feet deeper" than those dug by the Naftchizadas.[17] In reply, another member of the Naftchizada family recognized what the TPC's letter carefully skirted: the fact that, regardless of the depths of the wells they produced, the TPC's activities threatened to foreclose local residents' ongoing endeavor to commercially produce Kirkuk's oil and to supplant their right to do so on a more advanced level in the future. Emphasizing that Baba Gurgur was private land and that his family had documentation to prove their rights to the area, the replying family member stated, "Hundreds of natives of Iraq and foreigners who own these estates together might one day as a natural right wish to exploit the petroleum from the lower layers as they are currently exploiting the upper ones."[18]

In December 1928, more than a year after the successful digging of Well No. 1, the absentee family patriarch Nazim Beg Naftchizada directed a much more forceful letter to the TPC director from his residence in Istanbul, protesting the TPC's exploitation and use of oil at Baba Gurgur. He cited what he considered universally recognized concepts of property rights and repeated the claim that the Naftchizada family had ample documentation verifying their entitlement. At one point he underscored the longevity of the family's connection to the land, claiming that they had owned the oil-bearing areas since long before the Ottoman era and conveying the perceived enormity of the TPC's transgression: "I wonder how and on the basis of what right your company violates and encroaches upon my legitimate rights, rights that even the most despotic tyrants and invaders of the Middle Ages spared."

Nazim Beg's letter also claimed that the Iraqi government could not be trusted to be "impartial and neutral" in any matter concerning his family because he had favored the former Mosul *vilayet*'s inclusion in Turkey and had been part of the Turkish delegation during the visit from the League of Nations Mosul Commission. Boldly, he cited the Mosul Commission's own statement in its report that those in the Mosul *vilayet* region who were politically "compromised" deserved safeguarding, including the right to leave the country. He reasoned on that basis that the Iraqi government's actions on matters related to the oil-bearing areas that his family owned, including its convention with the

TPC, therefore had "no legal value." Nazim Beg concluded with a demand that the TPC cease its activities, close its wells, and provide him with compensation for the oil already extracted.[19]

Although the Naftchizadas' efforts to regain their rights to Kirkuk's oil from the TPC were never likely to succeed, the dispute is significant for several reasons. First, it illustrates that at least one prominent group of Kirkukis had a well-established concept of their ownership of oil as a resource with the potential for further development. This idea was furthermore grounded in a concept of their legal rights to certain lands. The British narrative of the beginning of large-scale petroleum production misrepresents this connection between Kirkukis, local oil, and local land. It stresses the fear that the townspeople and nearby villagers felt when witnessing the first gusher, thereby implying that the substance was alien to them on a visceral level, and then focuses on their presumed gratitude for Western intervention to develop it. Second, Nazim Beg's categorization of his elite Turkmen family as politically "compromised" in the context of the Baba Gurgur dispute implied that the Iraqi government threatened their rights in a manner that went beyond simply denying their entitlement to oil revenues. This contention corresponds with the idea that remains common among Turkmens that the Anglo-Iraqi Mandate government was actively punishing their community for their perceived insubordination to King Faysal. Third, the dispute demonstrates that Kirkuk's oil industry was born into controversy. These early divergences between Kirkukis, the oil company, the provincial government, and Baghdad would proceed for decades and would indelibly affect Kirkuk's local politics.

The early behavior of the company in relation to the economy of the global oil market would also prove to have a local impact, because curtailed production threatened the urban labor force. In general, the TPC's constituent companies, all of which had interests in many other parts of the world, wished to exploit and export oil as slowly as possible while still meeting global demand to prevent a decline in international oil prices.[20] In 1930 the company, newly renamed the Iraq Petroleum Company (IPC), started to consider laying off a large fraction of its drillers within the constraints of its existing convention, which regulated the company's activity by mandating a minimum amount of drilling per year. One memorandum proposed restricting drilling hours to the daytime and introducing a more complicated (and therefore slower and less productive) drilling procedure in certain areas, with the goal of reducing expenditures and heading off the Iraqi government's attempt at an "open-door formula."[21]

Then, in 1931, the company negotiated a revision of the convention. Crucially, they pushed for the deletion of the original version's Article 5, which contained the exploration requirement. Article 5 also threatened the company's monopoly over Iraqi oil by opening up the lease of certain plots of land to competition. In the negotiations over the revision, the drilling obligation had proven to be a particularly contentious point between the company and the Iraqi government. After suggesting changes to Article 5, the company managed to have it removed entirely from the final version signed in March 1931. The head of the Ministry of Economics and Communications, Muzahim al-Pachachi, resigned in protest of the fact that the revised convention was less advantageous to Iraq.[22] All these efforts were characteristic of the IPC's inclination throughout the 1930s to delay the pace of oil production in Iraq, a tendency that its cartel status undergirded.[23]

As of January 1931 the IPC employed more than 2,300 workers throughout Iraq. Nearly 2,000 of them were native Iraqis,[24] and most of them were working at Baba Gurgur. Because the total population of urban Kirkuk could not have grown too far beyond its estimated magnitude of 25,000 in the mid-1920s at that point, IPC employees must have already constituted a large fraction of Kirkuk's labor force among men of working age. Recognizing Kirkuk as "the best labour centre outside of Baghdad and Mosul" and considering its proximity to the oil field, the IPC moved their headquarters there from their previous location in Tuz Khurmatu in March 1931.[25] However, they had already begun dismissing hundreds of workers as early as February of that year.[26] After the revision of their convention later that month, the IPC, no longer encumbered with exploration requirements, continued its layoffs while proposing a temporary stop to most of its drilling operations. In August 1931 a Royal Air Force officer stationed in Kirkuk reported that crime was increasing there as a result of growing unemployment.[27] By October 1931, when the virtual suspension of drilling went into effect, the company had let go more than 1,400 of its Iraqi workers in Kirkuk. At that point, it employed only 514 Iraqis throughout the country.[28]

Both IPC and British government officials correctly anticipated that the Kirkuk layoffs would result in a backlash from the Iraqi government, press, and population at large. Even internal communications among these British officials, who were broadly in agreement with one another in their support for the company's actions, assumed a defensive tone. They cited the deletion of Article 5 to justify the dismissals and argued that there was no need to explore further until after the construction of a pipeline to the Mediterranean Sea, which would allow Kirkuk's oil to be exported to the world market, was completed.[29]

Indeed, as one British official noted, the company also had no urgent need to keep exploring because they were "free from competition."[30] The reduction of the IPC's workforce provoked a negative reaction among Iraqis throughout 1931; a letter from an IPC official at the company's headquarters in Kirkuk late in that year recalled that the Iraqi government's director of oil affairs had "on more than one occasion mentioned the anxiety felt in local circles at the continued fall in employment."[31] In contrast, IPC officials felt earnestly and fervently that suspending drilling operations was the best option moving forward from a business standpoint. As Sir John Cadman, the IPC chairman in London, wrote to company official G. W. Dunkley:

> In view of possible criticism arising from the necessary slowing up of operations, particularly drilling in Iraq itself, I am anxious that if and as suitable occasions present themselves, you should do all you can to enlighten those around you, and in Baghdad, as to the reasons for such a course. . . . Nothing could, of course, be more reasonable, or more consistent with the principles of sound commercial development.[32]

The IPC therefore thought that their task was to convince Iraqis, or what one official called "the Iraqi mind," that this was, in fact, the most rational path.[33] The British government agreed, suggesting that "a certain amount of advance propaganda" could address the problem of Iraqi opposition.[34] Accordingly, an article titled "The Pipe-Line" appeared in the *Times of Mesopotamia*, an Anglo-Iraqi English-language newspaper, on 28 September 1931 that assured readers that the IPC was committed to continuing its work in Iraq. The article illogically attributed the reduction in Kirkuk's workforce to "the attention being lent by the company to the extension of the oil pipe-line to the Mediterranean." In other words, the public British stance on the layoffs was that they were the result of a diversion in the company's focus; unlike internal discussion of the issue, the article did not try to make a case for the supposed commercial wisdom of this approach, instead choosing to center on a refutation of the claim that the company was suspending its activities throughout Iraq.[35]

The IPC's operations in Kirkuk therefore continued to be contentious in their early years. From the beginning of the company's activities, the IPC, British government officials, Iraqi officials, and Kirkukis had competing visions of the company's obligation to the local population. In general, Iraqis believed that the IPC had a duty to employ Kirkuk's labor force as long as it was both contractually and publicly committed to large-scale oil production.

The Iraqi government would continue to adopt a similar attitude about the IPC's responsibilities to Kirkuk even after expropriating nearly all its concession after the end of the monarchy. British officials and the IPC's expatriate executives were not in accord with the Iraqis with regard to labor affairs or legal obligations, instead thinking exclusively about how to maintain high oil prices and preserve the IPC's monopoly, even if doing so required modifying the legal framework under which they were operating. Once again, a divergence both in concepts and aims marked the relationship between corporate and British imperial concerns on the one hand and the interests of local officials and notables on the other. In addition, the 1931 layoffs were an early sign of the extensive political and economic influence that the IPC would soon wield in Kirkuk. This influential position served as a site for the emergence of discrete local political interests in Kirkuk among Kirkukis, Iraqis, and expatriates alike.

As always, the official British presence in Kirkuk was intertwined with and occasionally indistinguishable from the presence of the IPC. After Iraq's admission to the League of Nations in 1932, the terms of the Anglo-Iraqi Treaty of 1930, which preserved British interests in Iraq, came into effect. Britain's activities in Iraq shifted from the purview of the Colonial Office to that of the Foreign Office. The British government maintained considerable sway over Iraqi politics and policy through the strategic placement of powerful diplomats and through the maintenance of Royal Air Force bases in the country. These practices were typical examples of the system of "informal empire" throughout former British colonies.[36] Soon after dismantling the apparatus of the Mandate in 1932, the Foreign Office opened a vice consulate in Kirkuk, professing in internal communications that it did so in the interest of keeping track of Kurdish separatist activity. This outpost subsequently closed for unknown reasons in 1936.[37] Officials associated with the British embassy in Baghdad, such as land-settlement officer Wallace Lyon and education consultant John Brady, continued to operate in Kirkuk intermittently and kept up a close relationship with the IPC.

In May 1941 British troops reoccupied Iraq, restoring to power pro-Western establishment politicians who had been temporarily marginalized by pro-German forces and bringing British government influence back to Kirkuk in its full capacity, including the eventual reestablishment of a vice consulate.[38] The strategic concerns that partly motivated the British invasion of 1941 were omnipresent in communications from Kirkuk, where protecting the oil fields from possible Axis encroachment was a primary concern, including extensive plans for the demolition of wells if an enemy takeover proved inevitable. Kirkuk's oil was essential for British military operations in Iraq; the IPC provided fuel for military vehicles directly from its own installations.[39]

PROVINCIAL TOWN TO OIL CITY: KIRKUK'S DEMOGRAPHICS IN THE MID-TWENTIETH CENTURY

The IPC's emergence also permanently changed Kirkuk's urban fabric and demographic composition. In general, Iraq's population grew rapidly in the early to mid-twentieth century, as was typical of developing countries in that time period. Urban areas experienced most of this growth, expanding at an unprecedented rate as impoverished rural inhabitants formerly engaged in agriculture moved into cities in search of work. This phenomenon was also common throughout the developing world, including in and around Middle Eastern metropolises such as Damascus and Cairo.[40] In Iraq, one of the factors that precipitated rural-to-urban movement was a vastly unequal land registration system that concentrated landownership among tribal shaykhs and notables and dramatically exploited sharecroppers. The 1933 Law Governing the Rights and Duties of Cultivators was particularly punitive to cultivators because it had the potential to hold them responsible for anything that could go wrong with the crops they worked on, trapping them in debt to landowners. The global depression that began in 1929 exacerbated the effects of this system by lowering the prices of agricultural products, thereby reducing the revenue yielded from land and forcing cultivators to move to urban areas to seek other means of making a living.[41]

In the period between 1918 and the 1950s, Kirkuk experienced the effects of Iraq's trend of rural-to-urban migration in an especially pronounced way. A 1958 report on Kirkuk by the urban planning firm Doxiadis Associates found that the population of the city of Kirkuk was increasing at an annual rate of 5.9%, whereas the average annual rate of increase in the populations of Iraqi *liwa'* capitals altogether (i.e., including Kirkuk) was 5.3% and Iraq's overall population growth rate was 3%.[42] A close examination of the data relevant to Kirkuk in the two full and reliable Iraqi population censuses of the mid-twentieth century, conducted in 1947 and in 1957, reveals population growth patterns consistent with the regional trend of rural-to-urban migration and with the accumulation of an urban industrial labor force.

To begin, it should be noted that it is difficult to compare these censuses with full statistical rigor. The two censuses did not consistently measure the

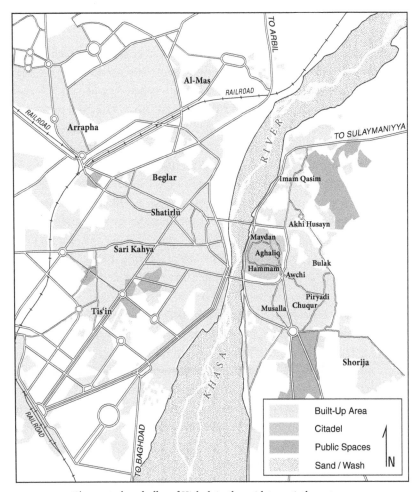

FIGURE 7. The central *mahallas* of Kirkuk in the mid-twentieth century.

same population categories. For example, the 1957 census contains an analysis of Kirkuk's population by native language, whereas the 1947 census does not. In addition, the definitions of the urban *mahalla*s (neighborhoods or quarters) of Kirkuk and of the province's *qada*'s (provincial subdivisions) apparently changed over the course of ten years (Figure 7). Some *mahalla*s and *qada*'s appear in one census but not the other. The versions of these censuses that I consulted were not accompanied by maps, which could have clarified these issues.[43] Nonetheless, a comparison of the populations of some urban *mahalla*s and provincial *qada*'s whose boundaries are unlikely to have changed illuminates the particular ways in which Kirkuk's urban demographics changed in the three decades following the discovery of oil.

As previously mentioned, various officials had estimated Kirkuk's urban population to be around 25,000 in the mid-1920s. Two decades later the 1947 census found that Kirkuk's urban population was just over 68,000.[44] A 1948 British government report estimated that Kirkuki IPC workers and their families numbered about 30,000 at that time, therefore implying that nearly half of the city's inhabitants were directly or indirectly reliant on the oil company for their livelihood.[45] The 1957 census found Kirkuk's urban population to be over 120,000.[46] While the urban population grew especially fast, increasing by 76% between 1947 and 1957, the population of the areas of Kirkuk's provincial subdivision outside the city—that is, the villages immediately surrounding urban Kirkuk, as well as the town of Altun Kopri—grew by about 39%, from 73,000 to 101,000, in the same time period.[47] By way of contrast, the population of the mostly rural *qada'* of Chamchamal, located between Kirkuk and Sulaymaniyya, increased by only 15% from 1947 to 1957.[48]

The inhabitants of these rural areas regularly moved to Kirkuk in search of work with the IPC whenever a harvest was poor, as indicated by the tone of a June 1947 report by the British vice-consul in Kirkuk, who suggested an ipso facto connection between such events: "The damage done by locusts has brought peasants from the outlying villages of Kirkuk flocking to the I.P.C. Employment offices."[49] Many migrants to the city were from outside Kirkuk altogether; in 1947, 28% of the urban population of Kirkuk had been born in places other than the Kirkuk *liwa'*. By 1957 the proportion of people in the city who were from outside the Kirkuk *liwa'* had decreased to 22%, but, of course, the absolute number of nonnatives had increased along with the rest of the population. In the *liwa'* as a whole, including all other towns and rural areas, the percentage of the population from outside Kirkuk in both 1947 and 1957 was 9%, confirming that most migrants from other parts of Iraq (and expatriates from other countries) settled in Kirkuk city. The largest numbers of non-Kirkuki migrants came from Baghdad and from mostly Kurdish-speaking *liwa'*s in relatively close proximity to Kirkuk, including Mosul, Sulaymaniyya, Arbil, and Diyala.[50]

The fact that migrants seeking work with the IPC largely drove urban Kirkuk's population growth is further indicated by the sex ratio of the population. There were more men than women throughout the city in this time period; indeed, men predominated among the migrants from outside Kirkuk. In 1925, not long after World War I and the disastrous effects of the Mesopotamian campaign, C. J.

Edmonds estimated that the number of women in Kirkuk was about 10% greater than the number of men.[51] Yet by 1947 the population of the city of Kirkuk was 54% male and 46% female.[52] In 1957 the proportions had evened out slightly to 52% male and 48% female; however, unlike in 1947, men outnumbered women in every single urban *mahalla*.[53] The sex distribution of the population of the Chamchamal *qada'* once again illustrates the dissimilarity between Kirkuk and nearby rural areas; Chamchamal had roughly equal numbers of men and women in 1957, with a difference of just 1.5% between them.[54] The presence of a predominantly male population that maintained a majority over the course of one decade is consistent with the fact that a large percentage of urban Kirkukis were employed in an extractive industry. Naturally, it followed that other industries and types of labor and commerce would expand to provide services to the growing population, which in turn may have fueled further immigration. The IPC itself started to encourage local enterprise in the 1950s by beginning to solicit local services, as will be discussed in Chapter 4.

Another indication of the expansion of industry and new forms of commerce is that the population of the citadel, the Turkish-speaking traditional heart of Kirkuk, was barely growing compared with the population of the rest of the city and was steadily declining as a share of the city's total population. Between 1947 and 1957 the populations of the three *mahallas* that made up the citadel—Maydan, Aghaliq, and Hammam Muslim—grew by only 2%, from 5,712 to 5,826, and their percentage of the city's population as a whole dwindled from just over 8% to just under 5%.[55] In stark contrast, the *mahalla* of Shorija (al-Shurja) experienced more rapid growth than any other part of the city between 1947 and 1957. Shorija, a newer neighborhood, was located southeast of the citadel and its surrounding *mahallas* that had constituted Kirkuk's Ottoman-era core on the east bank of the Khasa River (Figure 8). Although it was just within the municipal boundary and, on its western side, was quite close to the *mahallas* of Piryadi (which housed the city's Jewish quarter), Chuqur, and Musalla, it was still infrastructurally disconnected from the other inhabited areas of the city as late as the mid-1950s.[56]

Shorija's population more than tripled, from 2,365 to 7,711, between 1947 and 1957, amounting to an increase of 226%. No other *mahalla* in Kirkuk experienced a comparable rate of growth.[57] Its residents were mostly Kurdish migrants to urban Kirkuk from rural areas. A Kirkuki Kurd who now lives in London described 1940s-era Shorija as a Kurdish "shantytown" where, in his view, no non-Kurds would have wanted to live. He recalled that the populations of the much

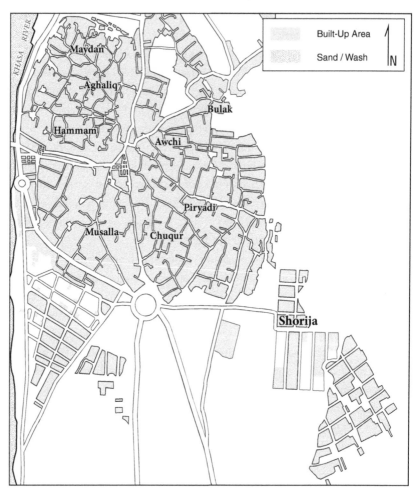

FIGURE 8. Kirkuk's southeast quadrant in accordance with the extent of the urban fabric in the mid-twentieth century. The citadel is visible in the upper left-hand corner of the map, and the *mahalla* of Shorija takes up most of the lower right. A stark contrast is evident between the gridlike streets and blocks of Shorija and the irregular configurations, by modern construction standards, of the centuries-old *mahalla*s around the citadel.

older neighboring *mahalla*s that surrounded the citadel were mostly Turkmen, an observation that makes intuitive sense in light of the fact that Turkish speakers had historically dominated urban Kirkuk.[58] The remarkable expansion of Shorija demonstrates that rural-to-urban migration, especially of Kurds, was one of the most striking patterns in Kirkuk's urban population growth. It also further confirms the observation that, as was often the case with urban immigrants in many other places, these newly arrived Kirkukis were disproportionately poor and tended to live in harsh conditions.

Migration into Kirkuk also brought an end to the demographic primacy of the Turkish-speaking community, a fact that is affirmed by a frequently cited table in the 1957 census that analyzes the province's population with reference to "mother tongue" (*lughat al-umm*). Although those identified as Turkish speakers still constituted a plurality of the urban population at over 45,000, the census identified more than 40,000 Kurdish speakers and 27,000 Arabic speakers in the city.[59]

My conversations with those who lived in or spent time working in Kirkuk in the mid-twentieth century have typically revealed memories that these communities were spatially divided within the city at that time, though the precise nature of these divisions differs from telling to telling. As mentioned, the city's historic core on the east side of the Khasa River was most likely predominantly populated by self-identified Turkmens, while the rapidly expanding nearby *mahalla* of Shorija was clearly Kurdish. Notwithstanding, one former IPC employee recalled that Kurds tended to live on the "left," or west, side of the river; he verified that Turkmens tended to live on the "right" side, as did Assyrians.[60] Another former IPC employee, speaking in English but using an Arabic term, described the city as being divided into "ethnic *mahallat*."[61] A former American consul to Kirkuk, Lee F. Dinsmore, who lived there in the 1950s, offered the opposing view that "Kirkuk's population lived in a mixed environment," clarifying that what he meant by this was that there were no "strictly located or agreed-upon subdivisions" at the time.[62] These perspectives indicate that there is a general sense among Kirkuk's current and former inhabitants that urban geography and ethnolinguistic communities were linked—as they were in many other world cities—at least as early as the mid-twentieth century, but it is clear that such divisions were neither rigid nor widely agreed on.

Unsurprisingly, the geographies of ethnicity in Kirkuk, both urban and rural, constitute one of the most controversial and enduring topics of discussion in analyses of its twentieth-century history. Present-day histories of Kirkuk, especially those written by Kurdish nationalist scholars, often charge that the Iraqi government began the process of Arabizing the Kirkuk region as early as the 1930s. These texts point to the inauguration of an irrigation project in the Hawija region southwest of urban Kirkuk as a seminal moment in the attempt to bolster Arab influence in the province. The Hawija project stemmed from the Iraqi government's official approach to rural agricultural policy in the period after the British Mandate ended in 1932. This approach was based on the premise that the transition from subsistence agriculture to settled agriculture was central to economic development. The government's policies also privileged the interests of shaykhs, concentrating the agricultural rights to arable lands among a relatively small number of tribal notables.[63]

It was in this context that the Iraqi government, starting in the mid-1930s, constructed an irrigation system in Hawija using water from the nearby Lesser Zab River. Beginning in 1940, the government granted nomadic Arab tribes the rights to agricultural utilization of plots of land in Hawija, thereby allowing them to settle there. Even though the land tenure system in Iraq was complex and contestable, the Hawija plots appear to have consistently fallen under the category of *miri sirf*, or state-owned land for which the government retained the entitlement to determine exploitation rights under all circumstances. In 1950 the Iraqi government launched a new *miri sirf* cultivation project in Hawija.[64]

It is difficult to confirm (and impossible to refute) the idea that the Iraqi government undertook the Hawija project to change Kirkuk's demographics. On one hand, it is undeniable that Iraqi irrigation projects, like irrigation projects in many other parts of the developing world, typically carried the goal of settling a certain group of people in a particular region. It is clear that officials involved in every branch of Iraq's politics would have been cognizant of the effects that this settling would have on the region in which it took place.[65] One American agricultural economist who spent time in Iraq wrote that in the case of *miri sirf* distributions in the southern region of Dujayla in the 1940s, some settlers had to go through a rigorous application process with the Iraqi government, which then chose whom to grant rights to on the basis of such factors as age and marital status.[66] Therefore the notion that the Iraqi central government engaged in demographic engineering by placing carefully chosen Arabs in the Kirkuk province for strategic reasons is plausible. This is especially true in light of the fact that this settlement would have put Arabs in close proximity to the oil pipeline from Baba Gurgur to the Mediterranean Sea, thereby ensuring, at least in theory, that the pipeline would not fall into Kurdish rebel hands.

On the other hand, the population of Hawija from the 1930s to the 1950s was only a small component of the population of the Kirkuk province and did not alter its demographic balance significantly. Even if, as Kurdish politician and author Nouri Talabany claims, there were over 27,000 tribal Arabs in Hawija in 1957,[67] this number means little compared to the enormous growth that was taking place in urban Kirkuk.[68] As mentioned, the 1947 and 1957 censuses indicate that the proportion of native-born inhabitants of the Kirkuk *liwa'* as a whole was 91% (and higher in rural areas alone), whereas in the city it ranged from 72% to 78%. The settlement of Arab tribes in Hawija was also not engineered well enough to be free of inherent security problems—there were violent disputes between different tribes over the rights to newly irrigated areas in the 1940s.[69]

Overall, even though the settlement of Arab tribes in Hawija certainly appears, with the benefit of hindsight, to have foreshadowed the gerrymandering of Kirkuk that began a few decades later, Kirkuk's oil-fueled urban growth in the same time period proved to be a much more momentous factor in demographic shifts and geographic change in the province. Nonetheless, the Hawija project is significant as a sign of Baghdad's continued attempts to consolidate its influence in the northern part of the country. In this case it did so by asserting its control over *miri sirf* lands and by establishing the potential for commercial agriculture in the region under the auspices of the central government.

THE SALIENCE, AND LIMITS, OF ETHNICITY IN POST-MANDATE KIRKUK

In the early period of Iraqi independence and British semicolonial influence following the end of the Mandate, Kirkuk's politics were characterized by the continuing permeation of Baghdad's presence through its many state-making efforts. Baghdad-centered political discourse also gained a foothold in Kirkuk while the ethnicization of group identities steadily intensified. Broadly, political disputes in Kirkuk pitted those who supported centralized Iraqi power against those who had separatist tendencies, as they had during the Mandate era. Since the 1930s the strongest separatist faction was the Kurdish nationalist movement, which continued to actively defy Baghdad and carried some influence in Kirkuk. Arab influence also grew in Kirkuk, whereas Turkmens expressed a communal consciousness, a sense of collective loss, and opposition to the Kurdish movement. As a result, stances for and against centralized power tended to fall along more sharply defined ethnic lines in the post-Mandate monarchy era than they had before. The ways in which different communities of Kirkukis were mobilized in accordance with ethnic group identities could be called ethnic nationalisms—at least, in a budding form. These political developments took place among burgeoning Iraqi narratives of independence and anti-imperialism that had different effects in Kirkuk than they did in Baghdad.[70] They also occurred in the context of emergent pan-Arab nationalism in monarchic Iraq, suggesting that the development of ethnic nationalisms was a statewide trend.

Educational institutions in Kirkuk were one of the most noteworthy fronts on which the Iraqi central government strove to increase its influence, particularly with regard to the language of instruction. From the beginning of the British occupation of Kirkuk and the rest of the former Mosul *vilayet*, British officials had condoned the Arabization of primary and secondary education, which was conducted in Turkish at that time, as a way of integrating the region into Iraq. For instance, in 1919 the British officer in charge of educational affairs in Iraq, Humphrey Bowman, wrote about the difficulty of finding "schoolmasters who can teach Arabic" in Kirkuk, a task that he thought was necessary because Arabic would be "the language of commerce and intercourse" going forward.[71] The Language Law of 1931, Baghdad's controversially limited compromise with the Kurds with regard to education and political representation, specifically stated that primary education in each *qada'* should be conducted in the language spoken by the majority of students therein, but it did not make any stipulations for secondary education.[72] Therefore, by the early 1930s, although Turkish remained the dominant language of primary instruction throughout the Kirkuk *liwa'* in accordance with the Language Law, education at the secondary level was usually in Arabic.[73] For girls' primary schools in Kirkuk, an Iraqi government memorandum explained that the presence of Arabic-speaking staff members was the result of a lack of qualified Turkmen and Kurdish female teachers.[74] This example, along with the circumvention built into the Language Law, demonstrates that Baghdad's approach to education policy in Kirkuk in early independent Iraq consisted of gradually allowing primarily Arabic-speaking teachers to assume positions of authority within the confines of a framework that acknowledged but did little to address the professed interests of non-Arabs. By the mid-1940s primary education in Kirkuk's public schools was conducted in Arabic as well.[75]

These shifts are reflected in the languages used in the Kirkuk municipality's weekly newspaper, *Kerkük/Karkuk*. (Its name can be transliterated into English either way, because the city's name is spelled the same in Turkish and Arabic when using Arabic lettering, and the newspaper printed in both of those languages as well as Kurdish.)[76] When it was established in 1926, and as late as 1931, the paper described itself as a Turkish- and Kurdish-language paper. Turkish dominated the front page, but occasional notices in Arabic also appeared.[77] By 1937 the editors described the paper as a weekly newspaper about "everything," and the content was still predominantly in Turkish.[78] By the 1950s the front page and most of the paper's content were in Arabic.[79]

The Iraqi Turkmen dialect of Turkish continued to be, and still is, one of the primary vernacular languages in Kirkuk, but the use of Arabic had risen in prevalence by 1955 to the point that the IPC was offering its expatriate workers classes in colloquial Iraqi Arabic so they could communicate with Kirkukis.[80] This would have been unlikely to happen just three decades earlier, when a working knowledge of Turkish or Kurdish was essential for British officials who were serving in Kirkuk. At that time, Arabic was considerably more marginal, even "foreign."[81] Consequently, by the 1950s some Kurdish teachers in northern Iraq were unable to teach in Kurdish because they had been educated in Arabic themselves, even in such historically Kurdish-majority areas as Sulaymaniyya.[82] The lack of Kurdish-language education was a constant point of contention between Kurdish leaders and the Iraqi central government in the years following the end of the Mandate. Kurdish pressure from outside Kirkuk led to some nominal attempts to address this issue, including in Kurdish-majority areas of the Kirkuk *liwa'*.[83]

Neither Kirkuk's Turkmens nor any other group appear to have made a correspondingly strong effort to promote Turkish-language education in this era, though the use of Turkish—or, at least, vernacular spoken Turkmani—continued to some extent in an ad hoc manner among teachers and pupils who were colinguists. The Assyrian-American scholar Edward Odisho, a longtime professor of linguistics who grew up in Kirkuk, recalls that his elementary education in 1940s Kirkuk was officially in Arabic but that teachers sometimes taught him and his fellow students in Turkmani when they knew that the entire class could understand it.[84] The Arabization of education—and, gradually, of much of Kirkukis' vernacular communication—was the predictable result of the process of Kirkuk's deepening relationship with Baghdad through the process of Iraqi state making. This was a linguistic shift that Baghdad facilitated; the resistance that it faced from Kirkukis, at this stage, was limited and disorganized.

The ongoing integration of Kirkuk also furthered a politics of loyalty to an Arab-led, Baghdad-centered Iraq among some notables and local authorities that hastened the emergence of intercommunal fault lines. Kirkuk's position on the

frontier between majority-Kurdish-speaking and majority-Arabic-speaking areas of
Iraq was a key aspect of this process. For both Baghdad and the Kurdish nationalist
movement, as well as for British authorities after the reoccupation of Iraq in 1941,
Kirkuk increasingly served as a strategic and political nexus of communication
between Iraq's divided regions even though it was distant from the violent tribal
unrest that caused turmoil in other parts of the country. The existing pattern of
Kurdish revolts against the Iraqi central government continued throughout the
1930s and 1940s as Kurdish nationalism grew in strength. Kurdish separatist action came to be led by the Barzani tribe, which was centered in the Barzan region
about 165 kilometers north of Kirkuk. Both the British embassy in Baghdad and the
emergent leader of the Kurdish movement, Mustafa Barzani, corresponded actively
with the British political advisers stationed in the city of Kirkuk after 1941.[85] The
political advisers' primary tasks included keeping a close watch on the Kurdish
insurgency through meetings with local officials and Kurdish leaders themselves,
conveying the desires of British diplomats through letters to Kurdish leaders, and
acting as the conduit through which these leaders attempted to communicate with
the British embassy about their interests and demands.[86] As previously discussed,
Kirkuk's geographic location had made it a logical base for military operations
against Shaykh Mahmud in the Mandate era; its military importance became further institutionalized over time, as it had been under the Ottomans.

As a result of Kirkuk's position and because of its large Kurdish population,
the province was also a natural site for competing influence between Kurdish
separatists and centralized power. One example of this conflict took place in
the spring of 1931, when both the Iraqi government and the then-prominent
Shaykh Mahmud attempted to control the affairs of Kurdish-speaking tribes in
the Kirkuk liwa' in different ways. The government tried to intervene to stop the
selection of a chief in the Jaf tribe whom it perceived as unfriendly to its interests.
Concurrently, Mahmud collected taxes from some tribes in the liwa'.[87] There is
also evidence that Kurdish nationalist organizations from outside Iraq viewed
Kirkuk as an important target for activity; for instance, in the late 1920s and early
1930s the international Kurdish organization Khoybun, based in Beirut, operated in Kirkuk and in areas to its northeast and northwest.[88] Despite the growing importance of external Kurdish nationalist movements in Kirkuk, however,
Kurdish nationalist activity that was actually native to Kirkuk was much more
limited and ephemeral. A group of Kurdish intellectuals and army officers formed
a party in favor of Kurdish self-determination, the Hiwa Party, in Kirkuk in 1937,
but it had dissolved by 1943 because of internal disagreements.[89] Furthermore,

although Kirkuki Kurds could occasionally be swayed by figures like Mahmud, the Kurdish rebellion did not spread to the Kirkuk *liwa'* in this time period.

Political trends emanating from Baghdad appeared in Kirkuk in a complicated interplay with these local dynamics. In 1931 prominent opposition parliamentarians joined together to form the Ikha' (Brotherhood) Party, whose popularity was then bolstered by Iraqis who were critical of British influence in the Iraqi government.[90] Evidently taking advantage of discontent with the continued British presence in Iraq, Kirkuki supporters of the Iraqi government, whom a British official in Kirkuk called "pro-Arab," distributed literature to local Kurds claiming that the concept of Kurdish independence was a British plot to ensnare gullible people.[91] This occurred shortly after a visit by the Iraqi interior minister to Kirkuk as part of a tour of northern *liwa*'s in which he appealed to a group of local notables "for unity and the sinking of racial and religious differences."[92] The continued Baghdad-based appointment of prominent Turkmens in government also progressively led to more incidents of ethnicized antagonism between Turkmens and Kurds. The most noteworthy of these Turkmens was ʿAbd al-Majid Beg Yaʿqubizada, the Kirkuki Turkmen notable and former *mutasarrif* of the Kirkuk *liwa'* who went on to serve as the *mutasarrif* of the Kurdish-majority Arbil and Sulaymaniyya *liwa*'s in the 1930s. He obtained his positions largely as a result of his ties to Jamil al-Midfaʿi, a member of the coterie of elite Arabs who circulated through Iraqi government ministries in the monarchy era. A British report on his administration in Arbil characterized it as "anti-Kurdish," and the writer worried that it had provoked resentment among Kurdish tribes, ultimately recommending that Yaʿqubizada be replaced by a Kurdish *mutasarrif*.[93]

On a popular level, though, Kirkuki Turkmens sometimes felt disempowered. In a historical-ethnographic reading of Turkish-language Iraqi poetry from the 1930s, Güldem Büyüksaraç finds that Turkmen poets exhibited a sense of loss stemming from their disengagement from a Turkish-dominated nation upon the creation and consolidation of Iraq. When a Turkish delegation of diplomats visited Kirkuk in 1937, according to later Turkmen accounts, they were greeted with "exuberant joy." Turkophile Kirkukis were subsequently arrested and imprisoned or exiled to southern Iraq for acts such as selling ephemera with the Turkish republic's star-and-crescent emblem.[94] In one instance in 1942, Turkmen students from Kirkuk sent a petition to the legation of the Republic of Turkey in Baghdad complaining that they were being mistreated by Arabs and Kurds at Kirkuk schools. According to a British summary of the petition, the students claimed:

(a) that they were prisoners of the Arabs and Kurds and, that though KIRKUK was a Turkish town, the Kurds were living a better life than they did and (b) that the Kurds were depriving them of their rights and were trying to instal a government of their own. The document went on to state that many of the students were excluded from the school, that ATATURK was abused in the school yard, and reference was made to fifty Turcoman students being sent away from school for a week by the headmaster, etc.[95]

The fact that these students complained to Turkish diplomats and specifically cited Kurds' and Arabs' purported disrespect for Mustafa Kemal Atatürk is telling. It indicates the power of the idea that Kirkuki Turkmens were facing hardships *as people with an inherited connection to Turkey* at the hands of members of other ethnic groups. The oblique mention of the Kurdish nationalist movement in this passage suggests that, in addition to exacerbating divisions between the Kurds and Baghdad, Kirkuki Turkmens had come to perceive ongoing Kurdish separatist activities as harmful to *their* community by this time. It is significant that a Turkmen notion of imminent Kurdish ascendancy as a threat existed by the 1940s; the fulfillment of this possibility on a local level in Kirkuk immediately following the 1958 revolution would go on to spark intercommunal violence.

Kirkuk's developing relationship with Baghdad in the post-Mandate monarchy era lent, on the whole, a growing salience to ethnolinguistic group identities. It is especially important to recognize the various divisive aspects of Baghdad's influence in Kirkuk because existing analyses of the flourishing of territorial-nationalist discourses and their offshoots in the twentieth-century Middle East often focus on how these ideas essentially *unified* people of different sectarian, ethnic, ideological, and/or familial backgrounds. Orit Bashkin, for instance, concentrates on the "shared universe of discourse" that Iraqi intellectuals created in the monarchy era.[96] Israel Gershoni and James Jankowski, writing about Egyptian discourses of the nation, analyze what they describe as the process of "collective self-definition."[97] This trend also exists in urbanist scholarship; for instance, in a study of Damascus during the era of the French Mandate, Philip Khoury demonstrates how the rise of Syrian nationalism and other extralocal foci of identity "began to corrode traditional ties to the quarter, family, clan, and confessional group."[98]

These arguments are cogent when applied to Middle Eastern metropolises but may be much less relevant outside them. Kirkuk, a provincial city located on a political and linguistic borderland, is a remarkably illustrative example of how centralizing power and the promotion of a politics of loyalty to the nascent nation in which a certain municipality is located can actually play a role in reinforcing urban social divisions and the distinctness of corresponding group identities. The development of ethnicized identities in Kirkuk was a central aspect of the evolution of the city's local political affairs. Kirkukis were increasingly invested in the local political domain as, throughout the oil era, the previous norm of patronage politics declined. Yet ethnicity in Kirkuk still had its limits. It was not the political practice through which the local population undertook its first major revolt against British influence after the end of the Mandate.

CONDITIONS "NOT FIT FOR CIVILIZED MEN": THE IRAQI COMMUNIST PARTY AND THE 1946 STRIKE

The combination of Baghdad's influence, growing political consciousness, and growing tensions in Kirkuk in relation to the IPC culminated in a catastrophic strike in 1946 that would shape the city's political and economic trajectory until 1958. The IPC was a key site where the British government pursued its interests in Kirkuk, albeit not without some conflict with company officials' desires. It was natural that the company would serve as the arena in which Kirkuk's post-Mandate political frictions would first become violently apparent, as it was an influential and even semi-sovereign entity in its own right that continuously shaped urban affairs. Notably, however, the organization that spearheaded the strike, the Iraqi Communist Party, did *not* emerge from or initially align with linguistic or confessional groups in Kirkuk. Instead, it mobilized workers on the basis of a nonsectarian form of anticolonialism in which the IPC served as a symbol of Western influence in Iraq.[99]

The idea of the company as a manifestation of imperialism resonated with Kirkukis because of the highly independent and aloof way in which the IPC operated in Kirkuk. This was a tendency that the Iraqi government bolstered. Baghdad's view of the nature of the company's position in the city is suggested by a letter from the Iraqi minister of economics and communications to the company written in April 1939 amid geopolitical turmoil and the immediate possibility of war in Europe. The minister indicated that, as far as the Iraqi government was concerned, the IPC was solely responsible for the defense of its oil fields against possible enemy air raids, including the purchase of anti-aircraft weapons.[100] In other words, the Iraqi government treated the company as though it were a separate governing body with complete authority, even in a military-strategic capacity, over its concession.

Given its powerful influence in Kirkuk, the company's isolation from its workers and from the everyday life of the city at this time was remarkable. The IPC's executives and their families, who were primarily British expatriates, lived in a company camp slightly northwest of the city, close to Baba Gurgur. Like many expatriate enclaves in the developing world, the camp had its own social facilities for expatriate and Iraqi staff-level employees. The company also had its own police force and airplane fleet. It operated private flights to other company sites, including Baghdad, Basra, and some areas outside Iraq. Employees could book seats on these flights for official purposes or for their family members' leisure; one former Iraqi staff-level employee recalls reserving seats on flights to Baghdad for his wife when she wanted to take a day trip to the capital to go shopping.[101]

The IPC's distance from the urban center of Kirkuk as well as the very notion of their dwelling as a "camp" or small transient territory was a physical manifestation of the social segregation that the IPC created and perpetuated in the city. This type of segregation, well known in colonial cities, was also a common phenomenon in the communities surrounding oil-producing areas in the Middle East during the era of foreign-owned oil companies.[102] Furthermore, the company's Iraqi workers did not reside anywhere near the company camp. The IPC's initial building plans in Kirkuk, made in 1930, indicate that they had planned to construct permanent housing in or near the company camp for a large proportion of their Iraqi employees, including up to 1,250 "labourers," a category presumably comprising daily-wage workers such as drillers.[103] It is unclear whether this plan ever came to fruition in any form. By the mid-1940s, however, the IPC's Iraqi workers in Kirkuk certainly did not have access to any permanent company-subsidized housing or transportation to and from the field.

British diplomats in Iraq and Foreign Office officials in London expressed concern about the lack of functional relations between the company and the local government specifically. For instance, on a visit to Kirkuk in October 1946, a British embassy counselor remarked that these relations were so poor that the IPC fields manager, M. S. Mainland, did not even know the name of the new *mutasarrif* of the Kirkuk province.[104] In general, British government officials were eager both to foster British political influence in Kirkuk and to ensure the involvement of the IPC in that process. IPC officials' responses to these efforts appear to have been tepid. One British official who visited Kirkuk in 1948 remarked that he was under the impression that the IPC actually discouraged social contacts between expatriates and members of the local community. He bluntly described the relationship between the IPC's management and local laborers using a racial slur suggesting that the Iraqi workers were degraded. This problem, the official wrote, was exacerbated by the differences in their living conditions and the executives' physical distance from the city.[105] The IPC's inattention to local interests was also reflected in its mostly nonexistent relations with its Kirkuki workforce up until the strike of 1946.[106]

A comparative lack of attention by the British government to labor issues in Kirkuk before 1946 suggests that despite their professed concerns about the previous trajectory of IPC-Kirkuki relations, they too did not notice any problems until the strike occurred. For instance, in a September 1945 letter to the foreign secretary, British embassy counselor G. H. Thompson noted that Iraq's labor conditions required improvement in general but that, as an exception, "the Oil Companies always take an enlightened and liberal view of their obligations to their workers."[107] Thompson's comment reflects the fact that British officials were not opposed to the appearance of certain kinds of progressive labor practices, even in imperial outposts. Indeed, Iraq had developed a relatively liberal set of labor laws by Middle Eastern standards, but they were not consistently implemented by the Iraqi government or by industries.[108] It is therefore not surprising that both British officials and the IPC were blindsided by the Kirkuk oil workers' strike of July 1946. The strike occurred after decades of government indifference and British obliviousness to Kirkuk's urban affairs.

In this environment of discontent, the presence of a large-scale industrial employer in Kirkuk provided an opportunity for labor organization to emerge in the city for the first time. The Iraqi government had outlawed strikes in 1932, using this law as a pretense to ban unions. Unions were otherwise not specifically prohibited under the labor system that had developed during the Mandate era. The government then began to sanction unions in 1944 but remained averse to their formation and activities.[109] Unions appeared in response to several immense difficulties that workers faced. Foremost among these were low wages, which had proven to be increasingly inadequate to cover the skyrocketing cost of living since the British invasion of 1941.[110] The lack of access to housing and transport was another major issue.

The attempt to form a union in the IPC in Kirkuk also followed a long-standing precedent of workers' organization in the Middle Eastern oil industry. Indeed, labor action had even previously taken place within the IPC itself at its Kirkuk-Haifa pipeline terminus in Mandate Palestine. Employees of the IPC in Haifa, a workforce made up of Palestinian Arabs and Jews, began to go on periodic strikes for higher wages in 1935 almost immediately after the inauguration of the pipeline. These strikes took place in the context of the highly active and complex local labor movement in Palestine.[111] The roots of labor organization in Haifa were quite different from those in 1940s Kirkuk, but in both cities the IPC provided fertile ground for actions stemming from both workers' grievances and idiosyncratic political circumstances.

As was the case in both Iraq and Iran, unionizing efforts in Middle Eastern oil companies were often inspired by communist methods. For instance, communists had played a key role in a strike in the Iranian oil town of Abadan as early as 1929. The Iraqi Communist Party, first formed in 1935, was not legally sanctioned by the Iraqi government, but it attracted a large following and gained considerable political power despite repeatedly facing suppression and censorship. Kirkuki IPC workers' actions began in 1937, when the IPC's workforce briefly went on strike twice as part of nationwide labor action in response to poor industrial working conditions; the Iraqi Communist Party played a role in spurring the general strike.[112] Significantly, the Iranian communist Tudeh Party later led a strike of oil workers that began days after the Kirkuk strike ended in 1946.[113] The exact nature of the connection between the Kirkuk and Abadan strikes of 1946, if any, remains unclear.[114] Nonetheless, both strikes reflect the fact that communists in the region, including those of the emergent Iraqi Communist Party, began to concentrate on organizing oil workers in the 1940s and found the local employees of these foreign-owned companies to be receptive to their efforts.

There were fifty-four active members of the Iraqi Communist Party in urban Kirkuk in the 1940s, constituting 5.3% of the party's total recorded nationwide membership (most of whom were located in Baghdad). One of these Kirkuki activists was in the party's central committee, and five more were at midlevel ranks. Two of the midlevel activists had worked for the party in other cities.[115] Organizational efforts in the IPC were led by an experienced member of the party from Baghdad, Hanna Ilyas. Along with some other Iraqi Communists, Ilyas had moved to Kirkuk and had specifically sought employment with the oil company as part of the party's operations.[116]

In January 1946 a pamphlet that was almost certainly authored by Iraqi Communist Party members, typifying the language they used and the specific grievances they often cited, circulated among IPC employees. The pamphlet decried the workers' low standard of living, contrasting it with the profits gleaned from the extraction of oil by "imperialistic foreigners." The pamphlet also stated that the workers' situation could "not be considered fit for any free and civilized man in the age of the atomic bomb," reflecting a desire to achieve a universally recognized form of modernity that would later characterize many of Iraq's development projects, including those in Kirkuk. The authors criticized their low wages, lack of housing and adequate food, and severe working conditions. They ended with a call for IPC workers to unionize.[117]

Under the tutelage of workers who were party members, the IPC's employees subsequently tried and failed to form a union, but they put together a fifteen-member workers' committee in June 1946. Though sanctioned by the company, five of its members were party operatives. When the company rejected the committee's demands for the improvement of workers' welfare through such measures as an increase in daily laborers' minimum wage, the right to unionize, and the creation of pensions, the by then well-organized party members successfully orchestrated a strike that began on 3 July 1946.[118] The ongoing labor action became a public event that was highly visible to Kirkukis outside the company, as striking workers gathered daily in Gawurbaghi (Gavurbağı), a large garden on the western outskirts of Kirkuk about a kilometer south of the company camp. The strike continued relatively uneventfully for over a week before its brutal suppression. On 12 July Kirkuk's *mutasarrif*, Hasan Fahmi, sent police to intervene in the strikers' gathering. The British vice-consul in Kirkuk acknowledged that he had suggested that Fahmi take this action because, in his words, "Force is the only language these people understand."[119] The police eventually opened fire. At least ten workers and perhaps as many as eighteen were killed, and many more were wounded.[120] The strike ended on 16 July, a day after the IPC agreed to raise the workers' minimum wages as a stopgap measure.[121]

The police's violent actions formally occurred on an Iraqi provincial official's order, but the British role in that order must have been widely suspected among Kirkukis; the vice-consul was unapologetic in private, lamenting only that the police had "fired between three hundred and four hundred rounds and had not knocked out a single important striker."[122] The strike's disastrous end backfired against the British establishment in Kirkuk, a fact of which IPC officials, British diplomats, and the Foreign Office were acutely conscious. The IPC and British government officials also feared the potency of communism among the company's Iraqi employees and hoped to work against it. Therefore, in response to the strike, the IPC immediately launched a series of urban development initiatives in collaboration with the local and provincial administrations and the central government. Some of these initiatives took place at the governments' prompting. The first major project, IPC workers' housing, was a direct response to the strike.

In subsequent months and years, political forces, development ideologies, and immediate necessity combined to draw the IPC, the British government, and different Iraqi administrations into educational projects, selective dialogue with oil workers, and citywide infrastructure projects. These projects, as well as the emergent discourse of Kirkuk as Iraq's oil city and a symbol of modernity, are the subject of the next chapter.

CONCLUSION

In the era of Kirkuk's initial rapid growth after the discovery of oil, its burgeoning local political domain gradually rendered obsolete the patronage politics that had characterized what had formerly been a provincial town reliant on external forces. These forces, especially the Iraqi central government and the British official presence in Iraq, certainly remained powerful in Kirkuk. But the city's affairs increasingly came to revolve around the oil industry, both as an institution and as a social and political agent. The IPC's presence spurred both the beginnings of communist organization and the dramatic demographic shifts that left the previously dominant Turkmen community, in particular, fearing its progressive loss of preeminence. Kirkuk's importance to Iraq as the center of its oil industry and the location of its only known supergiant oil field intensified Baghdad's motives for integrating the city and region into its domain, an effort that interacted with the local status quo in divisive ways.

Such state-making efforts tended to cause more political divisions that fell along ethnic lines than had been present during the Mandate era, but the most potent form of popular mobilization that emerged in the watershed moment of July 1946 was a nonsectarian, fundamentally unifying movement based on communist and anti-imperialist ideas. This trend demonstrates the complexity of the development of ethnicities in Kirkuk in the early years of Iraqi independence. Although they gained significance in certain contexts, they did not yet frame the city's political domain or determine most Kirkukis' interests. The next decade would see the construction of a distinct Kirkuki civic identity both inside and outside the region as the oil city became an ever more compelling symbol of Iraq's political-economic and ideological trajectory.

4 THE IDEOLOGY OF URBAN DEVELOPMENT

BY THE 1940S Kirkuk was a single-industry town, and a large percentage of the city's population worked for the Iraq Petroleum Company (IPC). This made the strain in the company's labor relations that had culminated in the 1946 strike an urgent problem of immense local import. Notably, the company responded by initiating local urban development projects in Kirkuk before the Iraqi government itself started to pursue large-scale development and modernization initiatives throughout the rest of the country in 1950. The presence of oil in Kirkuk therefore shaped both the process of development and its political and social implications. The IPC, the British government, and the Iraqi government operated on the assumption that urban development could counter the influence of communism and lead to the attainment of modernity. Their public expressions of the goals and achievements of development projects reinforced this ideological framework by stressing the advances made in infrastructure and housing as part of the undertaking of integrating Kirkuk into a Western-led capitalist system.

The oil company had greater access to capital, resources, materials, and technology than the Kirkuk municipality. This fact allowed the IPC to spearhead housing, water, and other public works projects, setting precedents for subsequent Iraqi governments to follow and inspiring similar schemes by other oil companies throughout the Middle East. As the site where Iraq's oil wealth was produced, Kirkuk was of vital importance to the Iraqi and British governments. Both Iraqi and British officials on several levels pressured the IPC to act in ways that would benefit their interests. In turn, the IPC sought to leverage its growing local political influence. Notwithstanding the aspects of these urban development projects that improved many Kirkukis' quality of life, segregation of ethnic groups in Kirkuk may have been hardened by the schemes' focus on creating a middle class that mostly excluded the growing Kurdish community. Kirkuk's local political domain and its communities' distinct group identities therefore became more salient in tandem with one another.

At the same time, the oil industry's needs fostered the growth of reading, writing, and printing activities in Kirkuk. Amid this flourishing of discourse, local and foreign writers alike began to evoke Kirkuk's ancient past while tracing the city's path to what they portrayed as a thriving present. They characterized this trajectory as the natural conclusion of thousands of years of history combined with the fortuitous discovery of plentiful natural resources and the helpful intervention of the IPC. Consciousness of the past and the promotion of modernization combined symbiotically in the concept of Kirkuk as the Iraqi "oil city." The discourses of the oil city not only bolstered urban development schemes but also created a space in which a Kirkuki civic identity grew alongside active efforts by the IPC and British authorities to ensure that oil workers were invested, literally and figuratively, in Kirkuk.

IPC HOUSING SCHEMES IN KIRKUK:
THE MAKING OF SMALL-SCALE CAPITALISTS

A twelve-year period of activity surrounding urban development projects in Kirkuk commenced in 1946 with a workers' housing scheme. The striking oil workers of July 1946 had made six demands that were similar to the demands made by the Communist-led workers' committee that preceded them. The first demand was that the IPC construct housing for its employees or, in the absence of doing so, grant them an allowance for their rent.[1] The notion of a large company providing housing for its workers was not unprecedented in Iraq; according to a 20 July 1946 letter from the British ambassador, Hugh Stonehewer Bird, to the Iraqi foreign minister, Fadhil al-Jamali, three Iraqi government-run companies housed their employees at the time. Indeed, as previously mentioned, the IPC itself had initially planned to provide housing for workers in the early 1930s. However, Stonehewer Bird's letter to al-Jamali held that expecting the IPC to provide such housing or a rent allowance was unreasonable and could lead to similar demands from workers in all sorts of other industries.[2]

At the same time, there was some internal British recognition that the strikers' demand for housing was fair and that fulfilling it might be necessary. The
Foreign Office and the Iraqi government, which were particularly concerned with
preventing further Communist Party exploitation of workers' grievances, immediately recognized while the strike was still ongoing that the strikers' concerns
about pay and housing were "legitimate."[3] In the aftermath of the Kirkuk strike,
the Iraqi parliament passed Law No. 29 of 1947, which required all companies
that employed more than 100 workers to provide housing for their employees.[4]
For its part, the IPC also came to acknowledge that, in the words of company
official H. H. Wheatley, "most of the Labour troubles at Kirkuk—although sometimes politically inspired—have resulted in showing up weaknesses in our provision of welfare and amenities." Writing in the context of an impending budget
cut that could have affected the company's housing plans, Wheatley warned that
the postponement of building would "have a very serious effect on our Labour."[5]
Consequently, by November 1946 the IPC had drawn up plans for workers' housing.[6] These rapid actions indicate that the political tensions created by oil were
inextricably intertwined with Kirkuk's urban affairs. To salvage their political
positions in the city, the Iraqi government, the British government, and the IPC
chose first to pursue urban development projects.

Just as important, though, the actions taken by these establishments illustrate
the ideological underpinnings of initial development efforts in Iraq. Specifically,
British officials sought to promote capitalist ideas in Kirkuk and to underscore
what they viewed as the "enlightened" Western approach to labor. For instance, in
mid-August 1946 British Embassy official Douglas L. Busk wrote to the Foreign
Office that housing schemes, among other projects, would be a necessary measure
to counter Communist influence. Busk noted that Britain had a "double interest" in
undertaking such projects: first, to address the "commercial concerns" of British-led
companies such as the IPC and, second, to maintain what he considered Britain's
status as "the world's pioneer in the promotion of social justice."[7] At the same time,
the IPC showed signs of leveraging their political influence in Kirkuk by fashion-
ing their Iraqi employees into "small-scale capitalists," a phrase used in a British
consular report describing an agreement between the IPC and the Eastern Bank to
allow Iraqi employees to set aside a portion of their wages in accounts with interest.
According to the consul, the IPC fields manager viewed the instilling of capitalism
in the workers as a way to "give them a stake in the stability of the country."[8]

Therefore, with a combination of political urgency and an ideological framework, within months of the strike construction began on the workers' housing

on IPC property northwest of Kirkuk's urban center. According to a 1950 British government report, the Arrapha Estate, named for the ancient Assyrian city whose site was near present-day Kirkuk, consisted of 246 "bungalows" for Iraqi personnel (Figure 9).[9] By 1955 there were over 450 houses.[10] By that time, there were about 6,200 monthly-rate and daily-rate employees of the IPC in Iraq, most of whom were native Iraqis in Kirkuk; hence the percentage of workers and their families housed by the company was still fairly small but growing.[11] Housing was allocated according to workers' family size.[12] A 1950 British government report by W. J. Hull described the Arrapha Estate houses, which were designed in London, as being "built of good local kiln-fired brick" (Figure 10). The houses consisted of three or four rooms and had ceiling fans; some of the more expensive houses had central heating. A large number of smaller, two-room houses were in the process of being built.[13] The estate eventually came to include grocers and other basic shops constructed by the company for the benefit of its residents.[14]

FIGURE 9. Aerial view of the Arrapha Estate in 1951. An IPC employee drew arrows on this photograph to indicate the locations of the houses that had been built so far (bifurcated arrow in center), the estate's shop units (left-most arrow), and the company camp's sports pavilion (arrow in bottom right). The expatriate executives' houses, ringed by gardens, are visible in the lower half of the photo. Source: BP Archive, File 49717. Reproduced with permission from the BP Archive.

Unsurprisingly, Hull also noted that the estate was "completely separated from Kirkuk town." He also observed that there was a serious shortage of housing in Kirkuk for those who were not in the IPC's employ.

> Until more is done either by the local authority or the I.P.C. or both, the contrast between the highly efficient modern industrial undertaking under foreign management, and the ramshackle oriental city will remain, and the sense of a sharp cleavage between the two may increase. It is a situation not without its dangers.[15]

Hull's characterization of the "modern" company camp in opposition to the "oriental" city reflects British officials' preoccupation with order and capitalist efficiency in urban growth. His observations correspond with the company's sense that uneasiness persisted in Kirkuk following the beginning of construction of the Arrapha Estate. As early as 1949, an IPC report had stressed that the company housing option should not be made "too attractive financially" for fear that this would create tensions between workers housed in Arrapha and those who continued to live in urban Kirkuk. The report recommended that the company continue to provide all workers, regardless of where they lived, with a "high cost-of-living" allowance.[16] The 1956 Iraqi housing census found that the average rent of a house in central Kirkuk was 5.251 Iraqi dinars per month, an amount easily covered by the IPC's allowance for daily-wage workers around that time.[17]

FIGURE 10. Homes and a road in the Arrapha Estate photographed by Constantinos Doxiadis in 1956, with local children in the street. Source: Constantinos A. Doxiadis, "23.1.56, Kirkuk City," Iraq Diary DOX.Q.8, 1956, Constantinos A. Doxiadis Archives, File 23875. © Constantinos and Emma Doxiadis Foundation. Reproduced with permission.

Still, these perceived tensions, combined with the desire on the part of the British government and the IPC to promote capitalism among the company's workers, led to the IPC's idea of initiating a "home ownership scheme." Though innovative in the context of the Middle East, the concept of the scheme derived from the building societies that had arisen in Industrial Revolution–era Britain and dominated the British mortgage market. Under this scheme "thrifty" Iraqi employees would obtain a loan from the Eastern Bank to buy plots of land in urban Kirkuk and build their own houses with the company's financial and logistical assistance, thereby becoming property owners. The home ownership scheme began to come to fruition in the fall of 1950.[18]

The IPC viewed the home ownership scheme as a way to link their aim of maintaining political leverage with their ideology of urban development. For instance, in January 1951 an IPC memorandum enumerated three principal reasons for the pursuit of the scheme; these reasons reflected the company's concerns with regard to its relationship with the city of Kirkuk and the political practices and beliefs of its workers. First, the company wanted to make a visible contribution to Kirkuk economically, because the city did not exhibit the benefits of the IPC's "cash disbursements" to the Iraqi government, which generally went to Baghdad. Second, the company believed that the scheme would relieve them of the costly burden of a major expansion of the Arrapha Estate. Third, they thought that the scheme would "encourage the employee to make good use of his wages in the improvement of his standard of living and give him a positive stake in the community of the town of which he is a member."[19] Less than a month later, IPC official P. R. A. Ensor marked the IPC's shift in priorities when, in a letter to the company's general management in Tripoli, he asserted, "In Kirkuk we must regard [the home ownership scheme] as the more important" housing project.[20] Ultimately, the scheme proved to be successful enough in the company's view that the IPC and its associated firms later duplicated it in other parts of the Middle East, including Syria and the United Arab Emirates.[21] The American-owned Arabian American Oil Company (ARAMCO) in Saudi Arabia also went on to inaugurate a similar scheme in 1953.[22]

By the end of 1954, 202 houses had been built and 19 purchased in Kirkuk under the scheme.[23] A 1955 IPC map indicates that the plots of land purchased or in the process of being purchased under the home ownership scheme were overwhelmingly on the west side of the Khasa River in newer *mahallas* rather than in the older *mahallas* in and around the citadel on the east side, implying that the scheme aimed primarily to build in areas that were not yet integrated into the urban fabric and that it would not replace any historic buildings. The largest concentrations of these plots of land were in *mahallas* in northwestern Kirkuk that were relatively close to the company camp, particularly al-Mas and Beglar. Some collections of plots were also located in *mahallas* closer to the center of the city or the railway station in the southwest, such as Shatirlu, Sari Kahya, and Tis'in. Plots associated with the scheme on the east side of the river were few, more scattered, and generally in newer areas on the outskirts of the older neighborhoods. However, the poor and rapidly growing Kurdish neighborhood of Shorija, unlike most of Kirkuk's younger *mahallas*, had no plots of land associated with the IPC's home ownership scheme at this time.[24] The fact that the IPC was not constructing in Shorija is indicative of the home ownership scheme's focus on creating a middle class.

Shorija's separation from IPC housing construction, both physically and socioeconomically, is also consistent with a pattern of inequalities in urban Kirkuk corresponding to ethnic group identities that long predated the presence of the IPC but was exacerbated by its hiring practices. A former IPC staff member whom I interviewed echoed anecdotal reports that Kirkuki IPC employees in clerical positions like his own were mostly of either Turkmen or Assyrian origin. This outcome is predictable in light of the Turkmens' historically higher socioeconomic status in Kirkuk and the Assyrians' longtime association, whether it was advantageous to them or not, with British authorities. On the other hand, the Kurds and Arabs who worked for the IPC were usually poorer and tended to hold daily-wage unskilled labor positions, though some worked in skilled labor or as technicians.[25] Some authors, including Nouri Talabany, claim that Kurds made up a much smaller proportion of the company's workforce as a whole relative to their strength in Kirkuk's population.[26] Because the IPC does not appear to have kept track of or even internally discussed its employees' ethnic backgrounds in any official capacity, this claim is difficult to verify or refute with any precision.[27] Talabany reiterates a frequent argument about the IPC's impact in Kirkuk, namely, that its hiring patterns indicated a policy of ethnic discrimination against Kurds that was tied to Baghdad's efforts to increase Arab influence and marginalize Kurds in the Kirkuk region.[28] The apparent relative absence of Kurds in the higher levels of the company may indeed have been tied to quiet prejudices on the part of British company officials, given the common local assumption that Kurds were uneducated, but there is no evidence that it was a policy deliberately engineered by the Iraqi government.

The common question of whether or not the IPC and the Iraqi government deliberately followed hiring practices that were prejudicial to Kurds as part of the project to bolster Arab influence in Kirkuk cannot be answered definitively. This question, in its bluntness, also misses a subtler and equally insidious dynamic: the inadvertent ethnicization of employment categories in the IPC would have aggravated the socioeconomic stratification in Kirkuk that already corresponded to group identities. In the IPC this stratification was so pervasive that its ethnicization would have even resulted in the physical separation of workers of different linguistic and confessional groups in the company's facilities. For example, there were separate cafeterias for staff and laborers. The company's hospital at the K1 pumping station had three distinct wards for daily-rate, monthly-rate, and covenanted employees in addition to the medically necessary maternity and outpatient wards.[29] The IPC's fostering of a middle class of skilled and clerical workers, who were kept apart from daily-wage workers and who disproportionately consisted of members of politically or socioeconomically privileged ethnic groups, likely contributed to solidifying group identities and deteriorating intercommunal relations.

The home ownership scheme's absence in Kirkuk's fastest growing, predominantly Kurdish *mahalla* signals the possible influence of this phenomenon on the urban spatial distribution of different ethnic groups. The hypothesis that the segregation of employees at different levels of the company may have been indicative of evolving identity-based disaggregation in urban Kirkuk on a larger scale is also supported by the verifiable ethnoreligious composition of the IPC's housing schemes. The demographics of these projects are suggestive of how attitudes toward them were probably affected by the relationship that different communities had with British authorities in Iraq. A 1953 company report observed that the employees who took up residence in the Arrapha Estate, which was close to where the expatriates lived, were mostly "Christians," whereas the majority of IPC workers who purchased houses in urban Kirkuk under the home ownership scheme up to that time were "Muslims." According to the report, the company had offered houses in the Arrapha Estate to more than 600 employees, and only 68 Muslims had accepted the offer. The report did not mention linguistic groups, but Kirkuk's confessional categories generally fell along lines of ethnic self-identity. In view of Kirkuk's demographic patterns, it is clear that the Christians living in the Arrapha Estate were mostly Chaldo-Assyrians and that the "Muslim" category comprised the vast majority of self-identified Turkmens, Arabs, and Kurds. Indeed, locals nicknamed the Arrapha Estate the "Assyrian Village," and the neighborhood is associated with Chaldo-Assyrians to this day.[30] One IPC official noted that this apparent self-segregation of religious groups into different parts of the city could not "be viewed without disquiet." Echoing British diplomats' concerns from several years earlier, the same official also warned that expanding the company camp northwest of the city would exacerbate the company's disconnect from urban Kirkuk and engender "envy" among the "townsfolk," forming "a focus of resentment against the foreigner."[31]

The IPC's housing schemes therefore did not ameliorate the greatest contributing factor to the unrest that undergirded the 1946 strike: the separation of the company camp from the city's historic urban fabric and the corresponding segregation between expatriates and locals. The schemes might have also, despite their relatively small scale, contributed to divisions between local communities, in particular, the insulation of Chaldo-Assyrians from Kirkuk's urban space and the marginalization of Kurds within the city. As I argued in Chapter 3, spatial divisions between Kirkuk's communities existed but were probably neither rigid nor institutionalized in the era of the Hashemite monarchy. But by the time of the 1958 revolution, the distinctions between ethnic groups, especially Turkmens and Kurds, had become salient enough to fuel a cycle of intercommunal strife.

The ethnicized stratification of IPC employment categories in the 1940s and 1950s—specifically, in light of the links these groupings had with housing plans and the attempt to engineer a middle class of "small-scale capitalists"—demands a close reading, despite a lack of conclusive evidence as to the exact nature of these divisions. Part of the difficulty of this question stems from the fact that Kirkuk, unlike Middle Eastern oil cities that were designed by companies from the ground up with overt ethnic segregation, had an old urban fabric and a lengthy history of intercommunal relations with which the IPC's presence interacted.[32] In any case, there is reason to believe that both the provision of suburban company housing and the urban home ownership scheme would have catalyzed the separation of Kirkuk's ethnic communities in a manner that was linked with these communities' socioeconomic statuses and their relations with British and Iraqi authorities.

DOXIADIS AND THE IRAQI GOVERNMENT'S
MODERNIZATION PLANS IN KIRKUK

Another source of discontent in Kirkuk was the fact that the Iraqi government failed to take the initiative to pursue much-needed urban development projects in the provinces. In particular, it allowed the capital generated by the IPC to be spent on enterprises that ultimately benefited Baghdad rather than Kirkuk.[33] When the Iraqi government first turned its attention to large-scale development projects in 1950 after negotiating a new revenue-sharing agreement with the IPC, it focused strongly on the agricultural sector and on rural areas with little, if any, attention to urban issues outside Baghdad. These projects were administered by the Iraqi Development Board, which was created by an act of parliament in 1950. The board was a group of several full-time executives, including two foreign "experts" (one British and one American), who oversaw the spending of the 70% of Iraq's oil revenues that the Iraqi government had set aside for development. The Development Board defined multiple areas, including transportation and industry, in which it planned to invest its funds, but it ultimately concentrated most of its efforts on irrigation and flood control.[34]

This tendency changed to some extent in 1955 in the aftermath of an Iraqi government report on the Development Board's activities authored by a British civil servant, Lord Salter. Salter criticized the development initiatives for failing to make tangible improvements in the lives of ordinary Iraqis, and he expressed concern at the resulting popular resentment.[35] The Iraqi government's interest in diversifying its development projects led it to commission the Greek architect and urban planner Constantinos A. Doxiadis and his fledgling firm, Doxiadis Associates, to design master plans for the modernization of major Iraqi cities, including Kirkuk. Doxiadis's work in Iraq proved to be an early career stage in what would eventually become a large-scale international practice.

The Iraqi government selected Doxiadis to lead its urban development projects because his planning philosophy corresponded with prevailing ideas among Western governments and institutions about achieving modernization through rational, scientific economic development. This philosophy, which he called "ekistics," or "the science of human settlements," claimed to be apolitical.[36] In one of his articles on economic development, Doxiadis argued that a highly systematic approach to construction in provincial areas, with a focus on housing projects, was the key to fighting the "war of liberation from poverty" in the developing world by building settlements that could "integrate all functions towards the emergence of a better and richer life for the people."[37] In other words, it was urban "science" that would alleviate the suffering of the poor, not, for example, labor strikes. Accordingly, Doxiadis's approach also encompassed what Pascal Menoret describes as "containment urbanism," or the attempt to "prevent rural migrants from falling for communism" through the construction of features such as wide roads that facilitated state control of cities.[38]

In keeping with their prescriptive method, Doxiadis Associates created plans for Kirkuk that were ambitious and unrealistic; their master plan for the city

was in keeping with the theory of ekistics rather than with the principle of seeking practical solutions to concrete problems.[39] Nonetheless, these efforts are an
indication of the goals that the Iraqi government wanted to achieve in rapidly
growing cities such as Kirkuk that had large numbers of people, especially recent
migrants, living in poverty. Doxiadis's firm envisioned a radical reorganization of
the nondifferentiated city into separate residential and commercial zones, which
they described as a means to impose "control" on its "haphazard" growth. They
also called for the creation of open communal spaces (including in the citadel),
networks of wide streets, and the construction of nearly 3,000 houses in different
parts of the city and other areas of the Kirkuk province by 1965.[40]

In the end, Doxiadis Associates made little headway toward achieving their
stated goals. By the time the revolutionary government in Iraq forced the firm to
abandon their projects and leave the country in 1959, they had only overseen the
building of 309 houses and some "corresponding community facilities" in urban
Kirkuk.[41] The part of Doxiadis's initial housing plan that his firm successfully
implemented expanded the city's inhabited area in the northeast only slightly
along the road to the city of Sulaymaniyya. Aside from the relatively limited
construction, it is unclear how the Iraqi government planned to pursue housing
projects like the one in Kirkuk from an administrative standpoint once the houses
were built. The government did not establish a legal or organizational framework
for the allotment of the housing that resulted from such projects.[42]

The significance of Doxiadis's plans in Kirkuk lies instead in the fact that they
were the first projects sponsored by the Iraqi government to develop Kirkuk's
built environment separately from the IPC. Like the IPC's housing schemes,
Doxiadis's plans are especially remarkable for their underlying ideology: the
notion that scientific urban planning could bring about modernity in provincial
cities. In addition, they were the first housing plans intended to benefit Kirkukis
who were not on the payroll of the oil company and the first plans that adopted
a broad social and civic scope, aiming far beyond the fostering of a middle class.
It is notable that Doxiadis's approach to housing in Kirkuk took into account
the precedent of the IPC housing projects. On a 1956 visit to the city, Doxiadis
studied the Arrapha Estate as an example of a recently constructed "high standard settlement" in Kirkuk, but he lamented what he viewed as its inefficient
utilization of space and unpaved roads.[43]

The available details of Doxiadis's approach to the Kirkuk housing projects
also provide a valuable glimpse into the factors underlying the Kirkuki demand
for urban development. For instance, when Doxiadis visited Kirkuk in December

1955, he met with the provincial *mutasarrif* and other officials, including a representative of the Iraqi Mortgage Bank. The officials noted that the city was in particularly dire need of "low-income group housing for labourers and farmers," most of whom had moved into Kirkuk in recent years from the rural hinterland and from other parts of Iraq. Farmers, in particular, were moving into the city under urgent circumstances because of a lack of water in the countryside at that time, and some of them exhibited a preference for working for the IPC or construction contractors once they arrived.[44] This rural-to-urban influx mirrored the pattern of population growth in Baghdad, which was the focus of Doxiadis's Iraqi urban planning. In Baghdad the government was especially insistent that Doxiadis's housing plans should attempt to eliminate the intercommunal divisions that had been exacerbated by rural migrants. However, Doxiadis Associates ultimately avoided addressing this issue in the capital.[45] Similarly, the firm's master plan for Kirkuk generally emphasized improving the built environment in response to population growth without specifically addressing any of the reasons for migration into the city that Iraqi officials had discussed with Doxiadis.[46] Despite the Iraqi central government's approval of Doxiadis's methods, there was a disparity between his approach, which was rooted in making cities rational, and the urban issues that local officials found most pressing.

Therefore, just as rapid population growth in the capital presented daunting social and economic challenges that government-commissioned housing efforts did not fully take into account, so too did growth in the provincial oil city produce poor living conditions for many immigrants that the Iraqi government's plans, funded by newly acquired oil revenues, did not improve. The subtext of both the government's housing scheme and the IPC's schemes was the notion that the achievement of modernity was inextricable from the growth of capitalism and the pursuit of economic development. These ideological dynamics were a common feature of the politics of urbanism throughout the region, especially in Middle Eastern oil cities, around the mid-twentieth century. This is indicated by the eventual spread of the concept of the home ownership scheme and the expansion of Doxiadis's activities into other Middle Eastern countries, including Iran, Saudi Arabia, Libya, and Syria.[47]

LEVERAGING POWER THROUGH PUBLIC UTILITIES:
THE KIRKUK WATER SCHEME

The IPC's relations with local government officials in the Kirkuk municipality and province were also a crucial component of the progress of development projects, yielding an arena in which local power politics distinct from external trends burgeoned. Nowhere are these dynamics more apparent than in the company's provision of infrastructure needs to the city. The IPC had established an early precedent for sharing their resources, particularly water, with the municipality of Kirkuk. In 1930 the company initially derived its water supply by sinking wells in the Khasa River. When these wells became insufficient for the company's expanding operations, the IPC bequeathed them to the Kirkuk municipality and proceeded to build a system to obtain water from the much larger Lesser Zab River.[48] By the time of the 1946 strike, the IPC's former wells had also proven to be inadequate for Kirkuk's rapidly growing population. Following the strike, Kirkuk's provincial government saw an opportunity to solicit further help from the IPC in obtaining water for the municipality after the company turned their attention to development projects.

The *mutasarrif* of Kirkuk province, 'Abd al-Jalil Parto, first contacted IPC officials about this matter in September 1946, when he asked the company, in one official's paraphrase, to "do everything possible to assist the Kirkuk Municipality to overcome the seasonal shortage of drinking water." The IPC's managing director assured Parto that the company would use its own equipment and newly built pipelines to pump the water it could spare from its own supplies—a maximum of 500,000 gallons a day during the hottest part of the summer—into a new municipal water tank. In further correspondence during project delays, Parto repeatedly emphasized the city's dire need for water and the fact that Kirkukis had begun to complain about the water shortage, putting pressure on company officials. Upon the project's completion in May 1947, both Parto and the Iraqi interior minister wrote to the IPC to thank them effusively for their "service" and "gift free of charge" to "the people of Kirkuk Town."[49]

This correspondence occurred when Parto was concerned about the financial relationship between the Kirkuk municipality and the central government in Baghdad with regard to local projects. In a meeting with the British ambassador in October 1946, the *mutasarrif* expressed apprehension about the fact that, although the central treasury held an allotted budget for the municipality of 50,000 Iraqi dinars per year, the municipality found it "extremely difficult" to obtain permission from Baghdad to use the funds locally to undertake, for example, a public transportation scheme. Parto also suggested that he would like either the British government or the IPC to help in obtaining film projectors for the new Kirkuk cinema. In response the ambassador emphasized that Parto was the one responsible "to badger the Central Government" about these problems and that

Kirkuk should not expect the IPC or the British government to address such issues; British officials did not want the relationship between them and Kirkuk to be "all give on our side and all take on" the *mutasarrif*'s.[50] In his 1950 report on the IPC oil fields in Kirkuk, Hull noted that the municipality was "well off," their budget having increased to about 60,000 or 70,000 Iraqi dinars per year. He was critical of local officials for not doing more to address public health problems, among other pressing issues. However, he did not take into account possible difficulties in the relationship between Kirkuk and Baghdad.[51] The relationship between the capital and the oil city was also troubled because, as previously mentioned, the Iraqi Development Board was primarily focusing its efforts on the agricultural sector, especially on rural flood control projects. In 1952, when the IPC's endeavor to provide Kirkuk with water had evolved into a "municipal water scheme" to create a fully separate system for the municipality to obtain water from the Lesser Zab River, the company transferred nominal control over the project to the Development Board.[52] Nevertheless, the company continued to effectively operate the project, and in 1953 they drafted a formal agreement with the Development Board to bear part of the project's costs.[53]

The Iraqi central government encouraged the company's financial and material contribution to Kirkuk's municipal water scheme. For instance, the Iraqi minister of economics, Nadim al-Pachachi, suggested to the acting manager of the IPC in Baghdad in a 1951 meeting that the company should "consider making a definite monetary contribution" toward the cost of the scheme not because the board lacked ample money to fund it but because, "in the opinion of the Prime Minister" of Iraq, it would be "a gesture which would bring wide publicity to the Company's advantage, and which should show the people of Iraq the extent to which the Company was now interesting itself in the general progress and development of the country."[54] In 1952 the Development Board indicated to the IPC that it wanted the IPC to publicize its commitment to contributing part of the cost of the water scheme through its upcoming ceremonies associated with the increase of oil production to 25 million tons per year. Most suggestively, according to M. S. Mainland, this highly visible promotion of the IPC's role in the project would "provide the reply to the question—asked by both the Government and the Development Board—as to what contribution the Company were prepared to make."[55] Iraqi newspapers that were sympathetic to British influence in Iraq rewarded the IPC's contributions to Kirkuk with positive attention, as in a 1950 article in the newspaper *al-Sha'b*, written by a correspondent in "the black-gold city," praising the IPC's provision of electricity.[56]

For their part, IPC officials in Kirkuk indicated repeatedly that continued engagement in and full cooperation with the demands of the project were necessary to maintain good political relations with the local government. For instance, in 1948 the IPC official H. H. Wheatley wrote that supplying water to Kirkuk was, "whether we like it or not . . . as much a necessity as our industrial requirements."[57] In 1950, when contemplating an expansion of the project that the city had requested, fields manager Mainland described it as "a measure of insurance against further demands for water from the Municipality."[58] In contrast, IPC officials in London were lukewarm about the prospect of spending an increasing amount of company money on the scheme; Mainland responded that doing so was an "obligation."[59] Once the scheme was in the process of coming under Iraqi control, however, the company's description of its political interests took on a tone that was less defensive and more politically strategic. In 1951 Mainland favored the company's continued participation in the scheme by arguing that it would be useful for the IPC to exercise some control over Kirkuk's infrastructure to maintain a strong position in relation to the municipal government in the face of potential political difficulties. "By placing the Kirkuk Town Water supply under operations which we control," he wrote in a dispatch to the IPC in London, "we shall be establishing some community of interest between ourselves and the municipality in the matter of public services which may be valuable should labour or living conditions become difficult in Kirkuk."[60] As the IPC became progressively more involved in Kirkuk's economic development, it began to wield its resulting influence in the city more deliberately. By this time, the IPC's infrastructure projects had made the transition from essentially ad hoc attempts by the IPC at improving relations with Kirkuk to fully realized political endeavors in which the local and central Iraqi governments were also participating.

The Kirkuk municipal water scheme illuminates yet another facet of the IPC's role in Kirkuk's everyday social and political life. In addition to its effects on Kirkuk's economy, its physical layout, and its communities, the company became an ever more integral part of the municipal and provincial governments' activities. When it initiated a development project, it often did so in advance of Baghdad's participation—a fact that Baghdad used to its advantage. The IPC's interactions with the municipality simultaneously increased its power on a local level and lent greater potency to the provincial oil city's civic domain by creating a set of political dynamics in which older forms of patronage politics and reliance on Baghdad became less relevant.

VOCATIONAL TRAINING AND "GENUINE" UNIONIZING:
THE IPC'S HUMAN CONCERNS

The IPC's "sociological" interest in Kirkuk, as one British diplomat put it, was not limited to improving Kirkukis' standard of living through housing and infrastructure schemes.[61] It also included continuing concerns with the lack of interaction between IPC expatriates and the local population. In particular, the British government was preoccupied with the goal of improving the IPC's relations with its workers because the company was the largest employer in the city and as such monopolized its labor affairs. Hull, in his 1950 report on the IPC, indicated that, as the *mutasarrif* had informed him, unemployment in Kirkuk resulted primarily from the company's periodic layoffs. Because the company ultimately aimed to employ fewer daily-rate laborers as its production increased to 25 million tons per year, there was little prospect that this situation would improve.[62] Political friction therefore spurred interventions in the form of the establishment of social, and particularly educational, institutions aimed especially at oil workers.

The British government first attempted to create an educational enterprise in Kirkuk by establishing the British Institute in 1946. The British Institute was operated by the British Council, an organization funded by the Foreign Office for the purpose of promoting British influence worldwide through targeted cultural projects. Although Kirkuk was smaller than Iraq's three historically important metropolises of Baghdad, Basra, and Mosul (where the Institute also had branches), it also attracted the attention of the British Council as an important site for public diplomacy. The Institute offered classes in English, held occasional lectures and social functions, and screened films. Initial missteps led to adjustments; for instance, the Institute eventually began to provide explanations in Arabic during their screenings of English-language films because the vast majority of Kirkukis could not understand English.

But the very presence of the immensely powerful oil company, which enhanced Kirkuk's significance to Britain, distorted the usual approach of British diplomatic activities by creating a competing force with which the British Institute had to contend. Although the Institute had limited successes in involving members of the community, particularly in the English classes, the British Council eventually deemed it a failure and closed it in 1948. One of the Institute's main complaints was that IPC officials were not sufficiently involved in its activities, despite attempts to solicit their help and interest; upon its closing, the Institute's director lamented the IPC's "luxurious seclusion."[63]

Whereas the British Council failed to secure the IPC's involvement in providing educational services to the Kirkuk community, the Iraqi government succeeded in doing so through consistent pressure. The government indicated to IPC officials as early as 1948 that they were obligated to provide their workers with vocational education, and it continued to stress this expectation during negotiations with the company at least until 1953.[64] Accordingly, the IPC started a two-year course for the company's artisans in 1948. They expanded their educational offerings in 1951 with an apprentice training scheme for the technical training of 15- and 16-year-old boys with a primary education. In 1953 they inaugurated an adult training scheme for older students. The IPC also started a training scheme in cooperation with the Iraqi government in 1951 that would prepare students to study at a British university by the end of the course.[65] About a dozen Iraqi students per year from the Kirkuk institute were sent to the United Kingdom as part of a scholarship program to study in exchange for a commitment to working for either the Iraqi government or the IPC.[66] By about 1955 the IPC offered seven different types of educational courses, including technical training, language training in both Arabic and English, and other types of vocational training such as typewriting.[67]

The IPC initiated these schemes with the intention of increasing the number of Iraqi employees in higher-ranking positions, especially in skilled labor and management, which were then held mostly by expatriates.[68] The political implications of increasing the presence of British-trained Iraqis at higher levels of the company were subtle but significant to both the company's management and the Iraqi government, both of which wished to head off any further unrest. The company in particular viewed these programs as part of an "obligation" to their workers.[69] A former IPC staff member recalls that in the beginning, the apprentice training scheme primarily attracted Christians, in a pattern that paralleled the demographics of the Arrapha Estate; the children of skilled and clerical workers who were closer to the mostly British expatriates than the laborers were given preference. Gradually, however, the variety of education programs reached many Muslim employees, including daily-wage workers and their children. The number of Muslims in clerical positions grew, and some of the Muslims who had been educated through the British university scholarship program and appointed to staff-level positions chose to live in the Arrapha Estate. The scholarship program also allowed a larger number of Kurds to become trained as engineers than had been the case previously, allowing them to take up highly skilled positions in the company.[70]

Despite the company's efforts to assuage the sensibilities of the workforce, British authorities continued to be suspicious of external influences that might further damage the relationship between the IPC and its workers. This fear was not unfounded. For example, Iraqi Communist Party communications intercepted by British intelligence in 1949 indicated that the Communists were still actively attempting to organize Kirkuk's oil workers.[71] British and Iraqi officials alike were also apprehensive of the Communists' potential to act as a conduit for Soviet influence in Iraq.[72] Consequently, beginning as early as July 1946, when the workers' strike was still ongoing, British diplomats repeatedly emphasized the importance of establishing what they usually called "genuine trades unions" among oil workers and other laborers in Kirkuk. This was their term for workers' unions friendly to the British and the IPC. One Foreign Office official in London was more explicit about the inorganic process of forming these types of unions, suggesting that, if possible, "we should endeavour . . . to put into control of labour unions at Kirkuk, and any other potential focus of trouble, labour leaders who are known to have anti-Communist views."[73] The company's own role in this process was markedly passive. Mainland, the IPC fields manager, indicated that he agreed with the idea of forming such unions only when urged to assent by the British ambassador.[74]

In any case, efforts to form these kinds of pseudo-union organizations were not successful. One report indicated that those whom the company called the "best workers" wanted nothing to do with unionizing after the disastrous end of the July 1946 strike.[75] "Genuine" unions aside, the IPC did eventually succeed in forming "joint consultative and welfare committees" of oil workers. Unlike the first Communist-led workers' committee that eventually led the 1946 strike, these committees met uneventfully on a regular basis with company officials to discuss the housing schemes and other welfare provisions, such as transportation, that affected IPC workers. Thirteen or fourteen of these committees operated in Kirkuk in the mid-1950s. From the company's perspective these committees were "a useful two-way channel of communication,"[76] but it is unclear whether they put IPC workers in a position to make any progress regarding issues that affected them.

IPC officials remained uneasy with the idea of their Kirkuki workers engaging in consultative activities that were out of their direct control, as indicated by an episode that took place in 1950. The International Labour Organization (ILO) held a conference that year in Geneva, and the British adviser to the Iraqi Ministry of Social Affairs, W. J. Hull, recommended that the Iraqi government send a delegation of Iraqi oil workers to the conference selected from the joint consultative committees in Kirkuk and at other oil fields. The IPC fields manager in Kirkuk at the time, P. R. A. Ensor, told Hull upon learning of the idea that he thought it would be "quite premature" to send any IPC workers to an international conference.[77] Hull nevertheless tried to find at least one oil worker in Kirkuk whom he deemed appropriate to represent Iraqi oil workers as part of a delegation. Despite the IPC's hesitation with this plan, Hull managed to find an English-speaking employee in Kirkuk who was a member of one of the joint consultative committees and whom he thought was suitable. However, the Iraqi government failed to support him, eventually sending a delegation to Geneva that did not represent the workers.[78]

The positions that the Iraqi government, the British government, and the IPC assumed in this episode reflected their attitudes toward engagement with Iraqi oil workers. The IPC remained reluctant to deal with their workers and with Iraqis in general on any explicitly political level even though they were closely involved with urban development, including human development efforts that made some headway toward giving valuable educational access to less privileged employees. On the other hand, British governmental representatives were keen to take clear, public steps to co-opt workers politically, using the company as a key site for their ongoing imperial project in Iraq. The Iraqi government in Baghdad maintained its distance from the politics of labor in Kirkuk even while urging the IPC to provide more benefits to their workers. The oil city's human and labor affairs, caught between the politics of the Iraqi and British governments and the IPC's interests as a mostly private enterprise, developed in occasionally unpredictable ways. But they brought about a growing number of opportunities, however conditional, for Kirkukis outside the local government to learn new skills, achieve literacy, and engage with the oil company politically. Those opportunities contributed to the growth of a distinct domain of local politics.

KIRKUK'S CIVIC IDENTITY: MODERNITY IN THE OIL CITY

Another aspect of the British and IPC political strategy in Kirkuk was the publicizing of their housing, infrastructure, and human-centered projects, particularly those that were led by the IPC. British public promotion of development in Kirkuk dovetailed with the Iraqi government's own ritual celebration of Development Board projects in periodic events such as the ceremonial Development Week in Baghdad.[79] The discourses of modernity that resulted from these efforts prioritized the city of Kirkuk as a focus of identity, holding that the prosperity the oil company had brought to the city was a distinctly Kirkuki achievement and source of pride.

These discourses coincided with a rise in literacy and the consequent expansion of Kirkuk's literary culture. A large new public library was built in Kirkuk sometime in the 1950s, and there was also a local library owned by the Muslim Brotherhood. In addition, beginning around this time, the IPC kept a library of mostly English-language books in the Arrapha Estate. In 1952 the local office of the United States Information Service also established a library of English-language materials in the city center under the direction of Lee F. Dinsmore, who would go on to serve as American consul in Kirkuk in the late 1950s. Along with the libraries, by the 1950s several bookstores in Kirkuk sold books and periodicals in multiple languages, including Arabic, Kurdish, Turkish, and English; some of the periodicals were themselves multilingual.[80] The members of the writing collective eventually known as the Kirkuk Group, who were among Iraq's most influential literary figures in the 1960s, came of age during this era, and a couple of them have subsequently noted that their interest in literature was first piqued by what they were able to read at these libraries and bookstores.[81] In a conversation with me, an Iraqi former IPC employee also fondly recalled, without my prompting, the history books he used to read at the library in the Arrapha Estate.[82] As the small percentage of literate people slowly grew and literary activity, however relatively limited, began to thrive in the oil city, Kirkukis and other Iraqis adopted and modified British-led discourses of oil-enabled modernity in the process of constructing a Kirkuki civic identity.

Beginning in 1951, the IPC strove to generate positive publicity for itself by promoting its housing projects and other works in Kirkuk through articles in its new monthly magazines: *Iraq Petroleum* and its Arabic-language companion publication, *Ahl al-Naft*. To some extent, these magazines were formed in the mold of the American magazine *Life*; they featured high-quality photographs on most pages, occasional crossword puzzles and cartoons, and human interest news stories from all the countries where the IPC operated. The English-language *Iraq Petroleum* emphasized the highlights of expatriate life in the Kirkuk oil fields, such as theater troupes and golf tournaments, for the benefit of a foreign audience.[83] When the magazine's focus turned to the city of Kirkuk, it celebrated the fact that development schemes using oil revenues had, in the words of one article, "transformed [Kirkuk] almost completely into a modern industrial suburbia."[84] The magazine's writers were particularly preoccupied with the ceremonies that ritualized this transformation, featuring photographs of Iraqi officials cutting ribbons to inaugurate new technology.[85]

According to the viewpoint expressed in these articles, Kirkuk's industry embodied its modernity and, as a result, its newfound identity. Another article referred to the oil fields' "B" power station, from which the company also provided the municipality with electricity, as the "beating heart of Kirkuk's industrialism."[86] Moreover, a common trope in *Iraq Petroleum* was the active contrasting of Kirkuk's long documented history and its relatively economically advanced present. In an article titled "Kirkuk Bridges the Centuries," a writer named Anne Kitchen depicted the contrast for readers.

> The most interesting feature to be noted in Kirkuk today is the fascinating juxtaposition of new and old from every conceivable view-point—the smith pursuing his craft in traditional fashion next door to the shopkeeper selling radios; Western dress jostling alongside Kurdish costume; it strikes the eye over and over again, and it is a clear sign of the times. For Kirkuk today is in the process of turning itself into a very modern and progressive town. . . . So today, while the dust blows across the shattered palaces of Babylon, and through the ruins of Nineveh, their splendour departed, their story written and finished, a town of similar great age, Kirkuk, is already well on the way towards establishing itself as a centre of outstanding importance in modern Iraq.[87]

As in many Western discussions of the "juxtaposition of new and old" in the Middle East, Kitchen simultaneously praised Kirkuk's long history while intimating that the region's "splendour" had remained untapped for generations, requiring a Western-led intervention to revive it in modern form.

The prevalence of this theme extended to many other Western portrayals of Kirkuk and of the oil-bearing parts of the Middle East in general. For instance, an American oil company's promotional film about the construction of the Kirkuk-Baniyas pipeline, which opened in 1952, begins by evoking the common idea that Kirkuk's natural gas fires were the biblical "fiery furnace." It concludes with a voiceover delivering the following monologue over a transition from a Western-style classical soundtrack to the quiet background of a traditional Middle Eastern oud.

> It was in the Middle East that Western civilization had its beginnings. Culture and commerce attained high levels there two thousand years ago, but later went into a decline. Now, with the aid of the Westerners who inherited and expanded

the scientific and cultural knowledge of the Middle East, the modern citizens of these ancient lands have gained enormously in material wealth and in a resurgence of industrial activity based in large measure on the development of petroleum reserves that would otherwise have lain dormant for long years to come.[88]

Ahl al-Naft, though targeting an Arabic-speaking audience with slightly different content, wholeheartedly embraced and used this temporal juxtaposition theme in its treatment of Kirkuk. The February 1958 issue featured a poem about Kirkuk titled "The Eternal Fire" (*al-Nar al-Khalida*), a reference to the perpetual natural gas fires of Baba Gurgur. The poem was credited to a writer named Bashir Mustafa.

> Kirkuk, O city of black gold,
> This flame of yours does not have a hearth
> as though your insides burned
> blazingly, bursting forth from a closed heart
> that complains with tongues of flame superiorly
> and the superiority of the complainers is the greatest glory
> and it draws with the lights the clearest picture
> of what grief and rebellion it suffers
> Kirkuk, I don't know! Did the verse of a poet
> shake my conscience unintentionally?
> Or my devil, which worships the Magi,
> saw, near the flame, the holiest temple![89]

In this poem Mustafa uses a form and meter common in classical Arabic poetry. The poet's references at the end of the poem to his "devil" (*shaytani*) and to the worship of the Magi are further indications of his engagement with pre-Islamic literary tropes. These archaic elements contrast starkly with Iraqi literary trends of the period in which the poem was written and published. Beginning in the late 1940s, the Iraqi poets Badr Shakir al-Sayyab and Nazik al-Mala'ika led the Arabic literary world in challenging traditional poetic forms through their innovative use of free verse.[90] In this context Mustafa's work comes across as bombastic, and his persistent descriptions of the Baba Gurgur fires with reference to Kirkuk create an unusually dramatic image of the city as volatile and passionate. The most striking aspect of the poem is the poet's reverence for Kirkuk's mineral resources. The fires that Mustafa glorifies are the surface-level manifestation of Kirkuk's natural gas. His concluding suggestion that he may have been moved to write the poem because the city of Kirkuk is "the holiest temple" emphasizes that this temple is "near the flame," the proof of the city's riches. The poem juxtaposes ancient images with the modern city; the phrase "city of black gold" comes to invoke both.

The inclusion of a poem about Kirkuk also reflects *Ahl al-Naft*'s more sustained focus on culture and, correspondingly, on cultural developments that would have been of interest to its pan-Arab readership. For instance, the August 1957 issue featured an article about the growing prevalence of drawing and painting in Kirkuk and of recent exhibitions to promote artists' work, describing these as a trend that augured a bright future; the article was called "An Artistic Movement in the City of Black Gold."[91] The IPC's magazines thus elevated various aspects of Kirkuk's history and the evolution of its society and economy while repeatedly and explicitly linking these attributes to the oil industry. In doing so, they sought to define distinctive elements of Kirkuki experience and to make the case that these elements were tied to oil modernity.

The tropes that the IPC magazines incorporated also appeared in the work of Arabic-language writers who were unaffiliated with the oil company. Iraqis writing about Kirkuk in Arabic used many of the same themes that characterized texts such as "The Eternal Fire." One example of the kinds of works about Kirkuk's past and present that began to appear in this era is a volume in a series of biographical dictionaries by 'Abd al-Majid Fahmi Hasan, an Iraqi Arab journalist, titled *Dalil Tarikh Mashahir al-Alwiya al-'Iraqiyya* (The Guide to the History of the Notables of the Iraqi *Liwa*'s).[92] Biographical dictionaries of provincial cities in the Islamicate world first appeared around the tenth century, when power in the Islamic caliphate had started to decentralize, lending greater political weight to areas on the margins of the empire.[93] The publication of the second volume in Hasan's series, a guide to the Kirkuk *liwa'*, in 1947 coincided with a growing interest in Kirkuk promoted not by a decline in Baghdad's leverage, as the medieval pattern might suggest, but rather by Kirkuk's own newfound prominence economically in Iraq. Hasan's series also coincided with a flourishing of intellectual production in Baghdad, especially in social and political history and geography, which stressed a separate Iraqi-territorial identity.[94] With respect to Kirkuk, this trend manifested as an interest in the city's distinct local identity as it was intertwined with its production of oil.

Hasan's series of biographical dictionaries was licensed by the Iraqi government's Directorate General of Propaganda. His volume on Kirkuk is correspondingly friendly to Baghdad and British interests in its tone.[95] The book combines the classic elements of a geographically localized biographical dictionary with chapters on the city and its hinterland that reflect its contemporary significance and its well-established identification with the production and export of oil. In keeping with the long-held customs of the genre, the dictionary contains detailed profiles of the preeminent male inhabitants of Kirkuk and surrounding areas along with histories and descriptions of elite Turkmen families and notable Kurdish and Arab tribes of the *liwa*'.[96] The earlier sections of the book, however, consist of exhaustive articles on Kirkuk's political history, geography, climate, agriculture, and particularly its oil industry. The book's introduction narrates a typical day in the journey of a train transporting passengers, mail, and goods northward from Baghdad and imagines it approaching, at nightfall, "the lights of glowing electric lamps and the tongues of the eternal fire." It continues:

> This is Kirkuk, the city of oil and factories, the axis of movement and activity, the center of one of Iraq's greatest *liwa*'s with respect to its present and its past, and the source of the enormous canal of oil that flows effusively toward the west . . . so that black gold pours into the white Mediterranean Sea.[97]

From the outset, Hasan frames the volume by juxtaposing evocations of Kirkuk's past, particularly the "eternal fire," with descriptions of the modernized, industrialized trappings of its present and the oil that has enabled them. Throughout the book he continues to stress the extent to which the city of Kirkuk has experienced dramatic changes between the past and the present; for instance, Hasan portrays the city as having become "overfilled with masses" of many types of professionals after the establishment of the oil industry encouraged immigration.[98] Hasan thus validates, in the typically regional context of the biographical dictionary, a key aspect of the British narrative of Kirkuk's character.

In other parts of the book Hasan echoes a number of ideas about Kirkuk that solidified in British-led discourses in the early to mid-twentieth century. When describing the city's population, Hasan writes that there are "three ancient Eastern *qawmiyya*s [nationalities]" in Kirkuk, "and they are: the Arab, the Turkish and the Kurdish." He later mentions "the Armenians and the Nestorians"[99] in passing as "minorities" (*aqalliyyat*) in the *liwa*' while downplaying the significance of these groups by incorrectly implying that all of the city's "minorities" immigrated to Kirkuk after World War I. Hasan thereby maintains an intact and simplified tripartite model of Kirkuk's demographics reminiscent of the framework used in the era of the Mosul dispute.[100] Furthermore, in his discussion of the IPC, Hasan describes at length the "genius" of the company's negotiator in obtaining the company's initial concession in 1925 and touts the company's housing and water schemes. He concludes by stating emphatically that the IPC has greatly helped Kirkukis, especially its own workers.[101] The volume therefore indicates the extent to which British frameworks for understanding Kirkuk's people and the position of the oil industry in the city had become standard by the late 1940s in Arabic-language Iraqi discourses on Kirkuk among those who were aligned with the Baghdad and British establishments.

Around the same time, Kirkuki intellectuals also started to participate in constructing an image of Kirkuk as a city with a rich history juxtaposed with a prosperous present. The example of Matba'at al-Tatwij (Coronation Press) and a book about Kirkuk that it published, *Madha fi Karkuk* (What's in Kirkuk), illuminates how the process of self-fashioning a civic identity as Kirkukis was bound to the oil industry in multiple ways. In the mid-1950s Shamasha Youkhanan Moushi Lazar, a deacon in the Assyrian Church of the East and a resident of Kirkuk, founded Matba'at al-Tatwij as an English- and Arabic-language commercial printing outfit with the IPC as its main client. For the first two decades of its operation in Iraq, the IPC had imported nearly all the materials it required, both industrial and mundane, from the United Kingdom—a practice that was yet another symptom of its isolation from urban Kirkuk. In concert with its other efforts to create an urban middle class in the early 1950s, the company began to purchase its necessities locally to encourage enterprise in the city, and Lazar took the opportunity to establish a press in order to print the IPC's forms.[102] Eventually, the press began to publish scholarly and literary books. At the time there was relatively little printing activity in Kirkuk compared with Baghdad; consequently, the few extant works that were produced in Kirkuk in this era provide a unique window into the discourses of the city's mid-twentieth-century literary and academic culture.[103]

Madha fi Karkuk, an Arabic-language informational volume on Kirkuk's history, culture, and economy written by the Turkmen novelist and scholar Fahmi 'Arab Agha, was published in 1957. Overall, Agha adopts a more academic approach and tone than Hasan does; the book documents details about Kirkuk's local social and political life with an apparent view to making this information available for future learning and scholarship. For instance, Agha features extensive informational tables on Kirkuk's largest tribes and their geographic locations, the *mutasarrif*s of the Kirkuk *liwa'* and the years that they served, and the numbers of students and staff members in Kirkuk's primary and secondary schools.[104]

Unlike Hasan, Agha also documents the lives of ordinary Kirkukis, including photographs of women in a domestic arts class and the local women's branch of the Red Crescent organization.[105] Nevertheless, though he does not praise the IPC quite as fulsomely as Hasan does, Agha also emphasizes the central role of oil in Kirkuk's affairs, calling it "the fundamental axis for all aspects of life." He features a series of photographs of Kirkuki IPC employees enjoying the benefits that working for the company has provided them, including one of a man standing in front of his new house built under the auspices of the home ownership scheme (Figure 11).[106] Agha died shortly before completing the volume; a subsequent author named Fadil Muhammad Mulla Mustafa enabled its eventual publication and appended a short obituary paying tribute to Agha's immense knowledge and his command of both Arabic and Turkish.[107] As an example of writing by a prominent Kirkuki intellectual of the 1950s era, *Madha fi Karkuk* illustrates the intricate ways in which oil had become a part of Kirkuk's civic identity and demonstrates the growing interest among the city's writers and publishers in constructing Kirkuk as a discrete arena of history, economy, and culture.

But there were also long-established writing traditions in Kirkuk before the oil era, including many famous poets. For instance, Turkish-language poetry by Kirkuki Turkmen and other Iraqi Turkmen writers was a prominent form of

FIGURE 11. An IPC employee stands in front of his new house, purchased under the home ownership scheme. The original caption describes him as "looking at his future with confidence and peace of mind after building a modern nest for his children." Source: Agha and Mustafa, *Madha fi Karkuk*, between pp. 104 and 105. Reproduced with permission from Kirkuk Press.

local cultural production in the Ottoman era, and Iraqi Turkmen poets continued to write in the same classical forms throughout the twentieth century. In the mid-twentieth century these poems, like other writings from and about Kirkuk, exhibited a strong Kirkuki identity. The poems elevate the city in effusive verses that stress the Turkmen community's attachment to it as a "homeland." This identity is therefore tied to a particular form of Turkmen ethnonationalism that, in turn, relies on the city of Kirkuk as the figurative (and, arguably, geographic) heart of the Turkmen community. As Orit Bashkin argues, the Iraqi Turkmen concept of nation in this era was linked to a more universal Iraqi identity, but it "marked in most cases the city [of Kirkuk] rather than the state."[108]

The view of Kirkuk's oil expressed in these poems is also telling with regard to the contrast it forms to the portrayals of oil in the English- and Arabic-language writings on Kirkuk discussed earlier. Although Turkmen poets place emphasis on oil as a positive and lucrative element of Kirkuk's physical being, this enthusiasm is sometimes tempered by the way that the oil has been exploited. For instance, in a *ghazal* simply titled "Kerkük" and dated 9 February 1953, the Turkmen poet Hıdır Lütfi deplores the fact that Kirkuk has become "a source of wealth for foreign nations."[109] Even when local discourses appeared to echo British-led conceptions of Kirkuk, Kirkukis who were not in the patronage of the IPC or the Iraqi government retained their suspicion of external authority; they expressed a sense of injustice about foreigners' domination of the oil industry that was reminiscent of Nazim Beg Naftchizada's impassioned complaints to the company in the 1920s.

The ideas of Kirkuk as Iraq's "city of black gold," as a bridge between antiquity and modernity in which elements of both eras were visible, and as a focus of cultural identity became increasingly universal in the 1940s and 1950s. But they were also malleable and were not necessarily politically unifying, despite the IPC's attempts to promote local identification with Kirkuk as part of the project to build a middle class. After the 1958 revolution, Kurdish nationalists' attempts to identify Kirkuk's oil with the Kurds would further illustrate the manner in which a Kirkuki identity could serve as an axis for different rigid ethnic group identities rather than as a basis for intercommunal conviviality.

CONCLUSION

In the 1940s and 1950s Kirkuk's local politics came to the fore. With the inauguration of a variety of urban development initiatives, policymaking and political maneuvering within the municipal and provincial governments—and between these local authorities and various external entities—achieved a level of sophistication that signaled the culmination of Kirkuk's growth into a provincial metropolis in its own right. This domain was part of an arena that included a broader civic identity based on a sense of shared culture and history. By the time of the Iraqi revolution in 1958, Kirkuk had developed a distinctive local character in which Kirkukis were deeply invested. Kirkukis, partly following the lead of the IPC and British authorities, articulated an increasingly coherent concept of Kirkuk's past and of its purpose as an oil city: an example of Iraqi modernity and the lifeblood that made the country's economic development possible.

Between 1946 and 1958 Kirkuk's oil played a variety of roles in the city's political, economic, and social affairs as they related to urban development and local discourse. First, oil provided the means, both in terms of revenue and the industry's own infrastructure advancement, for the undertaking of housing, water, and electricity projects as well as the reading and printing of books. The post-1946 housing schemes aimed to undermine the influence of the Iraqi Communist Party by instilling the characteristics of the middle class—in particular, savings and property ownership—in oil workers while attempting to avoid further political difficulties by prioritizing building within the city. The home ownership scheme also had the stated goal of giving oil workers a "stake" in the Kirkuki "community"; the cultivation of civic identity was therefore crucial to the creation of a middle class. At the same time, the oil city served as a site for competition among and cooperation between governmental and private actors, both local and Western. Underpinning all these interactions were the ideologies that characterized British and Iraqi approaches to urbanism: capitalism and a desire to achieve "enlightened" modernity through development.

Ultimately, however, Kirkuk did not escape the pattern of social segregation and stratification common to Middle Eastern oil cities and other variations on the colonial metropolis. The IPC's and Iraqi government's urban development projects, which usually focused on building and benefiting a middle class, had little positive impact on the poor. Kirkukis living in poverty, who were disproportionately Kurdish and much less likely to be on the IPC's monthly-wage or covenanted payroll, grew in number throughout the 1950s, as indicated by the rapid growth of the *mahalla* of Shorija. The division between the formerly dominant Turkmen community and the incipiently powerful Kurdish community would prove to be the first major fault line to destabilize Kirkuk after the 1958 coup.

5 THE INTERCOMMUNAL FIGHT

THE COUP THAT ABOLISHED IRAQ'S MONARCHY in 1958 interacted with volatile local dynamics in Kirkuk in deadly ways. It pitted the city's ethnic communities and associated political consortiums against one another in a manner that had been unknown in its modern history. After 1958 the Kirkuki Turkmen and Kurdish communities, as well as the Baghdad-based Iraqi state, publicly staked their claims to the city of Kirkuk, its history, and its oil. They did so both verbally and violently in a manner that indicated the full formation of a distinct but divisive Kirkuki civic identity in which there was no room for negotiation between ethnic groups.

Over the course of the previous four decades, the oil city had grown to accommodate tens of thousands of mostly Kurdish poor rural migrants, while the city's formerly dominant Turkmen elite had declined in proportion and influence but generally maintained their higher socioeconomic status. The organization of politics along the lines of left or right and poor or elite in revolutionary Iraq therefore dramatically intensified the ethnopolitical mobilization in urban Kirkuk that had already been evident for decades, albeit in a weaker form.

Kirkukis referred to these ethnic groups using a variety of different terms in Arabic implying nationhood or race, including *qawm*, *qawmiyya*, *'unsur*, and *ahl*. Their calls for unity among the *qawmiyya*s (*qawmiyyat*) or *ahl*s (*ahali*) were a sign that those categories had become more discrete and divided rather than a sign of pluralism. The eventual rise of Arabist governments that aimed to consolidate the influence of Arabs in Kirkuk sharpened these ethnic divisions still further. More so than at any prior time in the era of the modern Iraqi state, Kirkukis' interests after 1958 came to depend on whether they were Kurdish, Turkmen, Arab, or Christian.

A COUP, A REVOLUTIONARY REGIME, AND ARAB-KURDISH "PARTNERSHIP"

At about 4:30 in the morning on 14 July 1958, two brigades of the Iraqi army led by Brigadier General ʿAbd al-Karim Qasim and Colonel ʿAbd al-Salam ʿArif that had been ordered to march to the Iraqi-Jordanian border instead entered and occupied Baghdad. Qasim and ʿArif were members of the Free Officers, a clandestine revolutionary movement that had formed within the army in the early 1950s; in the mid-1950s the group began to grow in influence and started to plot an eventual overthrow of the monarchy. At around 8:00 a.m. on 14 July some of the Free Officer–led forces took over the Royal Palace, killing the entire royal family, including the young King Faysal II and his older and more powerful cousin, Crown Prince ʿAbd al-Ilah. The following day, forces tracked down and killed the old regime's frequent former prime minister and most powerful establishment figure, Nuri al-Saʿid. By all accounts, the coup met no popular resistance. In fact, once ʿArif announced the formation of the republic on the radio at about 6:30 a.m., his proclamation was greeted by supportive crowds demonstrating—and, before long, destroying property—in the streets of Baghdad. To some extent, these crowds consisted of followers of various Iraqi opposition groups, including the banned Communist and Baʿth Parties, which ordered their constituents to demonstrate in support of the coup under pressure from the new military regime. Narratives of the Iraqi revolution written from the vantage point of Baghdad typically emphasize, whether positively or negatively, its short-lived but intense celebratory chaos that soon necessitated the imposition of martial law. Some stress the brutality of the events of 14 July and its aftermath, including the public mutilation of the corpses of ʿAbd al-Ilah and Nuri al-Saʿid, acts that most Iraqis and international observers found repugnant.[1]

In Kirkuk there were no serious acts of violence, but the city also reacted to news of the coup with excitement. Fadhil al-Azzawi, a Kirkuk Group novelist who was 18 years old in 1958, recalled the Kirkuk Group's early experiences in an autobiographical essay.

> When the republic was announced in Iraq while we were still students in school, we felt that our lives had begun with the revolution. Suddenly, we found ourselves in the middle of a sea of people: processions in the streets, signs every-

where, speakers in the squares, crowded coffeehouses like on holidays. . . . The city no longer slept. . . . The revolution appeared to us, we who were still at the beginning of our literary lives, to look like an endless celebration all year long.[2]

Al-Azzawi's account reflects his intimate engagement, as a young man coming into social consciousness, with Kirkuki society and private life. From his vantage point the entire city was consumed with revolutionary fervor. Externally, though, visible activity in Kirkuk on 14 July and the following days appears not to have exceeded normal levels to an extraordinary extent. British accounts suggest that 14 July was a quiet day in Kirkuk, though not entirely without incident; some youths took to the streets and ended up attacking and damaging two British cars. Power passed promptly and peacefully into the hands of the Iraqi army's 2nd Division, whose headquarters were in the city. According to a report by the British consul in Kirkuk written nearly one month later, the notables of the *liwa'* reacted to 14 July with little concern one way or the other, instead adopting a "wait and see" approach.[3] Of course, the British perception that the revolution was uneventful in Kirkuk may have stemmed partly from their relief at the new regime's quickly expressed intent not to nationalize the Iraq Petroleum Company (IPC). On 19 July the commander of the 2nd Division personally delivered a message to the head of the IPC, reassuring him that the new government was interested in keeping Iraq's oil flowing without disruption and indicating a desire on the part of the revolutionary government to cooperate with the company.[4] The coup's immediate effects in Kirkuk were therefore subtler than in Baghdad, but its long-term effects were yet to be felt.

The revolution's reverberations shook Kirkuk in full force once the new regime, led by Qasim styled as prime minister, moved toward acceptance of the political parties under which Kurds in Kirkuk and surrounding regions had begun organizing in the 1930s and 1940s. Specifically, Qasim's government allowed the Iraqi Communist Party and the Kurdistan Democratic Party (KDP), which were politically allied with one another in northern Iraq, to operate freely, leading to the ascendance of Kurdish nationalist interests. The KDP was led by Ibrahim Ahmad in Iraq and chaired by Mustafa Barzani in exile. Barzani had emerged as the most prominent member of his family and thus as the primary leader of a unified Kurdish movement, but he had been forced to leave Iraq under duress after the collapse of his rebellion in 1947 and was, in 1958, in the Soviet Union. Both the KDP and the Communist Party, aware of the Free Officers' potential friendliness to their ideologies and activities, endorsed the coup in one way or another. Two days after the coup, Ibrahim Ahmad proclaimed his party's support for Qasim's regime and optimism for the Kurds' future in Iraq in harmony with the Arabs.[5]

Thereafter, in its earliest phase, Qasim's government was careful not to take any steps that could alienate Kurds; instead, it began to explicitly attempt to appropriate them as allies. Some scholars suggest that Qasim's own background of mixed heritage—his father was Arab, his mother Feyli Kurdish—was a factor in this seemingly pluralistic vision for Iraq.[6] A new provisional Iraqi constitution, drafted just after the coup and announced by Qasim on 27 July, stated in its Article 3 that "Arabs and Kurds" were "partners in this nation [*watan*]" and that the government recognized the Kurds' "national [*qawmiyya*] rights within Iraqi unity." The term *watan* for "nation" in this case evoked Qasim's brand of Iraqi-territorial nationalism, as opposed to pan-Arab nationalism. The constitution therefore offered Iraq's Kurds clearly stated recognition as a distinct *qawmi* community, but one that was included in the *watan*, for the first time. The immediately preceding Article 2, however, stated that Iraq was "part of the Arab nation [*umma*]," a pan-Arabist idea, indicating the Free Officers' internal conflict between Iraqi-territorial nationalist and pan-Arabist sympathies in which the latter occasionally prevailed.[7] Nevertheless, the regime took a number of steps to satisfy the demands of Kurdish nationalists in its first months, such as the establishment of the Directorate General of Kurdish Studies within the Ministry of Education in May 1959 to address Kurds' expressed educational concerns.[8]

As mentioned, the Iraqi Communist Party also indicated its support for the coup by prompting supportive demonstrations among their followers starting on 14 July. For the sake of his own legitimacy, Qasim was soon obliged to co-opt the Communists, who had the strongest base of popular support in Iraq, an impressive fact in light of their previously clandestine existence.[9] The Communist Party had a predominantly Kurdish membership in northern Iraq, including Kirkuk, by 1958. The nature of the party's activities in Kirkuk had thus come to be ethnicized since the Communists' initial appearance in Kirkuk's political scene among IPC workers in 1946, in spite of the fact that the party's leadership in the city remained diverse and nonsectarian.[10] Kurdish Communist activity became potent enough in the 1950s that the U.S. Department of State established a United States Information Service office in Kirkuk in 1952. Its purpose was to promote American ideas and culture through various forms of propaganda in the Kurdish areas of northern Iraq, including rural areas in Kirkuk's hinterland and beyond, with the goal of limiting the Communist Party's leverage. The office, which the Department of State converted into a consulate in 1957, used Kirkuk as a base for keeping track of increasing levels of Communist activity among Kurds in northern Iraq on behalf of the American diplomatic delegation based in Baghdad.[11]

The Communists themselves also used Kirkuk as a pivotal post from which to distribute letters and literature originating in Baghdad to various areas in northern Iraq.[12] In the years leading up to the revolution, Kirkuk had become a crucial frontier for the Communists in an effort that, in northern Iraq, took on an increasingly Kurdish cast and exhibited ties with the Kurdish nationalist movement. For instance, the British consul in Kirkuk wrote in August 1958 that Communists there were "active with an independent Kurdistan line" and expressed an intent to align themselves with Barzani.[13]

The role of Kirkuk's Communists in local politics in the immediate aftermath of the July 1958 coup was therefore enabled not only by Qasim's fostering of the Communist Party but also by his broader promise of Arab-Kurdish "partnership" and consequent cooperation with the KDP. At this early stage in the trajectory of revolutionary Kirkuk, the fates of the Kurdish and Communist movements were closely intertwined. The initial ascent of these movements under the Qasim regime's tutelage led to the appointment of politically active Kurds who were members of either the Communist Party or the KDP to several important local government posts in Kirkuk, including the mayor's office and the leadership of the court.[14] Although Baghdad's relationship with both parties would dramatically change in the next year, the rise to power of a large number of organized, politically active Kurds set the stage for an immediate deterioration in Kirkuki intercommunal relations. The Western entities that were attempting to limit the growth of Communist influence in Kirkuk were mostly removed in November 1958, when the Qasim regime ordered the closing of all foreign diplomatic missions outside of Baghdad, Basra, and Karbala.[15] The American and British consulates in Kirkuk never reopened.

TURKMEN-KURDISH FRICTION AND THE CYCLE OF INTERCOMMUNAL VIOLENCE

Politically active Kurds tended to be aligned with either the KDP or the Communists. Most of Kirkuk's long-entrenched Turkmen elite aligned themselves with the opposing pole in the revolutionary regime: the pan-Arabists and Ba'thists, who, in Baghdad, were linked to 'Abd al-Salam 'Arif, the 14 July coup's co-leader and Qasim's rival, and Gamal Abdel Nasser, the Egyptian president of the United Arab Republic (UAR). The UAR, formed in February 1958, was a union of Egypt and Syria into one state, a political project with pan-Arabist aims. Given the hostility of most Turkmen notables to Arab leadership during the era of the British Mandate, their sympathy for pan-Arabist movements three decades later may initially seem counterintuitive. However, their support for these movements stemmed not from any sort of devotion to the idea of Iraqi unification with Egypt and Syria but rather from their perception of the ascent of organized Kurds in local government as a threat to Turkmens as a community.[16] In addition, Turkmen political activity, unlike that of many Kurds, was typically not organized under the auspices of trade unions. Turkmens tended to hold positions in the middle- and upper-class socioeconomic strata. They were highly represented among the city's merchants, businessmen, artisans, and landowners; as discussed before, they were also particularly numerous among the IPC's Iraqi staff. Kirkuki Kurds, who were disproportionately poor laborers, whether for the IPC or other industries, were more receptive to unionizing and therefore benefited directly from the rise of the Communist Party.[17] The socioeconomic differences between Kirkuk's two largest ethnic communities therefore solidified and politicized their preexisting divisions.

The increasingly flammable tensions between the Kirkuki Turkmen and Kurdish communities met their first spark in October 1958, when Mustafa Barzani, upon receiving a passport sent by Qasim through an emissary to his temporary domicile in Prague, returned to Iraq after eleven years in exile. Mustafa Barzani's rebellion had long been supported by the entire Barzani clan, and other members of the family had also been punished under the monarchy. In a symbolic initial step one week after the 14 July coup, the new government freed Mustafa Barzani's brother, Ahmad Barzani, from a Baghdad prison, where he had been incarcerated for twelve years. Ahmad Barzani passed through Kirkuk and Arbil on the way back to his family's native Barzan in far northeastern Iraq, receiving popular support in both cities. Similarly, when Mustafa Barzani returned to Baghdad on 6 October, the Communist Party and other parties aligned with Qasim ensured that a cheering crowd would greet him at the airport.[18]

Barzani then toured Iraq, arriving in Kirkuk on 25 October. In anticipation of his arrival, Kirkuki Kurds, possibly with official backing, had festooned the city with banners associating Barzani with Qasim. In this instance the public lionization of the Kurdish nationalist leader and privileging of the theme of Arab-Kurdish partnership proved to be too provocative to pass without incident. Turkmens who were angered by the festivities tore down the pro-Barzani banners, starting a riot. The Iraqi army's 2nd Division responded quickly by imposing a curfew, breaking up crowds, and jailing a large number of people.[19]

Two days after the riot, a plane dropped leaflets on Kirkuk, evidently with the 2nd Division's permission or coordination, containing a statement in Arabic by eight of the city's most prominent citizens.[20] The day after that, the same statement was printed in the city's newly established bilingual Arabic-Turkish newspaper *al-Bashir/Beşir Gazetesi* (named for a village south of the city whose inhabitants were predominantly Turkmen). Using many different terms to describe Kirkuk's communities, the statement was issued in the name of the "Committee for National [*Watani*] Cooperation in Kirkuk" and was addressed to "the peoples [*ahali*] of Kirkuk: Arab, Kurdish, Turkmen, Assyrian, and Armenian." The statement decried "colonizers" for fomenting "division and hostility" between Kirkuk's "nationalities [*qawmiyyat*]." Expressing full-throated support for Qasim's agenda of reform for Iraq, the statement called for unity among the five mentioned "peoples" in order "to preserve our republic." It urged Kirkuk's citizens to live in "brotherhood, cooperation, calm and tranquility, to go about your normal activities, and to fight rumors propagated by the agents of colonialism." The signatures at the bottom of the declaration do not specify any communal affiliations but feature family names well known as affiliated with the Kurdish and Turkmen communities, most famously, the Kurdish Talabani and Barzinji families and the Turkmen retired military officer Ata Khayrullah.[21] In other words, at least a few prominent non-Kurdish Kirkukis were willing to publicly align themselves with Qasim and politically active Kurds in the early months of the revolution.

A self-identified Turkmen political organization also issued a declaration in response to the riot in which they described the day's events as follows:

> On October 25, 1958, the patriot Barzani returned from Suleimaniyya to Kirkuk on his way to Baghdad. Extremist Kurds who came from outside Kirkuk exploited this occasion and provoked the residents of Kirkuk by their banners and outcries against Iraqi unity in general and Turcomans in particular. One of these outcries was "Kirkuk is the city of the Kurds, and let foreigners leave" and Kirkuk being a Turcoman city is an indisputable fact. They marched in the streets of Kirkuk raising hostile banners and chanting "Down with imperialism and its agents," pointing at passers-by and those in cafés.[22]

The declaration, purporting to represent the views of "democratic Turcomans," is careful to avoid criticizing Barzani or *Kirkuki* Kurds directly, instead attributing the most disturbing aspects of the day's demonstrations to external forces and asserting support for Qasim as well as making the statement, "Long live Arab-Kurd-Turcoman fraternity." In continuation of the theme of blaming outsiders for trouble in Kirkuk, the declaration implies that Western expatriates in Kirkuk played a role in the rioting. The document ends with the proclamation "Death to imperialism, [and] its reactionary agents," a sentiment that echoes the slogan apparently chanted by Kurdish demonstrators.[23] Government officials were eager to promote this popular idea, which seemed to excuse Kirkukis from any wrongdoing. A rumor quickly spread in Kirkuk that the American consulate had caused the rioting. This led the commander of the 2nd Division, Nazim al-Tabaqchali, to take steps to limit the Americans' movements under the assumption that they were functioning as spies.[24] The report on these events that is available for public view in the National Archives of the United Kingdom is extensively redacted, making it difficult to judge the plausibility of accusations of foreign intrigue.[25] In any case, the ordered closure of foreign consulates in the city less than a month later could not have come as a surprise.

In both declarations the pointedly inclusive *watani* language coexists with the tacit acknowledgment that friction had developed between the groups defined within. The Turkmen document's emphasis on the "indisputable fact" of Kirkuk's Turkmen character betrays the salience of ethnicized politics and its role in turning Barzani's visit into an episode of interethnic strife. Al-Tabaqchali would later testify that the army troops sent to control the rioting divided up along Kurdish-Turkmen lines and fought one another.[26] The British consul's report on the events verified the Turkmens' claim that Kurds from other areas, particularly Arbil and Sulaymaniyya, were among those feeding the unrest on 25 October; al-Tabaqchali's troops had to prevent them from entering the city as the day wore on.[27]

The events of October 1958 were significant because they marked the beginning of a cycle of intercommunal violence between the Turkmen and Kurdish communities of Kirkuk. Smaller but nonetheless severe confrontations occurred in the ensuing months. Amid continuous tensions, some Kirkukis hoarded arms; in December 1958 a prominent Turkmen, Ibrahim Naftchi, and an Assyrian army officer in Kirkuk were arrested for illegal possession of weapons.[28] Then, an attack by armed Kurds on a Turkmen neighborhood in January 1959 led to a series of events that left several dead.[29] The clash of 25 October 1958 was also one of the first public episodes in which the city of Kirkuk became a battleground for Kurdish activists from outside Kirkuk; they had previously concentrated their activities in mostly rural areas north and east of Kirkuk.

In addition to physical violence, intellectuals also drew battle lines in written discourse. One noteworthy episode of the Turkmen-Kurdish competition for Kirkuk took place in the Baghdad newspaper *al-Ahali* in March 1959. *Al-Ahali*, which was the official newspaper of the Baghdad-based National Democratic Party (NDP), had long been a medium for the opposition under the monarchy, arguing in favor of democratic principles and featuring a variety of leftist ideological commentaries.[30] It had been shut down under the monarchy in 1954 but resumed publication in December 1958. Although the NDP was in contact with the Free Officers before the revolution and allied with Qasim following the coup, al-Ahali did not always serve as a mouthpiece for the new regime, allowing it to become a venue for organic debate. On 1 March a Turkmen writer from Kirkuk named Shakir 'Umar published an article in al-Ahali under the title "The History of the Nations of Iraq" (Tarikh al-Aqwam fi al-'Iraq). The article never mentioned Kirkuk, but it was plainly a manifestation of the ethnopolitical ideas that Kirkuki Turkmens had begun to adopt in response to their perceived marginalization in the city that they had once dominated.

'Umar's extremely dubious central argument was that civilization in the Iraqi region, extending back for several millennia, was of Turkish origin. While repeatedly using the adjective Turkish to describe Iraqi and Mesopotamian people and places, 'Umar consistently included "Turkmen" in parentheses afterward, thereby tying Iraqi Turkish speakers' relatively recent distinct identity as "Turkmens" to a broader and much older Central Asian heritage that, he claimed, gave birth to Mesopotamia. 'Umar referred to the Sumerian people of ancient Mesopotamia as "Sumerian Turks (Turkmens)." He offered apocryphal Turkish etymologies for the names of Iraqi and Mesopotamian cities; for instance, he claimed that the name Sumer came from a Turkish word meaning "suck" or "absorb," though without trying to explain why this word would be used as a place name.[31] In an echo of the pan-Arabist ideas that had come to influence Kirkuki Turkmens, 'Umar anachronistically described the Assyrian empire and its capital city of Nineveh as "Arab," implying that "Arab" was synonymous with "Semitic." Most strikingly of all, 'Umar asserted that the Kurds were descendants of a branch of the Turks that had split off—a claim that seemed to link the Kurds and Turkmens on the surface but attempted to subordinate the Kurds historically.[32]

A Kurdish student who was studying history in Baghdad at the time, Kamal Muzhir Ahmad, read 'Umar's article in al-Ahali and was incensed. He proceeded to write an incredulous and often indignant six-part response to the article that was published in al-Ahali throughout the rest of March 1959.[33] Part of Ahmad's goal was to straightforwardly refute 'Umar's more egregious distortions of history, but his arguments and rhetoric also revealed the underlying hostility between Turkmens and Kurds that catalyzed the exchange. For instance, Ahmad claimed that ʿUmar believed the Kurds of Arbil and Kirkuk in particular were "Turks," although ʿUmar had not explicitly stated this. Ahmad's assertion indicates his attention to a subtext, whether imagined or real, of Turkmen claims to rightful authority over those cities. Ahmad then went so far as to claim that the Turkmen presence in Iraq dated back four centuries at the most, thereby accepting ʿUmar's framework in which legitimacy was determined by a community's longevity. Ahmad argued that the Iraqi Turkmens were the descendants of Turkish soldiers who had been settled there by the Ottomans along a line running southeast from Arbil to Mandali, with Kirkuk in between, in order to strengthen the Ottoman position in the region.[34]

Decades later, after a long career as a history professor at Baghdad University, Ahmad recalled having been told by a friend in Kirkuk that people there had purchased the issues of *al-Ahali* in which his articles appeared and, owing to a lack of copies, passed them around to each other. The exchange between ʿUmar and Ahmad also generated other responses, including public approval of Ahmad's articles by a prominent Kurdish historian in Mandali.[35] Ahmad told me that the high demand for these issues led to their being sold at a much higher price than usual: up to 100 fils per copy, whereas the newspaper typically sold for 16 fils.[36]

This series of articles in *al-Ahali* reveals a dimension of the conflict between Turkmens and Kurds over Kirkuk that is not obvious when considering intercommunal violence alone, namely, the investment that these groups had in claiming their historical legitimacy in opposition to one another throughout northern Iraq but especially in Kirkuk. Both intellectuals, ʿUmar and Ahmad, accepted the premise that the question of which ethnic group arrived first in the region was crucial to determining their rightful political positions. Each therefore tried to delegitimize the other's community by offering a doubtful theory of their origin that implied that they had been the ones to appear later. What is especially noteworthy throughout ʿUmar and Ahmad's exchange is the power of Kirkuk as a subtext to the arguments, even though the city itself is seldom mentioned in them. In his recollection of how ʿUmar's article had initially angered him, Ahmad incorrectly claimed that ʿUmar primarily argued that Kirkuk was a Turkmen city—a conclusion perhaps implied by the combination of ʿUmar's Kirkuki background and his premise that Iraqi civilization was Turkish—but this was never explicitly stated in the article.[37] As for ʿUmar, his retreat into a bizarrely chauvinistic Turkmen-centered ideology of Iraqi (and, it is implied, Kirkuki) identity was an early form of what Güldem Büyüksaraç has described as "melancholic resistance" rooted in a sense of loss and used as a survival mechanism.[38]

By 1959 Kirkuk's Kurdish and Turkmen communities exhibited crystallized and antagonistic group identities, even though prominent citizens of the city publicly spoke in favor of intercommunal unity in the face of colonialism. The denial of intergroup strife while simultaneously blaming intergroup strife on foreign agents remains a common feature of sectarianized politics in Iraq and elsewhere.[39] Political commentaries that alluded to the importance of fraternal coexistence were nevertheless irreconcilable because they were profoundly invested in the idea of a rightful "national" ownership of Kirkuk. Furthermore, Kurds from outside Kirkuk also increasingly had a stake in its ethnic characterization.

14 JULY 1959 AND ITS AFTERMATH:
THE FIRST ETHNIC BATTLE FOR KIRKUK

In the meantime, evolving tensions between Iraqi-territorial nationalists and pan-Arabists in the Baghdad government, as well as Qasim's increasingly troubled attempts to maintain a relationship with the Communists that worked to his advantage, permeated the Iraqi provinces and interacted with local fault lines. Two serious challenges to Qasim's authority by pan-Arabists with ties to Nasser, including an attempted coup in December 1958, set off a chain of events that benefited the Communist Party. Qasim took the opportunity to marginalize 'Arif, declare himself the "Sole Leader" of Iraq, and force several other pan-Arabists and Ba'thists out of government positions. The Communists and those who were aligned with them or sympathetic to them maneuvered to fill the vacuum both in the government and in various civilian organizations. As a result, by the beginning of 1959 the Iraqi Communist Party was approaching the apex of its power and influence.

Free Officers of several ideological affiliations who were allied with the Nasser-Ba'th axis, along with political and religious conservatives, were angry at Qasim's maltreatment of 'Arif and viewed the Communist Party's rise with trepidation. Soon, officers in the Mosul army garrison, led by 'Abd al-Wahhab al-Shawwaf, would hatch a plan for a revolt against Qasim under the assumption that it would be supported by the UAR and local tribesmen.[40] In February 1959 the Peace Partisans, a Communist-aligned leftist group, decided to hold a rally in the city of Mosul in the first week of March as a show of force in response to reliable rumors of an anti-Qasim plot. They announced their intent in the Iraqi Communist Party's newly authorized official newspaper, *Ittihad al-Sha'b*.

The Peace Partisans initially received Qasim's full approval, including support through the state media and even the scheduling of extra trains to allow an enormous influx of party members, sympathizers, and government supporters to get to the city.[41] Al-Shawwaf openly voiced his strong disapproval of the rally to Qasim, but the massive Communist-backed event nevertheless went ahead on 6 March. By 7 March it devolved into clashes that fell along numerous party and tribal lines loosely corresponding to the pro-Qasim and pro-UAR sides. On 8 March al-Shawwaf declared the planned revolt against Qasim, accusing him of having "betrayed" the revolution. He named Nazim al-Tabaqchali, Kirkuk's 2nd Division commander, as a supporter of the revolt. Four days of extremely violent and complex turmoil followed in Mosul in which about 200 people died; al-Shawwaf himself was killed on 9 March. Forces loyal to Qasim regained control on 12 March. Al-Tabaqchali and other suspected co-conspirators in the revolt were swiftly arrested and taken to Baghdad.[42]

The horrors of March 1959 proved to be a fleeting but tremendous gain for the Communist Party politically, including in Kirkuk. In the midst of a highly charged political and social atmosphere throughout Iraq in which competitions for authority were taking place at all levels in both physical and discursive spaces, the leader of the Kirkuk-based 2nd Division was imprisoned and charged with a capital crime, and his replacement was a Communist: Brigadier Dawud Salman 'Abbas al-Janabi, an Arab member of the Communist Party, who took over the command position on 14 March.[43]

However, despite Qasim's growing reliance on the Communists for support in the face of active insurgent opposition among his own troops, he had no intention of allowing them to grow so strong as to threaten his own nonpartisan position. He therefore began the uneasy process of achieving a balance between appeasing the Communist Party through certain appointments and policies while dismissing army officers with links to the Communists.[44] Meanwhile, during his tenure in Kirkuk, al-Janabi actively quelled the influence of those who opposed the Communists, shutting down Turkmen-run newspapers such as *al-Bashir/ Beşir Gazetesi* and exiling and imprisoning Turkmens who were openly against Qasim's government.[45]

On 1 July 1959, just a few months after ordering him to assume the command of the 2nd Division in Kirkuk, Qasim had al-Janabi fired. Al-Janabi was later arrested along with five other army officers who were suspected of Communist ties.[46] Meanwhile, in the wake of the Mosul disaster, provincial northern Iraq continued to be riven by clashes between people aligned with and against the Communists and between rival tribes, especially in predominantly Kurdish areas.[47] The events of the spring and early summer, beginning with Mosul and culminating in al-Janabi's arrest, agitated the overwhelmingly Kurdish popular base of the Communist Party in Kirkuk and, in turn, the mostly Turkmen local faction who opposed them. Both sides felt the need to publicly demonstrate their dominance over the city. On top of everything else, Kirkuk was suffering a high unemployment rate because of the suspension of development activities after the 1958 coup.[48] It was in this context that the worst episode of intercommunal violence in Kirkuk since the founding of the modern Iraqi state occurred on 14 July 1959, the first anniversary of the revolution.

The precise details of what happened on 14 July 1959 and the next couple of days vary widely in different tellings. Hanna Batatu's thorough analysis of the event, based on interviews and his one-time access to Kirkuk's municipal records, is generally considered the definitive and most reliable account.[49] Among the other versions of the story available for study are reports submitted to the British Foreign Office, which tended to be based on secondhand information because of the absence of a consulate in Kirkuk; a detailed memorandum by "Turkmen citizens" dated 18 July 1959, which has been reproduced in multiple books; and a detailed interview conducted by Güldem Büyüksaraç with a Kirkuki Turkmen expatriate in Turkey whom Büyüksaraç calls Resmiye Hanım, who was 11 years old when the violence occurred and witnessed it firsthand.[50] It is unsurprising that each account, including Batatu's, is subtly different in its interpretation of the events, and the variations correspond with the teller's political vantage point. As a result, many historians of Iraq have refrained from offering a detailed analysis of the events, simply noting that they were bloody and chaotic. In the words of one such historian, "Unfortunately, matters got out of hand."[51] However, a close reading of what occurred in Kirkuk is necessary to expose the specific ways in which intercommunal tensions presented primarily as claims to Kirkuk's civic identity and therefore to urban space.

For example, it is telling that, as in the case of the banners linking Barzani and Qasim that caused offense in October 1958, the clash of 14 July 1959 evolved out of a dispute over public visual symbols of political engagement and ascendancy that appeared in communal areas and were tied indirectly to socioeconomic class. In the months following the 1958 coup, organized groups in Kirkuk built a large number of triumphal arches in the city to express their support for the revolution and, in doing so, appropriate its popularity for their own interests. The hasty construction of these kinds of showy temporary structures was a common response to military victories in the region and had occurred in modern Iraq as early as 1933.[52] In revolutionary Kirkuk these arches became a point of pride, and therefore of competition, for those who erected them. Turkmens, who typically had more money, would even provoke the Kurdish community by building larger and more elaborate arches in the vicinity of arches that had been put up by Kurds.[53] The aforementioned Turkmen memorandum characterized the building of these celebratory arches as a primarily Turkmen endeavor intended to demonstrate their community's loyalty to the new regime, maintaining that Turkmens had built more than 130 arches featuring pictures of Qasim and Iraqi flags.[54] These details, whether or not they are accurate, reflect a forthright attempt by Turkmens to promote the notion that they, and not the Kurds and the Communists, were the genuine supporters of Qasim.

In the days preceding 14 July, local Kurdish affiliates of the Communist Party planned to further advance their claim to Kirkuk's public space by staging a demonstration in the city's traditional center on the anniversary of the revolution. The Turkmen community planned their own demonstration for the same day, apparently in response to the challenge. Kirkuk's chief of police, an Arab with Communist sympathies, wrote in a 15 July letter to Kirkuk's *mutasarrif* that "in view of the deep-rooted enmity between the Kurds and the Turkmen," the police took "appropriate precautionary measures" ahead of the planned marches.[55]

Accounts generally agree that the day began with peaceful, uneventful demonstrations that met in the center of the city (Figure 12). The processions paraded on two bridges across the Khasa River: a bridge near the location of the nineteenth-century stone bridge, which had been demolished in 1954, and a newly built bridge to its south.[56] The Turkmens were in traditional dress, and men, women, and children were among them. Some of the Turkmens seem to have been riding in decorated trucks, which the Kirkuk chief of police inexplicably described as "army vehicles." Accounts consistently state that they were unarmed.

At the same time, a procession of people carrying ropes was marching toward the Turkmen parade. The Kirkuk chief of police described the marchers as "soldiers," whereas Büyüksaraç's interviewee, Resmiye, described them simply as "Kurds" and "Communists."[57] This lack of clarity as to who the seemingly armed marchers were reveals the extent to which armed groups (including the army and civilian forces), Communist organizations, and Kurdish organizations had become blurred together in the popular imagination of revolutionary Kirkuk. Batatu speculates that these marchers may have belonged to military detachments that had been close to al-Janabi.[58] At the time, P. T. Hayman of the British embassy in Baghdad implied that they were commonly thought to be members of the Popular Resistance Force, a government-organized militia that

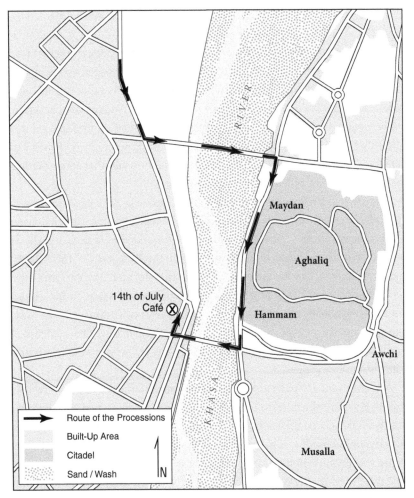

FIGURE 12. Locations of the events of 14 July 1959 in Kirkuk. Based on a map by Hanna Batatu, with corrections from other contemporary maps. Source: Batatu, *Old Social Classes*, 916.

had come to have Communist ties.[59] Although it is now impossible to know for certain whom they were representing, it is accepted in most accounts, including contemporary ones, that they were Kurdish. The implication that the Turkmens presented themselves as ornately dressed while the Kurds appeared in uniform and militarized also indicates the prevalence of commonly perceived differences in socioeconomic status between these groups, status differences that would mark them as having distinct political interests.

That evening, an altercation began in the vicinity of a well-known coffee-house, the 14th of July Café (recently named, of course, for the 1958 revolution), located near the older bridge on the west side of the Khasa, directly across from the citadel. More than one account states that the dispute began as a result of a visual element involving a political slogan. Hayman claimed that the offending object was "some Turkish writing on a decorative arch."[60] An account that appears to have originated with an American oil executive, based on multiple sources, claims that the owner of the 14th of July Café, a Turkmen named Osman, had displayed political slogans inside and outside his shop and that some Kurds of uncertain affiliation ordered him to remove them.[61]

There are also reasons to believe that this dispute at the café was primarily ethnically charged rather than a political or ideological dispute that happened to fall along ethnic lines. The American account makes the claim that, earlier in the day, "army trucks began blaring out insults to the Turkomen."[62] This memory bears a resemblance to Resmiye's recollection that the marchers carrying ropes were yelling "turani," a racial term for people of Central Asian Turkic descent that was occasionally used in Iraq at the time to refer to Turkmens.[63] The Turkmen demonstrators' choice to wear traditional clothing may well have intensified both the visual and ethnic dimensions of the rivalry between demonstrators from both ethnic groups.

At some point around 7 in the evening, shots of unknown origin were fired, causing a violent skirmish to break out. The Kurds were armed and therefore quickly overwhelmed the Turkmens. A mob killed Osman and publicly mutilated his body; one account says his body was hung from a tree, whereas others say the corpse was dragged in the streets in a manner reminiscent of the treatment of 'Abd al-Ilah and Nuri al-Sa'id one year earlier.[64] Osman's death was the beginning of a lengthy and grisly spectacle. The Kirkuk police chief wrote that about twenty other Turkmens were lynched that evening and that seventy Turkmen-owned businesses were looted.[65] The authors of the Turkmen memorandum written four days later thought that it was important to point out that the mob also tore down and burned some of the triumphal arches with Qasim's picture and Iraqi flags on them, indicating, they imply, a distinct lack of patriotism on the part of the Kurds.[66] That the competition between Kurds and Turkmens for political legitimacy in revolutionary Kirkuk continued in subtle ways in the immediate aftermath of a public bloodbath is remarkable.

There is little question that the violence consisted mostly of armed Kurds, whether civilian or affiliated with the military or a militia, attacking Turkmen civilians. Resmiye recalls that when the fighting began, she and other Turkmen children who had been part of the procession were led to nearby military head-quarters for their own safety. They hid there until about midnight while shots rang out all around them.[67] This memory corresponds with Hayman's report that "some of the Turkish community managed to barricade themselves inside an old fort."[68] In the meantime, people aligned with the attacking mob—who, by the Kirkuk police chief's account, were members of the Popular Resistance Force—broke into the Imam Qasim police station and took weapons from its arsenal. According to Batatu, a witness later testified that this group yelled an anti-Turkmen slogan as they emerged from the station with police rifles.[69]

For the next two days armed Kurds attacked Turkmen targets in Kirkuk's traditional core, where Turkmens remained the majority of the population. Many Turkmen men perceived to be hostile were detained and held hostage, and some were killed. Kurds from the local army division joined the fight, bombarding houses in the citadel with shells and destroying two Turkmen-owned cinemas.[70] A group of Communists from Kirkuk later claimed in a memorandum that the army had been fired on from these locations and was forced to return fire.[71] This allegation is not easily confirmed or disproved. Before the shelling of the citadel, Resmiye recalls, its residents, including her family, were warned that a bombardment was imminent and that they should evacuate the area. After Resmiye and her family took refuge at a relative's house outside the citadel, armed men captured and detained her father, uncle, and grandfather. These men and others were later found imprisoned in a school, having been deprived of food and water for a couple of days in the stifling July heat, though they were otherwise unharmed.[72] These details suggest that the attackers aimed to assert dominance over both Kirkuki Turkmens as people and the Kirkuk citadel as a historic symbol.

On 16 July forces from Baghdad finally arrived in Kirkuk and ordered the 2nd Division and the Popular Resistance Forces to return to their base or their homes. The violence came to an end by 17 July. Kurdish soldiers who had been firing on civilian targets were disarmed.[73] The final official count of the dead was 31, with about 130 injured; most of the people in both categories were Turkmens, and the actual number of dead was probably higher. Among the Turkmens killed was Ata Khayrullah, the Turkmen community leader who was one of the signatories to the October 1958 unity statement that appeared in *al-Bashir/Beşir Gazetesi*.[74] Twenty-four out of the 28 people who were eventually convicted of perpetrating these crimes were Kurds.[75]

The Kirkuk attacks riveted Iraq and devastated the standing of the Communist Party nationwide. Qasim took advantage of the horror of the events to crack down on the party by arresting hundreds of its members, shutting down various associated organizations, demobilizing hundreds of troops, and dismissing officers from Communist-influenced military units. He also had graphic photos of the victims displayed on national television and publicly used strong language against the accused perpetrators of the attacks, though he stopped short of explicitly denouncing the Communists as an organization. Nevertheless, July 1959 marked the beginning of the Iraqi Communist Party's fall from its apogee of influence.[76] Communists also lost their position within the KDP when Mustafa Barzani forced out executives who were sympathetic to the party.[77]

The Communist Party itself, whose central leadership had no role in the events, worked hard to distance itself from the perpetrators of violence against civilians, though, as mentioned before, at least some party members tried to argue that the Turkmens had opened fire on the 2nd Division. *Ittihad al-Sha'b* took a more hackneyed approach, blaming the initial shots that set off the violence on "conspirators" in a "colonialist plot."[78] Although vocal opposition to colonialism and imperialism had itself long been a prevalent local mode of political thought, this contention had remarkably little impact in the context of ethnicized political violence in the revolutionary era.

Qasim's curbing of the Communists in 1959 led to frequent killings of affiliates of the Communist Party throughout Iraq, particularly in the city of Mosul, where right-wing religious and political elements were especially influential. This "reign of terror," in Batatu's words, also spread to Kirkuk, where the massacre had created a deep-seated resentment of the Communist Party among much of the city's population. The influence of officers who were sympathetic to these anti-Communist purges was such that they were able to take place relatively openly. Iraqi politician Kamil al-Chadirchi even told Batatu that "well-known merchants of the city [of Mosul] offered as high as ten dinars for dead members of the party."[79]

The exact number of victims of these ideologically motivated killings in Kirkuk is probably impossible to know. One assassination, though, was widely reported at the time in international media: the shooting death of the well-known leftist Eugene Shamoun in August 1960. Shamoun was shot at least ten times on the doorstep of his home by multiple gunmen.[80] His legacy has persisted in the memory of many Kirkukis because of his prominence in the city as the owner of Eugene's Bookstore (Maktabat Yujin). The bookstore sold used books in English and a variety of Marxist and leftist works. It was an influential institution for Iraqi Communists and for Kirkuki intellectuals, including members of the Kirkuk Group.[81]

One of several members of the Kirkuk Group whom Shamoun influenced, the poet and journalist Anwar Al-Ghassani, wrote many years later that Shamoun's assassins had been "reactionary Turcoman thugs."[82] This detail, whether or not it is true, corresponds to the ethnicized political correlations most Kirkukis would have made at the time—for instance, the assumption that Turkmens were particularly predisposed to be politically conservative because of their instinct to preserve their historic position in Kirkuk and because of the association of communism with Kurds. However, Shamoun and his associates illustrate how these categories, despite their simple appearance, were much more complex at the margins.

Shamoun's own political activity, like that of so many forgotten victims of the city's violence, was not ethnicized or otherwise sectarian in nature. His preferred and professed self-identity is not indicated in contemporary sources, but his name indicates that he was of Christian, likely Chaldo-Assyrian, origin. The Kirkuk Group self-consciously characterized itself as multiethnic; for instance, Al-Ghassani himself was of mixed Turkmen and Arab heritage.[83] The polarization of revolutionary Iraq, and subsequently of Kirkuk, had little room for these nuances. Whereas nonsectarian communism had managed to briefly take hold among Kirkuki workers in the 1940s, overshadowing other political trends that revolved around ethnicity, such ideologies had since become subsumed under the rubrics of ethnic nationalisms in Kirkuk.

Indeed, one of the ramifications of the chaotic post-1959 political environment was the gradual exodus of a large percentage of the Kirkuki Chaldo-Assyrian community because the most powerful factions in Kirkuk did not serve their interests. Among those who did remain, there was a profound sense of alienation with the political changes that had taken place in Kirkuk. The late Daniel Benjamin, an Assyrian former IPC employee whose family owned a printing press in Kirkuk, recalled in an interview with me in 2011 that he used to print custom cards for his community for occasions such as Christmas and weddings, selling thousands per year during the monarchy era. After 1958 he was no longer able to sell them and still had a surplus of cards he had printed in 1957 when he left Kirkuk a decade later.[84] In the IPC Chaldo-Assyrian employees also tended to leave Kirkuk, transferring to positions in Baghdad or emigrating from Iraq entirely.[85]

I should note that many aspects of the events of July 1959 remain strongly contested. The most controversial question is whether or not the attacks on the Turkmen community were premeditated by those acting as representatives of Kurds or the Communists as a group. The belief that such an operation had long been planned by the Communists was common; for instance, al-Tabaqchali, the imprisoned former commander of the 2nd Division, mournfully told a lawyer upon hearing of the events that the Communists had been planning such a massacre since he had been in Kirkuk but that he had prevented them from carrying it out for as long as he was there.[86] Al-Tabaqchali continued to pursue this line while on trial for his alleged complicity in the Mosul violence, though he was ultimately unsuccessful. He was convicted and executed for his role in those events in September 1959.[87] The Turkmen memorandum submitted to Qasim on 18 July made a different claim that has since become very common among Turkmens: that the massacre was part of a "genocidal war against the Turkmen race [al-ʿunsur al-turkumani]."[88] Even Batatu makes the error of overemphasizing the presence of "inveterate enmity"—"almost instinctive," he suggests—between Kurds and Turkmens in the process of exonerating the Iraqi Communist Party of wrongdoing in the attacks.[89]

However, the attacks of July 1959 in Kirkuk were like the 1924 attack in that they were eruptions in the city's historic residential and commercial centers—even long after the urban fabric had expanded well beyond that core—that threw into relief the idiosyncratic ways in which local politics had developed in recent years. In this case the racialized language used by Turkmens to describe the event, considered along with the stark communal differences between the perpetrators and the victims regardless of their organizational affiliations, is salient. Namely, the strongest forces in Kirkuk's politics had shifted from alignment with a pro- or anti-centralization dichotomy to alignment with discrete and mutually hostile ethnic—or "racial"—categories. The new forces prioritized control over the city of Kirkuk itself, politically, historically, and symbolically, as a distinct and crucial political domain.

THE UNDOING OF THE IPC'S POSITION IN KIRKUK

The political dysfunction of the revolutionary era in Kirkuk affected the operations of the IPC. British influence throughout Iraq declined dramatically after the 1958 revolution, particularly after the expulsion of consuls in provincial areas, but the IPC remained as an outpost promoting a combination of imperial and private interests at its headquarters near Baba Gurgur. Government-led development projects with foreign involvement were suspended, but the IPC's internal projects, such as the home ownership scheme, continued.[90] The new regime, as previously mentioned, was quick to assure the company that it did not intend to nationalize the oil industry, but within a few weeks the Directorate General of Labour and Social Security made it clear that the revolutionary government intended to keep close track of the company's activities. In a 31 July 1958 letter the directorate requested that the IPC "do their best to avoid arbitrary disbandment of labourers" and demanded that no worker be fired without first consulting the directorate as to the reasons for the discharge. The IPC responded defensively that they reserved their right to let employees go, but the directorate repeated in further correspondence that they were to be informed of the reason given for any firing of an IPC worker.[91] In 1960 the government suspended the laying off of workers altogether under the stipulation of martial law.[92]

Iraq's revolutionary politics also affected hiring decisions and promotions, which often hinged on workers' political affiliations. In the early Qasim era the IPC was pressured into recruiting affiliates of the Communist Party, many of whom had recently been released from prison; when Qasim's relationship with the Communists soured, these new employees were often incarcerated again.[93] Just as individuals who had political connections that were advantageous (at a given moment, anyway) could gain employment, existing employees who lacked these connections found their attempts to rise in the company thwarted. For instance, Daniel Benjamin was working as the chief clerk of the IPC's stores department in 1958 and did not belong to any political party. He failed to receive a previously expected promotion to a covenanted staff position following the revolution. After nine years without receiving the promotion, he transferred to a job in Kuwait.[94]

Turkmens in particular faced dismissal from the IPC during the wave of Communist influence in 1959, often accompanied by accusations that they were pan-Turkists or Ba'thists.[95] Furthermore, these kinds of problems were pervasive outside the oil industry in Kirkuk. For example, at al-Tabaqchali's trial in August 1959, the director of a women's teaching college in Kirkuk who had been transferred there recently by Qasim testified that pan-Arabist, anti-Communist colleagues actively prevented her from doing her job. According to her account (which did not specify her ethnicity or any communal self-identity), she was nonpartisan, but students and staff nonetheless held a demonstration against her tenure and attacked her under the assumption that she was a Communist.[96] Even the contents of the IPC's private Arrapha Estate library changed with ascendant waves of political influence; Communists, pan-Arabists, and Ba'thists looted the library in succession and restocked it with texts that reflected their ideological inclinations.[97]

The Qasim regime's attempts to assert authority over the IPC's employment practices proved to be a major problem for the company once the government left no doubt that it intended to either prompt or force the company to relinquish the rights to most of the lands in its concession where exploration had not yet taken place. This move met with the approval of the Iraqi population, among whom resentment of the IPC's monopoly and its 50% share of the country's oil revenues was commonplace. When negotiations between the IPC and the government over what percentage of the lands to relinquish broke down in 1961, the legislature passed Law No. 80, shutting the company out of 99.5% of its previous concession outside of areas already being exploited.[98] The law immediately rendered redundant hundreds of employees in geophysical exploration nationwide and, in the company's view, created the possibility that 3,000 more employees engaged in jobs such as drilling would also prove to be surplus labor. The IPC futilely sought permission from the government to discharge these employees a few hundred at a time, even claiming that this intention reflected their good faith acceptance of the terms of Law No. 80, but Qasim declared publicly that he intended to preserve all Iraqis' jobs in the oil company. IPC officials feared the consequences of the impasse for the morale of their workforce and the subsequent negative political effects this mood could have, particularly because so many workers lived physically close to the headquarters in company housing.[99] The high rate of unemployment already prevailing in northern Iraq could not have helped. The IPC's G. W. Herridge openly admitted in a conversation at the British Embassy in Baghdad that the company was trying to "indoctrinate their Iraqi employees with the idea" that the problems caused by Law No. 80 were Qasim's fault.[100] Qasim's government also provoked the company's ire by trying to push along the undertaking of replacing expatriate staff with specially trained Iraqis, which both the company and the government termed "Iraqi-isation," through tactics such as obstructing visa processing and withdrawing foreign staff members' work permits without warning once it was determined that those individuals could be replaced by Iraqis.[101]

While the company viewed Qasim's oil and labor policies with a combination of annoyance, fear, and barely concealed disdain, the government exhibited a certain level of sincerity in its desire to continue to collaborate with the company, as indicated by its commitment to the ongoing Kirkuk urban water scheme for which the IPC provided material support and installations. However, like the monarchy-era government before it, the revolutionary regime attempted to coax the company into bearing the costs of as many aspects of the project as possible. In 1962 company official N. M. Ekserdjian complained in an internal letter that the Kirkuk municipality owed the IPC about £150,000 and was making no attempt to pay this debt or to make improvements to a well portion of the water system that would soon run dry, creating an emergency that, Ekserdjian warned, the municipality would probably expect the company to address. Ekserdjian suggested relieving the municipal government of its debt on the condition that they assumed all responsibility for the city's water supply, freeing the company of any future obligations.[102] This idea appears not to have been followed up by either the company or the municipality. On the contrary, after 'Arif had ousted both Qasim and the Ba'th in 1963, the new minister of oil contacted the company yet again with a request that the IPC bear the costs of a water project to expand upstream irrigation on the Lesser Zab without affecting the supplies of the company and the Kirkuk municipality. The IPC responded in a scathingly worded letter a few months later that it had no intention of doing so.[103]

In the absence of a government amenable to its interests, the oil company saw no need to continue its 1940s- and 1950s-era policy of cooperating with the local and national authorities to leverage its influence. The death of the collaborative, and mutually manipulative, relationship between the IPC and the government through development projects signaled the inexorable decline of the British position in revolutionary Iraq. The Iraqi government created a state-run oil company in 1966 and, under 'Abd al-Rahman 'Arif, bolstered its control over the development of oil fields through two laws passed in 1967.[104] Sclerotic negotiations eventually culminated in the nationalization of the IPC in 1972 under the second Ba'th republic.[105] From then on, as will be discussed in the next chapter, the formerly complex politics of oil workers' interests and oil-funded development in Kirkuk were entirely subjected to Baghdad's authority.

THE KURDISH WAR AND EMERGING
KURDISH CLAIMS TO KIRKUK

Another one of the most important political changes in Iraq after 1958, which appears especially momentous with the benefit of hindsight, was the addition of a notion of Kirkuk as a *Kurdish city* and as a crucial part of Kurdish ethnic identity to Kurdish nationalist discourses. Because this shift was subtle, it requires some explanation and qualification.

As discussed in previous chapters, notions of the Kirkuk *region*, a concept usually corresponding to the borders of the Kirkuk *liwa'*, as part of a loosely defined greater Kurdistan region dated back at least to the 1920s. Some Kirkuki Kurds, especially those in mostly Kurdish rural areas, had long explicitly expressed a desire to join such an entity. However, the largely Turkish-speaking *city* itself and the elements associated with urbanism—most notably, the oil industry—were not a significant battleground, whether geographically or ideologically, for Kurdish nationalists in the monarchy era. Moreover, the notion often encountered today that Kirkuk is the "heart of Kurdistan"[106] evidently did not exist yet to any consequential degree.

The character of Kurdish nationalist portrayals of Kirkuk and its oil changed quickly after the 1958 revolution, when Kurds started to explicitly stake their claims to Kirkuk as a Kurdish city. For instance, on 18 July 1958, just a few days after the 14 July coup, the British consul in Kirkuk reported that some prominent Kurds were promoting the idea that "Kirkuk oil is Kurdish oil" through cards they had made for an Islamic holiday.[107] It is not clear where the Kurds distributing these cards were located, but what is known about the October 1958 riots following Mustafa Barzani's visit suggests that it was Kurds from outside the city who spearheaded some of the most strident ethnonationalist sloganeering in Kirkuk. The Kurdish movement, which was centered in areas northeast of Kirkuk, began to permeate the city's political domain and was particularly invested in appropriating its trappings of urban modernity. The movement also came to distance itself from the Iraqi Communist Party, thereby severing ties with what had been a major nonsectarian ideological force among politically active Kurds.

The Kurdish separatist rebels associated with this movement, who were based in regions such as Barzan, did not use physical force in the Kirkuk area right away. They had avoided staging uprisings in the city of Kirkuk in its hinterland before 1958, or perhaps had simply failed to do so. But Kirkuk evolved into a battleground when war broke out between the Kurds and Baghdad in the early 1960s. The war was a consequence of the fact that, from the beginning, the new government had been loath to consider granting the Kurds the autonomy they demanded to any extent, despite its overtures to the KDP.[108] Relations between Qasim and Kurdish leaders therefore started to fall apart by early 1961. The Education Ministry's early gestures to Kurdish education notwithstanding, Qasim canceled a congress of Kurdish teachers in February 1961 and issued a corresponding declaration in which he claimed that the term *Kurd* had its origins in an ancient military honorific, thereby downplaying the legitimacy of Kurdish nationalist claims. This public statement reversed the trend that had started with the Kurds' recognition in the provisional constitution.[109]

In March 1961 the ongoing cycle of intercommunal violence in Kirkuk continued in a clash of obscure origin between Kurds and Turkmens that left 7 dead and more than 100 injured; the army had to take over the city and impose a curfew to control the chaos, as it had done in 1959.[110] In June and July 1961 Qasim's government made moves to consolidate its influence in the Kirkuk region by creating new administrative subdivisions, outlined in Republican Decrees 328 and 378, in the largely Arab areas of Riyad and Hawija west of urban Kirkuk. These areas were already part of the Kirkuk *liwa'*, but the establishment of two new administrative seats in Arab-majority areas near Kirkuk signaled a shift toward a new, ethnicized tactic in Baghdad's attempts to assert control over the city, a tactic that would eventually find its most extreme expression in the ethnically based expulsions and resettlements of the Ba'th era.[111]

That same summer, rebellion broke out in rural Kurdish areas north of Kirkuk. The unrest stemmed from discontent with the Agrarian Reform Law of September 1958, a signature piece of legislation that Qasim promoted to curb large-scale landownership and to redistribute landholdings among peasants. The law's implementation proceeded contentiously among tribal landowners in the Kurdish north. When Kurdish rebels ambushed an Iraqi army target in September 1961 and Qasim responded with airstrikes in Barzan, the KDP joined the uprising. The Communist Party denounced the rebellion, alienating many of its Kurdish members in the north; these people began to leave the party and align themselves with the rebels.[112] The KDP even began to make contacts with Qasim's pan-Arabist rivals, even though, from an ideological and practical standpoint, they did not constitute logical allies to the cause of Kurdish autonomy.[113] By this time, the notion of Arabs and Kurds as "partners" in Qasim's Iraq was effectively dead, and Kurds' political interests became ever more closely associated with their nationalist movement.

It was at this point that the Kurdish nationalist movement began to forthrightly demonstrate its physical presence in Kirkuk. In 1962, in the midst of the ongoing, brutal government campaign against the Kurds, Kurdish militants mounted an attack on the police force in 'Ayn Zala in northwestern Iraq. They killed several police officers and civilians; then, they kidnapped a British employee of the IPC, D. C. Dankworth, and two Iraqi employees. All three were eventually released unharmed. In the meantime, their captors covertly delivered messages from the hostages to IPC headquarters in Kirkuk, reflecting the extent of their penetration of the municipal boundaries. IPC general manager George Tod later remembered finding the notes "on the seat of my car, lying on a table, just lying about anywhere."[114]

A few weeks later, Kurdish militants kidnapped another group of IPC employees from an area an hour and a half's drive north of urban Kirkuk. These hostages included a British geologist, Frank Gosling; an Iraqi geologist, Adnan Samarrai; and three other Iraqis. The captives were treated well. In fact, Samarrai told me that Mustafa Barzani himself intentionally orchestrated their "guest" status to create a positive impression of the Kurdish movement.[115] Kurds abducted the leader of the village of Baba Gurgur, which was about 8 kilometers northwest of urban Kirkuk, shortly thereafter. IPC employees had never previously faced such threats, and a state of nervousness over the Kurdish rebellion prevailed. This anxiety was exacerbated by a perception that Iraqi security in the Kirkuk area was inadequate because of the commitment of troops to fighting the rebels elsewhere. It was also intensified by the fact that European staff members lived in the Baba Gurgur area and were therefore particularly close to the areas where militants were active.[116] In December 1962 expatriates in Kirkuk began to adhere to a curfew.[117] The government also increased armed protection of oil installations in Kirkuk in coordination with the army's 2nd Division.[118]

The heavy presence of the army in northern Iraq left strategically important points in Baghdad vulnerable to a coup just as the disputes between Qasim and his many rivals, especially 'Arif and the Ba'th Party, were coming to a head. On 8 February 1963 pan-Arabist and Ba'th officers seized key bases and the national radio station, declaring a revolution. 'Arif assumed the Iraqi presidency, though the Ba'th led the new regime. Unlike the 14 July 1958 coup, this announcement was met by massive popular opposition from Qasim's supporters, especially among Baghdad's urban poor, triggering two days of bloody fighting. The rebel officers forced their way into Qasim's quarters in the Ministry of Defense and summarily executed him on 9 February. The Ba'th government would eventually collapse in November, leaving an army autocracy under 'Arif's leadership in place.

Meanwhile, the intervening months witnessed a new wave of brutal suppression of Iraqi Communists. The regime publicly justified these acts as a warranted response to the events of 1959 in Mosul and Kirkuk, a reflection of the fact that anger over those attacks remained a well from which politicians in Baghdad could productively draw.[119] Indeed, just three days after the declaration of the new regime and two days after Qasim's execution, the Arab Communist former commander of the 2nd Division in Kirkuk, Dawud al-Janabi, was hanged.[120] Qasim had refrained from carrying out the death sentences of the mostly Kurdish Communists convicted of the crimes of July 1959 in Kirkuk, but the Ba'th did not hesitate to implement them, executing all twenty-eight men on 23 June. The government announced the executions on national radio and made a point of describing the criminals as Communists while reiterating the gruesome acts that the accused had been convicted of committing.[121]

The Ba'th also took a much harsher approach to the presence of Kurdish rebels in Kirkuk than Qasim had. In 1963 the army began to attack Kurdish civilians in urban Kirkuk's hinterland by razing villages that were close to the oil fields. Nouri Talabany documents the names of thirteen predominantly Kurdish villages that the first Ba'th government ordered destroyed in this manner.[122] In his unpublished memoir, George Tod describes one such incident that occurred sometime in early 1963. His account is worth quoting at length.

> One day the General in charge 'phoned me up and asked me to send him all our [i.e., the IPC's] earth moving equipment (about 50 pieces of power shovels, bulldozers, huge diggers etc.). . . . He told me he had orders from the President of the Republic in Baghdad to bull-doze down and destroy all houses of Kurds in Kirkuk. Outside villages had already been destroyed by fire but the town had so far been spared. . . . I refused. He said he would come with his men and take the machines. He did. That same night all Kurdish men were rounded up, put into cattle trucks on the railway and taken by train to Basrah. . . . At the same time . . . the army set about destroying and levelling out their habitations, throwing women and children on to the streets of Kirkuk with no shelter, food or means of getting it. For about a week the streets and the roads around our installations were littered with pathetic bundles of huddled bodies in their black robes, the women silent, the children crying.[123]

Tod's language in this passage—"all houses of Kurds in Kirkuk," "all Kurdish men"—is exaggerated, suggesting a fuzzy memory. Nevertheless, the incident he describes is, in its most significant details, corroborated by Talabany's records. It constituted a level of intrusion into the nearby outskirts of urban Kirkuk and the oil company's property by the Iraqi army that was, at that time, unprecedented in the history of the modern Iraqi state. This episode is a shocking example of the ethnicized targeting of civilian Kurds in Kirkuk as a way of suppressing the Kurdish nationalist movement.

As for the Kurdish movement's leadership, the KDP's establishment of good relations with the pan-Arabists briefly paid off, though the tenuous alliance between the groups soon fell apart. One of the KDP's younger executives, Jalal Talabani, led a Kurdish delegation accompanying the Iraqi Ba'th to an April 1963 conference in Cairo where the possibility, never realized, of Iraq joining Syria and Egypt in the UAR was addressed. Talabani issued a memorandum favoring a level of autonomy for the Kurds, an approach that he described as "decentralization." The Kurds' concerns were ultimately not recognized in the accord resulting from the conference.[124] The KDP put forth more forceful demands in late April; most notably, they insisted on the creation of an autonomous region that would include northern Iraq's oil fields, including those of Kirkuk, as well as the city of Kirkuk. The Ba'th responded with an unsparing offensive against Sulaymaniyya and areas north of Arbil and Kirkuk, though none within the Kirkuk *liwa'*.[125] Instead, their approach in Kirkuk, as well as in Arbil, was to expel Kurdish civilians from villages and replace them with Arab settlers. In late 1964, during a lull in the war in which large numbers of Kurds were returning to Kirkuk in dire circumstances, Iraqi prime minister Tahir Yahya claimed that the Kurds who had been displaced from Kirkuk villages could not be allowed to reclaim their homes because the Arab settlers were needed to keep an eye on "the imperialistic oil companies."[126] The method of using resettled civilian Arabs as proxies for Baghdad in Kirkuk had therefore evolved into an official government policy. Likewise, the twin notions that Kirkuk was the southern Kurdish frontier and that Kirkuk's oil was a Kurdish prerogative were firmly cemented in virtually all branches of organized Kurdish politics. Both the Kurdish movement and the Arab-led government in Baghdad had completed the transition to an ethnopolitical approach to controlling Kirkuk.

The polarization of Baghdad's and the Kurdish movement's fight for Kirkuk as a frontier drove wedges between the city's communities, engendering vicious divides that had profound emotional import. These external forces also began to interfere with the lives of all Kirkukis, permeating many of their mundane activities. They hurt business pursuits, interfered with employment, and even resulted in the looting of private property and violence against the politically marginalized. The divides were unavoidable in everyday written discourse too. By 1963 the municipality's weekly newspaper, *Kerkük/Karkuk*, was printed solely in Arabic and took an explicitly pan-Arabist editorial line. For example, a September 1963 issue commemorated the anniversary of the 1961 Syrian withdrawal from the UAR as a catastrophe and a threat to Arab unity. The same issue featured a

patriotic poem by Ramziyya Mayyas (Remziye Mayas), a Turkmen student at
Kirkuk High School for Girls, in which she described Kirkuk's "eternal fire" as
a weapon against colonialism.[127]

When describing the effects of the post-1958 Iraqi political scene on their
lives, my interlocutors typically conveyed a wry sense of the absurdity of it all, and
most who had a memory of the monarchy era either stated or implied that these
changes were a phenomenon with no direct precedent. George Tod poignantly
conveyed the reality of Kirkuki alienation in an anecdote about a dinner party
for IPC employees that he held at his house in the executive estate sometime in
the 1960s. During the party, the Iraqi army began to shell a Kurdish village just
north of the city. In the dark and from the vantage point of the hill where the
house was located, the explosions were clearly visible. "It was sad," Tod wrote,
"to have to witness it." Traumatized Kurdish guests left the party. Some Arab
guests "jeered," while others were embarrassed.[128]

It is perhaps not unexpected that, decades later, novels about Kirkuk written
by Kirkuki expatriates who are not Kurds tend to downplay or ignore the Kurdish
presence in the city.[129] Similarly, while being interviewed by Güldem Büyüksaraç
about her experiences in Kirkuk, the Turkmen emigrant Resmiye exclaimed
repeatedly, "There were no Kurds. Am I clear?"[130] I have also heard sentiments
of this sort voiced by an Assyrian from Kirkuk who grew up in Arrapha. These
Kirkukis do not mean to suggest, of course, that there were literally no Kurds
in the city. Rather, these viewpoints reflect the isolation of discrete ethnicized
social groups in Kirkuk that was exacerbated by their competing claims to the
city and by external, but uncomfortably proximal, warfare.

CONCLUSION

Over the course of the twentieth century, Kirkukis had experienced everything
from war and starvation to political tensions, gaping and growing socioeconomic inequalities, and uncertainty for the future. However, the violence that
destabilized both urban and rural Kirkuk after 1958 was of a different type. It
tore apart the region's social fabric along distinct lines of group identity. These
had become the basis for competing claims to Kirkuk's character and therefore to historical authority over the city and political authority over its institutions. Turkmens, who had lost their unquestioned political dominance over the
city and correctly sensed that their cultural dominance was also declining, felt
threatened. Kurds, boldly and sometimes brutally, began to assert their power,
eventually doing so through an ascendant nationalist movement. The horrors

of July 1959, which gripped the whole country, fed a cycle of intercommunal strife that continued well into the 1960s.

Meanwhile, Kirkuk became an ever more crucial borderland between the domains claimed by Baghdad and the Kurdish nationalist movement—a competition that penetrated the city and its oil for the first time in the revolutionary era, both in expressed ideas and in physical force. The turmoil of internal and external violence over and around Kirkuk created anxiety in the daily lives of Kirkukis in various pursuits and of all ages, worsening the distrust between communities and cementing ethnicity as a political practice. The extent to which distinct group identities had solidified in Kirkuk over the course of the twentieth century is starkly clear in light of the 1958 revolution. Similarly, it is evident that a divisive, rather than unifying, conception of Kirkuki identity had come to dominate local discourse.

6 NATIONALIZATION AND ARABIZATION

BY THE 1960S political mobilization using the concept of ethnicity, once rare, had become routine in Kirkuk's local political domain. It was increasingly common for individuals and groups to articulate their interests, their relationship to the city, and their relations with one another through their ethnic identities. As that practice developed and grew, so too did intercommunal tensions, ethnic violence, and the idea that ethnicized claims to power could not be reconciled with one another. However, this habitual method of politics had not yet reached its peak destructiveness during the regimes of 'Abd al-Karim Qasim and 'Abd al-Salam 'Arif. It would become especially poisonous once it coincided with the rule of an authoritarian regime that used ethnicity as shorthand for individuals' and communities' standing in relation to the state.

When the Ba'th Party seized power, Kirkukis responded to the new government's authoritarianism in a variety of ways. The party had affiliates of every ethnicity and religious sect, and its initial willingness to negotiate with Kurdish and Turkmen activists led to, at times, cautious cooperation. Over time, though, the party extended tight, multilayered control over all of Kirkuk's institutions and spaces—its governorate, its municipality, its oil company, much of its land—ultimately leaving Kirkukis with few tenable choices beyond collaboration, dangerous resistance, or exile. Once Iraq entered a state of "wartime,"[1] anyone who did not conform to the Ba'thist agenda was attacked. Ba'th-era discourse referred to ethnic groups as *qawmiyyas* (nationalities), continuing a trend that had grown in consistency in Kirkuk in the first decade of the republican era. The logic of dividing Iraqis in general and Kirkukis in particular into *qawmiyya*s for the purpose of governance relied on the assumption that one's *qawmiyya* determined one's loyalty to the state. All non-Arabs were persecuted under this logic, but Kurds suffered the highest costs.

The idea of *qawmiyya* as a primary form of identity was not exclusive to Ba'th administration in Iraq; on the contrary, this very word was at the ideological roots of the Ba'th Party. From its beginnings the Ba'th Party subscribed to a form of nationalism dependent on solidarities across a shared linguistic-communal identity of being Arab. The Iraqi Ba'th extended this idea by applying the governance logic of *qawmiyya* in a confrontational way. The initial project of "nationalizing" Kirkuk in order to integrate it into the state eventually gave way to a more explicit logic of ethnic cleansing, or "Arabization." In Kirkuk, a place with a recent history of segregation and mutual mistrust amid ethnic groups, this method of control produced the deadliest crimes of the Ba'th regime. In the 1980s Kirkuk would serve as the nerve center of the Anfal genocide.

THE BA'THIST SECURITY STRUCTURE IN KIRKUK AND THE OIL FIELDS

The death of 'Abd al-Salam 'Arif in a plane crash in 1966 left a power vacuum that enabled a second, and more durable, Ba'th coup on 17 July 1968. That coup was led by senior army officer Ahmad Hasan al-Bakr, a member of the Ba'th Party who had been involved in both the 1958 coup and the subsequent agitation against Qasim by the pan-Arabist branch of the military. Unlike the first Ba'th-led coup in 1963, which quickly collapsed, the second one in 1968 resulted in a successful extension of the party's control over the government and military. Al-Bakr was soon declared president of the republic. Saddam Hussein, a longtime Ba'thist who played a central role in the coup, soon became his most powerful deputy.

The Ba'th government, particularly after Saddam Hussein took over, created many layers of ideologically loyal armed forces outside the state's central military—"parallel militaries" or "anti-armies," both military-adjacent and paramilitary—to coup-proof the regime.[2] Some of these forces, such as the Popular Army and the Republican Guard (who reported directly to Saddam Hussein), are well known, but there were also other, more obscure ones. Kirkuk was home to the Iraqi army's First Corps (the army had been restructured since the days when Kirkuk was home to the Second Division) along with many other unaffiliated units.

A document detailing the "Ta'mim Branch" forces in Kirkuk, dating to late 2002, when Saddam Hussein was preparing for a threatened American-led invasion, gives a sense of the heavy structure of security in the governorate.[3] The leadership of the branch was divided into six divisions (*shu'ab*), each of which was further divided into somewhere between four and eight subdivisions (*firaq*). The names of these divisions and subdivisions sometimes give a sense of their mission. Two divisions were named for towns south of Kirkuk city, Daquq and al-Rashad, and another was the Ta'mim Women's Division (*shu'bat al-ta'mim al-niswiyya*). Others were given names that tapped into particular Ba'thist mythologies, such as the Qadisiyya Subdivision and the Mother of All Battles Subdivision (*firqat umm al-ma'arik*), after Saddam Hussein's names for the Iran-Iraq War and the 1991 Gulf War, and the Salah al-Din Subdivision, a reference to the anti-Crusader warrior from Saddam Hussein's hometown of Tikrit. (Umm al-Ma'arik was also the name of a newly created administrative subdivision just south of urban Kirkuk.)[4]

In addition to the Ta'mim Branch, an infantry division of the Republican Guard called al-'Abid was present in Kirkuk.[5] Most notoriously, the Popular Army had a base called Topzawa that covered 2 square miles just southwest of the city and played a central role in the Anfal genocide. The Ba'th regime also created Oil Protection Forces, which had a command in Kirkuk, to protect the oil fields; these forces ended up confronting Kurdish rebel attacks.[6] The security apparatus that the central government built to control Kirkuk over the years of Ba'th rule was therefore highly complex.

While the Iraqi government (and its enemies) continued to perceive Kirkuk as strategically crucial, by this time the Kirkuk oil field was no longer the most productive segment of Iraq's oil industry. Exploration in southern Iraq by the IPC's sister company, the Basra Petroleum Company (BPC), yielded discoveries of the Zubayr and Rumayla oil fields. Exports from these fields by way of Basra began in 1950 and 1954, respectively, and eventually surpassed those originating in Kirkuk. The Basra fields' immense potential bolstered Baghdad's position in relation to the IPC in the late 1960s. The strength of the southern oil fields also made Kirkuk less essential to the industry as a source of quality crude, leading to the egregious physical mismanagement of the Kirkuk field, including the use of injection of excess fluids to boost oil pumping rates.[7] After contentious negotiations and several confrontations, the Iraqi government under al-Bakr nationalized the IPC in 1972, eventually renaming the new state-owned entity the North Oil Company.[8] Therefore, under the second Ba'th republic, the company no longer acted as a competing center of political gravity in the local arena. Instead, it became yet another manifestation of Baghdad's ever-growing influence in Kirkuk.

A former employee of the North Oil Company told me that, after the Ba'th Party came to power, members of the party were first-priority hires for any job in the oil company. The applications of those who were not Ba'thists were routinely rejected. This employee had been born and raised in Kirkuk and worked for the company from the late 1960s until 1997 as a technician manager. He was not a member of the Ba'th Party. At one point in his career, he tried to transfer to another department within the company and was initially refused the transfer because of his unaffiliated status. He was eventually granted the transfer because of his extensive experience working in the oil fields. North Oil Company workers were also required to join a "union" that was controlled and managed as a branch of the government.[9] As we have seen, the presence of the oil industry in Kirkuk shaped the ways that Kirkukis related to each other and to the city, engendering political mobilization and sharpening the contours of ethnic identification. After 1972 the nationalized oil industry continued to influence the way that those living and working in Kirkuk aligned themselves politically—this time, as an instrument of the Ba'th's party-centered authoritarianism.

ETHNIC MOBILIZATION IN KIRKUK UNDER BA'THISM

In late 1968, soon after the Ba'th coup, relations deteriorated between al-Bakr and Kurdish nationalists led by Mustafa Barzani. Like his predecessors, al-Bakr inherited the conflict with the Kurdistan Democratic Party (KDP) and its attendant negotiation process. He made some early concessions to the party, such as appointing KDP members to the new government. But al-Bakr also took advantage of the intraparty conflict between Barzani and the faction of the KDP led by Jalal Talabani, who had disagreed with the ceasefire that Barzani negotiated with 'Abd al-Salam 'Arif in 1964. Hoping to leverage their power against both the Talabani faction and the Iraqi government, Barzani and his followers decided to approach this situation with a new show of force.[10] In December 1968 forces loyal to Barzani killed twenty people on a train from Kirkuk to Arbil.[11] Iraqi soldiers amassed in northern Iraq and confronted Kurdish rebels for months. These nationalist rebels were known among Kurds as *pêşmerge*—in Kurdish, "those who face death." The government described the operations against the *pêşmerge* as "police operations" and offered amnesty to soldiers for any crimes committed in their course.

In response, on 1 March 1969, Barzani's forces carried out a dramatic spectacle of an attack on a now-perennial target: the northern branch of the oil company, and, in particular, Kirkuk's crude oil stabilization plant. They used long-range mortars that could only have been supplied by an external funder (probably Iran, which backed the Kurdish movement substantially in this time period) and fired them with a precision that suggested formal training. The attack destroyed ten out of twelve of the plant's installations, temporarily reducing Kirkuk's output capacity by 70%.[12] By the time the KDP and the Iraqi government negotiated another temporary ceasefire and peace accord in 1970, there was no question that control over Kirkuk and its oil fields was a central Kurdish nationalist demand. The accord of 11 March 1970 did not grant the KDP that control but went further than previous Iraqi regimes' gestures to the Kurdish nationalist movement by acknowledging a right to autonomy in Kurdish-majority areas and the possibility of reversing the population transfers that were part of Arabization.

In recent analyses of the methods and taxonomies the Ba'th Party used to assess loyalty, scholars have found that the party's forms and official discourses were self-consciously nonsectarian, as evidenced by the fact that, with rare exceptions, they did not distinguish between Sunnis and Shi'is. This finding is significant when looking backward from post-2003 discourses in and about Iraq in which the Sunni-Shi'i divide has become highly politicized and predictive of partisan commitments, raising the question of how sectarianism might have been institutionalized in subtler ways in Ba'thist Iraq.[13] However, it must be emphasized that the prevalence of a Ba'thist nonsectarian mentality certainly did not extend to the Northern Bureau and its attitude toward *qawmiyya*s. Ba'th records from the Northern Bureau routinely included the *qawmiyya* of an individual under surveillance as a key piece of information along with full name, date of birth, and locations of origin and current residence.

This approach to intelligence gathering is evident in, for example, a batch of handwritten forms listing background information about students at the Kirkuk Technical Institute dating to the 1980s.[14] The students' full names were recorded, and each student was also assigned a number, evidently for filing purposes. The forms are relatively sparse, listing little beyond mundane and easily obtained information such as year of birth and place of origin. The party's priorities are reflected in the small amount of intelligence that they did gather, or attempted to gather, on each student: their political ties, their family's political ties, and their *qawmiyya*. Although the compilers of the forms were not always able to gather any information on political affiliations, sometimes listing these details as unobtainable, the *qawmiyya* is always present. In this particular batch every student is listed as Kurdish. This may indicate that the party focused specifically on surveillance of Kurdish students (or students they considered Kurdish) or that information gathered for background checks was filed according to *qawmiyya*.[15] Either way, it reflects the fact that the party used *qawmiyya* as a universal litmus test for potential loyalty or suspiciousness. Indeed, two men who applied to work as drivers for the North Oil Company, when filling out a section of a background check form that asked for their tribe (*al-ʿashira*), described themselves simply as "Kurdish." They seemed to intuit that this, rather than their tribe, was the aspect of their identity that would be most salient to those who would assess the form.[16]

The surveillance forms on Kurdish students at the Kirkuk Technical Institute also reveal the Baʿth Party's cultivation of and reliance on informants within each *qawmiyya*. One student, number 31, is described with an unusually neatly handwritten sheet specifying his mother's name (a less common piece of information in this batch), his previous location, his current location, and his place of birth, in addition to his Kurdish *qawmiyya*, his political affiliation (independent), and the standing of his extended family (good). As historians familiar with the Baʿth archive have consistently found, being politically independent in Iraq's one-party authoritarian state was a liability.[17] The sheet's anomalies are explained by the signature of the person who prepared it: not a government official but the head (*mukhtar*) of the village listed as the student's place of birth. This person was a fellow Kurd, someone who had probably known the student well for his whole life and was quite possibly a relative.[18]

From an examination of both the Baʿth archive and the long-known actions of the Iraqi government in the 1970s and 1980s, it is clear that Kurds bore the brunt of ethnicized surveillance and violence in the Saddam Hussein era. Nevertheless, the question remains: how did the Baʿth understand and apply the concept of *qawmiyya*, especially in a diverse city such as Kirkuk with a recent, burgeoning precedent of ethnicized politics? In Baʿth Iraq any kind of non-state-sanctioned ethnopolitical mobilization was a liability to those who participated in it, subjecting them to increased scrutiny and suspicion.

Alongside the growth of Kurdish nationalism, Turkmen literary and linguistic-communal consciousness flourished during Qasim's regime, which tried to build links with prominent Turkmens amid its crackdown on Kurdish and Communist political activity after the massacre of July 1959. Under the auspices of the Qasim government's Interior Ministry, a group of Turkmen intellectuals founded an organization called the Turkmen Brotherhood Association (Türkmen

Kardeşlik Ocağı) in Baghdad in 1960. It originated as a central government project but quickly established links to Kirkuk. As part of a series of books published
by the association to preserve Turkmen history and heritage, one of its primary
founders, a lawyer and writer named Ata Terzibaşı, published books documenting traditional expressions, songs, and folklore in Kirkuk's Turkmani dialect.[19]
Soon after the association's founding, in 1961, it began to publish a bilingual
Arabic- and Turkish-language literary magazine, *Kardeşlik* (Brotherhood), also
known by the alternative spelling *Kardaşlık*, which reflects how Kirkuki Turkmens pronounced it in their dialect, or by its Arabic name, *al-Ikha'*.[20] The magazine showcased different genres of Turkmen writing and reported on cultural
stories relevant to the Turkmen community. The organization was permitted to
publish its magazine and books on Turkmen heritage as long as its output was,
in the Iraqi government's words, "cultural" in nature, which officials considered
distinct from engaging in "political" activity.[21]

As political and social repression in Iraq intensified through the Ba'th era,
many Turkmens began to seek refuge in Turkey—Turkmens had moved northward in times of crisis as early as the period of the Mosul question, as in the
case of the defection of Nazim Beg Naftchizada—but they maintained links with
their relatives back home. The Iraqi Turkmen diaspora in Turkey, centered in
Istanbul, grew substantially during the Ba'th era and began to change Turkmen
practices within Iraq. Kirkuki Turkmens also traveled back and forth between
Turkey and Kirkuk.

The most notable transformation during this time affected Turkmens' written
language. Texts in Latinized, modernized Turkish started to make their way to
Kirkuk through Kirkukis' links with relatives and interlocutors to the north as
early as the 1930s, soon after the language reform spearheaded by Mustafa Kemal
Atatürk.[22] But through the late 1970s, written Turkish among Iraqi Turkmens,
including Kirkuki Turkish-language newspapers and the publications of the
Turkmen Brotherhood Association, retained the use of Ottoman-era Arabic
script. As Iraqi Turkmen communal identity became increasingly distinct from
that of Anatolian Turks over the course of the twentieth century (even as familial
and cultural connections to the Republic of Turkey continued), Turkmens tended
to refer to their language, when spoken locally or written in Arabic script, as
Turkmani rather than Turkish (*al-lugha al-turkumaniyya* in Arabic).

The 1970 accord with the Kurdish movement occurred at the same time
that al-Bakr's government was making similar gestures toward Turkmen organizations. In January 1970 the Iraqi government issued a resolution granting

Turkmens the rights of a *qawmiyya*, including language and cultural recognition. Referring to Turkmens as "the Turkmen minority" (*al-aqalliyya al-turkumani-yya*) and the language they speak as "Turkmani" (rather than Turkish), the resolution specified seven rights that the government would support, including the teaching of the Turkmani language in primary schools, the translation of school materials into Turkmani, the creation of a union for Turkmen litterateurs, and the growth of Turkmani-language programming on Kirkuk's local television.[23] *Kardeşlik*, which focused on the interests of Turkmens but gently toed a Ba'thist-friendly line, printed in its March-April 1970 issue the text of a cable from the Turkmen Brotherhood Association praising the "return of peace and stability to our beloved north" and the "fraternal *qawmiyyas*" (*al-qawmiyyat al-muta'akhiyya*), presumably referring to the March accord with the KDP. According to the magazine, the cable had been sent to al-Bakr, the Revolutionary Command Council (RCC), and the Iraqi media. Alongside this cable, the magazine approvingly announced the RCC-sponsored project of translating educational texts into Turkmani and listed the members of the committee that had been tapped to lead the project.[24]

Prominent Turkmen intellectuals were willing, in the early Ba'th era, to articulate their community's interests through ethnicity in accordance with the central government's approach to governance. But immediately a vast gulf opened between the language of the January 1970 Turkmen agreement and the actions of the government. For example, Kirkuk's provincial director of education, 'Izz al-Din Sardar, transferred Turkmen teachers away from predominantly Turkmen areas, sometimes outside the province, to places where the students did not speak Turkish—and then canceled Turkish-language classes in Turkmen areas on the basis of a lack of teachers able to teach in the language.[25] It was a move reminiscent of the Iraqi government's claim in the 1930s that the Arabization of primary education in the province stemmed from a lack of qualified Turkmen and Kurdish teachers.

The government's intentions to create a diluted, territorially limited, and thus less threatening Turkmen *qawmiyya* identity eventually came back around to affect *Kardeşlik*. The magazine initially published in only Turkmani and Arabic but began to add a third section in Latinized modern Turkish in 1964.[26] In 1971, just a year and a half after official recognition of the right of Turkmens to learn and produce culture in the Turkmani language, the Iraqi government banned the section of the magazine that was in Latinized Turkish.[27] Beginning with the September 1971 issue, and for the rest of its run, *Kardeşlik* had only Arabic and

Arabic-script Turkmani sections. *Kardeşlik* continued to publish for many more years, but its editorial committee was taken over by the RCC in 1977 and replaced with Ba'thist cronies who watered down considerably the magazine's original mission to promote a communal Turkmen identity.[28] Also in 1977, the Ba'th regime shut down a Turkish cultural center attached to the Turkish consulate in Kirkuk that taught Latinized Turkish.[29]

As Ba'thist purges accelerated during Saddam Hussein's regime, the steps to repress prominent and politically active Turkmens became even more extreme. The head of the Kirkuk Chamber of Commerce, a well-known Turkmen named Muhammad al-Salihi, had been executed in 1969, just before the Ba'th declaration of the 1970 resolution granting Turkmens recognition.[30] Other acts of violence followed. The most shocking act of intimidation took place in January 1980, when a retired army officer and former head of the Turkmen Brotherhood Association, 'Abdullah 'Abd al-Rahman, was executed along with three other notable members of the Turkmen community.[31]

Despite the Ba'th government's clear pattern of persecuting politically and culturally active Turkmens, the status of Turkmens in relation to the Ba'thist *qawmiyya* concept was ambiguous and somewhat different from that of Kurds. This is reflected in 'Ali Hasan al-Majid's candid, disturbing comments in a taped 1989 meeting as he reflected on what he had done to Kirkuk's demographics during the genocidal Anfal campaign.

> I would like to speak about two points: one, Arabization; and two, the shared zones between the Arab lands and the [Kurdish] Autonomous Region. The point that we are talking about is Kirkuk. When I came, the Arabs and Turkomans were not more than fifty-one percent of the total population of Kirkuk. Despite everything, I spent sixty million dinars until we reached the present situation.[32]

To Ba'thists, "Turkmen" was a distinct *qawmiyya* from "Arab," but it was not unusual for both *qawmiyya*s to be mentioned in the same breath when talking about Kirkuk. Baghdad had long used the patronage of elite Turkish-speaking Kirkukis as a bulwark against Kurdish nationalism in the city and its hinterland. By the late twentieth century, when the Iraqi government established a policy of treating ethnicities as formal groups with unitary interests, the Turkmen *qawmiyya* functioned as a useful demographic wedge. The Ba'thist relationship with the Turkmen *qawmiyya* varied depending on the context, whereas Kurdish *qawmiyya* interests were treated as intrinsically threatening to the state.

ARABIZING KIRKUK

With the 1970 accord with the KDP, the Ba'th regime temporarily slowed the 'Arif government's policy of demolishing predominantly Kurdish villages near Kirkuk to curb the Kurdish national movement. But the practices of the Kirkuk municipality continued to effectively force Kurds and Turkmens from Kirkuk into exile. It was routine for non-Arabs who sought to buy property in Kirkuk to be denied the right to do so, or they were denied permission to renovate structures that had severely deteriorated. The government also added neighborhoods to the city rapidly, including hundreds of units of housing that, as a result of discriminatory policies and practices, were effectively available only to Arabs.[33] This new built-up area vastly expanded the urban fabric toward the south and southwest, as though Baghdad were exerting a gravitational pull on the city (Figure 13). As a result of these and other grievances, Barzani and his forces took up arms against Baghdad again, only to have their efforts devastated by the Algiers Agreement between Iraq and Iran that concluded in December 1975. The accord normalized relations between the two countries, resulting in the end of Iranian support for the Kurdish rebellion. Barzani left Iraq permanently, eventually settling in the United States; he died of cancer a few years later.

During and after the collapse of the Kurdish rebellion, beginning around 1975, the RCC issued a slew of decrees intended to transform Kirkuk's geography and demographics. These included several attempts at gerrymandering, which also occurred in other parts of Iraq. Throughout the 1970s the Ba'th government reorganized Iraq's provinces into eighteen *muhafaza*s (governorates), often changing their names, altering their boundaries, and creating wholly new units. During this process, the Kirkuk province's boundaries were dramatically redrawn to exclude predominantly Kurdish and Turkmen areas. In 1975 Ahmad Hasan al-Bakr signed a decree removing Chamchamal and Kifri, both towns with close links to Kirkuk, from the province and redrawing them into the provinces of Sulaymaniyya and Diyala, respectively.[34] In 1976 the predominantly Turkmen city of Tuz Khurmatu, equally closely linked to Kirkuk, was redrawn into the Salah al-Din province to the south. Further revisions to provincial boundaries would attach largely Arab areas west and southwest of Kirkuk to the province, drawing its administrative territory physically closer to Baghdad.[35] In 1976 al-Bakr issued a decree renaming the Kirkuk province Ta'mim, or "nationalization."[36] The name was a reference to the nationalization of the oil company four years

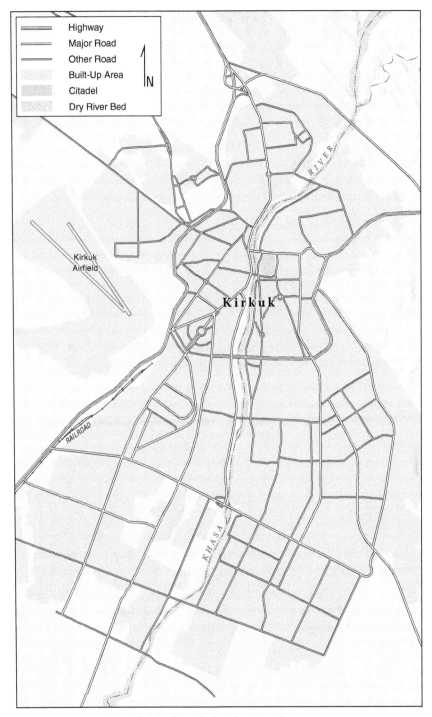

FIGURE 13. Extent of Kirkuk by the end of Ba'th Party rule.

earlier, emphasizing the penetration of the central government into a region where a foreign-owned company had previously wielded influence.

A new round of urban planning schemes, the kind of project previously spearheaded by the private oil company, accompanied Baghdad's permeation into Kirkuk. In 1973 the Ba'th regime had invited Doxiadis Associates (DA), the Greek architecture and urban planning firm, back to Iraq. After his early work in Iraq in the 1950s, Constantinos Doxiadis built a reputation as an urban planner of the developing world in an era of decolonization, modernization ideology, and consolidation of power by native regimes. Although Doxiadis, who died in 1975, was too ill to work on the new Iraq project himself, his firm continued to pursue urban planning commissions throughout South Asia, South America, Africa, and beyond. They brought the framework of ekistics, the "scientific" approach to controlled urban planning, to each of these projects. This time, however, DA's sole commission in Iraq was another master plan for Kirkuk, developed beginning in 1973. The Iraqi government publicized the project widely, holding exhibitions with DA representatives on the planning process in both Baghdad and Kirkuk. DA's project team appeared on a Kirkuk television program to discuss the plan in April 1974 and relied on Kirkuki students to administer a questionnaire on socioeconomic status to a sample of the city population. The final master plan was proposed at a public meeting with city and provincial officials in September 1974.[37]

DA's previous master plan of Kirkuk in the 1950s had focused on neighborhoods with a burgeoning middle class and had not proposed any major changes in Shorija, the poor neighborhood made up mostly of recent Kurdish migrants from the rural hinterland, or in the ancient citadel, whose population had stopped growing. By the Ba'th era Shorija was an infamous center of Kurdish resistance to the regime, and the citadel's residents were stewards of the city's historically Turkish-speaking culture.[38] Not coincidentally, the 1974 master plan touted potential transformations of both Shorija and the citadel as exemplary features. In the new plan Shorija was to be surrounded on all sides with large arterials that both connected it more thoroughly with the rest of the city and boxed it in, preventing further outward growth and making it easier to monitor. The plan eliminated two smaller arterials that ran through the neighborhood in a north-south direction, replacing them with buildings and pedestrian walkways, but it also proposed a new large arterial bisecting the neighborhood in an east-west direction that would cut through existing dense residential areas. DA's larger city plan proposed a similar systematic ringing of clusters of residential and commercial blocks with large arterials, fully integrating disconnected neighborhoods like Shorija into the urban fabric. The citadel was an exception; the project team designated it a special "conservation area" but also indicated that it needed to be "properly developed," perhaps with new housing, in order to be preserved.[39] In a 1976 interview in *Kardeşlik* (in one of its last issues produced without direct Ba'th Party intervention), one of the Kirkuk municipality's leading engineers outlined the city's urban development plans in response to several questions from the magazine about water, pavement, parks, and the future of the citadel. He described the plan to widen and pave roads throughout the city as a move intended to maintain "cleanliness."[40]

In the following years the systematic containment of Kirkuk's neighborhoods through building large arterials around them proceeded in a manner similar to what DA's master plan had prescribed. But Shorija was eventually incorporated into the city with a distinctly different tactic than that of DA's plan: the extension of a multilane highway in the northeastern part of the city, the highway that connected Kirkuk with Sulaymaniyya, south through the middle of the neighborhood (Figure 14). The highway was extended in a north-south direction through part of Shorija, then bent west and connected with the interprovincial highway on the west side of the city leading to Arbil, whereas these two highways had previously been unconnected and merged into local roads upon entering the city center.[41]

The tactic of building a highway through a crowded ethnic-minority neighborhood had previously been used in the postwar United States to disintegrate or even eliminate such communities. These construction projects required the destruction of tightly built houses and businesses to create space for multiple lanes, barriers, and ramps. Furthermore, they physically split apart close-knit populations.[42] The width of the highway, combined with Shorija's known pre-existing density, indicates that many homes must have been demolished in the course of this project. Baghdad provided minimal monetary compensation to Shorija residents who had their homes demolished as part of road construction and then prevented them from purchasing any other property in Kirkuk, forcing most of them out of the province.[43] This major infrastructural development was combined with the construction of dense neighborhoods on both sides of the Khasa River extending west and south, completely integrating what had been a marginal "Kurdish shantytown" on the southeastern outskirts of the city into what eventually became its northern half.

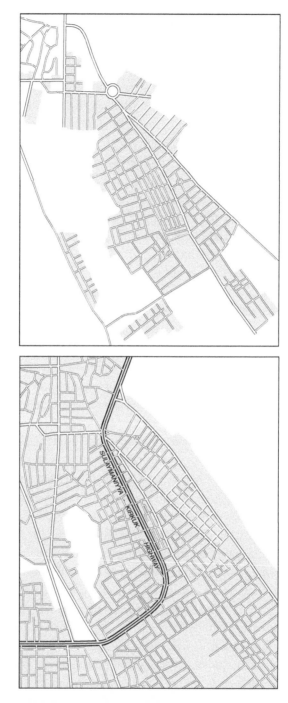

FIGURE 14. *Top*: Shorija in 1973. *Bottom*: Shorija c. 2003, years after the construction of the Kirkuk-Sulaymaniyya highway through its center. Source for the 1973 map: Sovetskaya Armiya, *Kirkuk* (Moscow: General'nyi Shtab, 1976). Source for the later map: Google Maps.

The RCC issued many decrees that turned over long lists of dozens of specific plots of land, both inside the city of Kirkuk and outside it in hinterland villages and agricultural areas, to the authority of the Ta'mim governorate, thereby repossessing them from either private owners or the Kirkuk municipality.[44] In the typical pattern of the Arabization campaign, people expropriated from their property received meager compensation in cash but were prevented from settling elsewhere within Kirkuk. During al-Bakr's presidency, the goal of *ta'mim* in Kirkuk was overt, but the policy of Arabization—*ta'rib*—was not. The fact that *ta'mim* and *ta'rib* went hand in hand was not lost, of course, on non-Arab Kirkukis. Under al-Bakr some place names in Turkish or Kurdish were changed to Arabic names, particularly ones that reflected Ba'thist ideology, such as claims to the legacy of triumphant battles. Along these lines, in 1976 many villages in the Qara Hasan area of the Ta'mim province were renamed, including two that were given the names al-Yarmuk (after the battle in which Muslims defeated the Byzantines in Syria) and al-Qadisiyya (after the battle in which Muslims defeated the Sasanians in Iran).[45] That said, the decrees of the RCC between 1975 and 1979 mainly implemented complicated procedures and regulations for construction and mortgages. These thickets of banal rules gave local officials, who had to be members of the Ba'th Party, considerable leverage in determining who could and could not continue to live in Kirkuk without mentioning *qawmiyya* in any way.[46]

The partial fog of plausible deniability obscuring Arabization in Kirkuk evaporated when al-Bakr stepped down from the presidency in 1979, allowing his deputy, Saddam Hussein, who had already been more powerful than him for some time, to assume the helm. One of Saddam Hussein's early decrees was an amnesty to allow certain Kurds affected by the collapse of the Kurdish rebellion to reintegrate into Iraq. But he then proceeded to issue another decree specifically excluding houses that had been confiscated from Kirkuki Kurds *qua* Kurds from this amnesty, even though previous confiscations of property had not specified the *qawmiyya* of those affected.[47] Soon afterward, in August 1980, Saddam Hussein signed a decision that did not contain any *qawmiyya* language but nevertheless, on behalf of the Ta'mim governorate, seized over 100 homes and shops in Kirkuk's urban *mahallas* long known to be predominantly Turkmen or Kurdish, such as Imam Qasim, Shatirlu, Sari Kahya, and Beglar.[48] Saddam Hussein continued to issue decrees bringing plots of land, mortgages, rents, and decisions pertaining to land tenure and usage under the direct control of the Ta'mim governorate and the Ba'th Party's Northern Bureau throughout the 1980s.[49]

Saddam Hussein's government provided incentives to move Arabs from southern Iraq to Kirkuk, including the provision of land for those who were landless,
which some of them willingly took.[50] Arabs who moved to Kirkuk from other
provinces were, *qua* Arabs, granted the official status of Kirkuk natives, in some
cases with forgery to suggest they had been present there for many years.[51] Some
non-Arabs, in order to be able to purchase property, were pressured into assimilation by being offered the ability to "correct" their *qawmiyya* to "Arab," which
they could do if they spoke the language (as nearly everyone in urban Kirkuk
did by that time). The "correction" policy was particularly coercive in the case of
Chaldo-Assyrians; because the Ba'th did not recognize them as a *qawmiyya*, their
choices were to declare themselves Arab or remain in an untenable, and dangerous, state of dissent in which they were considered by default to be "Christian
Kurds." New neighborhoods for Arab newcomers continued to be built in the
south, but Kirkuk's mostly non-Arab historic core areas in the northern half of
the city were neglected, with abandoned homes allowed to fall into disrepair and
neighborhoods deprived of infrastructural maintenance.[52]

Once the Ba'th regime's ethnic homogenization efforts in Kirkuk became
overt and deliberate rather than obscured by other pretenses, it sought to justify
and bolster those policies. It attempted to do so, as it did with many other repressive policies, through cultivating academic expertise. The government invested
in sending many accomplished Iraqi students and scholars abroad to complete
work in the social sciences. Not all these academics, however, ended up being
compliant with the party line.

In the late 1970s the Ministry of Higher Education and Scientific Research
funded the studies of a Kurdish linguist from Kirkuk, Mohammed Amin Qadir,
toward a PhD in sociolinguistics at the University of Aston in Birmingham on
the topic of Kirkukis' language usage. However, his comprehensive dissertation, completed in 1980, did not exhibit findings that were consistent with the
Ba'th goal of *ta'mim* in Kirkuk. After distributing questionnaires and conducting dozens of interviews, Qadir concluded that Kirkukis' language usage and
"language loyalty" had no correlation with their socioeconomic status. Rather,
the correlation of these factors with Kirkukis' "ethnic backgrounds" was "indisputable."[53] Any differences in dialect, in other words, had to be attributed to
intrinsic group differences of the sort that are not easily altered by the centralized
policies of an authoritarian government. Indeed, Qadir described "strict separation" among Kurds, Turkmens, and Arabs "despite the apparently cosmopolitan
nature of the town."

Qadir also focused specifically on Kirkuk's Kurdish community, describing them as "extremely proud" of their language, with "strong national feelings," and so accustomed to the use of Kurdish in daily life that the use of other languages in everyday conversations with one another would be perceived as snobbish. Their pride in their language, he wrote, stemmed from their "inhuman treatment . . . from the authorities of the different countries in which they live." Qadir was frank about the fact that, given the political circumstances of the time, non-Arab Kirkukis whom he interviewed were afraid to admit to him that Arabic was not their most fluent spoken language. Some even asked him to swear on the Qur'an that his research was "non-political" before responding to questions.[54]

Qadir's comments could only have aggravated the government officials who had funded his doctoral studies. He appears to have faced negative consequences as a result, though the exact nature of what happened to him remains unclear. Iraqi scholars I spoke to who were his contemporaries agree that he was pressured to leave the country, took refuge in another country in the Arab world, and died not long afterward sometime in the 1980s. One of my interlocutors, a Kirkuki Kurd who was working in British academia at the time Qadir completed his dissertation, believed that he had been killed in a targeted hit.[55]

HOW ANFAL RELIED ON KIRKUK

By the 1980s the uncomfortable-but-quiet 1975 status quo between Baghdad and the Kurdish nationalist movement brought about by Barzani's emigration and the Algiers Agreement had been completely overturned. While the Kurdish movement was largely underground or in exile, the KDP had new leadership under Barzani's sons, Mas'ud and Idris Barzani, and Jalal Talabani's leftist breakaway faction declared the formation of the Patriotic Union of Kurdistan (PUK). The PUK gained a foothold in Kirkuk by the mid-1980s and, to this day, remains the dominant strand of Kurdish politics there. A renowned PUK commander, Mama Rişa, was based in Kirkuk until his assassination there by the Ba'th regime in 1985.[56] Other, smaller factions of the Kurdish movement also sprang up, and often vicious infighting between these groups stalled the formation of a unified front for further negotiations or resistance.[57]

Meanwhile, in 1979 a revolution in Iran brought a Shi'i clerical republic to power, and animosity between the new government and Saddam Hussein escalated rapidly. In September 1980 Saddam Hussein dramatically tore up a copy of the Algiers Agreement on Iraqi television and sent troops across the formerly resolved border. This was the beginning of the Iran-Iraq War, the longest conventional ground war of the twentieth century. The war would end eight years later with the new consolidation of previously less stable governments in both Baghdad and Tehran, no territory gained on either side, and hundreds of thousands killed, maimed, and missing.

The various factions of the Iraqi Kurdish movement took different positions in the Iran-Iraq conflict, in a complex and shifting set of solidarities and enemy-of-my-enemy alignments. At one point, in 1983, the KDP assisted the Iranian regime with the capture of a border town in northeastern Iraq. Saddam Hussein and other Ba'th officials feared the possibility of a larger Iranian infiltration through the northeastern border, and so the government responded to this event with a brutal collective punishment. Beginning on 30 July 1983, security forces entered resettlement camps in the area of the border incursion where recently displaced Kurds from Barzan lived. They arrested and deported every man and adolescent boy they could find, numbering in the thousands. These "Barzani men" were disappeared; a fraction of them were found in a mass grave many years later in a remote desert area between Iraq, Kuwait, and Saudi Arabia.[58]

Amid their fear of security threats, the Ba'th regime extended its surveillance over every institution in Kirkuk. This is illustrated in a brief episode involving two mundane job applications.[59] In 1985 two men with roots in the Sulaymaniyya province applied for work as drivers for the North Oil Company. The job would allow them to access the oil depot in the 1 Haziran area in Kirkuk (named after the date of the nationalization of oil in 1972, 1 June) for civil purposes related to the transportation of fuel. Permission for performing this low-level job had to come directly from the Ba'th Party's Directorate of Security (mudiriyyat al-amn) in the Sulaymaniyya province, which had access to information about the men's political affiliations and activities and those of their family members. Both men filled out by hand the standard Identity Investigation Procedure Form, a form requesting information about their affiliations with tribes, professional and educational organizations, and political organizations, as well as the identity of various family members, including spouses, siblings, and paternal and maternal uncles. These forms, with photographs of the men attached, were then gathered by the North Oil Company's Directorate of Police and forwarded to the Sulaymaniyya Directorate of Security along with a petition of support for each man, both signed by two local officials certifying that the man in question lived in their jurisdiction.

The younger of the two men, born in 1967, described himself on the form as a nasir, or "supporter," of the Ba'th Party. This placed him one rank above the lowest rank of the party's membership—mu'ayyid, or "sympathizer." In northern Iraq, even the rank of *mu'ayyid* could take up to two to three years to reach because of more onerous requirements to achieve party membership than in the rest of the country.[60] That is, the younger man was already a well-established Ba'thist despite having just reached the age of majority, implying that he had joined the party as an adolescent.[61] He listed his current residence as a village in the Sulaymaniyya province and his tribal affiliation as Kurdish. He indicated no links with professional, educational, or other associations, though he described his extended family's political affiliation as "Ba'thist," like his own. The older of the two men, born in 1956, also described his residence as a village in Sulaymaniyya and his tribe as Kurdish, but he professed no political or professional ties on his behalf or on behalf of any member of his family. The oil company police sent the forms and petitions to the Ba'th security office in Sulaymaniyya with a cover letter dated 18 September 1985.

More than two months later, on 27 November 1985, the Sulaymaniyya office issued its decisions in a letter to the Directorate of Police for the North Oil Company. Both prospective drivers were described as "good in conduct and behavior and from the Kurdish *qawmiyya*." Only the younger of the two, however, was granted permission to enter the area of the 1 Haziran oil depot, on account of the fact that he was Ba'thist in affiliation "and none of his relatives are attached to the saboteurs [*al-mukharribin*]." The older man was described in the letter as "independent politically, among those who have returned to national alignment [*min al-'a'idin lil-saff al-watani*]." Having *returned* to "national alignment," though certainly better than being a dissident, led to a lower status, as did his lack of party affiliation. Even more damning, his brother was a deserter, or *harib*, linked with the PUK, and the man had not included this particular brother's name on his Identity Investigation Procedure Form. For these reasons the older man was denied entry to 1 Haziran and could not work as a driver for the oil company.

The Ba'th Party completely dictated movement through Kirkuk's industrial spaces. The two would-be drivers were from Sulaymaniyya and went through that province's party apparatus. But one can safely assume, despite the absence of comparable files from Kirkuk's Ba'th-era Directorate of Security (few have yet come to light),[62] that natives of Kirkuk would have found their movements similarly circumscribed. The fact that the party controlled employment at all levels of government, in educational institutions (even at the primary and secondary levels), and in the military has already been well established by those who have studied Ba'th Iraq.[63] It becomes clear upon further study of the Ba'th archive that the oil industry was another state institution whose employees, even in relatively menial jobs, were under a particularly intense form of scrutiny. The precautions that the party took before permitting anyone access to the area of an oil depot, even as a driver, were extraordinary in their attention to ideological loyalty.

The Ba'th Party had reason to be concerned about its ability to control Kirkuk's oil installations, because the Kurdish movement did, in fact, have its eyes on the oil company. In 1986 another Kurdish faction of *pêşmerge*, this time from the PUK, decided to assist an Iranian force in carrying out a more daring attack on the symbolic target of the Kirkuk oil fields and their Oil Protection Forces. With rockets provided by the Iranian government (as they probably had been in the similar attack in 1968), the *pêşmerge* carried out a dawn raid on the oil installations, causing minor damage, and then quickly retreated. In this case the damage was mainly psychological: Saddam Hussein's regime was taken aback by the successful infiltration, both physical and ideological, of an area so tightly secured that even low-level company employees had to be vetted for their affinity to the party.[64] The way that the regime eventually responded to these *pêşmerge* threats betrayed their assumption that Kurds, as an ethnic group, were a fifth column. Their approach to defense and the shoring up of power through the logic of *qawmiyya*—in which members of one "nationality" are inherently threatening to the unity and consolidation of the state—would lead to a predictable, and horrifying, conclusion in the Anfal genocide.

Anfal, the Arabic term used by the Ba'th to describe these campaigns, means "spoils," as in the spoils of war. Here, it was derived from a sura of the Qur'an on fighting and prevailing over the "disbelievers," the enemies of God and the Muslim community. The reference, like the repeated use of the names of the historical battles al-Qadisiyya and al-Yarmuk, reflects Saddam Hussein's penchant for Islamic symbolism. The Anfal campaigns broadly followed the pattern of the Arabization village destructions and the 1983 Barzani deportations—bulldozing and burning homes, arresting communities en masse with women and children separated from men, and taking them to prisons and concentration camps—but scaled up to terrifying proportions. They spanned many operations in the late 1980s, with a concentrated set of eight campaigns in 1988. The campaigns overwhelmingly targeted Kurds; in addition, they swept up some members of minorities who lived in predominantly Kurdish areas, particularly Chaldo-Assyrians and Yazidis, who did not conform to the Ba'thist concept of *qawmiyyas*.[65] Tens of thousands, and perhaps hundreds of thousands—men, women, and children—were disappeared.[66] Thousands of others were killed in direct aerial attacks on civilians, such as the chemical gas attack on the city of Halabja on 16 March 1988.

Notably, Anfal deportations did not occur in the city of Kirkuk or its immediate surroundings. Rather, the Ba'th Party was primarily concerned with villages
and towns in the hinterlands of Arbil, Sulaymaniyya, and Dohuk, quite far to
Kirkuk's north and east. Arabization policies and practices continued to displace
and disenfranchise non-Arab Kirkukis throughout this period, and individual
Kirkukis were certainly vulnerable to arrest, torture, and disappearance as a result
of Ba'thist persecution of dissidents in every part of Iraq. But Kirkuk itself was
not systematically targeted for the mass murder of Kurds. Instead, Kirkuk's role
in the Anfal genocide was that of headquarters: it was the vantage point from
which 'Ali Hasan al-Majid, Saddam Hussein's Tikriti cousin and the architect of
the genocide, conceived it and carried it out after being appointed head of the
Ba'th Party's Northern Bureau in 1987.[67]

Most infamously, Kirkuk was home to Topzawa (Figure 15), the enormous
camp on a Popular Army base just southwest of the city, where most Anfal
deportees spent a few days being processed, registered, and stripped of valu-
ables before being taken to other forms of detention. As a Human Rights Watch
researcher wrote after interviewing many survivors of the genocide, "For the
villagers who were trucked away from their burning villages by the army during
Anfal, all roads seemed to lead to Kirkuk, and to Topzawa."[68]

The images of the trip were seared into the minds of survivors. First, their
overcrowded trucks would make a brief stop at the Ba'th Party headquarters
in Kirkuk proper, and then they would proceed to the base. Once brought into
the camp, they were crammed into standing-room-only cells with no sanitation
and fed almost nothing. Confiscated personal items, both valuable and mundane, would be ripped away by guards and piled on the floor. First, males and
females were segregated from one another; then, males were further sorted by
perceived age, with the youngest and oldest spared some of the worst treatment
and military-age males subjected to cruel interrogation and dubious accusations
of *pêşmerge* affiliation. At times, as a form of psychological torture, children—
even infants in arms—would be taken away from their mothers, sometimes
temporarily, sometimes permanently.[69] Many survivors of Topzawa never saw
their relatives, especially young adult male relatives, again.

For decades, stretching back into the monarchy era, Kirkuk had served as
Baghdad's provincial nerve center from which military operations to control
Kurdish rebels were planned and executed. The Anfal genocide ensured that, in
the Iraqi Kurdish collective memory of persecution, Kirkuk would stand out,
even to Kurds who had no previous connection to the city (i.e., most of them).

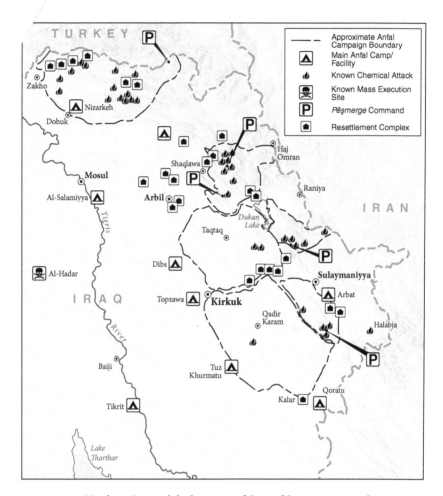

FIGURE 15. Northern Iraq and the locations of the Anfal campaigns in relation to Kirkuk. Based on data from RightsMaps.com, rightsmaps.com/html/anfalful.html (accessed 23 July 2018).

Furthermore, Anfal brought the city of Kirkuk under the direct purview of the Ba'th Party. In previous eras Kirkuk's security apparatus hinged on the local Iraqi army garrison, the police, and the oil company. The initial stage of Arabization relied on the governorate structure, placing much of the power to control who could own lands and live in dwellings with the Ta'mim governor. By 1987 both the means of violence and the authority of decision making in Kirkuk lay largely in the hands of the party bureau itself.

Once the party controlled Kirkuk, the Turkmen community was not spared from policies of mass displacement. In 1990 Saddam Hussein visited Kirkuk to announce a campaign to "clean" the citadel.[70] Kirkuk's citadel was, by that point, a subject of international academic study as one of the oldest continuously inhabited settlements in the world. An Iraqi architectural historian affiliated with the Ba'th government, Tariq al-Janabi, had begun in the late 1970s to study a famous monument in the citadel known locally as Yeşil Kümbet (Green Dome) or Gök Kümbet (Blue Dome). He published his work on this topic, and other work on medieval Iraqi architectural history, through the government's Directorate General of Antiquities. Al-Janabi was then invited to present his work on the Kirkuk citadel amid prominent scholars at a symposium held at the University of Edinburgh. In the proceedings from that conference, which were published in 1994, al-Janabi described the then-recent government activities in the Kirkuk citadel as "an ambitious project of conservation and restoration in Kirkuk." The goal of the project, he said, was "to clear and restore the existing monuments of the citadel of Kirkuk."[71]

Once again, Baghdad provided the Kirkuk municipality with millions of dinars, this time to compensate the hundreds of Turkish-speaking families— mostly Turkmen but some Kurdish, Arab, and Chaldean—whose homes were to be taken from them. The citadel was emptied out; the homes were mostly razed.[72] Al-Janabi's paper made no mention of these deportations, though his vague reference to "clearing" seems to allude to this aspect of the project, raising the obvious question of how such an action can be part of "conservation"—a question that seems not to have occurred to the book's editor. An act of ethnic cleansing in one of the world's oldest continuously inhabited places proceeded unhindered by operating under the cover of an ambitious "restoration" of antiquities sanctioned by Western experts.

CONCLUSION

On one hand, the Ba'thist logic of *qawmiyya* in Kirkuk fits with the pattern of the city's solidifying ethnic identities, segregation, and fragmentation over the course of the twentieth century. The Iraqi regime of the late twentieth century assumed that, individual collaborators aside, a community's loyalties could be predicted on the basis of their "nationality." In a city that had already experienced periodic explosions of intercommunal violence, Arabization and the Anfal genocide were outgrowths of the same trends. The Ba'th Party also exercised physical and ideological control over Kirkuk's urban spaces and oil infra-structure in a way that was consistent with, if more extreme than, the actions of prior governments.

Yet there is a key difference between the violence of the Ba'th era in Kirkuk and the violence of the first ten years of the Iraqi republic. Amid the turmoil of revolutionary Iraq, which sharpened political stakes but also opened up different kinds of mobilization, the possibility arose of making a claim to the city and asserting communal rights as a group—a possibility that manifested in the form of ethnic solidarities. In this environment different versions of Kirkuk's history could be articulated and argued over. Combined with the unresolved pain of previous grievances, those arguments could turn into pitched battles in the streets, or even, at worst, an intercommunal massacre. In Ba'th Iraq, as the state extended control over both material and discursive worlds—and then the party permeated and supplanted the state—the possibility of open political expression dramatically diminished. The horrors of Ba'th policy in Kirkuk were certainly a form of ethnic violence, but they were not intercommunal violence. Once the Ba'th regime was overthrown, new possibilities, and crises, in ethnopolitical mobilization would emerge.

CONCLUSION

AFTER THE 1991 GULF WAR a coalition led by the United States, the United Kingdom, and France established a no-fly zone in northern Iraq that allowed for the first formation of a self-governing Kurdish region in Iraq's history, the Kurdistan Regional Government (KRG). Kirkuk fell outside both the no-fly zone and the KRG area, remaining under the control of Saddam Hussein's government. The Arabization campaign—official harassment and intimidation of non-Arabs, seizure of their property, prohibition of their resettlement in Kirkuk, and pressure to change their *qawmiyya* to "Arab"—continued unabated through the 1990s. In the meantime, the KRG's claim to Kirkuk was not a unified one. For several years the Kurdish region was riven by civil war between its Kurdistan Democratic Party (KDP) and Patriotic Union of Kurdistan (PUK) factions. At the peak of this conflict, in 1996, Iraqi troops captured Arbil from the PUK for a few days, a move that KDP head Mas'ud Barzani welcomed. It was in this context that the PUK remained the dominant Kurdish nationalist force in Kirkuk.

The Arabization of Kirkuk and the horrors of the Anfal genocide only intensified the Kurdish movement's determination to claim the governorate as part of a proposed independent Kurdish region. In March 1991, during a series of uprisings against Saddam Hussein's government following the withdrawal of the American-led coalition of Operation Desert Storm, Kurdish *pêşmerge* forces took control of Kirkuk fleetingly before being forced out again by Iraqi army troops. During the American-led 2003 invasion, it was once again the *pêşmerge*—by now the official military of the KRG—who captured Kirkuk, this time on behalf of the coalition. They controlled the city for six months before withdrawing and leaving it in control of American troops, though they maintained an ongoing presence close to the city.[1] In the early months of post-Ba'th administration of Kirkuk, American officials who oversaw the formation of temporary provincial councils relied heavily on the notion that what they thought of as Kirkuk's "four major ethnic groups"—Kurdish, Turkmen, Arab, and Christian—needed to be equally represented, thereby institutionalizing the politics of ethnicity anew.[2] Similar identity-based formulas for political institutions, especially with regard to sectarian identities—Sunni versus Shi'i—prevailed elsewhere in American administration in Iraq. (Kirkukis also have Sunni and Shi'i communities, but these affiliations were not used in provincial politics after 2003, despite their use in most of the rest of the country.)

Before long, the councils were replaced by an elected provincial government whose ability to govern was hampered by severe factionalism along ethnicized lines. In this environment the KRG and its two leading parties, the KDP and the PUK, began to wield their authority in Kirkuk in more ways than ever before. Support for these parties, and for other Kurdish nationalist parties, grew in Kirkuk as Kurds who had been displaced during the eras of Arabization and Anfal moved back to their hometown with their children and families. Sometimes, these returnees were forced to live in terrible conditions, as they had no homes to return to; many of them squatted in Kirkuk's stadium or in decrepit abandoned offices of the Ba'th Party.[3] As had been the case previously, the PUK prevailed in influence locally, eventually leading to the election of a PUK-aligned provincial governor, Najmaldin Karim, in 2011.

The KRG's intelligence agency, Asayîş, started to operate in Kirkuk in a manner that intensified interethnic tensions. For instance, an investigation by reporters Steve Fainaru and Anthony Shadid in 2005 found that Asayîş agents and Kirkuki Kurdish police officers with ties to major Kurdish political parties were covertly orchestrating illegal abductions of Kirkuki Arabs and Turkmens to KRG prisons, where they were held without charges and often tortured.[4] In retaliation, militant groups made up mainly of Arabs targeted Kirkuk-based Asayîş agents in attacks, including a deadly series of car bombs in February 2011.[5]

The level of violence in Kirkuk at the height of Iraq's civil war was not as severe as it was in Baghdad, Basra, and Mosul, Iraq's largest cities. It was aimed in many different directions and was often of obscure origin; it would not be accurate to assume that it always stemmed from ethnic tensions. Kirkuk also experienced, like other Iraqi cities, the terrible scourge of random car bombs, rockets fired inexplicably into civilian areas, and other acts of terror with no clear message. Kirkukis periodically held street demonstrations and counter-demonstrations in which members of different ethnic groups would confront each other and wave their respective flags (including, in some cases, the Iraqi flag), but these typically did not descend into violence.[6] This fact is remarkable in light of the frightening degree of intercommunal warfare between Sunnis and Shiʿis that was consuming Baghdad at the same time.

On the other hand, there were some plainly targeted political killings. The Kirkuk headquarters of the major ethnonationalist parties—the KDP, the PUK, and the Iraqi Turkmen Front—were all attacked at different times. In a 2008 investigative article in the nonpartisan Kurdish magazine *Lvin*, a young Kirkuki Kurdish journalist, Soran Mama Hama, made an explosive accusation against Kirkuk's highest-ranking officers and bureaucrats, specifically singling out the KRG's ruling parties. He alleged that they were allowing brothels in which women were abused to run unchecked in the city in order to exploit those women for sexual bribes. Hama was assassinated in front of his home in Shorija shortly after the article's publication.[7]

The KRG's influence also grew in Kirkuk in subtler ways, including through the control of some of the city's infrastructure. For instance, in 2011 Kirkuk governor Najmaldin Karim negotiated an arrangement whereby the governorate's electrical grid became attached to Kurdistan's.[8] This deal came about in response to Kirkukis' continuous complaints about the city's sustained lack of functional utilities and sanitation. Journalists and scholars have consistently found through interviews with Kirkukis that concern with the lack of access to these kinds of basic services, as well as inadequate health care and education, is far more prevalent than concern with matters such as the implementation of Article 140 to resolve Kirkuk's status.[9] Much like the Iraq Petroleum Company (IPC) in an earlier era, the KRG came to command leverage over Kirkuk's electricity supply for reasons related to local politics—in this case, yielding the positive effect of a greater number of hours of electricity per day than in the regions connected to Baghdad's grid. Moreover, the KRG expressed its perception that it had a constitutional right to play a role in decisions regarding the development of the Kirkuk oil field.[10] This particularly bold intervention in local industrial affairs was a sign of the growth and evolution of the KRG's claim to Kirkuk.

Then, in 2014, Kurdish nationalist influence over Kirkuk reached a crucial tipping point in the city's modern history: outright capture without significant resistance from Baghdad. In early June the extremist militant organization known as the Islamic State captured the city of Mosul and pushed east and south, attacking both Iraqi and KRG targets. One of the *pêşmerge*'s responses was to move into Kirkuk. Remarkably, the Iraqi army vacated Kirkuk, leaving Kurdish forces in control of the city indefinitely. Baghdad then withheld Kirkuk's oil revenues from the province, creating an ongoing dispute with the provincial government. In the spring of 2017 the local government flew Kurdistan's flag over its buildings, sparking competing street demonstrations between flag-waving Turkmens and Kurds. In June 2017 reports surfaced that the Russian oil company Rosneft was in talks with the KRG to develop oil-bearing areas near Kirkuk, despite Baghdad's objections.[11] Weeks before a referendum to poll Kurdistan's inhabitants on the question of independence, scheduled for 25 September 2017, Kirkuk's provincial council voted to take part in the referendum. The meeting was boycotted by Turkmen and Arab representatives.[12] The leader of the Iraqi Turkmen Front, Arshad al-Salihi (Erşat Salihi), appeared on the Iraqi television channel al-'Ahd on the same day to decry the danger that Turkmens and Arabs were facing in Kirkuk and to demand that Baghdad provide security for the province.[13]

The Kurdistan independence referendum proceeded on 25 September 2017, including in Kirkuk, and produced the widely expected result: an overwhelming vote for independence. But the KRG did not break the results down by region, making it impossible to know how many Kirkukis had voted in favor of joining Kurdistan. Immediately after the vote, Baghdad threatened military action to retake disputed territories from Kurdish control.[14] Tensions in Kirkuk grew, as they had so many times before, to a fever pitch, both on the ground and on social media. On 14 October a dramatic video circulated on Twitter that showed Kurds in Kirkuk taking up arms and vowing to fight.[15] Then, early in the morning on 16 October, Iraqi forces began an operation to retake the city of Kirkuk.[16] Like the *pêşmerge* three years earlier, they did so quickly, facing remarkably little resistance despite the widespread anger and dismay of many Kirkuki Kurds. Kirkuk's governor, Najmaldin Karim, who had supported the independence referendum, was deposed.

Kirkuk's social and political trajectory has not always followed a predictable or straightforward path. At the turn of the twentieth century, it would have been impossible to predict that the market town of Kirkuk would eventually be some orders of magnitude larger and would end up caught between the pull of political entities based in, of all places, Arbil and Baghdad. Seventy years ago, the strongest trends in Kirkuk's local politics were centered on urban development and labor organization, not ethnic mobilization. In certain ways, though, its present-day circumstances fall into well-worn patterns. Today, both the KRG and the Iraqi central government are trying to integrate Kirkuk. As they do so, Kirkuk's national status—if we momentarily adopt the common assumption that cities need to have one—is no less ambiguous than it was nine decades ago, at which point the competition for its ownership was between Baghdad and London on one side and Ankara on the other.

Competing conceptions of Kirkuk's history are at the heart of this dispute, which is why I have sought to cut through those histories by asking new historical questions about Kirkuk's oil complex and ethnicity as a practice. The most widespread ethnonationalist mythologies surrounding Kirkuk leave little room for such intricacies. To be sure, these ideas should be understood as responses to historical traumas and political uncertainties and should be respected from that perspective. As Edward Said wrote with regard to Palestinians and Israelis, it is important to recognize the ethnic and nationalist narratives of oppressed people as "imperatives" and "try to reconcile them, rather than dismiss them as so much non-factual ideology."[17] But because these narratives, in the form of alleged expertise, have penetrated popular discussions and even, to some extent, the academic literature about Kirkuk,[18] it is necessary to take a moment to critically examine their factual claims.

The Kurdish nationalist idea of Kirkuk as the lost "Jerusalem" of the Kurdish people mischaracterizes the complexity of Kirkuki Kurdish interests for much of the twentieth century. In urban Kirkuk politically active Kurds did not outwardly and operatively align with the Barzani-led Kurdish national movement in large numbers until the revolutionary era after the 1958 coup. Urban Kirkuk and its hinterland were not physical battlegrounds for the Kurdish movement until that time, even though Kirkuk had previously been the main center of counterrevolutionary policing by Baghdad and British authorities. It is only since the late twentieth century that Kurds have come to constitute what appears to be a demographic majority—likely a narrow one—in both the city and the Kirkuk province. The impassioned notion that controlling Kirkuk is absolutely central to Kurdish sovereignty is, contrary to many Kurdish nationalists' claims, relatively recent.

Meanwhile, the Turkmen nationalist concept of Kirkuk as a Turkmen "ancestral capital" pervaded by Kurdish and Arab influence is poignant in light of many Turkmens' emigration to Turkey, their casualties in intercommunal and state violence, and the steady decline of the city's Turkish-language culture. Turkmen intellectuals have responded to these profound losses by publishing dozens of works of memory that exhaustively list and document mundane aspects of their lives in Kirkuk—the city's mosques, its Turkish-language singers and poets, its newspapers and publishing houses, and more. But Turkmen nationalist politicians tend to deny that their community is dwindling in number. They rely on unusually high estimates of Turkmens' demographic percentage in the Iraqi population, thereby choosing to play a game of numbers rather than arguing in favor of respect for all forms of difference. Subsequently, they demand impractical solutions to the Kirkuk crisis, such as an ethnically based "proportional" percentage power-sharing scheme split 32–32–32–4 between Turkmens, Kurds, Arabs, and Christians, respectively.[19] Therefore, much like the Kurdish nationalist perspective, the Turkmen nationalist perspective hews to dubious factual claims, producing unrealistic interpretations of Kirkuk's current circumstances.

And then there is the Iraqi nationalist idea, usually promoted by Arabs and sometimes by Turkmens and Chaldo-Assyrians, of fighting for Kirkuk as part of the struggle for the unity of a multiethnic Iraq. This idea may seem pleasantly pluralistic in the context of the pervasive sectarianism that has riven Iraq since 2003. Indeed, ordinary Iraqis who express it are often sincere about the principle of inclusiveness. However, a historical perspective makes it clear that this notion is inevitably loaded with the brutal legacy of Arabist policies that disenfranchised or displaced Kirkuk's Jewish, Kurdish, Turkmen, and Chaldo-Assyrian communities. It should be abundantly clear by now that integrating Kirkuk into Baghdad's domain has never actually been a diversity project. It is small wonder that Kurds, the community most consistently targeted and profoundly harmed by Arabization in Kirkuk, usually find the idea of remaining aligned with Baghdad hard to stomach.

Throughout this book I have focused on the development of ethnicity as a political practice in Kirkuk over the course of the twentieth century. By treating ethnicity as dynamic, I aim to question the ethnopolitical paradigm that currently dominates discussions of Kirkuk. First, it is underappreciated that, even now, political views in Kirkuk are not wholly predictable by self-identity. Soran Mama Hama was murdered after criticizing fellow Kurds. There are Turkmens and Chaldo-Assyrians aligned with all the major Kurdish parties; there are Kurds who reject both the KDP and the PUK. As the state-led ethnic cleansing of the Ba'th era demonstrated, ethnicized violence is not necessarily the same thing as intercommunal violence. It is time to open up lines of inquiry about Kirkuk's politics beyond ethnicity. The ethnopolitical paradigm remains useful for understanding the ways in which communities' collective stakes in the current crisis are articulated, but it is only one starting point in the effort to fully comprehend the intricacies of Kirkuk's local political domain. Its persistent use as an all-encompassing framework for understanding modern Kirkuk can, and sometimes does, lead to ahistorical and simplified analyses of the dispute by implying that it is solely a crisis of failed interethnic relations.

At worst, this paradigm can foreclose questions about other issues, such as the political economy of the dispute. For instance, it often reduces the role of oil in the conflict to a false dichotomy—either a coveted prize or an utterly irrelevant factor—or conceives of it as simply a curse rather than as a complex. Kirkuk's position as the heart of the oil industry declined steadily through the Ba'th era, and the notion of Kirkuki oil as Iraq's greatest cash treasure is ever more irrelevant. Today, Rumayla, not Kirkuk, is easily Iraq's single most productive oil field, exporting 1.4–1.5 million barrels per day. Estimates of Kirkuk's rate of production vary widely, but all are drastically lower than this number.[20]

One might ask instead, *how* do the oil industry and other sites of labor relations continue to shape the city's local politics and society? In what way does the historical *idea* of Kirkuk as Iraq's "city of black gold" (regardless of its actual production numbers) play into different actors' political calculations or emotive attachments? Another question might be about how Kirkuk's urban physical geography has evolved as large numbers of exiled Kurds have returned (or immigrated anew) to the city after the fall of the Ba'th. How has this process reproduced and reinforced spatial ethnic divisions?[21]

Within the context of ethnopolitics itself, it is necessary to consider the significance of the fact that certain claims to Kirkuk's status overlap despite having different ethnicized casts. Most notably, one could argue that the Arab and Turkmen "narratives" should not be viewed as distinct but rather as different forms of the same conception of Kirkuk, because they both hold that Kirkuk's status as an Iraqi city must not change.[22] The partial convergence of Arab and Turkmen claims to Kirkuk dates back to the 1950s, when prominent Turkmens first began to exhibit sympathy for pan-Arabist ideas.

Overuse of the ethnopolitical paradigm to the exclusion of other lines of inquiry can also lead to circular reasoning whereby certain subjects are only regarded as worthy of study if they fall within the paradigm. For instance, the interests and concerns of Chaldo-Assyrian Kirkukis have largely been left out of research on the Kirkuk crisis because, as a community, they are small in number; therefore, in this paradigm, they have no stake in controlling any of Kirkuk's institutions.[23] It only takes a moment's reflection, however, to realize that eth-nicities do not control institutions. Leaving Chaldo-Assyrians, Armenians, and other minority Kirkukis out of these discussions not only begs the question but also implies that Kirkuk is some sort of pie to be divided in one way or another between the ethnic communities who are big enough to be permitted to eat it. This has never been how cities work.

The omission of those who fall outside the tripartite Kurdish-Turkmen-Arab schema ignores the fact that paying close attention to these Kirkukis may be precisely the best way to understand the contours and limits of ethnopolitics, the roots of communal interests and anxieties, and how these phenomena are prone to shift over time. Accordingly, a close reading of the Chaldo-Assyrian narrative of Kirkuk's history might show that they, like Turkmens, often see the city as a sort of ancestral capital and fear the ramifications of their numerical and political decline as a community.[24] The similarities between Chaldo-Assyrian and Turkmen characterizations of Kirkuk suggest that such notions are not uniquely part of a "Turkmen narrative." Rather, they are natural consequences of the vicissitudes of urban change for more vulnerable communities that could also potentially affect marginalized Kirkukis along the lines of, for instance, class, religion, gender, or sexuality. This kind of human empathy is desperately needed in the current discourse on Kirkuk.

Indeed, one of the most striking features of recent ethnonationalist writ-ings on Kirkuk is the absence of any sense of how political, social, and eco-nomic trends over the course of the twentieth century subjected every Kirkuki to profound harm in some way, often simultaneously and for similar or identical reasons. Instead, by reading books such as the Kurdish-nationalist *The Kirkuk Region and Attempts to Change Its Ethnic Reality* or the Turkmen-nationalist *The Turcomans and Kirkuk*, one could come away with the impression that Kirkuk's politics have always been a zero-sum game in which one solid, clearly defined, unitary ethnic community loses catastrophically while the others avariciously pursue the region's oil.

This oversimplification in discourse on Kirkuk is inextricably linked with a lack of mutual understanding between Kirkukis of different ethnicities. Consider a Kirkuki Kurdish nationalist who is sincere in his conviction that Kirkuk is a crucial part of Kurdistan. He believes that the city's presence atop an oil field has prevented it from acceding to that status and has hurt the Kurds. On the other hand, an Arabic-speaking Kirkuki of Turkmen and Arab origin might be equally sincere in her belief that Kirkuk should remain part of a nonfederal Iraq under Baghdad's jurisdiction. She probably believes, as do most of those in Iraq who oppose Kurdish nationalism, that the Kurds are trying to annex Kirkuk solely to use its oil for economic and strategic purposes toward the goal of total independence.[25] She may even believe, in light of previous killings of Turkmens by Kurds, that Kurdish lamentation about genocide is a mere fig leaf. As long as each of these Kirkukis ascribes illegitimate motives to the other, empathy is impossible. Furthermore, as long as they each deny the central role of the oil complex in their own stances—regardless of whether or not they, individually, have vested interests in the oil industry—they will continue to question each other's motives.

Consequently, it might seem illogical that the other dominant trope in writings on Kirkuk is the idea that it is a "city of ethnic harmony." On closer examination, though, this notion can easily go hand in hand with the absence of intercommunal cooperation. The farcical essence of this paradox can be found in the meeting hall of Kirkuk's viciously divided provincial council. Kurdish representatives have dominated the council since its post-2003 formation, and Turkmen and Arab members have regularly boycotted its meetings over the years. The council's attenuated votes are held in front of an enormous rainbow-striped medallion proclaiming Kirkuk a "City of Brotherhood" in its three main languages (*kardeşlik şehri, madinat al-ta'akhi, şarî birayetî*).[26] Of course, the many Kirkukis whose personal socialities, or even immediate families, exist at the intersections of different groups may promote the idea of Kirkuk's cosmopolitanism with utmost sincerity. Such harmony—especially with regard to culture and language—may be a reality in their own lives, as it was in the life of Sargon Boulus, the Kirkuki poet who described his hometown as a "crucible" of "poetic chemistry."

However, the concept of Kirkuk as a city of ethnic harmony disregards the fact that multiethnic cities are not inherently tolerant simply by virtue of being diverse. On the contrary, urban segregation and mutual mistrust between communities—both of which built up slowly in Kirkuk between the 1920s and 1960s and then exploded during the Ba'th era—can symbiotically reinforce one another and lead to profound discord.[27] Idealizing cosmopolitanism in a vague way can, in the worst case, allow strident nationalists of all stripes to advance narrow-minded arguments while maintaining a patina of liberal inclusiveness and, at the same time, accusing those with different views of violating this ideal.

It is certainly heartening that Kirkukis come together for public festivals, standing side by side in different ethnic costumes. They read multilingual independent local news websites. Dozens of children from across the city have formed a parkour group that meets amid the ruins of the citadel, a place that is a central part of their heritage, to work on their techniques.[28] But none of these practices, even though they are habitual and dedicated, will solve Kirkuk's problems in the absence of truth telling and restitution by those in power. Shortly following his unilateral raising of the Kurdistan flag above Kirkuk's government buildings in 2017, Governor Karim claimed that the flag represented all ethnicities but that the Turkmen protests against the flag did not truly represent Turkmens.[29] Months later, when Iraqi troops retook the city, non-Kurdish Kirkukis rapidly replaced Kurdish flags with Iraqi ones, underscoring that *this* flag was the rightful symbol of multiethnic coexistence.[30] Too often, Kirkukis and other Iraqis advance exclusionary views while simultaneously insisting that they are the ones who are truly being inclusive.[31] As I have shown, the precedents for this behavior stretch back many decades.

Good faith efforts at concession of interests, withdrawal of blame, and recognition of each other's needs and grievances are required of all those who have a stake in the Kirkuk crisis, both locally and regionally, during the process of negotiation. Ethnonationalists, Iraqi nationalists, and all Kirkukis would do well to realize that acknowledging Kirkuk's painful history of ethnic fault lines and their relationship with the city's and hinterland's oil-fueled change—in other words, cultivating empathy—is a vital initial step toward reconciliation. Conflict in Kirkuk runs deep, but it must not be seen as the city's defining feature. One can only hope that a frank reckoning with this history, as well as with the legacy of oil in Kirkuk, might play a role in the city's future.

NOTE ON SOURCES
AND ARCHIVES

There is no such thing as objectivity in the writing of history. Although a historian should strive to speak the truth, claiming to present an "objective" narrative to counter accusations of bias does a disservice to the protagonists of that narrative and to the reader. Furthermore, the inherent subjectivity of history is as true of the sources from which we write as it is of the historian's perspective while writing. No archive is omniscient. Information can be fabricated, mistaken, accidentally omitted, or deliberately censored or purged. It can also be reorganized and cherry-picked according to the interests and agendas of the entity that creates the archive.

For example, the National Archives of the United Kingdom is infamous for "misplacing," or selectively removing from view, files pertaining to the history of the British Empire that may be incriminating in present political circumstances.[1] When I retrieved files from Britain's mid-twentieth-century Kirkuk consulate while doing research in these archives, I sometimes found them to be slim folders containing a few pages and a handwritten note indicating that most of the papers within them had been destroyed before declassification. I was unable, despite repeated attempts, to obtain the original version of a redacted 1958 report on events in Kirkuk through British Freedom of Information Act requests; in response to my second request, the Foreign and Commonwealth Office told me that releasing the full report would "risk prejudicing U.K. relations with, and interests in, countries in the region."[2] Similarly, when conducting research in the BP Archive at the University of Warwick, I was asked to submit my file requests three weeks ahead of time so that certain pages could be removed from them as necessary to make them suitable for public view.

In general, historians take these kinds of difficulties in stride when doing research. We form a habit of doing work in many kinds of sources and not reading any archive at face value. However, there are cases in which the creation and presentation of a particular archive result from acts and are attached to agendas that pose a grave ethical dilemma.

The case in point here is the Iraqi Ba'th Party's archives that the U.S. military seized from Iraq in 1991 and 2003: tens of millions of records documenting mass surveillance, inhuman crimes, and the mundane workings of a massive bureaucracy. These documents make up a large portion of the total extant Ba'th Party documents; the remainder of the Ba'th files still in Iraq are scattered among many different owners, including private individuals and Iraqi Kurdistan's ruling parties. The Iraq National Library and Archive has repeatedly demanded the return of the vast trove of U.S.-based files to Iraq, and Iraqi scholars have protested their removal publicly.[3] As of this writing, the overwhelming majority of the removed documents remain in the United States. Many of them have been scanned, and these digital files also reside solely in the United States. I cite some of the U.S.-based Ba'th files in Chapter 6 of this book.

The documents removed in 1991 are mostly from the security directorates of Sulaymaniyya, Dohuk, and Arbil and are known as the North Iraq Data Set (NIDS). The NIDS original files apparently were returned to the Kurdistan Regional Government in 2007.[4] The digital files remain exclusively in the custody of the Hoover Institution, a conservative think tank in Stanford, California, where they are accessible only on Hoover's own computers. The immense stash of millions of documents removed in 2003 ended up in the United States under the auspices of the Iraq Memory Foundation, a small organization founded by Brandeis University professor Kanan Makiya. Makiya, an Iraqi-born scholar of architecture and Middle Eastern studies, was a prominent supporter of the George W. Bush administration's invasion of Iraq. In 2008 the Iraq Memory Foundation turned over the papers in its possession and digital copies of them to the Hoover Institution, where they are now known as the Ba'th Regional Command Collection (BRCC). These files, like the NIDS, are only accessible in digital form at Hoover.

A smaller number of Ba'th records taken in 2003, including tapes of Saddam Hussein's meetings with his deputies, are housed at the National Defense University on the premises of Fort McNair, Washington, DC. There, over several years, they were gradually scanned, translated into English, and declassified in limited batches for researchers' use under the aegis of the Conflict Records Research Center (CRRC). Before the CRRC shut down, its stated mission was "to facilitate research using records captured during combat operations from countries, organizations, and individuals, now or once hostile to the United States."[5]

Accordingly, the CRRC's efforts were focused on making the files available to English-speaking researchers. The files could be viewed only in digitized form on the center's own computers. The database of the files was searchable only in English, and only the English translations (which were often poor, especially when they were produced by Arab Americans with no knowledge of the Iraqi dialect) could be reproduced for researchers to take off the premises. This made the CRRC's files useful to Americans who wanted to research Iraqi history without knowing any Arabic but rendered the trove effectively inaccessible to nearly all Iraqis. In 2015 the CRRC lost its funding, and, as of 2018, the documents are no longer accessible to the public at all. Furthermore, many millions of other Ba'th files remain in the custody of the U.S. Department of Defense (DOD) and have never been made public.[6]

In 2017 I learned from sociologist Wisam Alshaibi of a damning discovery he made in the Hoover archives. Stumbling upon a box of Kanan Makiya's personal papers that was apparently not supposed to be open to the public (it was promptly closed to public view afterward), Alshaibi found a collection of documents indicating that, beginning in 2004, the DOD had signed and renewed a multimillion-dollar contract with the Iraq Memory Foundation to produce records of information on Ba'th Iraq that would serve to bolster American and Iraqi support for the war effort. Some scholars have long suspected that the Hoover collection is presenting the Ba'th archives selectively to the public in a way that emphasizes Saddam Hussein regime's atrocities rather than, for example, the ways that the regime was weak, the ways that Iraqis were resistant and resilient in spite of it, or the extent to which it was supported by Western governments. Alshaibi's findings, which he is in the process of publishing, confirm this suspicion.[7]

When Alshaibi first publicized his discovery, I had already completed brief stints of research in the Ba'th archives at the CRRC and Hoover Institution in 2013 and 2015, and I had incorporated my findings into this book. Before 2013 I hesitated to use the U.S.-based Ba'th collections at all, but I also found researching the late twentieth century in Kirkuk without them to be prohibitively difficult. That year, I read Dina Khoury's then-new book *Iraq in Wartime*, a groundbreaking history of Iraqi state-society relations beginning with the Iran-Iraq War that is based primarily on the records that are now at the Hoover Institution. In her introduction Khoury grapples with the problem of using seized archives whose location in the United States prevents Iraqis from studying their own history. She argues that a researcher's use of a particular archive should not imply that the researcher condones the manner of its acquisition.

Ultimately, she concludes, using the Ba'th papers is valuable because it permits a "less ideologically charged" and more "critical" view of the inner workings of late-twentieth-century Iraq than that of any other postcolonial state in the Middle East.[8] In other words, access to these archives permits historians of Ba'th-era Iraq to read against the grain.

When I first decided to use these archives, the ethical dilemma before me primarily concerned whether or not a historian should use sensitive documents in the custody of an entity that has no right to claim ownership of them. Thinking about that question, I agreed with Khoury's reasoning. Through this reasoning, the use of these archives did not strike me as dramatically worse than the use of the colonial and corporate archives that I had already worked in extensively and whose selective composition I also did not condone. Furthermore, both the Hoover Institution and the CRRC require researchers to obtain approval for their plans from an Institutional Review Board to prevent the dissemination of ordinary Iraqis' personally identifying information that is so often found in the files, an ethical practice I found encouraging.

But I have come to realize that no matter how tenaciously we historians read against the grain of the U.S.-based Ba'th archives, we justify, at the very least, the continued existence and funding of these collections by using them. I did not use the DOD-funded Iraq Memory Foundation collection in my research; at the Hoover Institution, I used only the NIDS, whose originals are now somewhere in Iraq. But I did read files in the physical possession of the DOD at the National Defense University. I confess that, precisely because the DOD's role in the CRRC archive was overt, I did not think much about using it for my own purposes while paying little regard to the pro-war motivations of those who created it. Alshaibi's revelation that the DOD also covertly and lavishly funded the Iraq Memory Foundation, a small nonprofit that encourages donations on its website without mentioning its DOD links, has made those motivations harder to set aside.

When it comes to writing about Kirkuk, I face an additional ethical dilemma. Nearly every source I relied on to write about the Ba'th era was somehow problematic. For instance, I used a book collection of facsimiles of Ba'th files published by the Patriotic Union of Kurdistan that, like the Hoover and CRRC archives, contains unredacted documents with Kirkukis' personal information in them. My communications with individuals, though conducted carefully and without any questions intended to elicit painful accounts, were nevertheless fraught with the tensions of recalling events in a recent, disruptive era. Yet it would be dishonest for me to tell Kirkuk's story in the twentieth century without discussing the details of nationalization, Arabization, and the Anfal genocide and to give a sense of how Kirkukis lived with, through, and in spite of those campaigns—or were unable to. Those campaigns stemmed from precedents set in earlier eras in Kirkuk but also departed from that past in critical ways. My goal in writing this book has been to do justice to a place and its people whose history has been argued over but rarely engaged.

In an ethics statement the American Anthropological Association enjoins a principle of *first doing no harm* in research, stating that some lines of inquiry should not be pursued at all if they have the potential to be harmful.[9] I cite the view of anthropologists here because they have dealt with the ethics of knowledge production more explicitly than most professional historical associations have. On balance, I conclude that, had I disseminated a book claiming to be a history of Kirkuk that did not thoroughly and forthrightly contend with the Ba'th era, this would have had the potential to do harm by leading readers to inaccurate, even prejudiced, conclusions based on incomplete information. At the same time, I acknowledge that I have already done a certain amount of irreversible harm: legitimizing the demand for the Ba'th archives in the United States by signing my name on a daily ledger to use the collections at the Hoover Institution and the CRRC. A March 2018 *Stanford News* article proudly advertised that, up to that point, 170 researchers had used the Ba'th documents at the Hoover Institution. The press release marveled at the value of the documents to help "both scholars and governmental representatives better understand" the Ba'th regime's brutality, while making no mention of the fact that Iraqi scholars and officials are not among those who are able to do such research on their own history.[10] I am one of the 170 researchers whose work validates Hoover's continued holding of this collection.[11] That cannot be undone.

Every researcher who writes about Iraq, especially Ba'th-era Iraq, will have to make an individual ethical calculation. I understand that some readers will oppose the decision I have made to include citations from documents found at the Hoover Institution and the CRRC. These readers may reject any engagement with knowledge produced from the removed Ba'th archives as a form of "epistemic violence," as Sinan Antoon, quoting Gayatri Spivak, put it.[12] Conversely, others may take Dina Khoury's utilitarian approach, disagreeing with the idea that scholarship based on looted papers is inherently wrong as long as that scholarship is critical and advances our understanding of Iraq beyond what the creators of the archive intended. I stand on admittedly shaky middle ground between these positions.

Above all, I hope that the people of Kirkuk, many of whom are dear to me, benefit from the history that I have presented here. I take full responsibility for any and all of my shortcomings in meeting that goal. I have aimed to shed light on Kirkuk's stories with the insight and judiciousness that those stories are due.

NOTES

PREFACE

1. "Qanun Idarat al-Dawla al-'Iraqiyya fi-l-Fatra al-Intiqaliyya," *BBC Arabic*, 7 March 2004, news.bbc.co.uk/hi/arabic/middle_east_news/newsid_3538000/3538185 .stm (accessed 1 July 2018).

2. This quote is excerpted and translated from the longer text of the original article. "Dustur Jumhuriyyat al-'Iraq," www.cabinet.iq/PageViewer.aspx?id=2 (accessed 1 July 2018).

3. Campbell Robertson and Atheer Kakan, "Iraqi Parliament Returns to Tackle Issue of Election Law," *New York Times*, 9 September 2008, www.nytimes. com/2008/09/10/world/middleeast/10iraq.html?ref=middleeast (accessed 1 July 2018).

4. See, for instance, Zanger, "Refugees in Their Own Country."

5. L. Anderson and Stansfield, *Crisis in Kirkuk*, 140.

6. Karzan Sherabayani, *Return to Kirkuk: A Year in the Fire* (New York: Eagle Media, 2007), DVD.

7. Recent political-scientific studies of the Kirkuk issue include L. Anderson and Stansfield, *Crisis in Kirkuk*; Natali, "Settlers and State Building"; Romano, "Future of Kirkuk"; and Wolff, "Governing (in) Kirkuk."

8. L. Anderson and Stansfield, *Crisis in Kirkuk*, 56–86.

9. Sinan Salaheddin, "Bomb Kills 10 Iraqi Troops as Ethnic Tensions Rise," *Washington Post*, 14 March 2011, www.washingtonpost.com/wp-dyn/content/article/2011/03/14/AR2011031400652.html (accessed 1 July 2018).

10. See, for instance, Güçlü, "Who Owns Kirkuk?"

11. Soane, *To Mesopotamia and Kurdistan*, 120–24.

12. Al-Ma'ali, "al-Sha'ir Sarkun Bulus," 104.

INTRODUCTION

Some material from the Introduction and first five chapters of this book was previously published in Arbella Bet-Shlimon, "Group Identities, Oil, and the Local Political Domain in Kirkuk: A Historical Perspective," *Journal of Urban History* 38, no. 5 (2012): 914–31, © 2012; reprinted by permission of SAGE Publications.

1. Packer, *Assassins' Gate*, 337–40.

2. My use of the term *ethnolinguistic* reflects the prevalent basis of communal distinctions in Kirkuk. That said, the communal distinctions between Sunni and Shi'i— which most Iraqis would define as "sectarian" (*ta'ifi*), not "ethnic"—have also become significant in Kirkuk since 2003.

3. Google's Ngram Viewer, which searches millions of published texts to graph the rates of usage of particular words and phrases over time, indicates that the use of the word *ethnic* in English-language writing started to take off around 1940 and accelerated rapidly after about 1960. Ngram Viewer, books.google.com/ngrams /graph?content=ethnic&year_start=1800&year_end=2000&corpus=15&smoothing=3 &share=&direct_url=t1%3B%2Cethnic%3B%2Cco (accessed 30 June 2017).

4. Brubaker, *Ethnicity Without Groups*, 2. Brubaker's use of this language follows a similar formulation by E. P. Thompson with regard to class.

5. Bergholz, "Sudden Nationhood."

6. See, for instance, Natali, "Kirkuk Conundrum," 442.

7. See, for instance, Luke Baker, "Ancient Rivalries Vie for Dominance of Iraq's Kirkuk," *Washington Post*, 5 February 2004, www.washingtonpost.com/wp-dyn/articles/ A15048-2004Feb5.html (accessed 1 July 2018).

8. A similar, and better-known, false dichotomy about the role of oil in politics is also found in discussions of Western motivations for intervention in Iraq. It was particularly potent in the United States in debates surrounding the U.S.-led invasion of Iraq in 2003, when protesters' chants of "no blood for oil" were met with the defensive argument that the invasion had "literally nothing to do with oil" (in Secretary of Defense Donald Rumsfeld's words), which was sometimes countered by the argument that the war *was* "for oil" and that fighting Saddam Hussein for control of Iraqi petroleum was a perfectly legitimate cause. For a prominent example of the last argument, see Thomas Friedman, "A War for Oil?" *New York Times*, 5 January 2003, www.nytimes. com/2003/01/05/opinion/a-war-for-oil.html?src=pm (accessed 1 July 2018). These arguments all neglect the fact that the United States has never aimed to simply "take the oil" (in Donald Trump's words) from Iraq—forcibly seized oil is obviously not profitable for oil companies. They also neglect the fact that whether an invaded country's foremost natural resource plays a role in war planning is not typically up for debate.

9. Watts, "Resource Curse," 60–61.

10. Fuccaro, "Introduction."

11. The thorough two-volume official history of British Petroleum (now BP), based on BP's archival records and sponsored by the company, falls into this category. See Ferrier, *History of the British Petroleum Company* (vol. 1, covering 1901–1932); Bamberg, *History of the British Petroleum Company* (vol. 2, covering 1928–1954).

12. See, for instance, Frank, *Oil Empire*; Mitchell, *Carbon Democracy*; Santiago, *Ecology of Oil*; and Tinker Salas, *Enduring Legacy*.

13. Fuccaro, "Visions of the City."

14. See, for instance, Al-Nakib, *Kuwait Transformed*; Fuccaro, *Histories of City and State*; Limbert, *In the Time of Oil*; and Vitalis, *America's Kingdom*.

15. A conversation with Idan Barir in 2012 helped me to clarify this point with

regard to civic identity and politics in Kirkuk in the late Ottoman era. Barir's doctoral research at Tel Aviv University addresses Kirkuk's developing relations with the Ottoman state in the late nineteenth and early twentieth centuries.

16. See, for instance, Abdullah, *Merchants, Mamluks, and Murder*; Çetinsaya, *Ottoman Administration of Iraq*; D. R. Khoury, *State and Provincial Society*; and Shields, *Mosul Before Iraq*. With regard to the modern Iraqi state, two notable histories of provincial Iraq are Fuccaro, *The Other Kurds*; and Visser, *Basra*.

17. The political science literature on the Iraqi Kurds and the Kurdish national movement is extensive. Among the texts that are either historical in methodology or have a significant historical angle are Jwaideh, *Kurdish National Movement*; McDowall, *Modern History of the Kurds*; and van Bruinessen, *Agha, Shaikh, and State*.

18. See, for instance, Alsaden, "Baghdad Modernism"; Damluji, "Securing Democracy in Iraq"; D. R. Khoury, "Violence and Spatial Politics"; Marefat, "From Bauhaus to Baghdad"; and Pyla, "Back to the Future."

19. Duara, "Transnationalism," 38.

20. Duara, *Culture, Power, and the State*; Sahlins, *Boundaries*.

21. Examples include Dodge, *Inventing Iraq*; Simon, *Iraq Between the Two World Wars*; and Wien, *Iraqi Arab Nationalism*.

22. For instance, Orit Bashkin has written a chapter on the topic of "Iraq's others" that includes, among other discussions, an analysis of Iraqi Turkmen discourse. Bashkin, *The Other Iraq*, 157–93.

23. Zubaida, "Fragments Imagine the Nation."

24. B. Anderson, *Imagined Communities*.

25. See, for instance, Bashkin, *The Other Iraq*, 271–74; Davis, *Memories of State*, 277–78; and Zubaida, "Iraq," 344.

26. See, for instance, Haddad, *Sectarianism in Iraq*; and Kirmanj, *Identity and Nation*.

27. *Hyphenated* is a term Orit Bashkin uses to describe these kinds of combined identities, for example, Turkmen and Iraqi. See, for instance, Bashkin, *The Other Iraq*, 156, 178.

28. Judson, *Guardians of the Nation*, 3; Zahra, "Imagined Non-Communities."

29. Duara, *Culture, Power, and the State*, 1–6. Duara cites Charles Tilly as one of the originators of the term *state making*; see Tilly, *Formation of National States*.

30. Ussama Makdisi makes a similar argument with regard to the production of modern Lebanese sectarianism amid the colonial encounter and Ottoman policy. Makdisi, *Culture of Sectarianism*.

31. Batatu, *Old Social Classes*, 912–21. Another noteworthy chapter on Kirkuk in a larger book, by the journalist George Packer, examines the Ba'th campaign to Arabize Kirkuk and the uncertainties of the period immediately following the 2003 invasion; see Packer, *Assassin's Gate*, 333–69. British political adviser Emma Sky also recalls her time working for the Coalition Provisional Authority in Kirkuk in 2003 at some length in her memoir; see Sky, *The Unraveling*.

32. See, for instance, Ahmad, *Karkuk wa-Tawabi'uha*; Güçlü, *Turcomans and*

Kirkuk; Küzeci, *Kerkük Soykırımları*; Saatçi, *Urban Fabric*; Talabani, *Mintaqat Karkuk*; Talabany, *Arabization of the Kirkuk Region*; and Terzibaşı, *Kerkük Matbuat Tarihi*. One entertaining exception to this rule is a memoir by Henry D. Astarjian, an Armenian Kirkuki currently living in the United States who claims to illuminate the city's history and politics but provides few verifiable details: Astarjian, *Struggle for Kirkuk*.

33. See, for instance, Terzibaşı, *Kerkük Matbuat Tarihi*; and Terzibaşı, *Kerkük Hoyratları ve Manileri*. The latter book explores and documents two common forms of poetry in the Iraqi Turkmen literary tradition, whereas the former is a study of Kirkuki newspapers in Turkish. Also, 'Ismat Rafiq Sari Kahya, a Turkmen scholar, has written an encyclopedic, ethnographic book about Kirkuk's mosques: Sari Kahya, *Tarikh Jawamiʻ wa Masajid Karkuk*.

34. Markaz Karbala' lil-Buhuth wa-l-Dirasat, *Karkuk*.

35. Al-ʻAzzawi, *al-Ruh al-Hayya*, 279–317; Al-Ghassani, "The Rose and Its Fragrance"; al-Maʻali, "al-Shaʻir Sarkun Bulus." Al-Azzawi, Al-Ghassani, and Sargon Boulus also wrote reflective essays in 1992, after they had all left Iraq, addressing their experiences as young writers. These essays did not focus on the period when they were in Kirkuk but are nevertheless of interest. Al-ʻAzzawi, "Qissat Jil al-Sittinat fi al-ʻIraq"; Bulus, "al-Hajis al-Aqwa"; Al-Ghassani, "al-Sittinat, Hunaka, Huna, Hunalika."

36. Quoted in al-Maʻali, "al-Shaʻir Sarkun Bulus," 103–4.

37. Al-ʻAzzawi, *Akhir al-Malaʼika*. This novel has been translated into English: al-Azzawi, *The Last of the Angels*.

38. That said, the aforementioned municipality employee whom George Packer interviewed, Luna Dawood, claimed in 2004 to have saved many of the files that were earmarked for purging, and she showed Packer the room in which they were stored. Packer, *Assassins' Gate*, 337–40.

39. In 2004 the PUK published a collection of facsimiles of Baʻth documents that are presumably in their possession, some of which are addressed to officials in the "Taʼmim" (i.e., Kirkuk) governorate. Patriotic Union of Kurdistan, *Ethnic Cleansing Documents*. An essay by Mohammed Ihsan, a scholar who has worked as a minister for the KRG, cites Baʻth files pertaining to Kirkuk that he "gathered" while in that job: Ihsan, "Arabization as Genocide." For the most part, though, the locations of Baʻth-era files from Kirkuk, particularly its Security Directorate, are unknown. In this book's Note on Sources and Archives I discuss the fragmentation of the Baʻth archives in greater detail.

40. Benjamen, "Research at the Iraqi National Library and Archives."

41. A knowledgeable Kurdish scholar once told me in conversation that many politically active Kurds spent time in Kirkuk between 1958 and 1975 and wove accounts of their experiences there into memoirs that are written in Kurdish, but these books have thus far not been translated into any other language.

42. See, for instance, Frank, *Oil Empire*. In her work on disputed Alexandretta, Sarah Shields does not avoid the use of the term *ethnic* altogether but implies that the concept is a European transplant; she tends to use terms such as *Turcophile* in the place of *Turk*. Shields, *Fezzes in the River*.

43. The word *Turkmen*, when used to refer to members of the Iraqi Turkic eth-

nic group, is spelled in many different ways in English, including Turkman, Turkoman, Turkomen, and Turcoman. The plural is also confusing. The Arabic collective term for this group is *al-turkuman*, which is often simply transliterated into English in one way or another to describe members of the ethnic group as a whole. Further complicating matters is the fact that some English-language writers seem to erroneously think that the word *Turkmen* is analogous to "Englishmen" or "Irishmen." Like the authors of several (but not all) recently published academic works on Iraq that mention this group, as well as the *New York Times* and the *Washington Post*, I choose to use the singular *Turkmen* and plural *Turkmens*. These are the closest English renderings of the Turkish-language terms for this group (singular, Türkmen; plural, Türkmenler). However, whenever one of the other variant spellings or plurals is used in something I am quoting or the title of a work I am citing, I have rendered it as is without adding a flag such as "*sic.*"

44. One of the most prominent early uses of the term *Chaldo-Assyrian* was in the 2004 Law of Administration for the State of Iraq for the Transitional Period, which recognized the rights of "ChaldoAssyrians" [sic].

45. The history of the split between these confessional groups and the particularities of identity that have evolved from it are formidably complex issues far beyond the scope of this work. Two scholars who have different perspectives on these topics and who have written about them at length are Donabed, "Rethinking Nationalism"; and Hanoosh, "Politics of Minority."

CHAPTER 1

1. Saatçi, *Urban Fabric*, 19–20, 25.
2. Pfeiffer, *Nuzi and the Hurrians*, 553.
3. Kramers, "Kirkuk"; Walker, *Legend of Mar Qardagh*, 99–100.
4. Kramers, "Kirkuk."
5. Edmonds, *Kurds, Turks, and Arabs*, 267–68; Kramers, "Kirkuk."
6. For the Kurdish claims, see, for instance, Ahmad, *Karkuk wa-Tawabiʿuha*, 5. Ahmad claims that the Kurds are descended from two peoples who lived in or near the Kirkuk area in the third millennium BCE: the Hurrians and the Lullubians. Needless to say, claims of this sort are not only impossible to verify but also largely meaningless with regard to modern group identities. David McDowall describes nomadic tribes around Kirkuk as "Kurdish" even with reference to their status in the Sasanian era, but he also notes that the term *Kurd* was synonymous with *nomad* at the time and was not limited to its current ethnolinguistic meaning until the nineteenth century. McDowall, *Modern History of the Kurds*, 13, 21–23.
7. See, for instance, L. Anderson and Stansfield, *Crisis in Kirkuk*, 13–19.
8. For empiricist details about Kirkuk's various modern communities, including religious sects and tribes, see Edmonds, *Kurds, Turks, and Arabs*, 266–73.
9. Çetinsaya, *Ottoman Administration of Iraq*, 4–5; Edmonds, *Kurds, Turks, and Arabs*, 265–66.
10. I am using Albert Hourani's now-standard concept of the "politics of notables" in the late Ottoman era, discussed at length in Hourani, "Ottoman Reform," 41–68.

11. Çetinsaya, *Ottoman Administration of Iraq*, 4.

12. Longrigg, *Four Centuries of Modern Iraq*, 231–33.

13. For example, for an account of the Persian siege of Kirkuk in 1743, see Olson, *Siege of Mosul*, 123. Stephen Longrigg describes the many occasions that Persian forces threatened Kirkuk and/or Şehrizor; see, for instance, Longrigg, *Four Centuries of Modern Iraq*, 180–86.

14. For an account of the changing and differing alliances of the Kurdish Baban brothers in the Kirkuk area, see, for instance, Longrigg, *Four Centuries of Modern Iraq*, 182–83.

15. Longrigg, *Four Centuries of Modern Iraq*, 300.

16. Jwaideh, *Kurdish National Movement*, 54.

17. Klein, *Margins of Empire*, 1–6.

18. Ateş, *Ottoman-Iranian Borderlands*.

19. Çetinsaya, *Ottoman Administration of Iraq*, 45, 75.

20. Edmonds, *Kurds, Turks, and Arabs*, 290–95; Rasul, "Tatawwur al-Haraka al-Thaqafiyya fi Karkuk," 506–8. Shaykh Rida remains especially famous among Kurdish poets.

21. Çetinsaya, *Ottoman Administration of Iraq*, 74–76; Jwaideh, *Kurdish National Movement*, 75–76; van Bruinessen, *Agha, Shaikh, and State*, 221.

22. Çetinsaya, *Ottoman Administration of Iraq*, 63–64.

23. Çetinsaya, *Ottoman Administration of Iraq*, 65–66.

24. Çetinsaya, *Ottoman Administration of Iraq*, 86.

25. McDowall, *Modern History of the Kurds*, 97.

26. *Handbook of Mesopotamia*, vol. 3, *Central Mesopotamia with Southern Kurdistan and the Syrian Desert*, p. 375, British Library (BL), India Office Records (IOR), L/MIL/17/15/41/4.

27. "Copy of Memorandum No. 23919 dated 31st October 1918 from Civil Commissioner, Baghdad, to Major E. W. C. Noel," in Office of the Civil Commissioner, Baghdad, to the Secretary of State for India, London, 14 November 1918, BL, IOR, L/PS/10/619; *Handbook of Mesopotamia*, 3: 360.

28. Istanbul's nineteenth-century policy of extending its influence to other frontiers of the empire was arguably effective, or at least competent, in places where the central government did not compete with local notables or Western interference. See Rogan, *Frontiers of the State*, 17.

29. For an extensive compilation of quotations from many of these early accounts of Kirkuk, see Galletti, "Kirkuk." A discussion of French-language European travelers' accounts about Kirkuk can be found in Hakim, "Karkuk fi Kitabat al-Rahhala al-Fransiyyin."

30. Sarah Shields makes the same observation in writing about the Mosul *vilayet* in the nineteenth century. Shields, *Mosul Before Iraq*, 12–13.

31. Sykes, *Dar-Ul-Islam*, 186–200.

32. Soane, *To Mesopotamia and Kurdistan*, 120–39.

33. Letter, 1 April 1911, Gertrude Bell Archive, www.gerty.ncl.ac.uk/letter_details
.php?letter_id=1811 (accessed 1 July 2018).

34. Maunsell, "Mesopotamian Petroleum Field." For another example of a British
military figure's account of traveling to Kirkuk and presenting his findings to the Royal
Geographical Society, see Dickson, "Journeys in Kurdistan."

35. Roger Owen notes that individuals such as Sykes and Bell should not be con-
flated with professional members of the intelligence services. Owen, "British and French
Military Intelligence." For an example of official use of this information, see *Handbook
of Mesopotamia*, vol. 3, which cites Sykes and Soane, among others, with regard to
Kirkuk. Some of the other official texts cited in this section appear to have derived their
information from previous travelers' accounts.

36. *Handbook of Mesopotamia*, 3: 360.

37. Longrigg, *Iraq, 1900 to 1950*, 53.

38. *Handbook of Mesopotamia*, 3: 358.

39. Shields, *Mosul Before Iraq*, 101–2.

40. Political Officer, Kirkuk, to the Civil Commissioner, Baghdad, "Memorandum
No. K.1760/3/1 of 29-11-19," 29 November 1919, in Office of the Civil Commissioner,
Baghdad, to the Under-Secretary of State for India, London, BL, IOR, L/PS/10/821, File
2023-1919, Part 10.

41. Diary entry, 31 March 1911, Gertrude Bell Archive, www.gerty.ncl.ac.uk
/diary_details.php?diary_id=938 (accessed 1 July 2018).

42. Dickson, "Journeys in Kurdistan," 375.

43. C. C. Garbett, "Land Revenue Note on Kirkuk," 1919, Middle East Centre Archive (MECA), C. J. Edmonds Collection, GB 165-0095, Box 7, File 1.

44. Jean Otter, *Voyage en Turquie et en Perse*, cited in Hakim, "Karkuk fi Kitabat
al-Rahhala al-Fransiyyin," 143.

45. Hamilton, *Road Through Kurdistan*, 45–46.

46. Letter, 1 April 1911, Gertrude Bell Archive.

47. See, for instance, Sari Kahya, *Tarikh Jawamiʿ wa Masajid Karkuk*, 75.

48. Edmonds, *Kurds, Turks, and Arabs*, 265; Sari Kahya, *Tarikh Jawamiʿ wa Masajid Karkuk*, 54–57; "Kirkuk City," map, 1919, National Archives of the United Kingdom
(NAUK), Records of the War Office (WO), 302/553.

49. *Handbook of Mesopotamia*, 3: 359.

50. See, for instance, "Report No. 14, May 15–June 1," in Captain A. T. Wilson, Of-
ficiating Civil Commissioner, Baghdad, to the Political Secretary, India Office, London,
and the Secretary to the Government of India, in the Foreign and Political Department,
Simla, 8 June 1918, BL, IOR, L/PS/10/732. This report describes the process of oil production and transport in the town of Tuz Khurmatu. For a more general discussion
of the premodern oil trade in Kirkuk and neighboring areas, see Longrigg, *Oil in the
Middle East*, 10–11.

51. F. R. Maunsell, *Reconnaissances in Mesopotamia, Kurdistan, North-West Persia,
and Luristan from April to October 1888*, vol. 1, BL, Papers of George Nathaniel Curzon,
MSS Eur F 112/396/1; Owen, *Middle East*, 180–83.

52. Olson, *Siege of Mosul*, 30, 40n125.
53. Soane, *To Mesopotamia and Kurdistan*, 120.
54. Edmonds, *Kurds, Turks, and Arabs*, 266.
55. See, for instance, Soane, *To Mesopotamia and Kurdistan*, 122.
56. Bois et al., "Kurds, Kurdistan."
57. Edmonds, *Kurds, Turks, and Arabs*, 2–3.
58. Longrigg, *Iraq, 1900 to 1950*, 20.
59. Edmonds, *Kurds, Turks, and Arabs*, 2.
60. Precise demographics for this time period are unknown, particularly with regard to ethnicity and language, and the borders of subdivisions changed frequently. As will be discussed in Chapter 3, the 1957 census found that Kurdish-speaking people constituted a plurality in the Kirkuk *liwa'*. A 1925 British map with demographic numbers, possibly skewed by the British interest in retaining the Mosul *vilayet* as part of Iraq during League of Nations mediation, indicates that Kurds were the largest group in the Kirkuk *qada*, at about 41% of the population. "Annexure to Answer to Question II of the Supplementary Questionnaire," 1925, NAUK, MPKK 1/54/2. Overall, it is reasonable to assume that any administrative subdivision with Kirkuk as its seat in this time period would probably have had a Kurdish-speaking plurality.
61. S. H. Longrigg, "Kirkuk Progress Report, No. 2, for Period Ending November 29th, 1918," in Office of the Civil Commissioner, Baghdad, to the Under Secretary of State for India, London, 23 February 1919, BL, IOR, L/PS/10/619.
62. Edmonds, *Kurds, Turks, and Arabs*, 416.
63. Tepeyran, *Hatıralar*, 369.
64. Edmonds, *Kurds, Turks, and Arabs*, 266–67.
65. An extant 1947 biographical dictionary on Kirkuk, which will be discussed in Chapter 4, provides an overview of these tribes and others. See Hasan, *Dalil Tarikh Mashahir al-Alwiya al-'Iraqiyya*, 2: 60–66. By 1947, as I will argue later in this book, ethnic groupings had crystallized to a great extent. The heterogeneous nature of Kirkuk's countryside, discussed later, suggests that simplified ethnic descriptions of Kirkuk's tribes in earlier decades may not have been accurate.
66. Shields, "Interdependent Spaces."
67. Shields, "Interdependent Spaces," 44.
68. "Kirkuk City," map, NAUK, Records of the War Office (WO), WO 302/553.
69. Soane, *To Mesopotamia and Kurdistan*, 124.
70. Edmonds, *Kurds, Turks, and Arabs*, 266.
71. "Baghdad Wilayat Fortnightly Report No. 16, June 15th to July 1st, 1918," in Office of the Civil Commissioner, Baghdad, to the Director, Arab Bureau, Cairo, 23 November 1918, BL, IOR, L/PS/10/732.
72. Hourani's assessment of Mosul is in Hourani, "Ottoman Reform," 52. For a study of Mosuli Arabic culture in this era, see Kemp, "Power and Knowledge."
73. See, for instance, Political Officer, Kirkuk, to the Civil Commissioner, Baghdad, "Memorandum No. K.1760/3/1 of 29-11-19," BL, IOR, L/PS/10/821. This was also particularly true of the discourse surrounding the Mosul question, discussed later.

74. Klein, *Margins of Empire*, 14; Makdisi, *Culture of Sectarianism*.

75. Yapp, *Making of the Modern Middle East*, 332.

76. Longrigg, *Oil in the Middle East*, 17–21, 34.

77. Maunsell, "Mesopotamian Petroleum Field," 528–32.

78. E. H. Pascoe, "Oil in the Kirkuk Anticline," 26 February 1919, *Mesopotamia Geological Reports 1919*, BL, IOR, L/PS/10/815.

79. Kent, *Oil and Empire*, 15.

80. Yergin, *The Prize*, 185–88.

81. For the original map of the Sykes-Picot Agreement, see "Map of Eastern Turkey in Asia, Syria, and Western Persia," 1916, NAUK, MPK 1/426.

82. Sir Mark Sykes, "Meeting Held at 10 Downing Street," quoted in James Barr, *A Line in the Sand*, 7.

83. See, for instance, L. Anderson and Stansfield, *Crisis in Kirkuk*, 21; Shields, "Mosul," 219; Shwadran, *The Middle East*, 199; and Stivers, *Supremacy and Oil*, 23.

84. The differences between Sykes's, Picot's, and associated officials' expressed interests in oil or lack thereof are explained at length in Fitzgerald, "France's Middle Eastern Ambitions."

85. Fitzgerald, "France's Middle Eastern Ambitions," 715n56.

86. Sir Mark Sykes, "The Problem of the Near East," 20 June 1916, NAUK, Records of the Foreign Office (FO), FO 925/41378. Even after the negotiations, Sykes indicated that he wished the entire Mosul *vilayet*, which the British correctly believed held oil in its north, would be under British influence. Adelson, *Mark Sykes*, 279. Sykes did not live long enough to see this control established.

87. Kent, *Oil and Empire*, 122; Fitzgerald, "France's Middle Eastern Ambitions," 723.

88. Kent, *Oil and Empire*, 120–22.

89. Kent, *Oil and Empire*, 137–54; Stivers, *Supremacy and Oil*, 45, 87–88. The French shares in the TPC came from the shares that the German Deutsche Bank had lost as a consequence of the war.

90. C. C. Garbett, 29 October 1918, in Office of the Civil Commissioner, Baghdad, to the Secretary of State for India, London, 14 November 1918, BL, IOR, L/PS/10/619.

91. Garbett, 29 October 1918, BL, IOR, L/PS/10/619; Humphrey Bowman, 9 April 1919, in volume "April 1918 to August 1919," MECA, Humphrey Bowman Collection, GB165-0034, Box 3B.

92. "Telegram from Asst. Political Officer, Kirkuk, to Civil Commissioner, Baghdad, No. 7 dated 27-10-18"; and S. H. Longrigg, "Copy of Report No. K.6/8 dated 27–10–1918 from Asst. Political Officer, Kirkuk, to Civil Commissioner," 27 October 1918, both in Office of the Civil Commissioner, Baghdad, to the Secretary of State for India, London, 14 November 1918, BL, IOR, L/PS/10/619; "Note of Revival of Kurdistan," in Office of the Civil Commissioner, Baghdad, to the Director, Arab Bureau, Cairo, 1 January 1919, BL, IOR, L/PS/10/619; Longrigg, "Kirkuk Progress Report, No. 2," BL, IOR, L/PS/10/619.

93. "Kirkuk Administration Report for 1919," in Office of the Civil Commissioner,

Baghdad, to the Under Secretary of State for India, London, 29 April 1920, BL, IOR, L/PS/10/621; Terzibaşı, *Kerkük Matbuat Tarihi*, 78.

94.   Garbett, "Land Revenue Note on Kirkuk"; A. T. Wilson to Denys Bray, "Monthly Administrative Report No. 3, December 1st to January 1st, 1919," 9 January 1919, BL, IOR, L/PS/10/732. For an overview of some of the complexities of Middle Eastern property rights that are applicable to this era, see Roger Owen's introduction to Owen, *New Perspectives*, x–xiv.

95.   Longrigg, "Kirkuk Progress Report, No. 2."

96.   Garbett, "Land Revenue Note on Kirkuk."

97.   "Baghdad Wilayat Fortnightly Report No. 16," BL, IOR, L/PS/10/732.

98.   "Copy of Memorandum No. 1 dated 7th November 1918 from Political Officer, Kirkuk, to Asst. Political Officer, Kifri, Kirkuk, and Altum Keupri," in Office of the Civil Commissioner, Baghdad, to the Secretary of State for India, London, 14 November 1918, BL, IOR, L/PS/10/619.

99.   Noel was well known for this tendency among British officials. He further articulated his views on Kurdish independence in a 1919 report: E. W. C. Noel, "Note on the Kurdish Situation," July 1919, MECA, C. J. Edmonds Collection, GB 165-0095, Box 7, File 1.

100.   See, for instance, Khalaf, *Politics in Palestine*, 18–22.

101.   Garbett, "Land Revenue Note on Kirkuk."

102.   Later, during the Mandate era, Sir Henry Dobbs, the British high commissioner to Iraq, would draft a set of regulations on tribal disputes that was almost identical to the regulations he had abided by while working in India's North-West Frontier (today in Pakistan) and that rested on the concept of the "premodern tribesman," a figure who was seen as essentially the same whether in India or Iraq. Although Dobbs's North-West Frontier experience was especially influential, British officials in Iraq had served in other parts of India as well. Dodge, *Inventing Iraq*, xxiii, 92–95.

103.   Jwaideh, *Kurdish National Movement*, 165.

104.   Zürcher, *Turkey*, 169.

105.   Jwaideh, *Kurdish National Movement*, 147.

106.   Jwaideh, *Kurdish National Movement*, 163.

107.   Jwaideh, *Kurdish National Movement*, 161; McDowall, *Modern History of the Kurds*, 156.

108.   "Copy of Memorandum No. 23919," BL, IOR, L/PS/10/619.

109.   Jwaideh, *Kurdish National Movement*, 166–69.

110.   A. T. Wilson to the Political Secretary, India Office, London, "Monthly Administration Report No. 3, December 15, 1918, to Jan. 15, 1919," 24 January 1919, BL, IOR, L/PS/10/732.

111.   "Kirkuk Progress Report No. IV for Month Ending January 20th, 1919," in Office of the Civil Commissioner, Baghdad, to the Under Secretary of State for India, 19 May 1919, BL, IOR, L/PS/10/620.

112.   Jwaideh, *Kurdish National Movement*, 179.

113.   "Kirkuk Administration Report for 1919," BL, IOR, L/PS/10/621; Jwaideh, *Kurdish National Movement*, 180–82.

114. For instance, Saad Eskander's critical analysis of early British policy in Kurdistan states that one of the ways that the British misconstrued the region was to refer to "such Kurdish towns as Arbil and Kirkuk" as "Turkish." Although this may very well have been an inaccurate characterization of those towns, depending on the reasons for the use of such terminology, it is equally ill considered to simply regard Kirkuk in this era as "Kurdish." Eskander, "Britain's Policy in Southern Kurdistan," 160–61.

115. Longrigg, "Kirkuk Progress Report, No. 2," BL, IOR, L/PS/10/619.

116. A. T. Wilson to Denys Bray, "Monthly Administrative Report No. 2, November 15th to December 15th, 1918," 27 December 1918, BL, IOR, L/PS/10/732.

117. E. B. Soane, *Administration Report of Sulaymaniyah Division for 1919*, cited in McDowall, *Modern History of the Kurds*, 157.

118. "Copy of Memorandum No. 1 dated 7th November 1918," BL, IOR, L/PS/10/619.

119. Longrigg, "Kirkuk Progress Report, No. 2," BL, IOR, L/PS/10/619.

120. Dodge, *Inventing Iraq*, 63–81.

121. Longrigg, "Kirkuk Progress Report, No. 2," BL, IOR, L/PS/10/619.

122. "Kirkuk Administration Report for 1919," BL, IOR, L/PS/10/621.

123. S. H. Longrigg, "Kirkuk Divisional Council: Third Meeting, August 4th, 1920," BL, IOR, L/PS/10/821, File 2023-1919, Part 10.

124. McDowall, *Modern History of the Kurds*, 159.

125. S. H. Longrigg, in "Monthly Reports of Political Officers for April and May, 1920," in Office of the Civil Commissioner, Baghdad, to the Under Secretary of State for India, London, 20 July 1920, BL, IOR, L/PS/10/622.

126. S. H. Longrigg, in "Monthly Reports of Political Officers for June 1920," in Office of the Civil Commissioner, Baghdad, to the Under Secretary of State for India, London, 21 August 1920, BL, IOR, L/PS/10/622.

127. Haldane, *Insurrection in Mesopotamia*, 19–34.

128. High Commissioner for Mesopotamia to the Secretary of State for the Colonies, 17 August 1921, NAUK, Records of the Colonial Office (CO), CO 730/4.

129. High Commissioner for Mesopotamia to the Secretary of State for the Colonies, 21 June 1921, NAUK, CO 730/2; Secretary of State for the Colonies to the High Commissioner for Mesopotamia, 24 June 1921, NAUK, CO 730/2.

130. High Commissioner of Mesopotamia to the Secretary of State for the Colonies, Part 2, 5 July 1921, NAUK, CO 730/3.

131. High Commissioner of Mesopotamia to the Secretary of State for the Colonies, 9 July 1921, NAUK, CO 730/3.

132. "Secretary (M)," 9 July 1921, in "Future Administration of Mesopotamia: Proposed Inclusion of Kurdistan," 5 July 1921, NAUK, CO 730/3; Secretary of State for the Colonies to the High Commissioner for Mesopotamia, 9 July 1921, NAUK, CO 730/3.

133. High Commissioner of Mesopotamia to the Secretary of State for the Colonies, 11 July 1921, NAUK, CO 730/3.

134. Office of the Divisional Adviser, Mosul, to the Secretary to H.E. the High Commissioner, Baghdad, 22 August 1921, NAUK, CO 730/4.

135. Fieldhouse, *Kurds, Arabs and Britons*, 94–95.

136. "Mesopotamian Intelligence Report No. 1," 15 November 1920, in Office of the High Commissioner, Baghdad, to the Under Secretary of State for India, India Office, London, 3 December 1920, BL, IOR, L/PS/10/962.

137. Letter, 29 November 1920, Gertrude Bell Archive, www.gerty.ncl.ac.uk/letter _details.php?letter_id=438 (accessed 1 July 2018).

138. Al-Hurmuzi, *al-Turkuman fi al-'Iraq*, 28.

139. Letter, 8 July 1921, Gertrude Bell Archive, www.gerty.ncl.ac.uk/letter_details. php?letter_id=486 (accessed 1 July 2018).

140. High Commissioner, Baghdad, to Under Secretary of State for the Colonies, London, 13 June 1921, NAUK, CO 730/2.

141. High Commissioner of Mesopotamia to the Secretary of State for the Colonies, Part 2, 5 July 1921, NAUK, CO 730/3.

142. "Iraq Intelligence Report No. 18," in Colonial Office to the Under Secretary of State, India Office, 7 September 1921, BL, IOR, L/PS/10/962.

143. Edmonds, *Kurds, Turks, and Arabs*, 344.

144. "Iraq Intelligence Report No. 19," in Colonial Office to the Under Secretary of State, India Office, 13 October 1921, BL, IOR, L/PS/10/962.

145. "Iraq Intelligence Report No. 18," BL, IOR, L/PS/10/962.

146. "Iraq Intelligence Report No. 19," BL, IOR, L/PS/10/962.

147. Edmonds, *Kurds, Turks, and Arabs*, 118; McDowall, *Modern History of the Kurds*, 167.

148. "Iraq Intelligence Report No. 19," BL, IOR, L/PS/10/962.

149. Letter, 21 August 1921, Gertrude Bell Archive, www.gerty.ncl.ac.uk/letter_details .php?letter_id=500 (accessed 1 July 2018).

150. See, for instance, al-Hurmuzi, *al-Turkman fi al-'Iraq*, 28–29; and Küzeci, *Kerkük Soykırımları*, 37. Although these authors do not provide specific citations for this characterization of the event, their books are grounded in historical research from the perspective of the Turkish-speaking Kirkuki community.

151. "Iraq Intelligence Report No. 21," in Colonial Office to the Under Secretary of State, India Office, 15 September 1921, BL, IOR, L/PS/10/962.

152. Edmonds, *Kurds, Turks, and Arabs*, 118, 393.

153. Letter, 9 November 1921, Gertrude Bell Archive, www.gerty.ncl.ac.uk /letter_details.php?letter_id=519 (accessed 1 July 2018).

CHAPTER 2

1. Edmonds, *Kurds, Turks, and Arabs*, 245; Jwaideh, *Kurdish National Movement*, 188.

2. Sluglett, *Britain in Iraq*, 78.

3. Omissi, *Air Power*, 18–38.

4. Satia, "Defense of Inhumanity."

5. Edmonds, *Kurds, Turks, and Arabs*, 300.

6. "Memorandum on the Scheme for the Employment of the Forces of the Crown

in Mesopotamia," in A. Haldane, Baghdad, to the Secretary, War Office, London, 28 May 1920, British Library (BL), India Office Records (IOR), L/PS/10/766.

7. Satia, "Defense of Inhumanity," 34.

8. "Memorandum on the Scheme," BL, IOR, L/PS/10/766.

9. For more detailed information, see, for instance, C. J. Edmonds's extensive accounts of the operations dubbed Ranicol and Koicol that sought to put down rebellions in the Ranya and Sulaymaniyya districts in 1922 and 1923, respectively. Edmonds, *Kurds, Turks, and Arabs*, 244–62, 312–38.

10. Jwaideh, *Kurdish National Movement*, 198–99.

11. Edmonds, *Kurds, Turks, and Arabs*, 283, 389; Omissi, "Britain," 301–7.

12. C. J. Edmonds, "Kirkuk Liwa Report for Period 1 January to 31 January 1923," Middle East Centre Archive (MECA), C. J. Edmonds Collection, GB 165-0095, Box 1, File 1a; Edmonds, *Kurds, Turks, and Arabs*, 313.

13. McDowall, *Modern History of the Kurds*, 168.

14. C. J. Edmonds, "Confidential Report No. 4 of 1923 of the Kirkuk Liwa," MECA, C. J. Edmonds Collection, GB 165-0095, Box 1, File 1a; Edmonds, *Kurds, Turks, and Arabs*, 343–44.

15. William Stivers reaches the same conclusion. Stivers, *Supremacy and Oil*, 141–42.

16. Jwaideh, *Kurdish National Movement*, 202.

17. Edmonds to Cornwallis, 25 August 1923, MECA, C. J. Edmonds Collection, GB 165-0095, Box 1, File 1c; Edmonds, *Kurds, Turks, and Arabs*, 342–43.

18. Edmonds, *Kurds, Turks, and Arabs*, 266.

19. Edmonds, "Kirkuk Liwa Report."

20. Edmonds, *Kurds, Turks, and Arabs*, 78, 313.

21. Edmonds, *Kurds, Turks, and Arabs*, 317–18.

22. Edmonds to Cornwallis, 25 August 1923.

23. "Al Istiqlal No. 543 dated 23rd January 1925," in "Intelligence Report No. 3," 5 February 1925, National Archives of the United Kingdom (NAUK), Records of the Colonial Office (CO), CO 730/72.

24. Edmonds, *Kurds, Turks, and Arabs*, 389; Stafford, *Tragedy of the Assyrians*, 47. For examples of the uncritical repetition of the phrase "ran amok" by other scholars describing the event, see, for instance, Main, *Iraq from Mandate to Independence*, 152; Omissi, "Britain," 309; and Silverfarb, *Britain's Informal Empire*, 36.

25. See, for instance, al-Hurmuzi, *al-Turkman fi al-ʿIraq*, 29; and Küzeci, *Kerkük Soykırımları*, 37–39. Küzeci's book is an example of a source that calls the incident *Levi Katliamı*, or the "Levy Massacre." Another book by a Turkmen author written in English that characterizes the massacre as specifically targeting Turkmens as an ethnic group is Güçlü, *Turcomans and Kirkuk*, 78.

26. Büyüksaraç, "Poetics of Loss," 221.

27. H. A. Anson, "Special Report on the Recent Disturbances in Kirkuk," 8 May 1924, NAUK, Records of the Air Ministry (AIR), AIR 23/562.

28. Browne, *Iraq Levies*, 34.

29. Omissi, "Britain," 308–9.

30. Collections of these, transcribed and translated where necessary, are enclosed in Dobbs to Amery, 19 February 1925, NAUK, CO 730/72.

31. "Evidence of the 1st Witness, Lieut. P. Paulet King, 2nd Battalion 'Iraq Levies," in Dobbs to Amery, 19 February 1925, NAUK, CO 730/72.

32. The central market, or "Bazar," is indicated in these locations on a 1919 map of Kirkuk: "Kirkuk City," map, 1919, NAUK, Records of the War Office (WO), WO 302/553. The testimonies cited in this chapter also imply that this series of events began on the east side of the river near the stone bridge across the Khasa.

33. See, for instance, Anson, "Special Report on the Recent Disturbances in Kirkuk."

34. "Evidence of the 1st Witness, Lieut. P. Paulet King," NAUK, CO 730/72.

35. In a report dated 8 May 1924, Special Service Officer H. A. Anson noted that the "bazaar talk" in Kirkuk was full of speculation that the Levies would soon occupy Sulaymaniyya. Anson, "Special Report on the Recent Disturbances in Kirkuk."

36. "Evidence of the 1st Witness, Lieut. P. Paulet King"; and "Evidence of the 3rd Witness, Station House Officer Burgess, Kirkuk Police," in Dobbs to Amery, 19 February 1925, NAUK, CO 730/72.

37. "Evidence of the 1st Witness, Lieut. P. Paulet King," NAUK, CO 730/72.

38. "Evidence of the 2nd Witness, Captain W. E. N. Growden, Inspecting Officer of Police," in Dobbs to Amery, 19 February 1925, NAUK, CO 730/72.

39. "Evidence of the 5th Witness, Sergeant Wade, Transport Sergeant, 2nd Bn 'Iraq Levies," in Dobbs to Amery, 19 February 1925, NAUK, CO 730/72.

40. Nigel D. Davidson, report on Court's findings, in Dobbs to Amery, 19 February 1925, NAUK, CO 730/72.

41. "Evidence of the 7th Witness, Lieutenant A. T. O. Lees, Squadron Commander, 1st Levy Cavalry Regiment," in Dobbs to Amery, 19 February 1925, NAUK, CO 730/72.

42. "Evidence of the 15th Witness, Toma Hindi Effendi," in Dobbs to Amery, 19 February 1925, NAUK, CO 730/72.

43. Edmonds, *Kurds, Turks, and Arabs*, 266.

44. "Evidence of the 12th Witness, Inspector Hasan Effendi, Station House Officer, Kirkuk," in Dobbs to Amery, 19 February 1925, NAUK, CO 730/72.

45. "Evidence of the 13th Witness, Captain O. M. Fry, 2nd Battalion 'Iraq Levies," in Dobbs to Amery, 19 February 1925, NAUK, CO 730/72.

46. "Local Casualties," in Dobbs to Amery, 19 February 1925, NAUK, CO 730/72.

47. Testimonies appended to J. M. L. Renton, 9 May 1924, in Dobbs to Amery, 19 February 1925, NAUK, CO 730/72.

48. The lower estimate of the number of deaths, along with an analysis of all casualties, is found in "Local Casualties," NAUK, CO 730/72. For the higher estimate of the number of deaths, see, for instance, Stafford, *Tragedy of the Assyrians*, 67.

49. Yücel Güçlü cites other Turkmen authors as having estimated the number of victims to be as high as 280. See Güçlü, *Turcomans and Kirkuk*, 78. The plausibility of this claim is uncertain.

50. "Evidence of the 2nd Witness, Captain W. E. N. Growden," NAUK, CO 730/72; "Evidence of the 4th Witness, Dr. F. M. Halley, Civil Surgeon, Kirkuk," in Dobbs to Amery, 19 February 1925, NAUK, CO 730/72.

51. "Local Casualties," NAUK, CO 730/72; "Evidence of the 4th Witness, Dr. F. M. Halley," NAUK, CO 730/72. For the names of some of the victims, including women, see Küzeci, *Kerkük Soykırımları*, 42.

52. "Evidence of the 4th Witness, Dr. F. M. Halley," NAUK, CO 730/72.

53. "Evidence of the 13th Witness, Captain O. M. Fry," NAUK, CO 730/72.

54. Edmonds, *Kurds, Turks, and Arabs*, 389.

55. "Evidence of the 13th Witness, Captain O. M. Fry," NAUK, CO 730/72.

56. "Evidence of the 18th Witness, Captain A. F. Miller, Administrative Inspector," in Dobbs to Amery, 19 February 1925, NAUK, CO 730/72.

57. Testimonies appended to J. M. L. Renton, NAUK, CO 730/72.

58. Anson, "Special Report on the Recent Disturbances in Kirkuk."

59. See, for instance, Klein, *Margins of Empire*, 181.

60. Bergholz, "Sudden Nationhood."

61. Omissi, "Britain," 309.

62. Administrative Inspector Kirkuk to High Commissioner, 10 May 1924, NAUK, AIR 23/562.

63. J. G. Hearson to O.C., 2nd Bn., Iraq Levies, in Dobbs to Amery, 19 February 1925, NAUK, CO 730/72.

64. High Commissioner for Iraq to Amery, 18 March 1925, NAUK, CO 730/73.

65. Edmonds, *Kurds, Turks, and Arabs*, 389.

66. Memoranda in the frontmatter of "Outbreak at Kirkuk in May, 1924," 19 February 1925, NAUK, CO 730/72.

67. Anson, "Special Report on the Recent Disturbances in Kirkuk." Although the National Archives of the United Kingdom routinely censor colonial-era documents that are unflattering to the British government (as discussed in the Note on Sources and Archives), the documentation of these 1924 events is comparatively robust and does not appear to have been attenuated to hide British motives.

68. Stafford, *Tragedy of the Assyrians*, 197.

69. Georgeon, "De Mossoul à Kirkouk," 41.

70. High Commissioner of Mesopotamia to the Secretary of State for the Colonies, 5 July 1921, NAUK, CO 730/3.

71. "Procès-Verbal No. 3," 21 May 1924, in Schofield, *Arabian Boundary Disputes*, 9: 37–40. These negotiations were conducted in French; the translations of quotes here are my own.

72. "Memorandum on the Frontier Between Turkey and Irak," 14 August 1924, in Schofield, *Arabian Boundary Disputes*, 9: 58–67.

73. "Questionnaire for the British Government, with Answers," 29 November 1924, in Schofield, *Arabian Boundary Disputes*, 9: 120, 131.

74. For an in-depth analysis of the Wilsonian concept of self-determination and the ways in which various populations worldwide adopted it, see, for instance, Manela,

Wilsonian Moment. For a discussion of this concept in a Middle Eastern context, see, for instance, Shields, *Fezzes in the River*.

75. Untitled memorandum, 16 February 1925, MECA, C. J. Edmonds Collection, GB 165-0095, Box 1, File 2c; Office of Administrative Inspector, Kirkuk, to Liaison Officer to Mosul Frontier Commission, Mosul, 12 February 1925, MECA, C. J. Edmonds Collection, GB 165-0095, Box 1, File 2c.

76. Paulis to Edmonds, 16 February 1925, MECA, C. J. Edmonds Collection, GB 165-0095, Box 1, File 2a; also see Edmonds, *Kurds, Turks, and Arabs*, 415–16.

77. Office of Administrative Inspector, Kirkuk, to Liaison Officer, Frontier Commission, Kirkuk, 15 February 1925, MECA, C. J. Edmonds Collection, GB 165–0095, Box 1, File 2c.

78. Colonel A. Paulis, "Enquête en Irak: Journal Privé," cited in Shields, "From Millet to Nation."

79. Liaison Officer to the High Commissioner, 22 February 1925, MECA, C. J. Edmonds Collection, GB 165-0095, Box 1, File 2c.

80. H. A. Anson, "Notes on the Question of Kurdish Independence," 18 February 1926, MECA, C. J. Edmonds Collection, GB 165-0095, Box 3, File 2.

81. Liaison Officer to the High Commissioner, 22 February 1925, MECA, Edmonds Collection, GB 165-0095.

82. League of Nations, *Question of the Frontier*, 37, 77.

83. Office of Administrative Inspector, Kirkuk, to Liaison Officer to Frontier Enquiry Commission, Kirkuk, 25 February 1925, MECA, C. J. Edmonds Collection, GB 165-0095, Box 1, File 2c; Shields, "Mosul," 229.

84. Sarah Shields also reaches this conclusion. See Shields, "Mosul," 229.

85. "Kirkuk Administration Report for 1919," BL, IOR, L/PS/10/621; Political Officer, Kirkuk, to the Civil Commissioner, Baghdad, 22 March 1920, BL, IOR, L/PS/10/821, File 2023-1919, Part 10; Shields, "Mosul," 228, contains views from Paulis's diary of a Mosul merchant who complained that British goods would be privileged on a railroad.

86. Edmonds to the Secretary to H.E. the High Commissioner for Iraq, 7 March 1925, MECA, C. J. Edmonds Collection, GB 165-0095, Box 1, File 2c.

87. The Commission's 90-page report contains only two sentences about the possibility that the former Mosul *vilayet* would prove to be an "oil-bearing region." League of Nations, *Question of the Frontier*, 69.

88. See, for instance, Lindsay to MacDonald, 21 May 1924, in Schofield, *Arabian Boundary Disputes*, 9: 25–26.

89. This point is emphasized in, for instance, Sluglett, *Britain in Iraq*, 75–78. Based on his reading of official British documents, Peter Sluglett rejects the common notion that the British fought to include the Mosul *vilayet* region in Iraq because they were entertaining the idea of a strategic buffer between central Iraq and Turkey.

90. Penrose and Penrose, *Iraq*, 60–61.

91. "Note of a Conversation with Colonel Paulis on the Evening of the 22nd

January, 1925," in Dobbs to Amery, 27 January 1925, NAUK, CO 730/72; High Commissioner for Iraq to Secretary of State for the Colonies, 2 March 1925, NAUK, CO 730/73.

92. High Commissioner for Iraq to Secretary of State for the Colonies, 2 March 1925, NAUK, CO 730/73; "Intelligence Report No. 5," 5 March 1925, in Bell to the Under Secretary of State for the Colonies, 5 March 1925, NAUK, CO 730/73.

93. Penrose and Penrose, *Iraq*, 62–66; Stivers, *Supremacy and Oil*, 87–88.

94. "Treaty Between the U.K. and Iraq and Turkey"; Stivers, *Supremacy and Oil*, 166–72.

95. C. B. R. Pelly, "Report No. 17 for Period Ending 13 October 1931," 13 October 1931, NAUK, AIR 23/338.

96. C. B. R. Pelly to Air Staff Intelligence, 27 July 1931, NAUK, AIR 23/338.

97. See, for example, Note by J. H. Hall, 13 October 1930, NAUK, CO 730/157/6.

98. For an extensive discussion of the process of Iraq's admission to the League of Nations and the implications of its relationship with Britain for future independent states subject to informal imperialism, or "decolonization's Faustian bargain," see Pedersen, "Getting Out of Iraq."

99. Sluglett, *Britain in Iraq*, 128–29.

100. See, for instance, Ja'far al-'Askari to H. W. Young, 19 August 1930, NAUK, CO 730/157/5.

101. "Extract from Gazette No. 29," 23 May 1931, NAUK, CO 730/161/1.

102. Memorandum by K. Cornwallis, 4 February 1931, NAUK, CO 730/161/2.

103. F. H. Humphrys to Prime Minister, 29 May 1931, NAUK, CO 730/161/1; "Copy of Circular from His Excellency the Prime Minister to All Ministries," enclosed in Hull to G. W. Rendel, 30 October 1931, NAUK, Records of the Foreign Office (FO), FO 371/15318. The circular indicates that there were forty-nine non-Kurdish-speaking officials in the Kirkuk governorate, whereas the letter from Humphrys indicates that there were thirty-nine.

104. Hassanpour, *Nationalism and Language*, 312–16.

105. Sluglett, *Britain in Iraq*, 161–62.

106. R. Brooke-Popham to Lord Passfield, 3 September 1930, NAUK, CO 730/157/5.

107. G. C. Kitching to Sir Kinahan Cornwallis, 11 August 1930, NAUK, CO 730/157/5.

108. See, for example, Kurdish petition to the Prime Minister, 4 April 1929, MECA, C. J. Edmonds Collection, Box 3, File 2.

109. J. D. O'Malley, "Special Service Officer's Report for the Period Ending 28 April 1931," 28 April 1931, NAUK, AIR 23/338; J. D. O'Malley, "Special Service Officer's Report No. 5 for the Period Ending 5th May 1931," 5 May 1931, NAUK, AIR 23/338.

110. O'Malley, "Special Service Officer's Report No. 5," NAUK, AIR 23/338.

111. Anson, "Notes on the Question of Kurdish Independence."

112. "Extract from S. S. O. Sulaimani's Report No. I/1/2," 7 March 1929, NAUK, AIR 23/228.

CHAPTER 3

Portions of Chapters 3 and 4 appeared in Arbella Bet-Shlimon, "The Politics and Ideology of Urban Development in Iraq's Oil City: Kirkuk, 1946–58," *Comparative Studies of South Asia, Africa, and the Middle East* 33, no. 1 (2013): 26–40.

1. By the mid-twentieth century the company initially named the Anglo-Persian Oil Company had come to be known as British Petroleum. Today, it is simply called BP.

2. Longhurst, *Adventure in Oil*, 86.

3. "Qissat al-Bi'r al-Ula," *Ahl al-Naft*, October 1957, 7–8.

4. Longhurst, *Adventure in Oil*, 90; Yergin, *The Prize*, 188.

5. Longhurst, *Adventure in Oil*, 89.

6. "Turkish Petroleum Reports 50,000-Bbl. Gusher in Irak Area," *Oil and Gas Journal*, 10 November 1927, 45; Simpich and Moore, "Bombs over Bible Lands," 171.

7. Munif, *Cities of Salt*, 298–304.

8. "IPC Ceremonies, BBC Broadcast, 7th February 1935," BP Archive (BP), File 67881.

9. Longhurst, *Adventure in Oil*, 91.

10. Adnan Samarrai, interview, 1 June 2011.

11. Sluglett, *Britain in Iraq*, 137–38; Yergin, *The Prize*, 204.

12. The Iraq Petroleum Company holdings of the BP Archive at the University of Warwick in Coventry, which are cited throughout this work, are the remnants of the papers of the London office of the IPC. The papers of the IPC's Iraq headquarters are still in Iraq, though their status is unknown. As mentioned in the Introduction, at least some of them were lost to looting in 2003.

13. A well-known example of such challenges that is beyond the scope of this discussion is the claim made by the heirs of the late Sultan Abdülhamid II to lands that had been controlled by him through the Civil List, including Iraq's oil-bearing areas, before these lands' reversion to the Ottoman state in 1908. For a detailed account of this dispute from a perspective sympathetic to the heirs, see Sami, *Quest for Sultan Abdülhamid's Oil Assets*.

14. H. Dobbs to L. C. M. S. Amery, 19 March 1925, National Archives of the United Kingdom (NAUK), Records of the Colonial Office (CO), CO 730/74.

15. Longrigg, *Oil in the Middle East*, 68.

16. "Gouvernement d'Irak Tribunal de Première Instance de Kerkuk," 30 October 1926, BP, File 33519.

17. TPC General Manager to Salih Beg Naftchizadah, 28 July 1927, BP, File 33519.

18. Letter from Neftchi Halid Bey Zade, undated, BP, File 33519.

19. Neftchi Zadé Nazim to Turkish Petroleum Company, 26 December 1928, BP, File 33519. The quotations from this letter are my translations from the original French.

20. Penrose and Penrose, *Iraq*, 141–42.

21. Undated memorandum discussing drilling, c. late 1930, BP, File 164084.

22. Hubert Young to J. E. Shuckburgh, 24 April 1930, NAUK, Records of the Ministry of Power (POWE), POWE 33/381; Letter to W. B. Brown, 27 May 1930, NAUK,

POWE 33/381; John Cadman to Nuri Said Pasha, 15 October 1930, NAUK, POWE 33/381; F. H. Humphrys to Lord Passfield, 27 March 1931, NAUK, POWE 33/382.

23. For more details on this topic and an economic analysis of the IPC's behavior as a cartel-specific phenomenon, see Walter Adams et al., "Retarding the Development of Iraq's Oil Resources."

24. "Extract from Economic Report No. 3 for March 1931," NAUK, CO 730/161/12.

25. "Extract from Economic Report No. 3 for March 1931," NAUK, CO 730/161/12; Fields Manager, Iraq, to the Acting General Manager, London, 17 September 1930, BP, File 164084.

26. "Extract from Economic Report No. 4 for the Month of April, 1931," NAUK, CO 730/161/12.

27. C. B. R. Pelly, "Report No. 13 for Period Ending 17th August 1931," NAUK, Records of the Air Ministry (AIR), AIR 23/338.

28. "Extract from Economic Report No. 11 for the Month of November, 1931," NAUK, CO 730/161/12.

29. The 1931 revision of the IPC's convention required the construction of a pipeline to the Mediterranean Sea. Conflicting British and French preferences over whether the terminus of the pipeline was to be located in the Mandate territory of one country or the other resulted in a compromise in the form of a bifurcated line that would transport oil to both Haifa in Palestine and Tripoli in Lebanon. Construction on the pipeline would begin in 1932. Longrigg, *Oil in the Middle East*, 75–77.

30. J. H. Thomas, draft letter, 12 October 1931, NAUK, CO 730/161/12.

31. [W. E. Cole?] to Sir John Cadman, 4 November 1931, BP, File 72542.

32. Sir John Cadman to G. W. Dunkley, 29 October 1931, BP, File 72542.

33. G. W. Dunkley to Sir John Cadman, 20 November 1931, BP, File 72542.

34. J. E. W. Flood to Sir John Cadman, 12 October 1931, NAUK, CO 730/161/12.

35. "The Pipe-Line," *Times of Mesopotamia*, 28 September 1931, newspaper clipping in BP, File 72542.

36. An extensive discussion of British policy in Iraq in this time period is found in Silverfarb, *Britain's Informal Empire*.

37. Foreign Office to the Secretary to the Office of Works, 13 February 1933, NAUK, Records of the Office of Works and successors (WORK), WORK 10/53/1; C. Howard Smith to the Secretary to the Treasury, 18 March 1936, NAUK, WORK 10/53/1.

38. During the Anglo-Iraqi conflict of May 1941, Iraqi forces interned the few British government employees in Kirkuk, including Lyon and Brady, in IPC camps. For a fascinating account of these few weeks, see Brady, *Eastern Encounters*, 68–73.

39. See, for instance, "Draft for Demolition Scheme M.G.R.F. Tenth Army," undated (c. 1942), NAUK, Records of the War Office (WO), WO 201/1541.

40. See, for instance, P. S. Khoury, "Syrian Urban Politics"; and Raymond, *Cairo*, 339–74.

41. Penrose and Penrose, *Iraq*, 151–54, 174; Sassoon, *Economic Policy in Iraq*, 164; Sluglett, *Britain in Iraq*, 178–80.

42. Doxiadis Associates, *Future of Kirkuk*, 17.

43. Mudiriyyat al-Nufus al-ʿAmma, *Census of Iraq, 1947*; and Mudiriyyat al-Nufus al-ʿAmma, *al-Majmuʿa al-Ihsaʾiyya li-Tasjil ʿAm 1957*. The published copies of these censuses that I consulted are held in the Harvard University library system. It is likely that there are versions of these censuses archived elsewhere, such as in Baghdad, that contain further details.

44. Mudiriyyat al-Nufus al-ʿAmma, *Census of Iraq, 1947*, 2: 115.

45. M. T. Audsley, "Report on Visit to Iraq from 8th June to 10th July, 1948," NAUK, Records of the Foreign Office (FO), FO 371/68482.

46. Mudiriyyat al-Nufus al-ʿAmma, *al-Majmuʿa al-Ihsaʾiyya li-Tasjil ʿAm 1957*, 5: 154.

47. Mudiriyyat al-Nufus al-ʿAmma, *Census of Iraq, 1947*, 2: 115; Mudiriyyat al-Nufus al-ʿAmma, *al-Majmuʿa al-Ihsaʾiyya li-Tasjil ʿAm 1957*, 5: 139, 154.

48. Mudiriyyat al-Nufus al-ʿAmma, *Census of Iraq, 1947*, 2: 124; Mudiriyyat al-Nufus al-ʿAmma, *al-Majmuʿa al-Ihsaʾiyya li-Tasjil ʿAm 1957*, 5: 139.

49. "Political Summary for Kirkuk and Sulaimania Liwas—June 1947," 7 July 1947, NAUK, FO 624/117.

50. Mudiriyyat al-Nufus al-ʿAmma, *Census of Iraq, 1947*, 2: 115, 124, 134, 146; Mudiriyyat al-Nufus al-ʿAmma, *al-Majmuʿa al-Ihsaʾiyya li-Tasjil ʿAm 1957*, 5: 241.

51. Administrative Inspector, Kirkuk, to the Adviser to the Ministry of Interior, Baghdad, 9 January 1925, Middle East Centre Archive (MECA), C. J. Edmonds Collection, GB 165-0095, Box 3, File 2.

52. Mudiriyyat al-Nufus al-ʿAmma, *Census of Iraq, 1947*, 2: 115.

53. Mudiriyyat al-Nufus al-ʿAmma, *al-Majmuʿa al-Ihsaʾiyya li-Tasjil ʿAm 1957*, 5: 152–54.

54. Mudiriyyat al-Nufus al-ʿAmma, *al-Majmuʿa al-Ihsaʾiyya li-Tasjil ʿAm 1957*, 5: 162.

55. Mudiriyyat al-Nufus al-ʿAmma, *Census of Iraq, 1947*, 2: 101; Mudiriyyat al-Nufus al-ʿAmma, *al-Majmuʿa al-Ihsaʾiyya li-Tasjil ʿAm 1957*, 5: 154. Unlike the 1957 census, the 1947 census contains a figure on the page cited here for a *mahalla* called Hammam Masihi, or Christian Hammam (as distinct from Hammam Muslim). It appears that the population of the Christian part of Hammam was included as part of Hammam Muslim in the 1957 census. The analysis provided here assumes this is the case. Even if one were to omit the 1947 population of Hammam Masihi (732) from this analysis, the general pattern of the citadel's slower growth compared with the rest of the city and its declining share of the city's population still holds.

56. IPC Lands Department, "Kirkuk Town, 1955," map, BP, File 163897.

57. Mudiriyyat al-Nufus al-ʿAmma, *Census of Iraq, 1947*, 2: 101–02; Mudiriyyat al-Nufus al-ʿAmma, *al-Majmuʿa al-Ihsaʾiyya li-Tasjil ʿAm 1957*, 5: 152–54.

58. Kamal Majid, conversation, 26 June 2010.

59. Mudiriyyat al-Nufus al-ʿAmma, *al-Majmuʿa al-Ihsaʾiyya li-Tasjil ʿAm 1957*, 5: 243. Articles on the post-2003 Kirkuk crisis often cite this table and the 1957 Iraqi census's "mother tongue" figures in general, either in support of a particular ethnonationalist position or in the interest of outlining the main ethnopolitical narratives

of Kirkuk's rightful ownership. For an example of an article by a Kurdish politician that stresses the census's finding that the Kirkuk *liwa'* (as opposed to the city) had a Kurdish plurality, see Talabany, "Who Owns Kirkuk." For an example of an article by a diplomat of Turkmen origin that instead uses these figures to extrapolate a generous estimate of Iraq's modern Turkmen population, see Güçlü, "Who Owns Kirkuk." For an example of an article that indirectly cites the figures in this table in a discussion of the stakes of the Kirkuk crisis, see Rod Nordland, "Now It's a Census That Could Rip Iraq Apart," *New York Times*, 26 July 2009, www.nytimes.com/2009/07/26/weekinreview/26nordland.html.

60. Adnan Samarrai, interview, 9 June 2011.

61. George Yacu, interview, 8 June 2011.

62. Lee F. Dinsmore, personal correspondence, 3 May 2009.

63. Haj, *Making of Iraq*, 32–34.

64. Talabani, *Mintaqat Karkuk*, 42; Sassoon, *Economic Policy in Iraq*, 143; Warren E. Adams, "Pre-Revolutionary Decade of Land Reform," 269.

65. For instance, in the case of a Euphrates-based irrigation scheme in the southern half of the country, the British embassy in Baghdad went so far as to briefly consider settling Palestinian refugees in the irrigated area in the aftermath of the 1948 Arab-Israeli War to make up for a "lack of population" in the region. Henry B. Mack to Ernest Bevin, 30 October 1948, NAUK, FO 371/68468.

66. Warren E. Adams, "Pre-Revolutionary Decade of Land Reform," 269.

67. Nouri Talabany (Nuri Talabani) writes that there were 27,705 "members of settled Arab tribes" in Hawija in 1957 and cites the 1957 census as containing this figure, though without providing a page or table number: Talabani, *Mintaqat Karkuk*, 44. The version of the 1957 census I am consulting indicates that the *total* population of Hawija, regardless of mother tongue, was 26,981. Mudiriyyat al-Nufus al-'Amma, *al-Majmu'a al-Ihsa'iyya li-Tasjil 'Am 1957*, 5: 158.

68. Kamal Muzhir Ahmad, a Kurdish author advancing an argument for the Kurds' claim to Kirkuk's ownership, also reaches the conclusion that the Iraqi government did not, in fact, begin the Arabization of Kirkuk in the monarchy era. See Ahmad, *Karkuk wa-Tawabi'uha*, 79.

69. See, for instance, E. K. Wood, "Tribal and Political Weekly Intelligence Summary No. 74 for Week Ending 13th July 1942," 13 July 1942, NAUK, WO 208/1567.

70. For a detailed analysis of Iraqi nationalist discourses in this time period, see Bashkin, *The Other Iraq*, 52–86.

71. Humphrey Bowman, diary entry for 9 April 1919, in volume "April 1918 to August 1919," MECA, Humphrey Bowman Collection GB165-0034, Box 3B.

72. See, for instance, Ja'far al-'Askari to Major H. W. Young, 5 August 1930, NAUK, CO 730/157/5.

73. In addition to the Turkish-language schools, there were a few Kurdish-language schools in rural areas, and Jewish schools in urban Kirkuk conducted their instruction entirely in Arabic. Nuri al-Sa'id to H. W. Young, 7 November 1931, NAUK, CO 730/161/1; Hassanpour, *Nationalism and Language*, 311–12.

74. "Copy of Circular from His Excellency the Prime Minister to All Ministries," enclosed in Hull to G. W. Rendel, 30 October 1931, NAUK, FO 371/15318.

75. Edward Odisho, interview, 21 October 2015.

76. The city's name spelled in Sorani Kurdish with Arabic lettering is slightly different. The title of the newspaper uses a spelling that is consistent with Arabic and Turkmani Turkish.

77. *Kerkük/Karkuk*, no. 2670, 18 August 1931.

78. *Kerkük/Karkuk*, no. 644, 26 March 1937.

79. *Kerkük/Karkuk*, no. 1448, 21 January 1954.

80. Iraq Petroleum Company, "Guide to Kirkuk," 1955, BP, File 119015.

81. As mentioned in Chapter 2, the Mandate-era British official A. F. Miller spoke fluent Turkish and therefore had a close relationship with Kirkuk's Turkish-speaking notables. In his memoir C. J. Edmonds demonstrates a general knowledge of several Middle Eastern languages, but he was a specialist in Kurdish, a language he continued to write and lecture about long after retiring from military and government service. In 1919 Humphrey Bowman described Arabic in Kirkuk as being like a "foreign language": Bowman, 9 April 1919. This is undoubtedly an exaggeration but probably an accurate reflection of Arabic's tertiary status.

82. Hassanpour, *Nationalism and Language*, 316.

83. Many British records mention Kurdish grievances about education and the Iraqi government's responses in the 1930s and 1940s. For example, in connection with the Language Law, the Iraqi government proposed appointing a Kurdish education inspector who, it was suggested at one point, could oversee the Kurdish-majority *qada*'s of the Kirkuk *liwa*'. Ja'far al-'Askari to Major H. W. Young, 17 July 1930, NAUK, CO 730/157/5.

84. Edward Odisho, interview, 21 October 2015.

85. See, for instance, Mulla Mustafa Barzani to H.E. Colonel Lyon, 11 January 1944, NAUK, FO 624/66; Political Adviser's Office, Kirkuk, to Oriental Secretary, British Embassy, Baghdad, 29 August 1944, NAUK, FO 624/66; and "Minute Sheet," 8 April 1945, NAUK, FO 624/71.

86. See, for instance, Richard Wilson to H. Moore, 23 April 1945, NAUK, FO 624/71.

87. Special Service Officer, Sulaimani, "Report I/S/R for Period Ending March 8th 1931," 8 March 1931, NAUK, AIR 23/233; "Extract SSO Arbil Report No. 3 Dated 17/3," NAUK, AIR 23/233; Special Service Officer, Sulaimani, "Report No. I/S/R/2 Dated for Period Ending March 22nd 1931," 22 March 1931, NAUK, AIR 23/233.

88. Fuccaro, "Kurds and Kurdish Nationalism," 197n15.

89. Resool, "Reactive Nationalism," 101–2.

90. Tripp, *History of Iraq*, 69–71.

91. Special Service Office, Kirkuk, "Report No. 7 for Period Ending June 2nd, 1931," 2 June 1931, NAUK, AIR 23/338.

92. Special Service Office, Kirkuk, "Special Service Officer's Report No. 6 for the Period Ending 19th May 1931," 19 May 1931, NAUK, AIR 23/338.

93. Untitled copy of memorandum from Adviser to H.E., c. 1930, NAUK, CO 730/157/5; A. J. B. Chapman, "Annual Liaison Report for 1938," BP, File 162461.

94. Büyüksaraç, "Poetics of Loss," 140–43, 156–57.

95. E. K. Wood, "Tribal and Political Weekly Intelligence Summary No. 71," 22 June 1942, NAUK, WO 208/1567.

96. Bashkin, *The Other Iraq*, 7.

97. Gershoni and Jankowski, *Redefining the Egyptian Nation*, xi.

98. P. S. Khoury, "Syrian Urban Politics," 509.

99. Although *nonsectarian* often specifically means "not related to religious sects," I use the term here in a less literal sense: broadly, "not related to group identities, including ethnic ones."

100. Omar Nadhmi to the Iraq Petroleum Company, 30 April 1939, NAUK, FO 371/23215.

101. Adnan Samarrai, interview, 9 June 2011; George Yacu, interview, 8 June 2011.

102. Vitalis, *America's Kingdom*.

103. "Fields Gathering Line Scheme with Tentative Estimates," 13 June 1930, BP, File 164082.

104. "Oil: IPC Labour Welfare," 25 October 1946, NAUK, FO 624/105.

105. The official described the relationship between the IPC and Iraqi laborers as "outwardly that of 'sahibs' and 'niggers'" (here, *sahib* is an Arabic term for "master"). F. Wells, "Oil: Iraq Petroleum Coy.," 7 April 1948, NAUK, FO 624/130.

106. Even later reports, including a 1950 report, criticized the distance between IPC management and workers. See W. J. Hull, "Visit to IPC, Kirkuk Fields, 15–18 August 1950," August 1950, NAUK, Records of the Ministry of Labour and successors (LAB), LAB 13/672.

107. G. H. Thompson to Ernest Bevin, 28 September 1945, NAUK, LAB 13/193.

108. Sassoon, *Economic Policy in Iraq*, 260.

109. Sassoon, *Economic Policy in Iraq*, 256–60.

110. Tripp, *History of Iraq*, 113.

111. Lockman, *Comrades and Enemies*, 232–34, 327–32.

112. A. J. B. Chapman, "Annual Liaison Report for 1937," BP, File 162461; Batatu, *Old Social Classes*, 443–44.

113. For an in-depth study of the 1929 strike, see Cronin, "Popular Politics." The 1946 strike and the Tudeh Party's relationship with the urban working class in general are analyzed in Abrahamian, *Iran Between Two Revolutions*, 347–75.

114. There does not appear to have been a direct organizational link between these strikes, but their similar timing is unlikely to have been entirely coincidental because Iraqi and Iranian communists were in communication with one another. See Batatu, *Old Social Classes*, 579–80.

115. Batatu, *Old Social Classes*, 1188–89.

116. Batatu, *Old Social Classes*, 622.

117. "Iraq During the Year 1945," BP, File 162461; "Iraq During the Year 1946," BP, File 162461.

118. Batatu, *Old Social Classes*, 622–23.

119. Jones, "Poetics of Revolution," 274. Jones found this information in declassified U.S. Department of State files; it is not readily available in the U.K. archives.

120. Batatu, *Old Social Classes*, 624; R. Goddard-Wilson to Sir Hugh Stonehewer Bird, 7 May 1947, NAUK, FO 371/61637; Sir M. Peterson to Foreign Office, 25 July 1946, NAUK, FO 371/52456.

121. Batatu, *Old Social Classes*, 624.

122. Quoted in Jones, "Poetics of Revolution," 274.

CHAPTER 4

1. Hugh Stonehewer Bird to Ernest Bevin, 19 July 1946, National Archives of the United Kingdom (NAUK), Records of the Foreign Office (FO), FO 371/52456.

2. Hugh Stonehewer Bird to Fadhil al-Jamali, 20 July 1946, NAUK, FO 371/52456.

3. Foreign Office to Baghdad, 12 July 1946, NAUK, FO 371/52459.

4. Qubain, *Reconstruction of Iraq*, 247. However, Qubain notes that the law had not yet been enforced at the time of his writing in 1958.

5. H. H. Wheatley to Managing Director, 15 February 1949, BP Archive (BP), File 135819.

6. "Oil: IPC Labour Welfare," 21 November 1946, NAUK, FO 624/105.

7. Douglas L. Busk to Ernest Bevin, 13 August 1946, NAUK, Records of the Ministry of Labour and successors (LAB), LAB 13/193.

8. Guy H. Clarke, "Political Report for Kirkuk, Erbil, and Sulaimania Liwas—February 1950," 28 February 1950, NAUK, FO 624/186.

9. W. J. Hull, "Visit to IPC, Kirkuk Fields, 15–18 August 1950," August 1950, NAUK, LAB 13/672.

10. "Guide to Kirkuk," c. 1955, BP, File 119015.

11. "Personnel Statistics for 31st December 1954, All Areas Summary," BP, File 39649.

12. P. R. A. Ensor to Tripoli, 10 February 1951, BP, File 135818.

13. Hull, "Visit to IPC."

14. "Block of New Shops for Arrapha Estate," *Iraq Petroleum*, August 1953, 43.

15. Hull, "Visit to IPC."

16. W. V. Fuller, "Report on Kirkuk Housing Scheme," 25 August 1949, BP, File 135819. Fuller debates, based on advice from an Iraqi lawyer, whether or not workers should be charged rent at all.

17. "Monthly Rent of Houses and Rooms in I.D., Kirkuk Liwa (1956 Housing Census)," Iraq Reports R-QA 460-525, March 1957, Constantinos A. Doxiadis Archives (DA), file 23904. The cost-of-living allowance in 1954 ranged between 5.4 and 12.5 Iraqi dinars per month depending on the worker's wage. Baghdad to London, 6 April 1954, BP, File 163884.

18. "Notes on IPC Group Meeting on 9th November 1950," BP, File 60550; "Chairman's Speech for Inaugural Ceremony at Kirkuk," c. 1952, BP, File 65577.

19. H. S. Gibson, "House Building in Kirkuk Town," 30 January 1951, BP, File 135819.

20. P. R. A. Ensor to Tripoli, 10 February 1951, BP, File 135818.

21. See, for instance, documents in BP, File 163897, particularly C. K. O'Ferrall to A. F. Ensor, 4 November 1970, which discusses the Abu Dhabi scheme.

22. Seccombe and Lawless, *Work Camps and Company Towns*, 40.

23. "Industrial Relations, 1954," 26 April 1955, BP, File 39649.

24. IPC Lands Department, "Kirkuk Town, 1955," map, BP, File 163897.

25. George Yacu, interview, 3 June 2011.

26. Talabani, *Mintaqat Karkuk*, 41.

27. Officials did sometimes mention differences between Christian and Muslim workers; for instance, a 1953 report on a company educational scheme requiring young entrants to have had three years of secondary education expressed concern that Muslims were less likely to be able to fulfill this requirement. "Note on the Apprentice Entrance Examination," in "Project No. 43 (Revised): Kirkuk Training Institute," BP, File 166111. The Christian-Muslim distinction in the IPC is discussed later in this chapter.

28. See, for instance, L. Anderson and Stansfield, *Crisis in Kirkuk*, 32.

29. George Yacu, interview, 8 June 2011; "Programme for J. M. Pattinson's Visit to Kirkuk, Housing Production and Construction—Iraq Petroleum Co.," 22 October 1951, BP, File 49717.

30. Lenczowski, *Oil and State*, 233. For a brief sketch of the Arrapha Estate's demographic composition in the present day, see, for instance, L. Anderson and Stansfield, *Crisis in Kirkuk*, 89.

31. "Accommodation at Kirkuk," 6 January 1953, BP, File 135819.

32. For example, Ian Seccombe and Richard Lawless characterized the ethnic segregation perpetuated by the Anglo-Iranian Oil Company in the planned company town of Abadan, Iran, as "strict" and characterized by "sharp breaks between adjacent areas containing population groups of markedly different status" (Seccombe and Lawless, *Work Camps and Company Towns*, 55). For more on the topic of segregation in the AIOC's planned towns in Iran, see Crinson, "Abadan"; and Ehsani, "Social Engineering."

33. See, for instance, M. T. Audsley, "Report on Visit to Iraq from 8th June to 10th July, 1948," NAUK, FO 371/68482.

34. Khadduri, *Independent Iraq*, 352–57; Kingston, *Britain and the Politics of Modernization*, 103–4.

35. Salter, *Development of Iraq*. For other accounts of the Salter report's impact, see Gallman, *Iraq Under General Nuri*, 106–7; and Ionides, *Divide and Lose*, 119–26.

36. Pyla, "Back to the Future," 6–7.

37. C. A. Doxiadis, "No More Regional Planning: A Move Towards Regional Development Programs," 1958, DA, Articles-Papers 2509.

38. Menoret, "Development, Planning, and Urban Unrest," 276–77.

39. Similarly, Doxiadis envisioned using "traditional methods of construction" in his Baghdad housing projects in keeping with the idea of organic development, but this

idealized practice proved not to be possible at the scale of these projects. Sarkis, *Circa 1958*, 23–25.

40. Doxiadis Associates, *Future of Kirkuk*, 24, 49–53.

41. C. A. Panaghiotakis to H. E. the Mutasarrif, 28 June 1959, DA, Iraq Corr. C-QB 3984–4586, Archive File 24028; "Kirkuk Detailed Community Layout Plans," 1958–60, DA, Maps and Drawings 27676.

42. Ionides, *Divide and Lose*, 203–4.

43. Constantinos A. Doxiadis, "23.1.56, Kirkuk City," 1956, DA, Iraq Diary DOX.Q.8, Archive File 23875.

44. Constantinos A. Doxiadis, "7.12.55, The City of Kirkuk," 1955, DA, Iraq Diary DOX.Q.7, Archive File 23874.

45. Pyla, "Back to the Future," 12–13.

46. Doxiadis Associates, *Future of Kirkuk*, 40–46.

47. In the years following Doxiadis's early work in Iraq, Doxiadis Associates was commissioned to apply the idea of ekistics all over the Middle East and the developing world in general. Pyla, "Back to the Future," 3–4; Sarkis, *Circa 1958*, 23. The spread of the home ownership scheme is documented in, for instance, documents in BP, File 163897.

48. M. S. Mainland to Management, London, 25 February 1950, BP, File 163852.

49. M. S. Mainland to Douglas L. Busk, 12 December 1946; Abdul Jalil Parto to the Manager, 4 March 1947; Abdul Jalil Parto to Fields Manager, 8 April 1947; Abdul Jalil Parto to Fields Manager, 1 May 1947; Minister of Interior to the IPC Ltd., Kirkuk, 16 March 1947; all in BP, File 163852.

50. "Oil: IPC Labour Welfare," 25 October 1946, NAUK, FO 624/105.

51. Hull, "Visit to IPC."

52. General Management, Tripoli, to Managing Director, London, 20 August 1952, BP, File 163852.

53. "Agreement," enclosure in Chief Representative, Baghdad, to Management, London, 5 August 1953, BP, File 163852.

54. General Management, Tripoli, to Managing Director, London, 20 August 1952, BP, File 163852.

55. M. S. Mainland to Dr. C. T. Barner, 1 November 1952, BP, File 163852.

56. Article from *al-Sha'b*, 3 August 1950, as translated and enclosed in H. H. Wheatley to Sir John Cunningham et al., 29 August 1950, BP, File 135819.

57. H. H. Wheatley to E.A.S., 8 July 1948, BP, File 163852.

58. M. S. Mainland to Management, London, 25 February 1950, BP, File 163852.

59. L. V. A. Fowle to Fields Manager, Kirkuk, 10 March 1950, BP, File 163852; M. S. Mainland to Management, London, 5 April 1950, BP, File 163852.

60. General Manager, Kirkuk Fields, to Managing Director, London, 21 August 1951, BP, File 163852.

61. In 1947 a British diplomat in Baghdad used the term "sociological," albeit irregularly spelled as "socialogical," to describe the IPC's endeavors in Kirkuk that went

beyond the extraction, refinement, and export of oil. G. C. Pelham, "Foreign Office Minute," 28 August 1947, NAUK, FO 371/61676.

62. Hull, "Visit to IPC"; see also Acting Assistant Chief Personnel Officer to Fields Manager, 23 November 1949, BP, File 164177.

63. W. H. Earle, "British Institute, Kirkuk, Annual Report, 1946–47," 20 March 1947; and J. E. F. Gueritz, "Report of the Closing of the British Institute, Kirkuk, During the Quarter Ending 30th September, 1948," both in NAUK, Records of the British Council (BW), BW 39/10.

64. "Minutes of the Meeting of the Technical Sub-Committee of the Kirkuk Training Institute held at 214, Oxford Street on Thursday, 4th June 1953 at 11:00 a.m.," BP, File 163449.

65. London to the Groups, 5 July 1951; and "Apprentice Training Scheme / Kirkuk Training Centre," both in BP, File 15619; "Kirkuk Training Institute," April 1953, BP, File 166111.

66. Finnie, *Desert Enterprise*, 123.

67. "Guide to Kirkuk," BP, File 119015.

68. "Project No. 43: Kirkuk Training Scheme / Apprentice Training Centre," July 1951, BP, File 15619. As will be mentioned in Chapter 5, the Iraqi government and the IPC would eventually refer to this process as the "Iraqi-isation" of the company. See, for example, "New Iraq Labour Law," enclosed with [illegible] to Maxwell, 19 June 1958, BP, File 163884.

69. "Project No. 43," BP, File 15619.

70. George Yacu, interviews, 3 June 2011 and 8 June 2011.

71. Appendixes of "The Iraqi Communist Party (Supplementary Paper)," April 1949, NAUK, FO 371/75131.

72. See, for instance, Baghdad to Foreign Office, 19 July 1946, NAUK, FO 371/52459. This fear among Iraqi officials was strong enough that Iraq suspended relations with the Soviet Union in 1955. See Tripp, *History of Iraq*, 135.

73. Foreign Office to Bagdad, 12 July 1946, NAUK, FO 371/52459.

74. "Oil: IPC Labour Welfare," 25 October 1946, NAUK, FO 624/105.

75. Hugh Stonehewer Bird to Ernest Bevin, 25 October 1946, NAUK, LAB 13/193.

76. See, for instance, "Industrial Relations, 1954," 26 April 1955, BP, File 39649; and "Note of Information on Personnel Matters Reported to Board Meetings on 26th June, 1956," 10 July 1956, BP, File 39649.

77. W. J. Hull to Sir Guildhaume Myrddin-Evans, 3 September 1950, NAUK, FO 371/82505.

78. W. J. Hull to Sir Guildhaume Myrddin-Evans, 3 September 1950; Hull to Guildhaume Myrddin-Evans, 23 October 1950, NAUK, FO 371/82474.

79. See, for instance, Ionides, *Divide and Lose*, 198–99.

80. Agha and Mustafa, *Madha fi Karkuk*, facing 121; George Yacu, interview, 8 June 2011; Lee F. Dinsmore, personal correspondence, 3 May 2009; al-'Azzawi, *al-Ruh al-Hayya*, 279–80.

81. Antoon, "Remembering Sargon Boulus"; al-ʿAzzawi, *al-Ruh al-Hayya*, 280.

82. George Yacu, interview, 8 June 2011.

83. See, for instance, "Golf in the Fields of Kirkuk and Zubair," *Iraq Petroleum*, August 1952, 24–25.

84. "Kirkuk: The Domestic Scene," *Iraq Petroleum*, November 1957, 11–13.

85. See, for instance, "New Water Pump Station for Kirkuk," *Iraq Petroleum*, September 1956, 45.

86. "'B' Power Station: Beating Heart of Kirkuk's Industralism," *Iraq Petroleum*, December 1951, 5–9.

87. Anne Kitchen, "Kirkuk Bridges the Centuries," *Iraq Petroleum*, July 1954, 20–24.

88. *Kirkuk to Banias*, produced by Richard Finnie (Bechtel, 1952), VHS, ARC Identifier 656854, National Archives of the United States (NAUS), Records of the Central Intelligence Agency, Record Group 263.

89. Bashir Mustafa, "al-Nar al-Khalida," *Ahl al-Naft*, February 1958, 24. Copyright Iraq Petroleum Company; reproduced with permission. The translation, which conveys the literal meaning and does not attempt to duplicate the poem's prosody or meter, is my own.

90. See, for instance, DeYoung, *Placing the Poet*, 191–96.

91. Samih Nabil, "Haraka Fanniyya fi Madinat al-Dhahab al-Aswad," *Ahl al-Naft*, August 1957, 34–35.

92. Hasan, *Dalil Tarikh Mashahir al-Alwiya al-ʿIraqiyya*, 2. Nouri Talabany (Nuri Talabani) summarizes the contents of this volume from the perspective of the Kurdish nationalist case for Kirkuk's status in a 2002 article. See Talabani, "Karkuk."

93. Al-Qadi, "Biographical Dictionaries," 107–8.

94. Bashkin, *The Other Iraq*, 128–31.

95. The book's frontmatter states that its writing was undertaken in collaboration with "a staff made up of a select elite of young intellectuals" and mentions its licensing by the government. Hasan, *Dalil Tarikh Mashahir al-Alwiya al-ʿIraqiyya*, [iv]. For a discussion of state attempts to control intellectual production in this time period, see Bashkin, *The Other Iraq*, 92–93.

96. See, for instance, Hasan, *Dalil Tarikh Mashahir al-Alwiya al-ʿIraqiyya*, 60–65, 283–88.

97. Hasan, *Dalil Tarikh Mashahir al-Alwiya al-ʿIraqiyya*, 1. The contrast between "black" and "white" in this passage stems from the fact that the Arabic name for the Mediterranean Sea is literally the "White Middle Sea" (*al-bahr al-abyad al-mutawassit*).

98. Hasan, *Dalil Tarikh Mashahir al-Alwiya al-ʿIraqiyya*, 55.

99. "Nestorians" is another common term for Assyrians, specifically those belonging to the Assyrian Church of the East.

100. Hasan, *Dalil Tarikh Mashahir al-Alwiya al-ʿIraqiyya*, 57–58.

101. Hasan, *Dalil Tarikh Mashahir al-Alwiya al-ʿIraqiyya*, 28, 46–48.

102. Daniel Benjamin, interview, 27 June 2011; Benjamin, "Assyrian Printing Presses," 53.

103. When searching the online catalog of the Iraq National Library and Archive (INLA) on 12 April 2012, I was able to find only six books (including *What's in Kirkuk*) that were published in Kirkuk before 1960, as opposed to thousands from Baghdad. A WorldCat search on 12 April 2012 revealed a handful of other printed works from Kirkuk in this era that are not listed in the INLA catalog.

104. Agha and Mustafa, *Madha fi Karkuk*, 21, 23, 86–88.

105. Agha and Mustafa, *Madha fi Karkuk*, facing 33.

106. Agha and Mustafa, *Madha fi Karkuk*, 102, 104–5.

107. Agha and Mustafa, *Madha fi Karkuk*, backmatter.

108. Bashkin, *The Other Iraq*, 177–78.

109. Lütfi, "Kerkük," 42–43.

CHAPTER 5

1. Many works contain accounts of this coup, including Batatu, *Old Social Classes*, 800–807; Farouk-Sluglett and Sluglett, *Iraq Since 1958*, 49–50; Marr, *Modern History of Iraq*, 84–86; and Tripp, *History of Iraq*, 141–45.

2. Al-ʿAzzawi, *al-Ruh al-Hayya*, 305–6.

3. H. C. Whyte, "Report by H.M. Vice-Consul, Kirkuk," 8 August 1958, National Archives of the United Kingdom (NAUK), Records of the Foreign Office (FO), FO 371/134202.

4. J. C. C. Bennett to Levant Department, 20 July 1958, NAUK, FO 371/133879.

5. McDowall, *Modern History of the Kurds*, 302. An English translation of the KDP proclamation can be found in Barzani and Ferhadi, *Mustafa Barzani*, 174–75.

6. Tripp, *History of Iraq*, 146. The descriptor Feyli Kurdish is typically used for and by Persian-speaking Shiʿi Kurds originally from areas near the Iraqi-Iranian frontier.

7. "Al-Dustur al-Muʾaqqat li-ʿAm 1958," www.mesopot.com/mesopot/old/adad1/aldoustour1958.htm (accessed 1 July 2018). An English translation is found in Annex A to "Iraq Since the Revolution," 12 August 1958, NAUK, FO 371/134202.

8. Hassanpour, *Nationalism and Language*, 317.

9. Farouk-Sluglett and Sluglett, *Iraq Since 1958*, 54–55.

10. Fadhil al-Azzawi (Fadil al-ʿAzzawi) describes the Communist Party's leadership in Kirkuk as having consisted of "a mixture of Kurds, Arabs, Turkmens and Christians" in 1958. al-ʿAzzawi, *al-Ruh al-Hayya*, 307.

11. Dinsmore, "Regrets for a Minor American Role."

12. See, for instance, "The Iraqi Communist Party (Supplementary Paper)," April 1949, p. 34, NAUK, FO 371/75131; and "The Iraqi Communist Party (Supplementary Paper)," July 1949, p. 32, NAUK, FO 371/75131.

13. Whyte, "Report by H.M. Vice-Consul, Kirkuk."

14. Batatu, *Old Social Classes*, 914.

15. "Closure of Consulates," 13 November 1958, NAUK, FO 371/133136.

16. Al-ʿAzzawi, *al-Ruh al-Hayya*, 307; Kamal Majid, conversation, 26 June 2010.

17. Batatu, *Old Social Classes*, 913.

18. Barzani and Ferhadi, *Mustafa Barzani*, 178–83.

234 NOTES TO CHAPTER 5

19. H. N. Pullar to Selwyn Lloyd, 8 December 1958, NAUK, FO 371/133136.

20. Fritzlan, Baghdad, to Secretary of State, 4 November 1958, National Archives of the United States (NAUS), Department of State Central Files, 787.00/11-458.

21. "Bayan Lajnat al-Taʿawun al-Watani bi-Karkuk," al-Bashir, 28 October 1958, 10.

22. Barzani and Ferhadi, Mustafa Barzani, 349–50. The quotes here are from the English translation of the Turkmen organization's declaration as it appears in Barzani and Ferhadi's book, with irregularities preserved.

23. Barzani and Ferhadi, Mustafa Barzani, 350.

24. Pullar to Lloyd, 8 December 1958, NAUK, FO 371/133136; Robert S. McClellan, "Report on Recent Events in Kirkuk," 6 November 1958, NAUS, Department of State Central Files, 787.00/11-658.

25. The full original version of Pullar to Lloyd, NAUK, FO 371/133136, is held by the U.K. Foreign and Commonwealth Office. Two requests made under the provisions of the British Freedom of Information Act to see the full original document in 2010 and 2015 were unsuccessful. I further discuss my attempts to see this document in this book's Note on Sources and Archives.

26. Batatu, Old Social Classes, 913.

27. Pullar to Lloyd, NAUK, FO 371/133136.

28. Baghdad to Secretary of State, 30 December 1958, NAUS, Department of State Central Files, 787.00/12-3058.

29. BBC, 15 January 1959, cited in Batatu, Old Social Classes, 913.

30. For the early history of al-Ahali, see Bashkin, The Other Iraq, 62–69.

31. Shakir ʿUmar, "Tarikh al-Aqwam fi al-ʿIraq," al-Ahali 77, 1 March 1959, 3. ʿUmar was most likely referring to the Turkish verbs soğurmak (to absorb) and sorumak (to suck).

32. ʿUmar, "Tarikh al-Aqwam fi al-ʿIraq," 3.

33. Kamal Muzhir Ahmad's articles were "Radd ʿala Maqal Tarikh al-Aqwam fi al-ʿIraq, 1," al-Ahali 79, 3 March 1959, 3, 6; "Radd ʿala Maqal Tarikh al-Aqwam fi al-ʿIraq, 2," al-Ahali 80, 4 March 1959, 3; "Radd ʿala Maqal Tarikh al-Aqwam fi al-ʿIraq, 3," al-Ahali 81, 5 March 1959, 3; "Radd ʿala Maqal Tarikh al-Aqwam fi al-ʿIraq, 4," al-Ahali 83, 8 March 1959, 3, 6; "Radd ʿala Maqal Tarikh al-Aqwam fi al-ʿIraq, 5," al-Ahali 85, 10 March 1959, 3; and "Radd ʿala Maqal Tarikh al-Aqwam fi al-ʿIraq, 6," al-Ahali 88, 13 March 1959, 3, 7.

34. Ahmad, "Radd ʿala Maqal Tarikh al-Aqwam fi al-ʿIraq, 5."

35. Mufid Abdulla, "Dr Kamal Mazhar Ahmad: Every Kurd Would Love to See an Independent Homeland," KurdishMedia, 24 September 2006, web.archive.org /web/20100925151727/http://www.kurdmedia.com/article.aspx?id=13304 (accessed 1 July 2018).

36. Kamal Muzhir Ahmad, conversation, 16 June 2011.

37. Abdulla, "Dr Kamal Mazhar Ahmad."

38. Büyüksaraç, "Poetics of Loss," 110–51. Büyüksaraç is particularly interested in this expression of Turkmen identity as a form of resistance against the "normalizing

effects of Arab nationalism" in a later time period, particularly with regard to the legacy of Iraq's Baʿth era.

39. Fanar Haddad discusses this phenomenon at length with regard to contemporary Iraqi politics, but with a focus on the Sunni-Shiʿi split. See Haddad, *Sectarianism in Iraq*, 52–56.

40. Farouk-Sluglett and Sluglett, *Iraq Since 1958*, 58–67; Marr, *Modern History of Iraq*, 90–91.

41. Batatu, *Old Social Classes*, 879–80.

42. Batatu, *Old Social Classes*, 881–89; Farouk-Sluglett and Sluglett, *Iraq Since 1958*, 67–68.

43. Batatu, *Old Social Classes*, 914.

44. Farouk-Sluglett and Sluglett, *Iraq Since 1958*, 70.

45. Al-Hirmizi, *Turkmen Reality in Iraq*, 102–3.

46. H. Trevelyan to S. Lloyd, 9 July 1959, NAUK, FO 371/140919.

47. Humphrey Trevelyan to G. F. Hiller, 17 June 1959, NAUK, FO 371/140918.

48. P. T. Hayman to G. F. Hiller, 30 September 1959, NAUK, FO 371/140924.

49. Batatu, *Old Social Classes*, 912–21.

50. For accounts held in the British archives, see, for instance, P. T. Hayman to G. F. Hiller, 24 July 1959, NAUK, FO 371/140920; and Attachment to Copeland and Eichelberger to Colonel F. T. Davies, 30 July 1959, NAUK, FO 371/140921. The Turkmen memorandum of 18 July 1959, cited in al-ʿAni, *Tarikh al-Wizarat al-ʿIraqiyya*, is also found in English translation in al-Hirmizi, *Turkmen Reality in Iraq*, 110–18. Al-Hirmizi includes many documents relevant to the July 1959 events in his book verbatim. The Büyüksaraç interview with Resmiye is in Büyüksaraç, "Poetics of Loss," 205–10.

51. Marr, *Modern History of Iraq*, 94.

52. R. S. Stafford wrote that such arches were built in Mosul after the Iraqi army's "victory" over the Assyrians in Simele, where scores of civilians were killed in 1933. See Stafford, *Tragedy of the Assyrians*, 201. Kanan Makiya (Samir Al-Khalil) has suggested that these sorts of arches could be seen as precursors to "vulgar" constructions such as the Victory Arch monument built by Saddam Hussein consisting of two sets of enormous crossed swords held by disembodied forearms. See Al-Khalil, *The Monument*, 140n33.

53. Kamal Majid, conversation, 26 June 2010.

54. Memorandum by "Turkmen citizens," 18 July 1959, in Al-ʿAni, *Tarikh al-Wizarat al-ʿIraqiyya*, 3: 47–51. The content of this memorandum, which Al-ʿAni describes as a document held in the library of Khalil Ibrahim Husayn Al-Zawbaʿi (p. 51n1), seems to be similar to one that Hanna Batatu describes as "undated" and as having been written by two prominent Turkmen leaders. See Batatu, *Old Social Classes*, 914n10.

55. Letter no. 497 from Kirkuk chief of police, 15 July 1959, cited in Batatu, *Old Social Classes*, 915, 915n11.

56. Batatu, *Old Social Classes*, 916.

57. Letter no. 497, cited in Batatu, *Old Social Classes*, 915–17; Büyüksaraç, "Poetics of Loss," 207.

58. Batatu, *Old Social Classes*, 917.

59. Hayman to Hiller, NAUK, FO 371/140920.

60. Hayman to Hiller, NAUK, FO 371/140920.

61. Attachment to Copeland and Eichelberger, NAUK, FO 371/140921. The name of the ill-fated proprietor of the café is rendered in both Turkish (Osman) and transliterated Arabic (e.g., ʿUthman) spellings in various sources. I have opted for Osman not out of a prescriptive notion of his ethnic identity but because it is the spelling used in the Western account cited here, an account that was most likely rendering the name phonetically and therefore in accordance with Osman's probable preference.

62. Attachment to Copeland and Eichelberger, NAUK, FO 371/140921.

63. Büyüksaraç, "Poetics of Loss," 208.

64. Attachment to Copeland and Eichelberger, NAUK, FO 371/140921; Memorandum by "Turkmen citizens," in al-Hirmizi, *Turkmen Reality in Iraq*, 112.

65. Letter no. 497, cited in Batatu, *Old Social Classes*, 915.

66. Al-Hirmizi, *Turkmen Reality in Iraq*, 112; Letter no. 497, cited in Batatu, *Old Social Classes*, 915–17.

67. Büyüksaraç, "Poetics of Loss," 208.

68. Hayman to Hiller, NAUK, FO 371/140920.

69. Batatu, *Old Social Classes*, 917.

70. Batatu, *Old Social Classes*, 918.

71. "Memorandum Submitted to the Prime Minister by the Representatives of Democratic Organisations in Kirkuk," enclosure with Hayman to Hiller, NAUK, FO 371/140920.

72. Büyüksaraç, "Poetics of Loss," 208–10.

73. Hayman to Hiller, NAUK, FO 371/140920; Batatu, *Old Social Classes*, 918.

74. "Bayan Lajnat al-Taʿawun al-Watani bi-Karkuk," *al-Bashir*, 28 October 1958; Letter no. 497, cited in Batatu, *Old Social Classes*, 915.

75. Batatu, *Old Social Classes*, 912, 919; Farouk-Sluglett and Sluglett, *Iraq Since 1958*, 71.

76. Batatu, *Old Social Classes*, 919, 922–23; Farouk-Sluglett and Sluglett, *Iraq Since 1958*, 71–72.

77. Franzén, "From Ally to Foe," 172.

78. *Ittihad al-Shaʿb*, 20 July 1959, cited in al-ʿAni, *Tarikh al-Wizarat al-ʿIraqiyya*, 3: 43.

79. Batatu, *Old Social Classes*, 951.

80. "Communist Leader Shot Dead in Iraq," *The News and Courier*, 26 August 1960, news.google.com/newspapers?nid=2506&dat=19600826&id=BoNJAAAAIBAJ& sjid=xwsNAAAAIBAJ&pg=7061,4284616 (accessed 17 July 2012); "Communist Shot," *The Ottawa Citizen*, 27 August 1960, news.google.com/newspapers?nid=2194&dat=19 600827&id=X1ExAAAAIBAJ&sjid=euQFAAAAIBAJ&pg=4900,4951306 (accessed 17 July 2012).

81. Al-ʿAzzawi, *al-Ruh al-Hayya*, 280; Al-Ghassani, "Rose and Its Fragrance."

82. Al-Ghassani, "Rose and Its Fragrance."

83. Al-Ghassani, "Rose and Its Fragrance." For an obituary that highlights Al-Ghassani's mixed background, see "Anwar al-Ghassani, 1937–2009," *Banipal*, www.banipal .co.uk/contributors/388/anwar-al-ghassani/ (accessed 14 July 2012).

84. Daniel Benjamin, interview, 27 June 2011.

85. George Yacu, interview, 3 June 2011.

86. Mukhlis, *Mudhakkirat al-Tabaqjali*, 24.

87. Annex A, in Humphrey Trevelyan to Selwyn Lloyd, 14 October 1959, NAUK, FO 371/140931.

88. Memorandum by "Turkmen citizens," in al-'Ani, *Tarikh al-Wizarat al-'Iraqiyya*, 3: 47. This is my translation from the original Arabic. Arshad al-Hirmizi's translation of the memorandum inexplicably omits this racialized language. For another example of this kind of characterization of the July 1959 events, see, for instance, Küzeci, *Kerkük Soykırımları*, 51.

89. Batatu, *Old Social Classes*, 912, 914.

90. For example, as mentioned in Chapter 4, the government-sponsored housing scheme in Kirkuk under the auspices of Doxiadis Associates was suspended and the firm was forced to leave the country in 1959. Former IPC general manager George Tod mentions that the first house under the home ownership scheme was fully paid off in the mid-1960s. George Tod, *From Pillar to Post: The Autobiography of George Tod* (unpublished), 121, Middle East Centre Archive, George Tod Collection, GB 165-0349, File 2.

91. Directorate General of Labour and Social Security to IPC Ltd., 31 July 1958; and Chief Representative, Baghdad, to the Directorate General of Labour and Social Security, 26 August 1958, both enclosed in Chief Representative, Baghdad, to Iraq Petroleum Company, London, 6 September 1958, BP Archive (BP), File 163884; Directorate General of Labour and Social Security to IPC/MPC/BPC, 10 September 1958, enclosed in Chief Representative, Baghdad to Iraq Petroleum Company, London, 15 September 1958, BP, File 163884.

92. "Note on Personnel and Industrial Relations Matters in Iraq During 1961," June 1962, BP, File 39651.

93. George Yacu, interviews, 3 June 2011 and 8 June 2011.

94. Daniel Benjamin, interview, 27 June 2011.

95. George Yacu, interview, 8 June 2011.

96. Enclosure in Baghdad to Foreign Office, 14 August 1959, NAUK, FO 371/140930.

97. George Yacu, interview, 8 June 2011.

98. Farouk-Sluglett and Sluglett, *Iraq Since 1958*, 78. For the IPC's view of the negotiations, see, for instance, W. V. Fuller to Stockwell et al., 17 June 1959, BP, File 163300.

99. G. H. Herridge to N. R. Power, 30 August 1962, BP, File 39651; [illegible] to G. G. Stockwell, 31 August 1962, BP, File 39651.

100. Roger Allen to R. S. Crawford, 8 October 1962, NAUK, FO 371/164280.

101. "Note on Personnel and Industrial Relations Matters in Iraq During 1959," 21 June 1960, BP, File 39650.

102. N. M. Ekserdjian to General Division, 21 August 1962, BP, File 161974.

103. Abdul Aziz Al-Wattari to IPC Ltd., 25 November 1963, BP, File 161974; T. W. Elliott to D.G. of Oil Affairs, 4 March 1964, BP, File 161974.

104. Farouk-Sluglett and Sluglett, *Iraq Since 1958*, 100.

105. For more information on the processes that resulted in the IPC's nationalization, see Saul, "Masterly Inactivity"; and Wolfe-Hunnicutt, "End of the Concessionary Regime."

106. For instance, as encountered in the title of F. H. Khorshid, *Kirkuk: Qalb-e Kurdistan* [Kirkuk: Heart of Kurdistan], cited in Natali, "Kirkuk Conundrum," 443.

107. Hugh Pullar to Hadow, 18 July 1958, NAUK, FO 371/134255.

108. Farouk-Sluglett and Sluglett, *Iraq Since 1958*, 80.

109. Dann, *Iraq Under Qassem*, 333; Hassanpour, *Nationalism and Language*, 119.

110. "7 Slain in Iraqi Town," *New York Times*, 14 March 1961, 15.

111. "Republican Ordinance no. 328," *Weekly Gazette of the Republic of Iraq*, no. 39, 27 September 1961, 780–81; "Republican Ordinance no. 378," *Weekly Gazette of the Republic of Iraq*, no. 43, 25 October 1961, 847. Liam Anderson and Gareth Stansfield erroneously imply that these Arab subdivisions were *attached* to Kirkuk in 1961, thereby suggesting that these ordinances were an early form of the ethnically based gerrymandering of the provincial borders that would take place under the Ba'th regime in the 1970s. See L. Anderson and Stansfield, *Crisis in Kirkuk*, 28.

112. McDowall, *Modern History of the Kurds*, 309–11.

113. McDowall, *Modern History of the Kurds*, 312–13.

114. Tod, *From Pillar to Post*, 114–18.

115. Adnan Samarrai, interview, 9 June 2011. Frank Gosling's report on the ordeal is found in F. Gosling, 17 January 1963, NAUK, FO 371/170501. British journalist David Adamson met the captives while reporting on the Kurdish rebellion for the *Sunday Telegraph*; his account is found in Adamson, *Kurdish War*, 133–37. Adamson sardonically noted that, to the Kurdish captors, "the difference between 'guest' and detainee is a loose one."

116. Baghdad to Foreign Office, no. 831, 14 December 1962, NAUK, FO 371/164281; Baghdad to Foreign Office, no. 836, 15 December 1962, NAUK, FO 371/164281.

117. Eric Downton, "Europeans in Iraq Agree to Curfew," *Daily Telegraph*, 27 December 1962, newspaper clipping in NAUK, FO 371/164281.

118. Baghdad to Foreign Office, 31 December 1962, NAUK, FO 371/170501.

119. Farouk-Sluglett and Sluglett, *Iraq Since 1958*, 83–87.

120. al-Hirmizi, *Turkmen Reality in Iraq*, 109.

121. "28 Communists Executed by Iraq for 1959 Massacre," *New York Times*, 24 June 1963, 24.

122. Talabani, *Mintaqat Karkuk*, 54–55. One of the destroyed villages mentioned is Shoraw, the home village of Karzan Sherabayani, who talks about the incident in his documentary, also recalling that it happened in early 1963. See Sherabayani, *Return to Kirkuk*.

123. Tod, *From Pillar to Post*, 119.

124. Ahmad, *al-Kurd wa-Kurdistan*, 1: 688–710; McDowall, *Modern History of the Kurds*, 313. Ahmad's volume contains the full original text of Talabani's memorandum.

125. McDowall, *Modern History of the Kurds*, 314.

126. S. L. Egerton to M. St. E. Burton, 30 October 1964, NAUK, FO 371/175754; S. L. Egerton to M. St. E. Burton, 21 November 1964, NAUK, FO 371/175754.

127. *Karkuk*, 30 September 1963, Hoover Institution, North Iraq Data Set (NIDS), 1065364-1065373.

128. Tod, *From Pillar to Post*, 119.

129. Zeidel, "Iraqi Novel," 26.

130. Büyüksaraç, "Poetics of Loss," 208.

CHAPTER 6

1. D. R. Khoury, *Iraq in Wartime*.

2. Al-Marashi and Salama, *Iraq's Armed Forces*, 125.

3. Correspondence issued from Ta'mim Branch Command, 29 August 2002, Conflict Records Research Center (CRRC), SH-BATH-D-000-803.

4. L. Anderson and Stansfield, *Crisis in Kirkuk*, 31.

5. Tape of a conversation with Saddam Hussein, 1995, CRRC, SH-SHTP-A-001-463.

6. Human Rights Watch, *Bureaucracy of Repression*, 17.

7. L. Anderson and Stansfield, *Crisis in Kirkuk*, 45–46.

8. Farouk-Sluglett and Sluglett, *Iraq Since 1958*, 145–48.

9. Former employee of the North Oil Company, quoted by Ferida Danyal (another former employee of the company), interview, 29 September 2016. This individual wished to remain anonymous to protect family members who continue to live in Kirkuk and responded to written questions through an intermediary.

10. Tripp, *History of Iraq*, 172; Farouk-Sluglett and Sluglett, *Iraq Since 1958*, 128–29.

11. Farouk-Sluglett and Sluglett, *Iraq Since 1958*, 129.

12. Jean-Jacques Berreby, "A Second Front in Kurdistan?" *New Middle East*, May 1969, 44–45; Farouk-Sluglett and Sluglett, *Iraq Since 1958*, 129–30.

13. See, for example, Faust, *Ba'thification of Iraq*, 101.

14. Files from Kirkuk Art Institute [*sic*], c. 1986–1988, Hoover Institution, North Iraq Data Set (NIDS), 102022-102406.

15. Because of the haphazard organization of the digitized Ba'th archival files, it is virtually impossible to know for certain whether there are separate batches of surveillance files for students from the Kirkuk Technical Institute who are listed as being from other ethnic groups (unless, of course, another researcher happens upon them).

16. North Oil Company applications, 1985, Hoover Institution, NIDS, 1183170-1183186.

17. See, for example, Sassoon, *Saddam Hussein's Ba'th Party*, 204; and Faust, *Ba'thification of Iraq*, 98.

18. Files from Kirkuk Art Institute, Hoover Institution, NIDS, 102022–102406.

19. Terzibaşı, *Kerkük Havaları*; Terzibaşı, *Kerkük Eskiler Sözü*.

20. The standard spelling of the word for "brotherhood" in modern Anatolian Turkish (kardeşlik) is what the magazine editors used on their own covers. The Arabic name also appeared prominently on most covers.

21. Suphi Saatçi, personal communication, 26 July 2014.

22. Büyüksaraç, "Poetics of Loss," 156.

23. Facsimile of "Qirar Raqm 89 Sadir Min Majlis Qiyadat al-Thawra fi 24-1-1970," in al-Samanji, al-Tarikh al-Siyasi, 304.

24. Kardeşlik 9, no. 11–12 (1970): 13.

25. Al-Samanji, al-Tarikh al-Siyasi, 206.

26. Kardeşlik 4, no. 3 (1964).

27. "Iraqi Turks Seek Security," in U.S. Joint Publications Research Service, Translations on Near East 55112, no. 710 (4 February 1972): 59–61; Kardeşlik 11, no. 5 (1971).

28. "Kardeşlik Dergisi: Giriş," Kardeşlik (Ankara: Türkmeneli Vakfı Kültür Merkezi, 2009), DVD.

29. Büyüksaraç, "Poetics of Loss," 163.

30. Al-Samanji, al-Tarikh al-Siyasi, 286.

31. Al-Samanji, al-Tarikh al-Siyasi, 285.

32. Human Rights Watch, Genocide in Iraq, 353.

33. Talabani, Mintaqat Karkuk, 45–62.

34. Patriotic Union of Kurdistan, Ethnic Cleansing Documents, 16.

35. L. Anderson and Stansfield, Crisis in Kirkuk, 27–30; Talabani, Mintaqat Karkuk, 45–62.

36. Al-Samanji, al-Tarikh al-Siyasi, 307.

37. "IRAQ: Kirkuk Master Plan," D.A. Review 10, no. 89 (1974): 8–11; "IRAQ: Kirkuk Master Plan," D.A. Review 11, no. 91 (1975): 4–8.

38. Shorija's reputation is mentioned in, for example, Jacob Russell and Theresa Breuer, "Parkour Brings Iraqis Together," Aljazeera, 2015, interactive.aljazeera.com /aje/2015/kirkuk_parkour/index.html (accessed 16 September 2017). Mohammed Amin Qadir found in the late 1970s that 73% of the citadel's residents were Turkish/Turkmani speakers, a figure higher than in any other neighborhood by some distance. Qadir, "Linguistic Situation in Kirkuk," 8.

39. "IRAQ: Kirkuk Master Plan," D.A. Review 11, no. 91 (1975): 4–8. The differences between Kirkuk's extent in 1973 and the master plan can be measured by comparing the Doxiadis Associates maps with a detailed Soviet map of Kirkuk originally made in 1973. See Sovetskaya Armiya, Kirkuk.

40. Jawdat 'Ata Shakir, "Liqa' Ma' al-Ustadh Ibrahim Muhammad, Mudir Baladiyyat Karkuk bil-Wikala," Kardeşlik 16, no. 5–6 (1976): 10–11.

41. This containment of Shorija can be seen by comparing a Soviet map of Kirkuk originally made in 1973 with a map from a satellite view in the present day. Sovetskaya Armiya, Kirkuk; "Kirkuk, Iraq," map, Google Maps, maps.google.com (accessed 16 September 2017).

42. For example, the 15th Ward of Syracuse, New York, a poor neighborhood that was predominantly black, was destroyed in the 1950s by the construction of an urban

highway as part of an "urban renewal" campaign that was also overtly intended as a method of social control. DiMento and Ellis, *Changing Lanes*, 173–79.

43. Talabani, *Mintaqat Kirkuk*, 57.

44. See, for example, Patriotic Union of Kurdistan, *Ethnic Cleansing Documents*, 23–32.

45. Patriotic Union of Kurdistan, *Ethnic Cleansing Documents*, 21.

46. See, for example, Patriotic Union of Kurdistan, *Ethnic Cleansing Documents*, 22.

47. Patriotic Union of Kurdistan, *Ethnic Cleansing Documents*, 48.

48. Patriotic Union of Kurdistan, *Ethnic Cleansing Documents*, 49–54.

49. See also al-Samanji, *al-Tarikh al-Siyasi*, 210–11.

50. L. Anderson and Stansfield, *Crisis in Kirkuk*, 40.

51. L. Anderson and Stansfield, *Crisis in Kirkuk*, 38; Patriotic Union of Kurdistan, *Ethnic Cleansing Documents*, 207–8.

52. Donabed, *Reforging a Forgotten History*, 196–209; Packer, *Assassins' Gate*, 346. Saddam Hussein specified the definition of "Arab" as someone who can speak the Arabic language in, for example, a 2001 decree, though forced assimilation by means of "correction" of *qawmiyya* had already been happening for years at that point. See Patriotic Union of Kurdistan, *Ethnic Cleansing Documents*, 71.

53. Qadir, "Linguistic Situation in Kirkuk," abstract.

54. Qadir, "Linguistic Situation in Kirkuk," 67, 70–71, 89–90.

55. Kamal Majid, conversation, 26 June 2010. I received an account generally to the same effect of what is described here of Qadir's fate, but without the implication that Qadir's death was a homicide, from an Iraqi linguist who was a contemporary of his; this linguist did not give me permission for a more specific citation.

56. Resool, "Reactive Nationalism," 201.

57. McDowall, *Modern History of the Kurds*, 346.

58. Human Rights Watch, *Genocide in Iraq*, 39; Dave Johns, "1983: The Missing Barzanis," Frontline World, 24 January 2006, www.pbs.org/frontlineworld/stories /iraq501/events_barzanis.html (accessed 17 September 2017).

59. North Oil Company applications, 1985, Hoover Institution, NIDS, 1183170-1183186.

60. Sassoon, *Saddam Hussein's Ba'th Party*, 46.

61. In fact, this was not unheard of; in his research, Joseph Sassoon found a file on a party member who had joined at age 13. Sassoon, *Saddam Hussein's Ba'th Party*, 57.

62. In general, the whereabouts of Kirkuk's Ba'th-era Directorate of Security files are unknown. The 2004 collection of Ba'th documents published by the PUK contains a few letters addressed to officials in Ta'mim province, suggesting that the PUK is in possession of at least some of these files. See, for example, Patriotic Union of Kurdistan, *Ethnic Cleansing Documents*, 76.

63. See, for example, Nicholas Riccardi, "Iraqi Teachers Learn Hard Political Lesson," *Los Angeles Times*, 14 May 2004, articles.latimes.com/2004/may/14/world/fg -teachers14 (accessed 1 July 2018); and Sassoon, *Saddam Hussein's Ba'th Party*, 220.

64. Hiltermann, *Poisonous Affair*, 91–92.

65. Donabed, *Reforging a Forgotten History*, 200–201.

66. Human Rights Watch, *Genocide in Iraq*, xii.

67. D. R. Khoury, *Iraq in Wartime*, 118; Human Rights Watch, *Genocide in Iraq*, 52.

68. Human Rights Watch, *Genocide in Iraq*, 209.

69. Human Rights Watch, *Genocide in Iraq*, 209–17.

70. Packer, *Assassin's Gate*, 338–40.

71. Al-Janabi, "New Materials," 29–37.

72. Packer, *Assassin's Gate*, 338–40.

CONCLUSION

1. Mustafa Mahmud, "Iraq: Plan to Deploy Peshmerga to Kirkuk Alarms Minorities," *Radio Free Europe/Radio Liberty*, 8 August 2007, www.rferl.org/content/article /1078043.html (accessed 1 July 2018).

2. L. Anderson and Stansfield, *Crisis in Kirkuk*, 93–101.

3. Sherabayani, *Return to Kirkuk*.

4. Steve Fainaru and Anthony Shadid, "Kurdish Officials Sanction Abductions in Kirkuk," *Washington Post*, 15 June 2005, www.washingtonpost.com/wp-dyn/content /article/2005/06/14/AR2005061401828.html (accessed 1 July 2018).

5. Michael S. Schmidt, "Fatal Bombs in Iraq Seemed Aimed at Militia," *New York Times*, 9 February 2011, www.nytimes.com/2011/02/10/world/middleeast/10iraq.html (accessed 1 July 2018).

6. For instance, Karzan Sherabayani's documentary witnesses a 2005 demonstration in which Turkmens and Kurds wave competing flags. It is certainly emotional and contentious but not violent. Sherabayani, *Return to Kirkuk*.

7. Soran Mama Hama, "Prostitutes Conquer Kirkuk: A Report Written With Blood," *On Line Opinion*, 7 August 2008, www.onlineopinion.com.au/view .asp?article=7733&page=0 (accessed 1 July 2018).

8. Annie Gowen, "In Iraq, A New Breed of Returning Exile," *Washington Post*, 4 September 2011, www.washingtonpost.com/world/middle-east/in-iraq-a-new-breed-of -returning-exile/2011/08/24/gIQAnzSN2J_print.html (accessed 1 July 2018).

9. Gina Chon, "In Kirkuk, Ethnic Strife Takes Toll," *Wall Street Journal*, 25 February 2008, online.wsj.com/article/SB120390692899189767.html (accessed 1 July 2018); Natali, "Kirkuk Conundrum," 438, 443n13.

10. Kurdistan Regional Government, "Natural Resources Ministry."

11. David Sheppard and Henry Foy, "Rosneft in Talks to Develop Disputed Oilfields with Iraqi Kurdistan," *Financial Times*, 29 June 2017, www.ft.com/content/032819fe-5cd1 -11e7-9bc8-8055f264aa8b (accessed 1 July 2018).

12. "Kirkuk Votes to Take Part in Kurdish Independence Poll," *Aljazeera*, 29 August 2017, www.aljazeera.com/news/2017/08/kirkuk-votes-part-kurdish-independence -poll-170829134834287.html (accessed 1 July 2018).

13. "Al-Na'ib Arshad al-Salihi: Amn Turkuman Karkuk Fi Khatar wa-Nutalib bi-Himayat al-Muhafaza," *YouTube*, 29 August 2017, youtu.be/Pzq7404HMms (accessed 1 July 2018).

14. David Zucchino and Margaret Coker, "Iraq Escalates Dispute with Kurds, Threatening Military Action," *New York Times*, 27 September 2017, www.nytimes.com/2017 /09/27/world/middleeast/kurdistan-referendum-iraq.html (accessed 1 July 2018).

15. Rudaw English, Twitter post, 14 October 2017, twitter.com/RudawEnglish/status /919324814367707136 (accessed 14 October 2017).

16. David Zucchino, "Iraqi Forces Begin Assault Near Kurdish-Held City of Kirkuk," *New York Times*, 15 October 2017, www.nytimes.com/2017/10/15/world/middleeast /kurds-independence-iraq.html (accessed 1 July 2018).

17. Said, "Permission to Narrate," 47.

18. For instance, political scientist Brendan O'Leary approvingly cites Mas'ud Barzani's characterization of Kirkuk as "both a city of Kurdistan and of Iraq" in his argument that Kirkuk should accede to the KRG's region. See O'Leary, *How to Get Out of Iraq*, 160. Also, the *Middle East Quarterly* published two articles in 2007 featuring formulaic Kurdish and Turkmen nationalist arguments in the form of a point-counterpoint on the Kirkuk crisis; see Güçlü, "Who Owns Kirkuk"; and Talabany, "Who Owns Kirkuk."

19. For an example of a high estimate of Iraq's Turkmen population (in this case, claiming 8–10% of the total Iraqi population), see Güçlü, *Turcomans and Kirkuk*, 27–28. For more on the notion of the 32-32-32-4 scheme and its problems, see L. Anderson and Stansfield, *Crisis in Kirkuk*, 229–30.

20. Rumayla is also estimated to hold much greater reserves, particularly when grouped with several other smaller fields in the same region. Kirkuk's production declined from its 1980 peak rate of 1.2 million barrels per day because of war-related disruptions and failure to maintain the oil field, as well as the damage the field sustained as a result of injection. See Aref Mohammed, "Iraq Aims to Up Rumaila Oilfield Output to 1.5 mln bpd in 2018," *Reuters*, 29 November 2017, www.reuters.com/article/ uk-iraq-oil-rumaila/iraq-aims-to-up-rumaila-oilfield-output-to-1-5-mln-bpd-in-2018 -idUKKBN1DT29V (accessed 1 July 2018); Jassim and Goff, *Geology of Iraq*, 233; and U.S. Energy Information Administration, "Iraq: Country Analysis," www.eia.gov/beta /international/analysis.php?iso=IRQ (accessed 30 June 2018).

21. I am borrowing terminology from Mona Damluji, who argues that American policy in post-2003 Baghdad "actively reproduced, intensified, codified and spatially reinforced the significance of sectarian difference" (Damluji, "Securing Democracy in Iraq," 71).

22. Liam Anderson and Gareth Stansfield treat the "Turkmen perspective" and the "Arab perspective" in separate chapters but unify these two "group preferences" in their chapters on resolving the crisis. The significance of the simultaneous differences and convergences between these ethnic narratives is not fully explored. See, for example, L. Anderson and Stansfield, *Crisis in Kirkuk*, 56–70, 79–86, 204–33.

23. The justification that Anderson and Stansfield give for leaving Chaldo-Assyrians out of the substantive portion of their analysis is that this lacuna "reflects the naked political reality that Christian numbers are so low as to be irrelevant to any determination of Kirkuk's future status" (L. Anderson and Stansfield, *Crisis in Kirkuk*, 6).

24. Members of this community often stress the city's roots in the ancient Assyrian city of Arrapha and claim a connection to that heritage. Kirkuki Chaldo-Assyrians also continue to commemorate a pre-Islamic massacre of Christians in the citadel on an annual basis, an event that they connect to ongoing persecution in the present. See Mindy Belz, "A Fragile Light," *World Magazine*, 7 November 2009, world.wng.org/2009/10/a _fragile_light? (accessed 1 July 2018).

25. See, for instance, Güçlü, *Turcomans and Kirkuk*, 103.

26. This is visible in media photographs of their meetings. See, for instance, "Kirkuk Votes to Take Part in Kurdish Independence Poll," *Aljazeera*, 29 August 2017, www.aljazeera .com/news/2017/08/kirkuk-votes-part-kurdish-independence-poll-170829134834287 .html (accessed 1 July 2018).

27. Farah Al-Nakib makes a similar point in reference to Kuwait City, a highly diverse city (because of a long history of migration through the Persian Gulf and Indian Ocean arena) that has become segregated in the era of oil. She argues that city dwellers can become parochially minded and hostile to one another if they are not regularly brought into interactions of friendly difference. See Al-Nakib, *Kuwait Transformed*.

28. See, for instance, "Intilaq Fa"aliyyat Karkuk 'Asima lil-Thaqafa al-'Iraqiyya bi-Musharakat Muhafazat Iqlim Kurdistan," *al-Sumariya Niyuz*, 18 January 2010, web.archive .org/web/20101119093031/http://www.alsumarianews.com/ar/6/12525/news-details -.html (accessed 1 July 2018); and "Kirkuk University Students Celebrate National Clothes Day," *Kirkuk Now*, 9 March 2017, kirkuknow.com/english/?p=20824 (accessed 1 July 2018). *Kirkuk Now* is an example of a nonpartisan, multilingual local news website. The parkour group is described in Jacob Russell and Theresa Breuer, "Parkour Brings Iraqis Together," Aljazeera, 18 October 2015, interactive.aljazeera.com/aje/2015 /kirkuk_parkour/ (accessed 24 August 2018).

29. Ranj Sangawi, "Kirkuk Governor Speaks on Implications of Raising Kurdistan Flag," *Rudaw*, 7 April 2017, www.rudaw.net/english/kurdistan/07042017 (accessed 1 July 2018).

30. See, for instance, Steven Nabil, Twitter post, 23 October 2017, twitter.com /thestevennabil/status/922493412112080896 (accessed 23 October 2017).

31. Fanar Haddad also identifies this pattern, but primarily with regard to Sunni-Shi'i sectarianism. See Haddad, *Sectarianism in Iraq*.

SOURCES AND ARCHIVES

1. See, for instance, Ian Cobain, "Government Admits 'Losing' Thousands of Papers from National Archives," *The Guardian*, 26 December 2017, www.theguardian .com/uk-news/2017/dec/26/government-admits-losing-thousands-of-papers-from-national-archives (accessed 1 July 2018).

2. Mary Pring, letter to the author, 14 July 2015. The report I have tried repeatedly to see the full version of is H. N. Pullar to Selwyn Lloyd, 8 December 1958, National Archives of the United Kingdom (NAUK), Records of the Foreign Office (FO), FO 371/133136. This report is cited in Chapter 5. Those wishing to make their own

Freedom of Information requests to see the full version of this report can send an email containing that request to foi-dpa.imd@fco.gov.uk.

3. Caswell, "Thank You Very Much."

4. "Register of the Ḥizb al-Ba'th al-'Arabi al-Ishtiraki in Iraq [Ba'th Arab Socialist Party of Iraq] Records," Online Archive of California, www.oac.cdlib.org/findaid /ark:/13030/c84jocg3/entire_text/ (accessed 24 June 2018).

5. "Mission," Conflict Records Research Center, crrc.dodlive.mil/about/mission/ (accessed 24 June 2018).

6. Arbella Bet-Shlimon, "Preservation or Plunder? The ISIS Files and a History of Heritage Removal in Iraq," *Middle East Report Online*, 8 May 2018, www.merip.org /mero/mero050818 (accessed 1 July 2018); Maryam Saleh, "Protection or Plunder? A U.S. Journalist Took Thousands of ISIS Files Out of Iraq, Reigniting a Bitter Dispute Over the Theft of Iraqi History," *The Intercept*, 23 May 2018, theintercept.com/2018/05/23/isis-files -podcast-new-york-times-iraq/ (accessed 1 July 2018).

7. Alshaibi and Luft, "Resurrecting the Dead."

8. D. R. Khoury, *Iraq in Wartime*, 15.

9. American Anthropological Association, "Principles of Professional Responsibility," 1 November 2012, ethics.americananthro.org/category/statement/ (accessed 1 July 2018).

10. Clifton B. Parker, "Ba'ath Party Archives Reveal Brutality of Saddam Hussein's Rule," *Stanford News*, 29 March 2018, news.stanford.edu/2018/03/29/baath-party-archives -reveal-brutality-saddam-husseins-rule/ (accessed 1 July 2018).

11. Although the Hoover Institution and Stanford University Press are both affiliated with Stanford University, they are administered separately, and I have never had a relationship with the Hoover Institution beyond the use of its archives. My research trips to the Hoover Institution and this book's publication by Stanford University Press are wholly coincidental.

12. Avi Asher-Schapiro, "Who Gets to Tell Iraq's History?" *LRB Blog*, 15 June 2018, www.lrb.co.uk/blog/2018/06/15/avi-asher-schapiro/who-gets-to-tell-iraqs-history/ (accessed 1 July 2018).

BIBLIOGRAPHY

ARCHIVES

BP Archive, University of Warwick, Coventry, UK (BP)
    Archive of BP
    Archive of the Iraq Petroleum Company
British Library, London, UK (BL)
    India Office Records (IOR): L/MIL and L/PS
    Papers of George Nathaniel Curzon
Conflict Records Research Center (CRRC), National Defense University, Washington, DC
    Saddam Hussein Collection
Constantinos A. Doxiadis Archives, Athens, Greece (DA)
    Archive Files
    Articles-Papers
    Maps and Drawings
Hoover Institution, Stanford, CA
    North Iraq Data Set (NIDS)
Middle East Centre Archive, St. Antony's College, Oxford, UK (MECA)
    Humphrey Bowman Collection
    C. J. Edmonds Collection
    George Tod Collection
National Archives of the United Kingdom, London, UK (NAUK)
    Maps extracted from Foreign Office records: MPK 1, MPKK 1
    Records of the Air Ministry (Royal Air Force Overseas Commands): AIR 23
    Records of the British Council: BW 39
    Records of the Cabinet Office: CAB 84
    Records of the Colonial Office: CO 730
    Records of the Department of Scientific and Industrial Research: DSIR 4
    Records of the Foreign Office: FO 371, 624, 925

Records of the Ministry of Labour and successors: LAB 13

Records of the Ministry of Power and related bodies: POWE 33

Records of the Office of Works and successors: WORK 10

Records of the War Office: WO 201, 208, 302

National Archives of the United States at College Park, MD (NAUS)

Department of State Central Files: Record Group 59

Records of the Central Intelligence Agency: Record Group 263

Records of the Foreign Service Posts of the Department of State: Record Group 84

CORRESPONDENCE AND INTERVIEWS CITED BY NAME

Daniel Benjamin, Ferida Danyal, Lee F. Dinsmore, Kamal Majid, Kamal Muzhir Ahmad, Edward Odisho, Suphi Saatçi, Adnan Samarrai, George Yacu

NEWSPAPERS, MAGAZINES, AND OTHER NEWS MEDIA

al-Ahali

Ahl al-Naft

al-Bashir/Beşir Gazetesi

Iraq Petroleum

Kardeşlik/al-Ikha'

Kerkük/Karkuk

Los Angeles Times

National Geographic Magazine

New York Times

Oil & Gas Journal

Wall Street Journal

Washington Post

BOOKS, JOURNAL ARTICLES,
AND OTHER PUBLISHED SOURCES

Abdullah, Thabit. *Merchants, Mamluks, and Murder: The Political Economy of Trade in Eighteenth Century Basra.* Albany: State University of New York Press, 2001.

Abrahamian, Ervand. *Iran Between Two Revolutions.* Princeton, NJ: Princeton University Press, 1982.

Abu-Lughod, Janet L. "The Islamic City—Historic Myth, Islamic Essence, and Contemporary Relevance." *International Journal of Middle East Studies* 19, no. 2 (1987): 155–76.

Adams, Walter, James W. Brock, and John M. Blair. "Retarding the Development of Iraq's Oil Resources: An Episode in Oleaginous Diplomacy, 1927–1939." *Journal of Economic Issues* 27, no. 1 (1993): 69–93.

Adams, Warren E. "The Pre-Revolutionary Decade of Land Reform in Iraq." *Economic Development and Cultural Change* 11, no. 3 (1963): 267–88.

Adamson, David. *The Kurdish War*. London: George Allen & Unwin, 1964.

Adelson, Roger. *Mark Sykes: Portrait of an Amateur*. London: Cape, 1975.

Agha, Fahmi 'Arab, and Fadil Muhammad Mulla Mustafa. *Madha fi Karkuk*. Kirkuk: Matba'at al-Tatwij, 1957.

Ahmad, Kamal Muzhir. *Karkuk wa-Tawabi'uha: Hukm al-Tarikh wa-l-Damir*. Arbil: Matba'at Rinwin, n.d.

———. *al-Kurd wa-Kurdistan fi Daw' al-Watha'iq al-Sirriyya al-Britaniyya*, 2nd ed., Vol. 1. Arbil: n.p., 2009.

Akkoyunlu, Ziyat, and Suphi Saatçi, eds. *Irak Muasır Türk Şairleri Antolojisi*. Ankara: Kültür Bakanlığı, 1991.

al-'Ani, Nuri 'Abd al-Hamid. *Tarikh al-Wizarat al-'Iraqiyya fi al-'Ahd al-Jumhuri, 1958–1968*, vol. 3. Baghdad: Bayt al-Hikma, 2001.

al-'Azzawi, Fadhil. *The Last of the Angels*, trans. William M. Hutchins. Cairo: American University in Cairo Press, 2007.

al-'Azzawi, Fadil [Fadhil al-Azzawi]. *Akhir al-Mala'ika*. London: Riyad al-Rayyis, 1992.

———. "Qissat Jil al-Sittinat fi al-'Iraq." *Faradis* 4/5 (1992): 25–34.

———. *al-Ruh al-Hayya: Jil al-Sittinat fi al-'Iraq*. Damascus: Dar al-Mada, 1997.

Al-Ghassani, Anwar. "The Rose and Its Fragrance: The Kirkuk Group—Fifty Years of Presence in Iraqi Culture." 2003. al-ghassani.net/an-kirkuk-and-kirkuk-group/kirkuk-group-essay-2003.html (accessed 28 April 2010).

———. "al-Sittinat, Hunaka, Huna, Hunalika: al-Hubb, al-Hurriyya, al-Ma'rifa." *Faradis* 4/5 (1992): 55–62.

al-Hirmizi, Arshad. *The Turkmen Reality in Iraq*. Istanbul: Kerkük Vakfı, 2005.

al-Hurmuzi, Arshad [Arshad al-Hirmizi]. *al-Turkuman fi al-'Iraq: Dirasa Mujaza 'an Tarikh al-Turkuman fi al-'Iraq wa-Marahil Istitanihim wa-Aslihim*. Baghdad: Matabi' Dar al-Zaman, 1971.

al-Janabi, Tariq. "New Materials for a Study of Post-Saljuq Monuments in Iraq: The Mausoleum of the Green Dome at Kirkuk." In *The Art of the Saljuqs in Iran and Anatolia: Proceedings of a Symposium Held in Edinburgh in 1982*, ed. Robert Hillenbrand, 29–37. Costa Mesa: Mazda Publishers, 1994.

al-Khalil, Samir [Kanan Makiya]. *The Monument: Art, Vulgarity, and Responsibility in Iraq*. Berkeley: University of California Press, 1991.

al-Ma'ali, Khalid. "al-Sha'ir Sarkun Bulus." *'Uyun* 6, no. 12 (2001): 90–170.

Al-Marashi, Ibrahim, and Sammy Salama. *Iraq's Armed Forces: An Analytical History*. London: Routledge, 2008.

Al-Nakib, Farah. *Kuwait Transformed: A History of Oil and Urban Life*. Stanford, CA: Stanford University Press, 2016.

al-Qadi, Wadad. "Biographical Dictionaries: Inner Structure and Cultural Significance." In *The Book in the Islamic World: The Written Word and Communication in the Middle East*, ed. George N. Atiyeh, 93–122. Albany: State University of New York Press, 1995.

Alsaden, Amin. "Baghdad Modernism: Duplicity of Mirages and a Crisis of History." *WTD Magazine* 3 (2013): 16–22.

al-Samanji, ʿAziz Qadir. *al-Tarikh al-Siyasi li-Turkuman al-ʿIraq.* London: Dar al-Saqi, 1999.

Alshaibi, Wisam, and Aliza Luft. "Resurrecting the Dead: Kanan Makiya, the American Government, and the Exploitation of Baʿthist Atrocities in the Service of War in Iraq." In *Cultural Violence and the Destruction of Human Communities: New Theoretical Perspectives,* ed. F. R. Greenland and F. M. Göçek. London: Routledge, 2019 (in press).

Anderson, Benedict. *Imagined Communities: Reflections on the Origin and Spread of Nationalism,* 3rd ed. London: Verso, 2006.

Anderson, Liam, and Gareth Stansfield. *Crisis in Kirkuk: The Ethnopolitics of Conflict and Compromise.* Philadelphia: University of Pennsylvania Press, 2009.

Antoon, Sinan. "Remembering Sargon Boulus (1944–2007)." *Jadaliyya,* 22 October 2011. www.jadaliyya.com/pages/index/2925/remembering-sargon-boulus-%281944-2007%29 (accessed 1 July 2018).

Astarjian, Henry D. *The Struggle for Kirkuk: The Rise of Hussein, Oil, and the Death of Tolerance in Iraq.* Westport, CT: Praeger Security International, 2007.

Ateş, Sabri. *The Ottoman-Iranian Borderlands: Making a Boundary, 1843–1914.* Cambridge, UK: Cambridge University Press, 2013.

Bamberg, J. H. *The History of the British Petroleum Company,* Vol. 2, *The Anglo-Iranian Years, 1928–1954.* Cambridge, UK: Cambridge University Press, 1994.

Barr, James. *A Line in the Sand: The Anglo-French Struggle for the Middle East, 1914–1948.* New York: W. W. Norton, 2012.

Barzani, Massoud [Masʿud Barzani], and Ahmed Ferhadi. *Mustafa Barzani and the Kurdish Liberation Movement.* New York: Palgrave Macmillan, 2003.

Bashkin, Orit. *The Other Iraq: Pluralism and Culture in Hashemite Iraq.* Stanford, CA: Stanford University Press, 2009.

Batatu, Hanna. *The Old Social Classes and the Revolutionary Movements of Iraq: A Study of Iraq's Old Landed and Commercial Classes and of Its Communists, Baʿthists, and Free Officers.* Princeton, NJ: Princeton University Press, 1978.

Benjamen, Alda. "Research at the Iraqi National Library and Archives." *TAARII Newsletter* 7, no. 1 (2012): 13–14.

Benjamin, Daniel. "Assyrian Printing Presses in Iraq During the 20th Century." *Journal of Assyrian Academic Studies* 22, no. 2 (2008): 47–53.

Bergholz, Max. "Sudden Nationhood: The Microdynamics of Intercommunal Relations in Bosnia-Herzegovina After World War II." *American Historical Review* 118, no. 3 (2013): 679–707.

Bet-Shlimon, Arbella. "Group Identities, Oil, and the Local Political Domain in Kirkuk: A Historical Perspective." *Journal of Urban History* 38, no. 5 (2012): 914–31.

———. "Kirkuk, 1918–1968: Oil and the Politics of Identity in an Iraqi City." PhD diss., Harvard University, 2012.

———. "The Politics and Ideology of Urban Development in Iraq's Oil City: Kirkuk, 1946–1958." *Comparative Studies of South Asia, Africa, and the Middle East* 33, no. 1 (2013): 26–40.

———. "Preservation or Plunder? The ISIS Files and a History of Heritage Removal in Iraq." *Middle East Report Online*, 8 May 2018, www.merip.org/mero/mero050818 (accessed 1 July 2018).

Bois, Th., V. Minorsky, and D. N. MacKenzie. "Kurds, Kurdistan." In *Encyclopaedia of Islam*, 2nd ed., ed. P. Bearman, Th. Bianquis, C. E. Bosworth, E. van Donzel, and W. P. Heinrichs. Leiden: Brill Online, 2011. referenceworks.brillonline.com/entries/encyclopaedia-of-islam-2/kurds-kurdistan-COM_0544 (accessed 17 July 2012).

Brady, John. *Eastern Encounters: Memoirs of the Decade 1937–1946*. Braunton, UK: Merlin, 1992.

Browne, Brigadier J. Gilbert. *The Iraq Levies, 1915–1932*. London: Royal United Service Institution, 1932.

Brubaker, Rogers. *Ethnicity Without Groups*. Cambridge, MA: Harvard University Press, 2004.

Bulus, Sarkun [Sargon Boulus]. "al-Hajis al-Aqwa: Khawatir Hawl al-Sittinat." *Faradis* 4/5 (1992): 37–43.

Büyüksaraç, Güldem Baykal. "The Poetics of Loss and the Poetics of Melancholy: A Case Study on Iraqi Turkmen." PhD diss., Columbia University, 2010.

Caswell, Michelle. "'Thank You Very Much, Now Give Them Back': Cultural Property and the Fight Over the Iraqi Baath Party Records." *American Archivist* 74 (2011): 211–40.

Çetinsaya, Gökhan. *Ottoman Administration of Iraq, 1890–1908*. London: Routledge, 2006.

Cole, Juan. *Napoleon's Egypt: Invading the Middle East*. New York: Palgrave Macmillan, 2007.

Crinson, Mark. "Abadan: Planning and Architecture Under the Anglo-Iranian Oil Company." *Planning Perspectives* 12, no. 3 (1997): 341–59.

Cronin, Stephanie. "Popular Politics, the New State, and the Birth of the Iranian Working Class: The 1929 Abadan Oil Refinery Strike." *Middle Eastern Studies* 46, no. 5 (2010): 699–732.

Damluji, Mona. "'Securing Democracy in Iraq': Sectarian Politics and Segregation in Baghdad." *Traditional Dwellings and Settlements Review* 21, no. 2 (2010): 71–87.

Dann, Uriel. *Iraq Under Qassem: A Political History, 1958–1963*. New York: Praeger, 1969.

Davis, Eric. *Memories of State: Politics, History, and Collective Identity in Modern Iraq*. Berkeley: University of California Press, 2005.

DeYoung, Terri. *Placing the Poet: Badr Shakir al-Sayyab and Postcolonial Iraq*. Albany: State University of New York Press, 1998.

Dickson, Bertram. "Journeys in Kurdistan." *Geographical Journal* 35, no. 4 (1910): 357–78.

DiMento, Joseph F. C., and Cliff Ellis. *Changing Lanes: Visions and Histories of Urban Freeways*. Cambridge, MA: MIT Press, 2013.

Dinsmore, Lee F. "Regrets for a Minor American Role in a Major Kurdish Disaster." *Washington Report on Middle East Affairs*, May–June 1991. www.wrmea.com/index.php?option=com_content&view=article&id=1643 (accessed 1 July 2018).

Dodge, Toby. *Inventing Iraq: The Failure of Nation Building and a History Denied*. New York: Columbia University Press, 2003.

Donabed, Sargon. *Reforging a Forgotten History: Iraq and the Assyrians in the Twentieth Century*. Edinburgh: Edinburgh University Press, 2015.

———. "Rethinking Nationalism and an Appellative Conundrum: Historiography and Politics in Iraq." *National Identities* 14, no. 4 (2012): 407–31.

Doxiadis Associates. *The Future of Kirkuk: A Long-Term Program and a Master Plan for the Development of the City and Its Region*. Athens: Doxiadis Associates, 1958.

Duara, Prasenjit. *Culture, Power, and the State: Rural North China, 1900–1942*. Stanford, CA: Stanford University Press, 1988.

———. "Transnationalism and the Challenge to National Histories." In *Rethinking American History in a Global Age*, ed. Thomas Bender, 25–46. Berkeley: University of California Press, 2002.

Edmonds, C. J. *Kurds, Turks, and Arabs: Politics, Travel, and Research in North-Eastern Iraq, 1919–1925*. London: Oxford University Press, 1957.

Ehsani, Kaveh. "Social Engineering and the Contradictions of Modernization in Khuzestan's Company Towns: A Look at Abadan and Masjed-Soleyman." *International Review of Social History* 48 (2003): 361–99.

Eskander, Saad. "Britain's Policy in Southern Kurdistan: The Formation and the Termination of the First Kurdish Government, 1918–1919." *British Journal of Middle Eastern Studies* 27, no. 2 (2000): 139–63.

Farouk-Sluglett, Marion, and Peter Sluglett. *Iraq Since 1958: From Revolution to Dictatorship*. London: I. B. Tauris, 1987.

Faust, Aaron M. *The Ba'thification of Iraq: Saddam Hussein's Totalitarianism*. Austin: University of Texas Press, 2015.

Fawaz, Leila Tarazi. *Merchants and Migrants in Nineteenth-Century Beirut*. Cambridge, MA: Harvard University Press, 1983.

Ferrier, R. W. *The History of the British Petroleum Company*, vol. 1, *The Developing Years, 1901–1932*. Cambridge, UK: Cambridge University Press, 1982.

Fieldhouse, D. K., ed. *Kurds, Arabs, and Britons: The Memoir of Wallace Lyon in Iraq, 1918–44*. London: I. B. Tauris, 2002.

Finnie, David H. *Desert Enterprise: The Middle East Oil Industry in Its Local Environment*. Cambridge, MA: Harvard University Press, 1958.

Fitzgerald, Edward. "France's Middle Eastern Ambitions, the Sykes-Picot Negotiations, and the Oil Fields of Mosul, 1915–1918." *Journal of Modern History* 66, no. 4 (1994): 697–725.

Frank, Alison Fleig. *Oil Empire: Visions of Prosperity in Austrian Galicia*. Cambridge, MA: Harvard University Press, 2005.

Franzén, Johan. "From Ally to Foe: The Iraqi Communist Party and the Kurdish Question, 1958–1975." *British Journal of Middle Eastern Studies* 38, no. 2 (2011): 169–85.

Fuccaro, Nelida. *Histories of City and State in the Persian Gulf: Manama Since 1800.* Cambridge, UK: Cambridge University Press, 2009.

———. "Introduction: Histories of Oil and Urban Modernity in the Middle East." *Comparative Studies of South Asia, Africa, and the Middle East* 33, no. 1 (2013): 1–6.

———. "Kurds and Kurdish Nationalism in Mandatory Syria: Politics, Culture, and Identity." In *Essays on the Origins of Kurdish Nationalism,* ed. Abbas Vali, 191–217. Costa Mesa: Mazda, 2003.

———. *The Other Kurds: Yazidis in Colonial Iraq.* London: I. B. Tauris, 1999.

———. "Visions of the City: Urban Studies on the Gulf." *Middle East Studies Association Bulletin* 35, no. 2 (2001): 175–87.

Gallagher, John, and Ronald Robinson. "The Imperialism of Free Trade." *Economic History Review* 6, no. 1 (1953): 1–15.

Galletti, Mirella. "Kirkuk: The Pivot of Balance in Iraq Past and Present." *Journal of Assyrian Academic Studies* 19, no. 2 (2005): 21–52.

Gallman, Waldemar. *Iraq Under General Nuri: My Recollections of Nuri al-Said, 1954–1958.* Baltimore: Johns Hopkins University Press, 1964.

Georgeon, François. "De Mossoul à Kirkouk: La Turquie et la Question du Kurdistan Irakien." *Maghreb Machrek* 132 (1991): 38–49.

Gershoni, Israel, and James P. Jankowski. *Redefining the Egyptian Nation, 1930–1945.* Cambridge, UK: Cambridge University Press, 2002.

Güçlü, Yücel. *The Turcomans and Kirkuk.* Philadelphia: Xlibris, 2007.

———. "Who Owns Kirkuk? The Turkoman Case." *Middle East Quarterly* 14, no. 1 (2007): 79–86.

Haddad, Fanar. *Sectarianism in Iraq: Antagonistic Visions of Unity.* Oxford, UK: Oxford University Press, 2011.

Haj, Samira. *The Making of Iraq, 1900–1963: Capital, Power, and Ideology.* Albany: State University of New York Press, 1997.

Hakim, Halkut. "Karkuk fi Kitabat al-Rahhala al-Fransiyyin." In *Karkuk: Madinat al-Qawmiyyat al-Muta'akhiyya,* ed. Markaz Karbala' lil-Buhuth wa-l-Dirasat, 137–50. London: Markaz Karbala' lil-Buhuth wa-l-Dirasat, 2002.

Haldane, Sir Aylmer L. *The Insurrection in Mesopotamia, 1920.* Edinburgh: W. Blackwood & Sons, 1922.

Hamilton, A. M. *Road Through Kurdistan: Travels in Northern Iraq.* London: Tauris Parke Paperbacks, 2004.

Hanoosh, Yasmeen S. "The Politics of Minority: Chaldeans Between Iraq and America." PhD diss., University of Michigan, 2008.

Hasan, 'Abd al-Majid Fahmi. *Dalil Tarikh Mashahir al-Alwiya al-'Iraqiyya,* vol. 2, *Karkuk.* Baghdad: Matba'at al-Salam, 1947.

Hassanpour, Amir. *Nationalism and Language in Kurdistan, 1918–1985.* San Francisco: Mellen Research University Press, 1992.

Hiltermann, Joost. *A Poisonous Affair: America, Iraq, and the Gassing of Halabja*. Cambridge, UK: Cambridge University Press, 2007.

Hourani, Albert. "Ottoman Reform and the Politics of Notables." In *Beginnings of Modernization in the Middle East: The Nineteenth Century*, ed. William R. Polk and Richard L. Chambers, 41–68. Chicago: University of Chicago Press, 1968.

Human Rights Watch. *Bureaucracy of Repression: The Iraqi Government in Its Own Words*. New York: Human Rights Watch, 1994.

———. *Genocide in Iraq: The Anfal Campaign Against the Kurds*. New York: Human Rights Watch, 1993.

Ihsan, Mohammed. "Arabization as Genocide: The Case of the Disputed Territories of Iraq." In *The Kurdish Question Revisited*, ed. Gareth Stansfield and Mohammed Shareef, 375–92. Oxford: Oxford University Press, 2017.

International Crisis Group. *Oil for Soil: Toward a Grand Bargain on Iraq and the Kurds*. Middle East Report 80. Kirkuk/Brussels: International Crisis Group, 28 October 2008.

Ionides, Michael. *Divide and Lose: The Arab Revolt of 1955–1958*. London: Geoffrey Bles, 1960.

Jassim, Saad Z., and J. C. Goff, eds. *Geology of Iraq*. Prague: Dolin; and Brno: Moravian Museum, 2006.

Jones, Kevin. "The Poetics of Revolution: Cultures, Practices, and Politics of Anti-Colonialism in Iraq, 1932–1960." PhD diss., University of Michigan, 2013.

Judson, Pieter M. *Guardians of the Nation: Activists on the Language Frontiers of Imperial Austria*. Cambridge, MA: Harvard University Press, 2006.

Jwaideh, Wadie. *The Kurdish National Movement: Its Origins and Development*. Syracuse, NY: Syracuse University Press, 2006.

Kelidar, Abbas, ed. *The Integration of Modern Iraq*. New York: St. Martin's Press, 1979.

Kemp, Percy. "Power and Knowledge in Jalili Mosul." *Middle Eastern Studies* 19, no. 2 (1983): 201–12.

Kent, Marian. *Oil and Empire: British Policy and Mesopotamian Oil, 1900–1920*. London: Macmillan, 1976.

Khadduri, Majid. *Independent Iraq, 1932–1958: A Study in Iraqi Politics*, 2nd ed. London: Oxford University Press, 1960.

Khalaf, Issa. *Politics in Palestine: Arab Factionalism and Social Disintegration, 1939–1948*. Albany: State University of New York Press, 1991.

Khoury, Dina Rizk. *Iraq in Wartime: Soldiering, Martyrdom, and Remembrance*. Cambridge, UK: Cambridge University Press, 2013.

———. *State and Provincial Society in the Ottoman Empire: Mosul, 1540–1834*. Cambridge, UK: Cambridge University Press, 1997.

———. "Violence and Spatial Politics Between the Local and Imperial: Baghdad, 1778–1810." In *The Spaces of the Modern City: Imaginaries, Politics, and Everyday Life*, ed. Gyan Prakash and Kevin M. Kruse, 181–213. Princeton, NJ: Princeton University Press, 2008.

Khoury, Philip S. "Syrian Urban Politics in Transition: The Quarters of Damascus During the French Mandate." *International Journal of Middle East Studies* 16, no. 4 (1984): 507–40.

———. *Urban Notables and Arab Nationalism: The Politics of Damascus, 1860–1920.* Cambridge, UK: Cambridge University Press, 1983.

Kingston, Paul W. T. *Britain and the Politics of Modernization in the Middle East, 1945–1958.* Cambridge, UK: Cambridge University Press, 1996.

Kirmanj, Sherko. *Identity and Nation in Iraq.* Boulder, CO: Lynne Rienner, 2013.

Klein, Janet. *The Margins of Empire: Kurdish Militias in the Ottoman Tribal Zone.* Stanford, CA: Stanford University Press, 2011.

Kramers, J. H. "Kirkuk." In *Encyclopaedia of Islam*, 2nd ed., ed. P. Bearman, Th. Bianquis, C. E. Bosworth, E. van Donzel, and W. P. Heinrichs. Leiden: Brill Online, 2011. referenceworks.brillonline.com/entries/encyclopaedia-of-islam-2/kirkuk-SIM_4390 (accessed 17 July 2012).

Kurdistan Regional Government. "Natural Resources Ministry: Kirkuk Oil Field Development Requires Approval of KRG and Kirkuk Governorate." 26 March 2012. krg.org/articles/detail.asp?lngnr=12&smap=02010100&rnr=223&anr=43451 (accessed 17 July 2012).

Küzeci, Şemsettin. *Kerkük Soykırımları: Irak Türklerinin Uğradığı Katliamlar, 1920–2003.* Ankara: Teknoed Yayınları, 2004.

League of Nations. *Question of the Frontier Between Turkey and Iraq: Report Submitted to the Council by the Commission Instituted by the Council Resolution of September 30th, 1924.* Geneva: League of Nations, 1925.

Lenczowski, George. *Oil and State in the Middle East.* Ithaca, NY: Cornell University Press, 1960.

Limbert, Mandana E. *In the Time of Oil: Piety, Memory, and Social Life in an Omani Town.* Stanford, CA: Stanford University Press, 2010.

Lockman, Zachary. *Comrades and Enemies: Arab and Jewish Workers in Palestine, 1906–1948.* Berkeley: University of California Press, 1996.

Longhurst, Henry. *Adventure in Oil: The Story of British Petroleum.* London: Sidgwick & Jackson, 1959.

Longrigg, Stephen Hemsley. *Four Centuries of Modern Iraq.* Beirut: Librairie du Liban, 1968.

———. *Iraq, 1900 to 1950: A Political, Social, and Economic History.* London: Oxford University Press, 1953.

———. *Oil in the Middle East: Its Discovery and Development*, 3rd ed. London: Oxford University Press, 1968.

Lütfi, Hıdır. "Kerkük." In *Irak Muasır Türk Şairleri Antolojisi*, ed. Ziyat Akkoyunlu and Suphi Saatçi, 42–43. Ankara: Kültür Bakanlığı, 1991.

Main, Ernest. *Iraq from Mandate to Independence.* London: George Allen & Unwin, 1935.

Makdisi, Ussama. *The Culture of Sectarianism: Community, History, and Violence in Nineteenth-Century Ottoman Lebanon.* Berkeley: University of California Press, 2000.

Manela, Erez. *The Wilsonian Moment: Self-Determination and the International Origins of Anticolonial Nationalism.* Oxford: Oxford University Press, 2007.

Marefat, Mina. "From Bauhaus to Baghdad: The Politics of Building the Total University." *TAARII Newsletter* 3, no. 2 (2008): 2–12.

Markaz Karbala' lil-Buhuth wa-l-Dirasat, ed. *Karkuk: Madinat al-Qawmiyyat al-Muta'akhiyya*. London: Markaz Karbala' lil-Buhuth wa-l-Dirasat, 2002.

Marr, Phebe. *The Modern History of Iraq*, 2nd ed. Boulder, CO: Westview Press, 2004.

Maunsell, F. R. "The Mesopotamian Petroleum Field." *Geographical Journal* 9, no. 5 (1897): 528–32.

McDowall, David. *A Modern History of the Kurds*, 3rd ed. London: I. B. Tauris, 2004.

Menoret, Pascal. "Development, Planning, and Urban Unrest in Saudi Arabia." *The Muslim World* 101, no. 2 (2011): 269–85.

Mitchell, Timothy. *Carbon Democracy: Political Power in the Age of Oil*. London: Verso, 2011.

Monroe, Elizabeth. *Britain's Moment in the Middle East, 1914–1956*. London: Chatto & Windus, 1963.

Moore, James. "Between Cosmopolitanism and Nationalism: The Strange Death of Liberal Alexandria." *Journal of Urban History* 38, no. 5 (2012): 879–900.

Mudiriyyat al-Nufus al-ʻAmma. *Census of Iraq, 1947*, vol. 2. Baghdad: Government of Iraq, 1954.

———. *al-Majmuʻa al-Ihsa'iyya li-Tasjil ʻAm 1957*, vol. 5. Baghdad: Wizarat al-Dakhiliyya, 1962.

Mukhlis, Jasim. *Mudhakkirat al-Tabaqjali wa-Dhikrayat Jasim Mukhlis al-Muhami*. Baghdad: Matbaʻat al-Zaman, 1985.

Munif, Abdelrahman. *Cities of Salt*, trans. Peter Theroux. New York: Vintage International, 1989.

Natali, Denise. "The Kirkuk Conundrum." *Ethnopolitics* 7, no. 4 (2008): 433–43.

———. "Settlers and State Building: The Kirkuk Case." In *Settlers in Contested Lands: Territorial Disputes and Ethnic Conflicts*, ed. Oded Haklai and Neophytos Loizides, 114–40. Stanford, CA: Stanford University Press, 2015.

O'Leary, Brendan. *How to Get Out of Iraq with Integrity*. Philadelphia: University of Pennsylvania Press, 2009.

Olson, Robert W. *The Siege of Mosul and Ottoman-Persian Relations, 1718–1743: A Study of Rebellion in the Capital and War in the Provinces of the Ottoman Empire*. Bloomington: Indiana University Research Center for the Language Sciences, 1975.

Omissi, David. *Air Power and Colonial Control: The Royal Air Force, 1919–1939*. Manchester, UK: Manchester University Press, 1990.

———. "Britain, the Assyrians, and the Iraq Levies, 1919–1932." *Journal of Imperial and Commonwealth History* 17, no. 3 (1989): 301–22.

Owen, Roger. "British and French Military Intelligence in Syria and Palestine, 1914–1918: Myths and Reality." *British Journal of Middle Eastern Studies* 38, no. 1 (2011): 1–6.

———. *The Middle East in the World Economy, 1800–1914*, 2nd ed. London: I. B. Tauris, 1993.

———, ed. *New Perspectives on Property and Land in the Middle East.* Cambridge, MA: Center for Middle Eastern Studies of Harvard University, Harvard University Press, 2000.

Packer, George. *The Assassin's Gate: America in Iraq.* New York: Farrar, Straus & Giroux, 2005.

Patriotic Union of Kurdistan. *Ethnic Cleansing Documents in Kurdistan-Iraq.* Kirkuk: Patriotic Union of Kurdistan, Kirkuk Organization Center, 2004.

Pedersen, Susan. "Getting Out of Iraq—in 1932: The League of Nations and the Road to Normative Statehood." *American Historical Review* 115, no. 4 (2010): 975–1000.

Penrose, Edith, and E. F. Penrose. *Iraq: International Relations and National Development.* London: Ernest Benn, 1978.

Pfeiffer, Robert H. *Nuzi and the Hurrians: The Excavations at Nuzi (Kirkuk, Iraq) and Their Contribution to Our Knowledge of the History of the Hurrians.* Washington, DC: Government Printing Office, 1936.

Pyla, Panayiota. "Back to the Future: Doxiadis's Plans for Baghdad." *Journal of Planning History* 7, no. 1 (2008): 3–19.

Qadir, Mohammed Amin. "The Linguistic Situation in Kirkuk: A Sociolinguistic Study." PhD diss., University of Aston in Birmingham, 1980.

Qubain, Fahim I. *The Reconstruction of Iraq: 1950–1957.* New York: Praeger, 1958.

Rasul, 'Izz al-Din Mustafa. "Tatawwur al-Haraka al-Thaqafiyya fi Karkuk—al-Shaykh Rida al-Talabani Namudhajan." In *Karkuk: Madinat al-Qawmiyyat al-Muta'akhiyya,* ed. Markaz Karbala' lil-Buhuth wa-l-Dirasat, 506–30. London: Markaz Karbala' lil-Buhuth wa-l-Dirasat, 2002.

Raymond, André. *Cairo,* trans. Willard Wood. Cambridge, MA: Harvard University Press, 2000.

Resool, Shorsh Mustafa. "Reactive Nationalism in a Homogenizing State: The Kurdish Nationalism Movement in Ba'thist Iraq, 1963–2003." PhD diss., University of Exeter, 2012.

Rogan, Eugene L. *Frontiers of the State in the Late Ottoman Empire: Transjordan, 1850–1921.* Cambridge, UK: Cambridge University Press, 1999.

Romano, David. "The Future of Kirkuk." *Ethnopolitics* 6, no. 2 (2007): 265–83.

Saatçi, Suphi. *The Urban Fabric and Traditional Houses of Kirkuk,* trans. Mehmet Bengü Uluengin. Istanbul: Kerkük Vakfı, 2007.

Sahlins, Peter. *Boundaries: The Making of France and Spain in the Pyrenees.* Berkeley: University of California Press, 1989.

Said, Edward. "Permission to Narrate." *Journal of Palestine Studies* 13, no. 3 (1984): 27–48.

Salter, Lord. *The Development of Iraq.* Iraq Development Board, 1955.

Sami, E. Mahmud. *The Quest for Sultan Abdülhamid's Oil Assets: His Heirs' Legal Battle for Their Rights.* Istanbul: Isis, 2006.

Santiago, Myrna I. *The Ecology of Oil: Environment, Labor, and the Mexican Revolution, 1900–1938.* Cambridge, UK: Cambridge University Press, 2006.

Sari Kahya, 'Ismat Rafiq. *Tarikh Jawami' wa Masajid Karkuk*. London: Dar al-Hikma, 2015.

Sarkis, Hashim. *Circa 1958: Lebanon in the Pictures and Plans of Constantinos Doxiadis*. Beirut: Dar An-Nahar, 2003.

Sassoon, Joseph. *Economic Policy in Iraq, 1932–1950*. London: F. Cass, 1987.

———. *Saddam Hussein's Ba'th Party: Inside an Authoritarian Regime*. Cambridge, UK: Cambridge University Press, 2012.

Satia, Priya. "The Defense of Inhumanity: Air Control and the British Idea of Arabia." *American Historical Review* 111, no. 1 (2006): 16–51.

Saul, Samir. "Masterly Inactivity as Brinkmanship: The Iraq Petroleum Company's Route to Nationalization, 1958–1972." *International History Review* 29, no. 4 (2007): 746–92.

Schofield, Richard N., ed. *Arabian Boundary Disputes*, vol. 9. Slough, UK: Archive Editions, 1992.

Seccombe, Ian, and Richard Lawless. *Work Camps and Company Towns: Settlement Patterns and the Gulf Oil Industry*. Durham, UK: University of Durham, Centre for Middle Eastern and Islamic Studies, 1987.

Sherabayani, Karzan. *Return to Kirkuk: A Year in the Fire*. New York: Eagle Media, 2007. DVD.

Shields, Sarah D. *Fezzes in the River: Identity Politics and European Diplomacy in the Middle East on the Eve of World War II*. Oxford, UK: Oxford University Press, 2011.

———. *From Millet to Nation: The Limits of Consociational Resolutions for Middle East Conflict*. EUI Working Paper 2010/84. Fiesole, Italy: European University Institute, 2010.

———. "Interdependent Spaces: Relations Between the City and the Countryside in the Nineteenth Century." In *The Urban Social History of the Middle East, 1750–1950*, ed. Peter Sluglett, 43–66. Syracuse, NY: Syracuse University Press, 2008.

———. *Mosul Before Iraq: Like Bees Making Five-Sided Cells*. Albany: State University of New York Press, 2000.

———. "Mosul, the Ottoman Legacy, and the League of Nations." *International Journal of Contemporary Iraqi Studies* 3, no. 2 (2009): 217–30.

Shwadran, Benjamin. *The Middle East, Oil, and the Great Powers*. Jerusalem: Israel Universities Press, 1973.

Silverfarb, Daniel. *Britain's Informal Empire in the Middle East: A Case Study of Iraq, 1929–1941*. New York: Oxford University Press, 1986.

Simon, Reeva. *Iraq Between the Two World Wars: The Militarist Origins of Tyranny*. New York: Columbia University Press, 2004.

Simpich, Frederick, and W. Robert Moore. "Bombs over Bible Lands." *National Geographic Magazine* 80, no. 2 (August 1941): 141–80.

Sky, Emma. *The Unraveling: High Hopes and Missed Opportunities in Iraq*. New York: Public Affairs, 2015.

Sluglett, Peter. *Britain in Iraq: Contriving King and Country*. London: I. B. Tauris, 2007.

Soane, E. B. *To Mesopotamia and Kurdistan in Disguise: With Historical Notices of the Kurdish Tribes and the Chaldeans of Kurdistan*. London: John Murray, 1912.

Sovetskaya Armiya. *Kirkuk*. Moscow: General'nyi Shtab, 1976.

Stafford, R. S. *The Tragedy of the Assyrians*. London: George Allen & Unwin, 1935.

Stivers, William. *Supremacy and Oil: Iraq, Turkey, and the Anglo-American World Order, 1918–1930*. Ithaca, NY: Cornell University Press, 1982.

Sykes, Mark. *Dar-Ul-Islam: A Record of a Journey Through Ten of the Asiatic Provinces of Turkey*. London: Bickers & Son, 1904.

Talabani, Nuri [Nouri Talabany]. "Karkuk fi Mawsu'a 'Iraqiyya Sadira 'Am 1947." In *Karkuk: Madinat al-Qawmiyyat al-Muta'akhiyya*, ed. Markaz Karbala' lil-Buhuth wa-l-Dirasat, 229–55. London: Markaz Karbala' lil-Buhuth wa-l-Dirasat, 2002.

——. *Mintaqat Karkuk Wa-Muhawalat Taghyir Waqi'iha al-Qawmi*. Arbil: Dar Aras, 2004.

Talabany, Nouri. *Arabization of the Kirkuk Region*. Arbil: Aras Press, 2004.

——. "Who Owns Kirkuk? The Kurdish Case." *Middle East Quarterly* 14, no. 1 (2007): 75–78.

Tepeyran, Ebubekir Hâzım. *Hatıralar*, 2nd ed. Istanbul: Pera Turizm ve Ticaret, 1998.

Terzibaşı, Ata. *Kerkük Eskiler Sozü*. Baghdad: Zaman Basımevi, 1962.

——. *Kerkük Havaları*. Baghdad: Rabıta Basımevi, 1961.

——. *Kerkük Hoyratları ve Manileri*. Istanbul: Ötüken Yayınevi, 1975.

——. *Kerkük Matbuat Tarihi*, 2nd ed. Istanbul: Kerkük Vakfı, 2005.

Tilly, Charles, ed. *The Formation of National States in Western Europe*. Princeton, NJ: Princeton University Press, 1975.

Tinker Salas, Miguel. *The Enduring Legacy: Oil, Culture, and Society in Venezuela*. Durham, NC: Duke University Press, 2009.

"Treaty Between the United Kingdom and Iraq and Turkey Regarding the Settlement of the Frontier Between Turkey and Iraq, Together with Notes Exchanged." *American Journal of International Law* 21, no. 4 (suppl.) (1927): 136–43.

Tripp, Charles. *A History of Iraq*, 3rd ed. Cambridge, UK: Cambridge University Press, 2007.

U.S. Energy Information Administration. "Iraq: Country Analysis." www.eia.gov/countries/cab.cfm?fips=IZ (accessed 14 July 2012).

van Bruinessen, Martin. *Agha, Shaikh, and State: The Social and Political Structures of Kurdistan*. London: Zed Books, 1992.

Visser, Reidar. *Basra, the Failed Gulf State: Separatism and Nationalism in Southern Iraq*. Piscataway, NJ: Transaction, 2005.

Visser, Reidar, and Gareth Stansfield, eds. *An Iraq of Its Regions: Cornerstones of a Federal Democracy?* New York: Columbia University Press, 2008.

Vitalis, Robert. *America's Kingdom: Mythmaking on the Saudi Oil Frontier*. Stanford, CA: Stanford University Press, 2007.

Walker, Joel Thomas. *The Legend of Mar Qardagh: Narrative and Christian Heroism in Late Antique Iraq*. Berkeley: University of California Press, 2006.

Watts, Michael. "Resource Curse? Governmentality, Oil, and Power in the Niger Delta, Nigeria." *Geopolitics* 9, no. 1 (2004): 50–80.

Wien, Peter. *Iraqi Arab Nationalism: Authoritarian, Totalitarian, and Pro-Fascist Inclinations, 1932–1941.* London: Routledge, 2006.

Wolfe-Hunnicutt, Brandon. "The End of the Concessionary Regime: Oil and American Power in Iraq, 1958–1972." PhD diss., Stanford University, 2011.

Wolff, Stefan. "Governing (in) Kirkuk: Resolving the Status of a Disputed Territory in Post-American Iraq." *International Affairs* 86, no. 6 (2010): 1361–79.

Yapp, M. E. *The Making of the Modern Middle East, 1792–1923.* London: Longman, 1987.

Yergin, Daniel. *The Prize: The Epic Quest for Oil, Money, and Power.* New York: Simon & Schuster, 1991.

Zahra, Tara. "Imagined Non-Communities: National Indifference as a Category of Analysis." *Slavic Review* 69, no. 1 (2010): 93–119.

Zanger, Maggy. "Refugees in Their Own Country." *Middle East Report* 32, no. 222 (2002): 40–43.

Zeidel, Ronen. "The Iraqi Novel and the Kurds." *Review of Middle Eastern Studies* 45, no. 1 (2011): 19–34.

Zubaida, Sami. "The Fragments Imagine the Nation: The Case of Iraq." *International Journal of Middle East Studies* 34, no. 2 (2002): 205–15.

———. "Iraq: History, Memory, Culture." *International Journal of Middle East Studies* 44, no. 2 (2012): 333–45.

Zürcher, Erik J. *Turkey: A Modern History.* London: I. B. Tauris, 1998.

INDEX

Language Law of 1931, 74, 75, 96,
226n83
Languages: academic research on, 180–
81; ethnicity and, 3, 16, 180–81; mul-
tilingualism, xvii, 3, 9, 10, 10 (fig.),
12, 15, 22, 74; Neo-Aramaic, 16–17,
30, 61. *See also* Arabic language;
Kurdish language; Turkish language
Lausanne Conference, 54, 55
Law Governing the Rights and Duties of
Cultivators (1933), 88
Lazar, Shamasha Youkhanan Moushi, 131
League of Nations: admission of Iraq,
73, 74, 75, 87; mandate system, 51;
Mosul Commission, 67–72; Mosul
dispute and, 55–56
Leftists, 152–53. *See also* Iraqi Commu-
nist Party
Libraries, 126, 155–56
Limbert, Mandana E., 7
Literary culture, 12, 126, 131, 152–53.
See also Writers
Longhurst, Henry, 80–81
Longrigg, Stephen Hemsley, 23, 30, 36,
41, 42, 43
Lütfi, Hıdır, 133
Lvin, 191
Lyon, Wallace, 45, 87, 223n38

Madha fi Karkuk (What's in Kirkuk),
131–32
Mahallas (neighborhoods or quarters):
central, 89 (fig.), 92 (fig.); ethnic residential patterns, 93–94, 114, 179; new,
91–93, 112–13, 174, 180; population
growth, 89–90, 91–93. *See also* Shorija
Mainland, M. S., 102, 120, 121, 124
Makiya, Kanan, 200, 201
Maps of Kirkuk: central *mahallas*, 89
(fig.), 92 (fig.); events of May 1924,
62 (fig.); in 1919, 27 (fig.); region, xiv
(fig.); southeast quadrant, 92 (fig.),
178 (fig.)

Markets, 31, 61–62
Matbaʿat al-Tatwij (Coronation Press),
131
Maunsell, F. R., 26, 33–34
Menoret, Pascal, 116
Mesopotamian campaign (World War I),
19, 34, 36–37
Middle class, 108, 113, 114, 115, 131,
133, 134
Migration: to Kirkuk, 21, 79, 90–93, 135;
rural-urban, 79, 88, 90–93, 118
Miller, A. F., 56, 226n81
Ministry of Defense, 160
Ministry of Economics and Communica-
tion, 85
Ministry of Education, 138
Ministry of Higher Education and Scien-
tific Research, 180
Ministry of Oil, 13–14
Modernization, 7, 108, 116, 118, 126–27,
134. *See also* Urban development
Mosques, 28
Mosul: Arabic-language culture, 32; army
revolt against Qasim, 145–46; Assyrians, 59; in French zone of influence,
34, 35–36; Islamic State capture of,
xv, 192; Ottoman rule, 24, 32; as part
of Kurdistan, 30; roads, 26–27; violence against communists, 152
Mosul Commission, 67–72, 83
Mosul *vilayet*: British control, 36, 39–42,
44, 52–56, 67; British interest in,
26; governors, 24; integration into
Iraq, 48, 73; Kurdish tribes, 24, 30;
oil fields, 28–29, 33–34, 70–73; opposition to centralized authority,
57; Ottoman rule, 22, 24–25; trade,
70; Turkish claims, 39, 44, 46, 52,
54, 65–67; Turkish-Iraqi conflict in
1920s, 51, 54, 55, 65–72
Munif, Abdelrahman, *Cities of Salt*, 81
Muslim Brotherhood, 126
Muslims, Arrapha Estate residents, 114,

Lightning Source UK Ltd.
Milton Keynes UK
UKHW012259060720
366021UK00015B/97